Democracy and the Origins of the American Regulatory State

The Institution for Social and Policy Studies at Yale University
The Yale ISPS Series

Democracy and the Origins of the American Regulatory State

Samuel DeCanio

Yale UNIVERSITY PRESS

NEW HAVEN AND LONDON

Published with assistance from the Louis Stern Memorial Fund.

Yale University Press books may be purchased in quantity for educational, business,
or promotional use. For information, please e-mail sales.press@yale.edu (U.S. office)
or sales@yaleup.co.uk (U.K. office).

Set in Adobe Garamond type by Newgen North America.
Printed in the United States of America.

Library of Congress Control Number: 2015933606
ISBN 978-0-300-19878-2 (pbk: alk. paper)

A catalogue record for this book is available from the British Library.

This paper meets the requirements of ANSI/NISO Z39.48-1992 (Permanence of Paper).

10 9 8 7 6 5 4 3 2 1

For my father

Contents

Acknowledgments

This book began as my doctoral dissertation, written under the supervision of Gregory Caldeira, Lawrence Baum, Dean Lacy, and Kathleen McGraw. While a number of people helped me complete the project in various ways, Daniel Wirls and Jeffry Burnam deserve a special note of thanks for helping me secure lecturing positions as I was finishing the project; this book never would have been completed without their help.

A number of people read the manuscript and offered suggestions as it developed. Stephen Skowronek deserves special acknowledgment. Skowronek's research has helped shape the discipline of political science, and his writing continues to be a model of historically and theoretically informed scholarship. Steve read multiple versions of the manuscript and offered a range of detailed comments and suggestions that strengthened the manuscript significantly.

I also owe a considerable debt of gratitude to David Mayhew. Like Steve, David offered extensive comments and suggestions. As the project neared completion, David offered a particularly helpful set of suggestions that significantly improved the manuscript's content and organization.

Richard Bensel also deserves a special note of thanks. Richard's writings introduced me to the study of American political development, and demonstrated what is possible when appreciation for theory is blended with careful attention to historical facts. Richard read various papers and chapters over the years, and he always generously offered extensive commentary and suggestions. Richard also deserves recognition for suggesting the current title of the book.

The manuscript was subjected to a round of constructive criticism during a conference that took place at Yale University in the fall of 2011. Three wise men, Richard Bensel, Paul Quirk, and Adam Tooze, served as discussants and offered close commentary and numerous suggestions. In addition to providing their own recommendations, Jacob Hacker, Stephen Skowronek, and Steven Smith secured generous funding through Yale's Center for the Study of American Politics, Yale's Institution for Social and Policy Studies, the Yale Center for the Study of Representative Institutions, and Yale's Department of Political Science.

Many others offered helpful comments on specific chapters as they developed. I have been lucky to receive feedback from Jamie Briskin, David Broockman, Greg Caldeira, Seth Center, Daniel DiSalvo, Dennis Drabelle, Phil Gorski, Richard Jensen, Richard John, Sigrun Kahl, Keith Poole, Charles Postel, Nancy Rosenbluth, Morgan Marietta, Nuno Monteiro, Franklin Noll, Elizabeth Sanders, Lucais Sewell, Corwin D. Smidt, Peter Swenson, Tariq Thachil, Adam Tooze, and Richard White. Ryan Berg offered research assistance on short notice, and both David Trihn and Kate Bermingham read the entire manuscript and provided helpful comments. My editor, William Frucht, and Jaya Chatterjee at Yale University Press ensured that the whole process for the manuscript was helpful and constructive. Special thanks to Otto Bohlmann for carefully editing the entire manuscript and correcting innumerable errors before it went into production.

Several people also generously offered me housing as I traveled to various archives. Sid Iyer and Anne Horstman Iyer deserve a special note of thanks for hosting me for far longer than I deserved. Much of the archival work I did at the Library of Congress and the National Archives would not have been possible without their generosity. Others who deserve special thanks for housing me include Kevin Miles, John Gliedman, Margot Adler, Tanner Whitney, Amanda Miller, Ian Kimmerly, and Randy and Jan Miller. Special thanks to Katrina Wehmeyer for her love and support as the project neared completion.

Finally, where would I be without the invaluable Jeffrey Friedman! Jeff's writings in his journal, *Critical Review,* were responsible for initially sparking my interest in democratic politics and the problem of the state. Jeff offered encouragement when conditions seemed darkest, and I have been lucky to have access to his meticulous editing and feedback ever since the original idea for the book was formed during a discussion in New York in the summer of 1998.

Introduction

This book contains two arguments, one historical and the other theoretical. The historical argument seeks to explain the creation of the American regulatory state in the late nineteenth century; the theoretical argument examines the implications that high levels of voter ignorance have for democratic politics and the autonomy of modern states.

The historical argument examines how political and media elites helped build the American state's bureaucratic regulatory authority in the final decades of the nineteenth century, and argues that such authority initially emerged in the Treasury Department and the Interstate Commerce Commission. Although many scholars have examined conflicts over monetary policy and railroad regulation during the nineteenth century, I argue that autonomous elites created a new state to accomplish unpopular policy objectives, and that the state that emerged from these conflicts had lasting implications for American politics.

In addition to this historical argument, I develop a theory of the state that challenges widespread assumptions regarding the nature of political power in modern democracies. Although democracy is believed to ensure voters' influence over modern politics, I argue that high levels of public ignorance grant democratic states significant autonomy from society, allowing implementation of policies that do not reflect social demands or preferences. By suggesting that voter ignorance may prevent societal control of the state, my theoretical argument challenges both commonsense assumptions regarding political power in modern societies and academic theories of democracy.

Before I turn to my argument, it is necessary to provide a brief methodological discussion of my explanatory objectives. Historically oriented political science has come under intense scrutiny, and important questions have been raised regarding the role of historical data for the social scientific project, and the relationship between case selection and the validity of inferences drawn from specific historical periods. Three general challenges face historically oriented social science: (1) the nature of the generalizations drawn from discrete historical cases, (2) problems with making causal inferences from a small number of observations, and (3) the criteria used for case selection.

Social scientific theories often attempt to construct generalizations that are valid across time and place.[1] Although understanding general patterns or "laws" of social behavior is critical for any analysis, understanding general patterns and typical behavioral responses remains a *preliminary* step necessary for the analysis of historical data.[2] Indeed, my argument is predicated upon the assumption that a characteristic feature of social analysis is *developmental;* involving questions regarding why specific institutions emerged at specific times and not others.[3] Efforts to explain the emergence of certain developmental patterns must be guided by theoretical assumptions regarding social behavior. However, my focus on explaining the origins of a new developmental pattern assumed by a specific type of state is an explanatory objective that is distinct from identifying general laws of social behavior.[4]

As I examine a transformation in state authority that takes place under a specific set of historical conditions, certain characteristics of my cases must briefly be mentioned. Although social scientists recommend selecting cases to induce variation across independent and dependent variables, my primary objective is to explain why a new type of state was created at a specific point, and is not simply to "test" a theoretical argument. My cases were not selected to induce variation across variables, nor do I examine cases where bureaucratic regulatory authority failed to emerge. Rather, I selected my cases because they were the initial instances of a new type of state that had important implications for popular control of democratic politics.[5]

There are two problems with selecting cases to ensure variation across independent and dependent variables. First, not all theories and historical transformations are equally important: their importance can only be determined through their association with cultural values. This methodological issue is conceptually distinct from questions associated with variation and questions associated with causality and "tests" of a theory. Hardly specific to the social sciences, *all* scientific inquiry is predicated upon assumptions regarding the value or "meaning" of the patterns scientists seek to explain.[6]

Second, selecting cases to generate variation across variables is a problematic method for isolating causality when a limited number of observations are being examined.[7] Expanding the number of cases under examination is no guarantee this problem of isolating causality will be overcome, because doing so expands the number of possible confounding variables, thereby failing to overcome the problem that the inclusion of additional cases is supposed to overcome in the first place.[8]

One way to overcome this problem is to use experimental methods that allow the manipulation of treatment and control groups to determine causal relationships among independent and dependent variables.[9] Although social scientists have increasingly adopted experimental methodological techniques, elite decision making—a key subject of analysis in this book—rarely allows assignment of treatment and control. Furthermore, important historical events rarely occur in the context of natural experiments, and when a small number of decisions are responsible for new developmental patterns, the application of experimental methods becomes even less appropriate.

If we seek causal explanations for developmental sequences associated with important cultural values, and if we do not merely study phenomena that generate variation on independent and dependent variables, occur as a result of quasi-natural experiments, or facilitate the application of statistical methods, one must adopt methodological techniques, such as process tracing and historical counterfactuals, that are appropriate for studying elite phenomena with small numbers of cases.[10]

This book studies three cases that influenced the creation of the American regulatory state. First, I examine how conflicts over the gold standard influenced American party ideology and state formation. This section of the argument considers how the Northern Civil War funding operations and partisan conflict over the gold standard influenced the Treasury Department's administrative capacity, and suggests that the Treasury Department was empowered to exercise powers preceding the subsequent emergence of central banking authority that occurred later in American history.

My second case examines the politics of free silver and inflationary demands for the free coinage of silver at the ratio of 16 to 1. This section discusses how voter ignorance influenced political decisions and the myths surrounding the free silver issue during the 1870s through the 1890s. Unlike my other cases, my examination of the silver issue does not directly focus on American state formation. Instead, this case examines how conflicts over free silver influenced the Democratic Party's demands for federal economic intervention, inaugurating a shift in the ideology of the Democratic Party with important implications for American politics.

The third case examines how railroad regulation influenced American state formation. This section focuses on the creation of the Interstate Commerce Commission (ICC), one of America's first independent commissions that regulated the American railroad industry. Instead of focusing on public opinion or the demands of organized economic groups, this case examines how the contested election of 1876, and the political bargain that became known as the Compromise of 1877, influenced railroad regulation and the creation of the ICC. Even though there are important differences among these cases, each played an important role in influencing party ideologies and the creation of the American regulatory state.

Although I do not examine cases where this type of state authority failed to emerge, the historical conditions surrounding these cases constitute "most difficult" tests of my theoretical argument for four reasons.[11] First, I focus on how elected officials, and not unelected judges or bureaucrats, operated autonomously from public opinion and electoral demands. As elected officials are those officials most exposed to elections and public opinion, I examine actors that should be most sensitive to democratic pressures, and not those whose positions are removed from influence by public opinion.

This focus, however, has important implications for the inferences we draw from these cases. For if elected officials enjoy ignorance-induced autonomy from society, unelected officials may enjoy even greater levels of autonomy because they do not directly face electoral pressures. Indeed, my focus on elected officials may *understate* the autonomy of the more numerous bureaucratic officials staffing modern states.

Second, I focus on two policies—monetary policy and railroad regulation —that were among the most contentious issues of the late nineteenth century. Instead of studying the far more numerous policies that never solicited public attention or became topics during elections, I examine two issues that generated widespread media coverage and popular attention. If state elites enjoyed autonomy over contentious policy decisions, state autonomy may be even more pervasive for the far more numerous, and less visible, policies that receive little media attention or popular interest.

Third, the historical period I examine (1860s–1890s) is a particularly unlikely arena to find evidence of state autonomy. Unlike contemporary America, where around 50 percent of the public does not vote in presidential elections, late nineteenth century America exhibited a vibrant participatory political culture where more than 80 percent of the electorate participated in elections at all levels of government. This period's extensive political participation has led many to conclude this was a uniquely democratic moment in American politics. If elites were able to elude popular control and manipulate public opinion during a period of rampant political engagement, democratic states may enjoy even greater autonomy when voters are apathetic and disengaged.

Fourth, the restricted scope of government during this period should have made it relatively easy for voters to become politically informed. Nineteenth-century policy debates were relatively simple, often merely involving such questions as whether more or less money should be put into circulation or whether railroads should be prevented from charging different prices based upon the distance they shipped goods. As the scope and complexity of government has expanded dramatically since the late nineteenth century, the thousands of public decisions and proliferation of governmental regulatory agencies that has occurred have compounded the amount of information voters need to become informed. If political elites acted autonomously when the scope and complexity of government was limited, state autonomy may be more extensive when the scope and complexity of government is expansive.

Aside from revealing this period's importance for American politics, these issues indicate that studying representation in the late nineteenth century may also help illuminate certain aspects of contemporary American politics. For since the nineteenth century, Americans' political engagement has declined while the scope and complexity of government has expanded. If my argument about the relationship between voter ignorance and state autonomy is correct, contemporary democratic states may enjoy even more autonomy than they did in prior historical periods because voters have become more apathetic and democratic politics involves regulatory issues that are more numerous and complex than they were in earlier periods of American history.

I should note that while my historical argument is limited to explaining the origins of American state authority, my theoretical argument is predicated upon general propositions that make it applicable beyond the American case. However, the specific way that voter-ignorance-induced state autonomy influences different democracies in specific historical episodes cannot be extrapolated from my theoretical argument. Rather, it is only possible to develop certain general propositions to serve as preliminary assumptions to guide empirical inquiry into how voter ignorance and state autonomy vary in different contexts and settings.

Using underutilized manuscript collections, and drawing new interpretations from these sources, this book offers a new explanation for the creation of the American regulatory state. Aside from explaining this institutional development, I develop a theory of state autonomy in democratic societies with implications for understanding how political power is exercised in the society that emerged from these historical transformations.

CHAPTER SUMMARY

Let me say something about the structure of the book and the role each chapter plays in my general argument. Each empirical chapter's introduction summarizes the chapter's objectives, and is followed by historical material organized around questions determined by the theory. Each empirical chapter concludes with a counterfactual discussion of what would have happened if voters had been informed, or if the events the chapter examines had not occurred, or had occurred in a different way.[12]

The individual chapters of the book are organized as follows. Chapter 1 conceptually distinguishes the specific historical transformation I seek to explain, the creation of a new type of American state. It is critical to note the numerous studies documenting the existence of governance and administration in the antebellum republic, especially at the state and local levels. Despite recognizing the numerous cases of active governance and administration that existed prior to the Civil War, chapter 1 argues that the postbellum American state exhibited three novel characteristics distinguishing it from prior forms of American government.

First, the *level* of government was altered, and new forms of authority were placed in the hands of federal, not state or local, officials. Second, there was a shift in authority between the *branches* of government, as power shifted from legislatures and courts to executive bureaucrats and independent commissions. Third, the federal state pursued regulatory objectives that were distinct from prior forms of government, increasingly focused on *regulating* the market price system and not simply facilitating industrialization or engaging in distributive actions such as postal delivery. The combination of these three characteristics constituted a new type of state that was increasingly applied to the American economy, marking a divergence from prior forms of American governance.

My discussion of this institutional shift is embedded within a discussion of party ideologies before the Civil War, a discussion that examines the political parties' positions on such issues as federal power, the role of respective branches of government, and the types of government action they endorsed. In addition to discussing the institutional characteristics of the state that emerged following the Civil War, this chapter examines the ideological belief systems of political parties in the second (1828–1854) and third (1854–1896) American party systems. This discussion is intended to clarify both the institutional shift I focus on explaining and the changing components of the party ideologies associated with this shift in state power.

Chapter 2 presents a theory of the state that argues widespread public ignorance grants democratic states autonomy from society. This chapter makes three arguments regarding the consequences high levels of voter ignorance have for modern democratic political systems: I argue that public ignorance grants democratic states autonomy from society, allows elite manipulation of public opinion, and facilitates regulatory capture. Although this theory is applied to the context of nineteenth-century American state formation, its simplicity makes it generally applicable to the analysis of modern democratic states, especially since certain changes that have occurred since the nineteenth century, such as an expanded scope and complexity of government, have made it more difficult for anyone to become politically informed.

Chapter 3 begins the historical analysis by examining how Civil War finance policy influenced American state formation. This chapter considers Northern war finance in the context of Eastern financiers' preferences and demands, and argues that the public was largely unaware of how the federal government financed the Civil War. Although this chapter examines how war influenced

American state formation, it is also used to establish certain conditions that are important for the following chapter, which focuses on how voter ignorance created opportunities for certain politicians to manipulate public opinion in the elections following the conclusion of the Civil War.

Chapter 4 analyzes how public ignorance influenced elections and monetary policy in the immediate postbellum period. Recognizing that the Democrats' associations with secession made them electorally vulnerable, Midwestern Democrats George Pendleton and Clement Vallandigham began demanding inflationary monetary policies to introduce an economic issue that was isolated from secession, the Civil War, and the "bloody shirt." Doing so required these Democrats to popularize fictitious claims regarding their preferred policies, the positions they took during Civil War, and the positions of bankers and members of the Republican Party. However, since voters had little understanding of the government's Civil War funding operations, or various political and economic groups' positions toward such funding methods, Pendleton's message was more persuasive than it would have been had voters been informed.

Chapter 5 examines the election of 1868 and argues that despite winning the presidency, the Republican Party was convinced that the Democrats had reintroduced monetary policy into postbellum American political debate and had placed the Republicans on the unpopular side of the issue. In addition to influencing the specific issue positions occupying political debate, the Democrats' new monetary activism inaugurated a new willingness to use the federal government to intervene in the economy.

Although the Democrats initially focused on increasing the volume of paper "greenbacks" in circulation, in the early 1870s collapsing silver prices created the possibility that inflationary monetary policy could reenter political debate in the form of silver, and not paper, currency. The politics of free silver would become deeply associated with the Populist Party, William Jennings Bryan's candidacy in the presidential election of 1896, and the ideological development of the Democratic Party. Indeed, when Bryan used the Democratic platform of 1896 to endorse free silver and the proactive government action necessary for inflationary monetary policy, he completed the Democrats' transition to endorsing federal regulation of the economy.

Aside from influencing Bryan and the election of 1896, the free silver issue has been used as evidence of Americans' willingness to endorse paranoid conspiracy theories. This argument was famously made in Richard Hofstadter's essay "The Paranoid Style of American Politics," and was further developed in

The Age of Reform. Hofstadter claimed there was little evidence supporting the Populists' claims that bankers bribed public officials to remove silver currency from circulation, and subsequent studies by Irwin Unger, Allen Weinstein, and Milton Friedman and Anna Schwartz shared Hofstadter's conclusion that the Populists exhibited paranoid and irrational tendencies.

Chapter 6 argues that the studies echoing Hofstadter's claims have erroneously dismissed the Populists' suspicions of conspiratorial dealings. This chapter claims that the Populists' central contention—that a banker bribed a key official to influence silver policy—is far more accurate than has been realized. The chapter examines how William C. Ralston, president of the Bank of California, paid thousands of dollars to Henry Linderman, the official who wrote the Coinage Act of 1873, the legislation that the Populists claimed was influenced by bankers and bribery and was denounced as the "Crime of '73." Rather than being based upon circumstantial evidence, this chapter presents evidence from Ralston's correspondence detailing his payments to Linderman, including one of the actual checks he paid Linderman with, which were preserved in Ralston's papers.

Ralston's involvement in the Coinage Act's passage requires a revision of our understanding of the Populists and the ideological transformation that Bryan's candidacy inaugurated. Furthermore, the errors in the subsequent historiography, and the fact that Ralston's involvement in finance policy was unknown to practically every major study of this period, have broader ramifications for our understanding of issues involving dissemination of information in modern societies, the nature of conspiracy theories and myths, and the difficulties facing anyone attempting to understand political events. Although chapter 6 examines how public ignorance distorts democratic representation, the chapter also suggests that talented elites with high incentives to become informed face the same epistemological problems confronting voters, difficulties that frustrate anyone's efforts to understand or accurately reconstruct political events.

Thus, in addition to helping improve our understanding of certain political events during this period, chapter 6 serves as a critique of elites' ability to understand political events, indicating that the problems posed by public ignorance cannot be eliminated by simplistic recommendations such as increasing education or the wider dissemination of factual data. Indeed, the fact that the suspicions of the Populists and many nineteenth-century Americans were, in a sense, more accurate than the academic studies that followed indicates that popular understanding may, in certain instances, be more accurate than elite understanding of political events.

Chapter 7 examines how the Panic of 1873 resulted in a final wave of popular support for greenback inflation, leading to a Democratic House majority for the first time since the conclusion of the Civil War. In this context, lame-duck Republicans drafted a bill delegating monetary policy to the Treasury Department to prevent the incoming House Democratic majority from implementing inflationary currency policies. Delegation to the Treasury Department was a critical moment in American state formation, marking one of the initial instances where federal bureaucrats were granted regulatory authority over the national economy. Hardly a response to interest group pressure or public opinion, this decision was a desperate effort by certain conservatives who sought to resume the gold standard despite recognizing its widespread unpopularity.

Chapter 8 examines how, a mere two years after the Democrats' victory in 1874, a victory that was widely interpreted as a mandate for currency inflation, both parties endorsed the gold standard in the presidential election of 1876. This policy convergence was influenced by the strategy Rutherford Hayes used to emerge as an unexpected candidate for the Republican nomination. Despite the Republicans' dire electoral situation, Hayes recognized that if he could win the Ohio gubernatorial election of 1875 he could become the Republican presidential nominee for the election of 1876.

Aware of the unpopularity of the Republicans' economic policy positions, Hayes exploited voter ignorance in the Ohio gubernatorial election of 1875 by claiming that the Ohio Democrats sought to impose Catholic religious instruction on the Ohio public schools. Although there was no basis for these claims, Hayes successfully drew public attention away from his unpopular economic policies, and after he won the Ohio election, he secured the Republican presidential nomination for the election of 1876, which he subsequently won. Hayes's 1875 victory in Ohio caused a convergence in the parties' monetary positions in the subsequent presidential election, ensuring the country would resume the gold standard regardless of which party won the election of 1876.

Chapter 9 examines how the election of 1876 was thrown into controversy when it became unclear which party had carried certain Southern states. This chapter focuses on how the Republicans promised certain Southern Democrats railroad subsidies to extend Thomas Scott's Texas and Pacific Railroad into their districts in exchange for making Hayes president. Initially documented by C. Vann Woodward in *Reunion and Reaction: The Compromise of 1877 and the End of Reconstruction,* the Compromise of 1877 collapsed after

Hayes became president and refused to fulfill his vague promises to aid Scott's railroad.

Aside from robbing Southern Democrats of railroad subsidies, the collapse of the Compromise of 1877 led Texas Democrat John Reagan to introduce legislation to help Scott's railroad empire and deliver railroad developments to Reagan's district. Although few understood why Reagan was suddenly championing railroad regulation, his bill generated support from agrarian groups and other House Democrats. While various studies have argued that railroad regulation was a result of popular opposition to the railroads, shippers' demands, or the railroads themselves, political pressures associated with the collapse of the Compromise of 1877 led Reagan to introduce his important bill.

Although Reagan championed railroad regulation to pursue short-term political objectives, his bill tapped into widespread dissatisfaction with the railroads, leading him to advocate railroad regulation long after the factors that had led him to introduce his bill subsided. However important the Reagan bill was for regulating the railroads, the ultimate product of the railroad issue was the creation of an independent regulatory commission, even though Reagan never sought to use his bill to create such an entity. In this sense, Reagan and the interests that endorsed his bill were not responsible for the effects railroad regulation had upon American state formation. It took a second set of actors to propose creating an administrative agency to regulate the railroad industry, an institutional development that Reagan consistently opposed.

Chapter 10 explains how Reagan's bill caused a reaction among members of the liberal reform faction of the Republican Party who endorsed creating an independent commission to blunt the more radical implications of Reagan's bill. Liberal reformers hoped expert commissioners would make more effective regulatory decisions than legislatures, and also hoped commissioners would disseminate impartial information to help voters make rational decisions. Liberal reformers' endorsement of a regulatory commission was influenced by their pessimism regarding the public's understanding of the complex forces that were transforming the American economy.

Chapter 11 examines the free silver movement and how William Jennings Bryan's demands for the free coinage of silver marked the Democrats' final turn toward federal regulatory activism. This chapter discusses how some of Ralston's allies either remained silent regarding their actions on Ralston's behalf or popularized fictitious claims regarding the forces responsible for the Coinage Act of 1873. The chapter focuses on the actions of one of Ralston's allies, Nevada Republican William Stewart, who became a prominent leader of the free silver movement even though he had assisted Ralston with the Coinage Act.

Chapter 12 discusses how populist social demands led certain liberal reformers and Republicans to endorse bureaucracy as a means of resisting public opinion and in an attempt to educate voters. This chapter suggests that public opinion was not demanding the creation of bureaucracies or the specific policies the Treasury Department and the Interstate Commerce Commission were implementing. The chapter argues that, far from responding to popular demands, certain conservatives empowered bureaucracies to implement policies they believed were deeply unpopular. In this sense the American regulatory state cannot be explained as a product of popular outrage toward industrialization. Although the public was increasingly turning to democratic politics to protect it from the forces of industrialization, the bureaucratic institutions that were created in response to these demands were not intended to satisfy popular policy preferences but were instead intended to remove political decisions from popular control and implement policies that elites of all political orientations recognized were unpopular.

The book's concluding chapter is divided into two sections. The first section discusses the effects these specific historical transformations had for subsequent episodes of American political development. The second section steps back from the details of the historical argument and reflects on the more general ramifications this book has for our understanding of democratic politics.

Specifically, the second section of the Conclusion focuses on discussing how the informational problems that existed in the nineteenth century have only been exacerbated by certain political conditions in contemporary America. For since the nineteenth century, Americans have become increasingly apathetic and politically ignorant, while the expanding scope of the administrative state has made it progressively more difficult for anyone to become informed. As the state has come to regulate an increasing number of economic and social relationships, the sheer number of public decisions has multiplied. This has made it impossible for anyone to become informed of what government is doing, and has rendered the state increasingly autonomous from society, while also empowering political elites who disseminate explanations of politics for popular consumption. This indicates that American society has changed in ways that have only made it more difficult for contemporary voters to become informed, indicating that this book's theoretical argument may be more applicable to explaining political events in our contemporary democracies than in prior periods of American political development.

Chapter 1 The Modern Regulatory State

Since the nineteenth century scholars have focused on studying two developments that have transformed the modern world. On the one hand, they have sought to understand the conditions that led to the rise of capitalism, the engine of economic growth that has altered every society it has touched. Yet on the other hand, as markets have proliferated and societies industrialized, there has been a corresponding expansion in another object of scholarly investigation: the modern state.

Modern states are engaged in a wide variety of regulatory and redistributive actions; they possess enormous coercive powers, have extensive financial resources, and impose a range of regulatory decisions upon their economies. Given these attributes, and their derivation of legitimacy from the consent of the governed, modern states are among the most powerful human organizations ever created. The study of the modern state's origins, development, and tendencies has occupied countless scholars operating from a range of theoretical traditions.[1]

This book examines the origins of a specific type of state authority that initially emerged in late nineteenth-century America. I do not examine all types of state activity, nor do I suggest that America's specific developmental sequence necessarily resembled other areas of the Western world. I do not examine the numerous cases of local and state government action that existed throughout the nineteenth century, and I ignore the development of the state's military capacity, its taxation powers, and its varied social welfare functions. Instead, I focus on explaining the initial instances where the American state acquired bureaucratic regulatory authority over the market economy, and am specifically interested in assessing popular control over this institutional development.

This focus might initially seem odd, for America is often depicted as a stateless society, a laggard in terms of political development.[2] This view of America is often due to comparisons with European states that developed powerful bureaucracies, systems of public credit, and standing armies prior to mass democratization.[3] Different European states exhibited different types of bureaucratization: in certain countries corporatist class and occupational alliances checked state authority; other countries were influenced by the institutional legacies of the Catholic Church. Great Britain and the Low Countries developed legal-rational bureaucracies and systems of public credit necessary for imperial expansion.[4] Nor was the rise of the bureaucratic state simply a European development. In Ming China vast bureaucracies promulgated regulations delineated by Confucian religious doctrine. Before the centralization of Chinese political authority, bureaucracies extracted resources to finance war against neighboring states, leading to the creation of legal-rational bureaucracies prior to the emergence of such bureaucracies in Europe.[5]

While premodern states were influenced by variables associated with war and revenue extraction, modern democratic states pursue regulatory functions distinguishing them from prior forms of government. Instead of having to subjugate recalcitrant principalities, separate state revenue from the private control of the nobility, or impose religious homogeneity upon society, modern democratic states regulate market economies in ways that are markedly different from those of their predemocratic predecessors.

This is partially due to the economic conditions surrounding modern states. Modern states are immersed in market economies that are qualitatively more rationalized, and quantitatively more extensive, than those of their premodern predecessors. As the regulation of market economies requires significant technical expertise, modern states have assumed a distinct form, employing career civil servants in functionally specialized bureaucracies empowered with discretion by their legislative principals.[6]

Aside from the nature of their administrative decisions, perhaps the single most striking feature of modern democratic states is the sheer scope of their regulatory operations. Exhibiting numerous bureaucratic agencies and quasi-public corporations, producing disparate goods and services, consuming between one-third and one-half of their societies' GDP, employing nearly a quarter of the civilian labor force, and possessing highly developed coercive capacities, modern states' actions are more varied and more extensive—in the range of regulations they promulgate and in the number of officials they employ—than prior forms of governance. Indeed, the expanding scope of decisions made by democratic states has been described as a "defining characteristic of our times," a characteristic shared by every democracy in the Western world.[7]

Aside from their unique organizational characteristics, modern states are also distinct from their premodern predecessors due to the source of their legitimacy. Although modern states appeal to popular ambivalence over the antagonistic values embodied by democratic politics and market economies, modern states are legitimized by their democratic characteristics—by elections and the power of public opinion.[8]

The democratic basis of modern states' legitimacy has a number of implications for popular control of politics. Instead of being able to ignore public opinion or suppress societal dissent through force of arms, democracy is believed to ensure that states respond to popular demands and interests. Indeed, some suggest democracy makes it difficult to distinguish the state from the society it claims to represent.[9] As Richard T. Ely noted some time ago, in democracies it appears that "the state is not something apart from us and outside us, but is we ourselves."[10] By combining democratic electoral institutions with discretionary regulatory bureaucracies, modern states exhibit a combination of characteristics unique to the modern world.[11]

Despite the unprecedented power of modern states, elections and public opinion are believed to ensure that democratic states remain responsive to the societies they govern. This assumption is prevalent in popular political culture, and is exhibited by both scholarly theories of democracy and historical studies of American political development. Indeed, unlike Europe, where industrialization and state centralization preceded democratization, the American state was created in the nineteenth century when more than 80 percent of eligible voters were participating in elections at all levels of government.[12]

As America's participatory political culture was the "one area" where nineteenth-century America was "profoundly different" from European societies,[13] it seems difficult to study American political economy without acknowledging the influence of public opinion and electoral demands.[14] For when popular participation is robust—as it was throughout the nineteenth century—it seems natural to assume that democratic states respond to societal demands "because they must."[15] By assuming democracy ensures societal control of the state, studies of American political development "dissolve any stark analytic separation between state and society," as the nineteenth century's competitive electoral environment and vibrant partisan political culture appear to have limited state autonomy from society.[16]

Some argue that the influence of popular demands extended beyond elected officials to unelected bureaucrats as well.[17] Bureaucrats allegedly required "sustained ties" to voters and organized social groups to ensure successful policy implementation.[18] With nineteenth-century American government closely monitored by voters, and facing unprecedented levels of electoral participation, "sweeping assertions" of democratic responsiveness are often found in studies of this period.[19]

There are, however, several facts that, when examined from this theoretical consensus, are difficult to explain. Clearly, by the end of the nineteenth century voters were turning to democratic politics to ameliorate the effects of inequality and industrialization. Yet prior to the Civil War "few if any of the common people regarded government as a means by which economic and social power might be redistributed or the problems of their lives resolved."[20] Oddly, some have noted that before the Civil War the disadvantaged economic groups that led demands for the state's expansion had expressed opposition to positive visions of the federal government. Before the war it was "among subsistence farmers in the most remote and economically underdeveloped regions of states" that the "doctrine of a negative state . . . became . . . [a] dogma."[21]

Although various late nineteenth-century electoral groups demanded legislation to counteract the effects of markets and industrialization, the writings of antebellum Democrats such as Orestes Brownson, Thomas Hart Benton, and William Leggett express views of government diametrically opposed to these demands.[22] While many have documented exceptions to these attitudes, "the tendency of democratic politics"—where contemporaries would expect to find the disadvantaged demanding government action—was in fact "to let more and more alone."[23] Thus although subsequent reformers championed redistribution, social programs, and various forms of market regulation, antebellum Democrats "envisioned no such programs."[24]

One can, of course, find exceptions to this trend. For example, Thomas Skidmore, theoretician of the New York Working Men's Party, is regularly cited as a precursor to New Deal liberalism.[25] Skidmore is interesting, however, precisely because he "was not a typical artisan who espoused 'representative' views," for when he advocated property redistribution in *The Rights of Man to Property*, he was "savagely attacked" by members of the labor movement and conservatives who were critical of it.[26] Although some claim liberal ideas are "deeply imbedded," albeit "carefully hidden," in the writings of antebellum labor radicals, these ideas have been difficult to find.[27]

This is not to suggest that antebellum Americans ignored economic grievances or failed to advocate political remedies during periods of hardship. Writers such as George Fitzhugh produced scathing critiques of capitalism and industrialization.[28] The remedies suggested by these critics, however, were often qualitatively different from those espoused by subsequent reformers. Antebellum agrarian and labor organizations denounced poverty, working conditions, economic exploitation, and inequality—and then demanded free trade and the gold standard; Fitzhugh indicted Northern industrialization and endorsed slavery and racial apartheid; Fourier socialists denounced mechanization and poverty only to recommend creating phalanxes in local townships.

Antebellum Americans' attitudes become even more perplexing when we examine the Democrats' Whig opponents. While contemporary conservatives' opposition to state intervention seems natural and self-evident, before the Civil War affluent Protestant Whigs sought to provide "centralized direction to social policy."[29] Hardly championing a negative state, the antebellum Whigs endorsed Henry Clay's "American System" and its combination of a protective tariff, a national bank, and government support for internal improvements to facilitate industrial development. Oddly, it was only after the Civil War that "the idea of a positive relationship between government and economic life . . . [fell] out of favor among those who underwrote the conservative program."[30] Despite government efforts to promote industrial development, "*interestingly*, a laissez-faire critique of government . . . *did not* surface" during this period among the affluent Protestant Whigs.[31]

Antebellum attitudes "appear illogical" to commentators today because they reverse the means that have become associated with specific cultural values and ends.[32] For it was the Whigs, and their affluent Protestant constituents, who supported state-led industrialization and positive government action, while ethnic and religious minorities, laborers, marginal agrarians, and the poor supported the Democrats and their commitment to nonintervention.[33] Indeed, it was this paradoxical combination of ideas that progressives such as Herbert Croly sought to replace with a new nationalist culture and a state that would wield Hamiltonian means to achieve Jeffersonian ends.

Antebellum Americans' attitudinal configuration has been described as an "unresolved paradox," a "massive confusion of political traditions" so severe that, in the words of one historian, it apparently "reverses the facts."[34] Yet at some point these assumptions were transformed, and as marginal economic groups began demanding the state take a more proactive role in American social life, there was a corresponding institutional transformation as the American state began empowering independent commissions and federal bureaucracies to regulate the industrial market economy.

It is, of course, necessary to recognize important exceptions to these generalizations, for antebellum Democrats were not simply advocates of laissez-faire, and at no point has America ever resembled a "night-watchman" state. Although the intellectual positions of various writers often express skepticism toward federal power, the actions of antebellum government were far more active than such rhetoric suggests. Jacksonian Democrats endorsed programs such as federal appropriations for the Cumberland Road and the improvement of harbors and lighthouses, and the antigovernment rhetoric of Jacksonian Democrats was often at variance with their actions in office, especially at the state and local levels.[35]

Indeed, antebellum America was hardly "stateless," for state and local governments regulated numerous activities, ranging from banking and internal improvements to education.[36] Yet when all the exceptions are catalogued it is clear that the scope of *federal* action remained restricted, and yet it is the federal government that has experienced a great expansion.[37] As the American state existed in a political culture hostile to enlarging federal authority, there were "few advances in its services and activities" during this period.[38]

At some point in the late nineteenth century, however, a transformation of popular attitudes clearly occurred, and this attitudinal reversal influenced American state formation. Once the public began demanding federal regulation of the economy, the expansion of state authority appeared to be a "near-automatic response" to industrialization; for with every new market discovered, developed, and exploited, corporations were seen to be "fit subjects for regulation."[39] But while the creation of the American regulatory state is often attributed to popular demands, it is unclear why the assumptions that structured American politics throughout the first and second party systems were abandoned.

It is possible that this attitudinal reversal was a response to changes in the American economy. With the demise of artisanal modes of production, the proliferation of production for markets, industrialization, the rise of the modern corporation, and a transportation revolution that transformed isolated "island communities" into an economically integrated society, voters may have turned to the federal government to control the impersonal economic forces that were increasingly influencing their lives.[40]

Changes in the American economy do not, however, appear to be correlated with this attitudinal reversal. Between 1839 and 1859 the value added by manufacturing and agricultural output grew by more than 270 percent.[41] Surging industrial productivity and trade among the country's major industrial centers were linked by a canal system and regional railroads, long before the Golden Spike was driven at Promontory Point.[42] Before the Civil War, rising levels of industrial production, the creation of stock markets, and improvements in communication technology occurred nationally, integrating capital markets and causing a convergence in short-term interest rates that extended to the South by the 1840s.[43]

Although a virtual "market revolution" occurred decades prior to the Civil War, this economic transformation did not create a corresponding ideological shift among the political parties.[44] Even if we assume that voters' demands for federal action were a response to the intensification of these economic transformations after the Civil War, we cannot explain the *type* of regulatory state that emerged from these transformations. Although nineteenth-century Americans came to demand a greater role for government in the economy, the radical groups that led these demands, such as the Granger movement and the Populists, opposed the *type* of state that emerged: federal, regulatory, and bureaucratic.[45]

Although labor and agrarian groups often called for increasing the federal government's role over the economy, they did not call for an expansion of *bureaucratic* authority. In cases where antebellum labor theoreticians demanded proactive government action, they tended to endorse legislative decrees such as general incorporation laws or the ten-hour workday, measures requiring little administrative regulation. Recognizing the novelty of these attitudes, labor historian David Montgomery has suggested that the general "incapacity to envision the state as an administrative agency" was indicative of a "mental limitation" exhibited by many Americans during this period.[46]

Yet here we encounter another paradox: although the Whigs endorsed state-led industrialization, they drew upon an intellectual tradition that demanded subordinating the executive to the legislature.[47] The opinions of Whigs such as Adams, Webster, and Clay on the tariff and internal improvements exhibit hostility toward executive power, indicating that although the Whigs endorsed an activist state they did not endorse expanding *bureaucratic* authority.[48] Given the disjuncture between these political attitudes and institutional forms, the creation of the American bureaucratic state has been described as a "major anomaly" that remains "*the* paradox" of American political development, for popular demands "deeply hostile to bureaucracy" appear to have "produced a great bureaucratic expansion."[49]

This indicates that the expansion of bureaucratic authority is an *institutional* innovation that requires explanation.[50] Although bureaucracy has become a ubiquitous feature of the American state, before the Civil War there was widespread "distrust of professionalized administration and complex administrative machinery," and expert administration was believed to be neither "necessary or desirable."[51] Since many believed discretionary administrative action to be "unequal and impolitic but also coercive and evil," the "strict limitation of executive discretion was a cardinal principle" endorsed by many Americans.[52] The empowerment of regulatory bureaucracies with discretionary authority poses an additional paradox for understanding American political development, for this regulatory technique was not widely used prior to the Civil War.[53]

This claim is admittedly imprecise; it is critical to recognize that the development of American bureaucratic institutions was not a linear process, and that both state and federal bureaucrats took a range of positive actions before the Civil War.[54] Furthermore, it is important to recognize that the Federalists developed defenses of executive authority,[55] and bureaucrats exercised discretion in decisions ranging from Treasury assessment of imports, mail delivery, granting patents, military procurement, and Indian affairs.[56]

As Jerry Mashaw has demonstrated, within the Treasury Department an independent commission regulated steamboat safety and developed a coherent body of administrative law years before the Civil War.[57] In addition, the General Land Office sold vast tracts of Western land, and the U.S. Postal Service developed a professionalized bureaucracy with significant independence from

Congress.[58] Within the Treasury Department, Alexander Hamilton resorted to open market financing operations and developed the principles subsequently codified in Bagehot's rule to combat the Panic of 1792, and after the veto of the recharter of the Second Bank of the United States Treasury officials enjoyed discretion when depositing federal funds in state banks.[59] In addition to these examples of federal administration, bureaucratic commissions at the state level administered various government enterprises, such as Ohio's canal system and various states' railroads, and New York used commissions to set toll rates and sell bonds to finance and operate the Erie Canal.

Yet while there clearly were cases of bureaucratic action before the Civil War, these actions were typically not focused on the specific *type* of government action that this book examines. Specifically, these actions did not focus on the *regulation* of markets, nor did they seek to achieve economic fairness; instead they focused on distributive issues such as mail delivery, the collection of tariff revenue, land sales, and promotional efforts to encourage economic development, especially at the state and local levels.

Generally, antebellum bureaucratic actions did not seek to regulate markets or enhance the efficiency of the market price mechanism. Nor is this entirely surprising, for despite rampant economic development, the antebellum American economy had not become national, there were no transcontinental railroads, and, as scholars such as Alfred Chandler Jr., Martin Sklar, and Robert Wiebe have documented, the development of national corporations and the demise of locally oriented proprietary exchange did not occur until the turn of the century.

Furthermore, even after recognizing the numerous cases of antebellum administrative authority, it remains unclear why such authority was often used for such limited objectives. If administrative action, independent commissions, and executive discretion existed before the Civil War, why was such authority used for mundane purposes such as mail delivery and steamboat boiler safety inspections? Indeed, once we recognize that administrative discretion existed in antebellum America, it becomes even more puzzling that such authority was not used to regulate markets or ensure greater degrees of economic fairness.

For example, the Treasury Department's incipient forms of discretion remained transient and were used infrequently—for example, to retire war debt, to select banks to hold federal funds, or to issue a limited amount of noncirculating interest-bearing currency. Instead of implementing a coherent monetary policy or appropriating the regulatory authority enjoyed by the Second

Bank of the United States, America witnessed the veto of the recharter of the Second Bank of the United States, the distribution of federal funds among state banks, and then attempts to divorce the federal government from private banking with the Independent Treasury system and the specie circular.[60]

Although the Treasury Department technically could manipulate the money supply through its control over deposits in state banks, Jerry Mashaw recognizes that by 1836 Congress had intervened to regulate the use of federal deposits in ways that "sharply limited" the Treasury's ability to regulate the money supply, and took various actions that "seriously inhibited the Treasury's flexibility" over financial regulation.[61] Instead of delegating responsibility for a coherent monetary policy to the treasury secretary, Congress required that federal surpluses be deposited in state banks on the inflexible basis of their relative representation in Congress.

Even if independent regulatory authority existed in the Treasury Department's influence over Western banks, such authority was not used to direct any coherent monetary policy.[62] Indeed, the idea of exercising central banking functions did not exist until the late nineteenth century.[63] Although the Second Bank of the United States (BUS) exercised certain central banking functions through its control over the redemption of state bank notes, the Second BUS was a quasi-public corporation that was only loosely controlled by public officials.[64] Furthermore, perhaps the single most important aspect of the Second BUS is that it was *destroyed,* and hence, did not serve as a subsequent model of institutional development.

Furthermore, there was *active opposition* to independent action by the Treasury Department's own officials. Treasury secretaries such as Levi Woodbury are notable for their commitments to limiting the Treasury's authority, eliminating their discretion over the disbursement of federal monies in private banks, empowering state legislatures, and refusing to endorse any coherent monetary policy.[65] Instead of seeking independent policy authority, Woodbury's annual reports of the Treasury Department "repeatedly urged" that Congress make "full and explicit statutory provisions on all . . . important points," and called for "duly restricting executive discretion" enjoyed by the Treasury Department.[66]

Although the antebellum state was active and enjoyed discretion in certain realms, these powers were expanded in novel ways after the Civil War.[67] Instead of simply focusing on promotional and distributional policies, and instead of empowering state and local governments, the American state increasingly exercised authority at a new *level* (federal), empowered a specific *branch* of government (executive bureaucrats and independent commissions), and wielded authority for specific *purposes* (regulation of markets). As Martin Sklar has suggested, these three characteristics constituted a new kind of state that was increasingly applied in ways that had lasting implications for American politics.[68]

There are two principal problems with existing explanations of this transformation in American government. First, the economic conditions that existed during this period did not mark the initial emergence of capitalism as an economic mode of production. Production for markets, the rise of proprietary enterprises, and industrialization began before the Civil War and then underwent a period of consolidation at the turn of the century.[69] This indicates that the origins and subsequent consolidation of American capitalism occurred before and then after the period that I am arguing saw the initial emergence of the regulatory state.

Second, although populist social groups such as the Grange, the Greenback Party, and the Populists demanded expanding federal authority over the economy, these groups initially *opposed* expanding the power of federal bureaucracy in American economic life.[70] Furthermore, aside from opposing the bureaucratic institutional form the state took, these groups opposed the *policies* these newly empowered bureaucracies implemented. Specifically, populist agrarian groups opposed the Treasury Department's resumption of the gold standard, and they objected to the Interstate Commerce Commission's discretionary exemptions allowing railroads to engage in "reasonable" forms of price discrimination. Such opposition indicates that the social movements that are often used to explain the transformation of the American state were opposed to the empowerment of federal bureaucracies, and to the specific policies these bureaucracies implemented.

This book argues that the timing, and bureaucratic characteristics, of this new American state cannot be attributed to underlying economic forces, electoral demands, or the demands of powerful economic groups. Such arguments fail to explain the timing of the transformations I am examining, they cannot explain the specific type of state that emerged in the late nineteenth century, and they rest upon unrealistic assumptions regarding democratic state's responsiveness to public opinion and electoral demands.

It is critical to recognize, however, that my focus is on explaining the *timing* of the emergence of this form of state authority, and the bureaucratic-regulatory *characteristics* that this authority assumed. I am *not* arguing that this type of state would *never* have emerged were it not for specific decisions and individuals that I examine. Nor am I attempting to deny the active presence of state and local governments before the Civil War. Rather, my focus is on explaining why a specific type of regulatory state emerged in American during the late nineteenth century.

To explain this transformation in American state authority, however, we must expand our focus beyond the confines of political institutions and incorporate the analysis of a partisan-ideological shift that occurred during this period. Specifically, the creation of the American state was influenced by the emergence of popular demands for regulating the economy, an event deeply associated with the ideological development of the Democratic Party. I argue that this ideological reversal spurred an institutional innovation—namely, the delegation of discretionary authority to federal bureaucracies, which was introduced by a faction of Republicans who were attempting to prevent populist economic demands from influencing political decisions.

By delegating authority to federal bureaucracies, certain Republicans hoped they could remove political decisions from popular control and implement policies they recognized were widely unpopular. As federal bureaucracies acquired discretionary regulatory authority over the economy, these transformations generated an institutional technique that became a ubiquitous feature of American governance. Hardly intended to fulfill popular demands and desires, this institutional innovation was initially a conservative response to the shifting positions of the Democratic Party.

Chapter 2 State Autonomy in Democratic Societies

By explaining the origins of certain ideological and institutional transformations, this book seeks to answer specific historical questions about the origins of the American regulatory state. However, these empirical objectives are embedded within a broader theoretical argument. Explaining the partisan reversal that occurred, and the corresponding institutional reaction this reversal generated, requires recognizing that democratic states often enjoy a degree of autonomy from the societies they rule.

Positing that democratic states enjoy autonomy from society may seem counterintuitive, especially for modern citizens who typically assume that elections render government responsive to public opinion. Indeed, this assumption is widespread in both popular political culture and scholarly theories of democracy. Despite exhibiting innumerable distinctions and disparate predictions, pluralist, neo-Marxist, rational choice, and public choice theorists assume that democracy renders the state responsive to social preferences, electoral coalitions, and public opinion.[1] Indeed, even scholars adopting a "state-centered" perspective of modern government often assume that democracy limits the state's autonomy from society.[2]

Despite its widespread acceptance, I argue that this assumption, and the theories that adopt it, offer inaccurate accounts of how states exercise political power in modern democracies. Instead of assuming that democracy ensures societal control of the state, my principal theoretical claim is that the source of modern states' legitimacy—democracy—virtually ensures that society will not control the state, since the putative agent of control, the electorate, cannot be informed about the tasks undertaken by modern governments.[3]

Despite recognizing certain important dissimilarities, I argue that public ignorance influences democratic politics in a manner similar to how anarchy structures the international state system. This analogy focuses on the nature of these variables and their relevance for understanding the behavior of "units" populating each competitive system. Unlike classical realist and neorealist theorists of international relations, I make no assumptions regarding the motives or objectives that states or voters pursue. Nor do I make any assumptions regarding the rationality of the units (states, parties) populating each system of political competition. My analogy between public ignorance and anarchy is related to how both of these underlying conditions structure political competition in important and predictable ways.[4]

Before I proceed further, it is necessary to define certain terms. Although there are numerous definitions of democracy, I follow Joseph Schumpeter and define democracy as a method of governance where state elites are chosen on the basis of the competitive struggle for votes.[5] I define the state as a group of individuals from whose decisions there is no legitimate appeal within a defined territory.[6] Unlike Max Weber, I do not define the state solely by its monopoly of legitimate coercion. The state's monopoly of legitimate coercion is merely a *means* the state uses to secure the type of authority that is specific to it. However, it is the state's capacity to make decisions that cannot be appealed, not the state's monopoly over legitimate coercion, that conceptually distinguishes the state from social organizations such as religious organizations and private firms.[7]

Since many of my claims involve the scope, nature, and causes of state autonomy, the term "state autonomy" must be defined, especially since I employ this term in a way that is different from other state theorists. I define states as acting autonomously when they implement policies that do not merely reflect popular demands or electoral pressures.[8] This conceptualization of state autonomy is distinct from Marxist state theorists who focus on the state's independence from social classes, and neo-Weberians, such as Theda Skocpol, who attribute state autonomy to the state's institutional capacities, such as standing armies, loyal bureaucracies, and access to taxation revenue.[9]

The concept of state autonomy, as originally derived from Marx and Engels, was a simple empirical observation that states occasionally enjoyed a degree of independence from economic classes, an observation further developed in debates between instrumentalist and structural neo-Marxist state theorists.[10] Marxist state theorists attribute state autonomy to the temporary weakness, or equilibrium, of class power, even if such weakness merely results in the state's acting in the long-term interests of dominant economic groups. Despite offering insights into the nature of various predemocratic governments, state autonomy from social and economic classes is not the principal focus of my analyses, even though I do examine the preferences of various economic groups to establish their influence over public decisions.

My principal focus, however, is on state autonomy *from the electorate;* I am particularly concerned with how the public's knowledge of politics, and not the power of economic groups, social classes, or states' access to resources and institutions, influences state autonomy. Unlike other state theorists, I attribute state autonomy to behavioral variables associated with the public's knowledge of politics and not to the relative strength of economic classes or the state's institutional capacities. My theory of state autonomy focuses on the informational division of labor between elites and the public, and on elites' dissemination of explanations for events that influence popular conceptions of politics.

It is important to note that I do not argue that public opinion and electoral demands never *influence* politics, nor do I argue that public officials are inattentive to public opinion. Despite recognizing that popular demands may influence election outcomes and remove parties from power, the crude messages and explanations which elites disseminate, and which influence public opinion, are made persuasive by the public's ignorance and voters' resulting inability to recognize distortions and falsehoods.

According to this conceptualization, state autonomy is derived from voter ignorance of politics, and not from the economic structure of society, the interests of powerful corporate groups, the state's position in the international state system, or its control of powerful institutional resources. Indeed, the institutional characteristics neo-Weberian state theorists use to explain state autonomy are treated here as the objects of historical explanation, and not as independent variables responsible for state autonomy.

Unfortunately, public ignorance has been described as one of the strongest findings of the social sciences. Although democracy is often assumed to ensure that states respond to social demands, voters are typically ignorant of basic political information, such as the names of their representatives, the policies governments implement, or the effects policies have upon society.[11] Usually only about half of Americans can name a single congressional candidate running for office, only 10 percent can name a policy their representative has supported, and 70 percent cannot name their senators.[12]

Voters are also ignorant of major policy debates. In the 1980s, 70 percent of Americans could not describe *Roe v. Wade;* in 1972, only 22 percent of Americans knew what Watergate was about; in 1985, only 31 percent knew what affirmative action was.[13] In 1964, in the middle of the Cold War, 64 percent of the American public did not know that the Soviet Union was not a member of NATO; and in 1948 a majority of Americans were unaware that the Berlin airlift was occurring.[14]

Although most findings of public ignorance are derived from twentieth-century survey research, there is evidence that voters were poorly informed in earlier periods of American history as well. Richard Bensel's study of contested nineteenth-century elections finds that some voters could not identify Abraham Lincoln a few years after the Civil War and were often ignorant of basic facts, such as the location of the South and the fact that children could not be older than their parents.[15] Finding that ethnic and religious identities, and not abstract economic issues, often determined nineteenth-century American political behavior, Ronald Formisano concludes that studies of this period must recognize that "mass political knowledge [was] . . . low and . . . voting . . . generally lacked issue orientation."[16]

Recognizing that nineteenth-century Americans were often poorly informed, Robert Wiebe argues such ignorance was politically consequential as well. Wiebe suggests that the salience of ethnocultural identities for nineteenth-century mass politics created a bifurcated political culture, separating the issues occupying mass electoral politics from the economic policy debates that were the principal focus of public officials' actions in office.[17] Many argue that public ignorance is hardly limited to contemporary American politics but was widespread in earlier periods of American history as well.

Since voter awareness of the state's actions is a prerequisite for popular control of government, high levels of voter ignorance may grant democratic states autonomy from popular control. As Angus Campbell, Philip Converse, Warren Miller, and Donald Stokes recognized some time ago, voter ignorance may grant "great freedom" to public officials simply because the existence, implementation, and effects of public decisions are largely unknown to modern electorates.[18]

However, voter ignorance of empirical information, such as the names of elected officials and their actions in office, is only one aspect of the information problem facing modern electorates. For knowledge of empirical information is not adequate to ensure that voters understand politics; they must also have correct theories to accurately interpret the empirical information they acquire. If accurate scientific theories are complex, or involve counterintuitive causal relationships between variables that are difficult to explain, public ignorance of empirical information may represent only one aspect of the knowledge problems facing democratic publics.

It is important to emphasize that I am not arguing that these forms of ignorance must be overcome before voters can influence politics, as this would establish an unrealistic standard for democratic representation to occur. Indeed, it is unrealistic to expect anyone, voters and experts alike, to acquire the information and theoretical understanding necessary to understand modern political decisions. Instead, various information shortcuts and decision heuristics, such as the positions of liked or disliked social groups, information from daily life, the miracle of aggregation, value orientations, and retrospective evaluations, are believed to allow voters to make reasonable political decisions "as if" they were derived from larger amounts of information.[19]

Unfortunately, information shortcuts may not ensure democratic responsiveness, for four reasons. First, heuristics, such as the positions of social groups, can be manipulated by political elites in ways that frustrate popular accountability. Second, retrospective voting may not ensure popular control of government, because the policy decisions, parties, and politicians responsible for social conditions may be indirect and uncertain. Third, the miracle of aggregation may not cancel out voters' judgmental errors, because the distribution of errors within public opinion is not random. Finally, political elites may be able to popularize simple explanations for social events that inaccurately attribute policy effects to public decisions in ways that frustrate popular control and comprehension of politics.

I must emphasize that my conception of state autonomy does not argue that voters cannot *influence* politics, and it does not require that voters attain detailed understanding of political decisions to limit the state's autonomy. Rather, I recognize that public opinion may influence officials' calculations and policy decisions, and elections may remove parties and politicians from power in

ways that have significant effects on the political system. Even if public opinion is manipulated, orchestrated, or framed by elites, the public's manipulated
opinions may still influence politics and constrain state elites.

I do not seek to ignore, or minimize, such arguments, nor do I argue that
the state is never influenced by public opinion. Rather, I argue that such instances of opinion manipulation and mobilization, while influencing politics,
may also enhance state autonomy if public officials successfully popularize
inaccurate explanations for politics that prevent voters from recognizing and
penalizing the officials responsible for certain decisions. Regardless of whether
opinion manipulation constrains or enhances state autonomy, understanding
opinion manipulation requires recognizing how political elites interact with
a poorly informed electorate, and how public ignorance of political information provides the underlying condition that allows elites to manipulate public
opinion in the first place.

Yet recognizing that public opinion may influence politics does not establish that the public *controls* public policy, the actions of politicians, or the
social conditions voters seek to manipulate. For example, if a party is removed
from power because voters mistakenly believe the party was responsible for a
policy that it actually did not implement, voters may influence the state without controlling it. Similarly, if voters seek to penalize politicians responsible
for implementing an unpopular policy but cannot identify the politicians responsible for the policy, voters may lack the information necessary to control
the government's policy outputs even though their electoral decisions may
influence the politicians and parties that hold power.

While democracy is believed to ensure societal control of the state, voter
ignorance may grant democratic states autonomy from society even when they
face elections and the power of public opinion. I argue that public ignorance
has three principal effects on democratic politics: voter ignorance causes state
autonomy, facilitates elite manipulation of public opinion, and may permit
regulatory capture in ways that cannot be explained by existing theories.

PUBLIC IGNORANCE AND STATE AUTONOMY

Unlike existing theories of state autonomy, and contrary to widespread assumptions regarding democratic politics, this book argues that voter ignorance ensures that the majority of state regulatory operations are conducted
autonomously from popular awareness or control. In its most basic form,

public ignorance causes state autonomy simply because voters are unaware of states' decisions and hence are incapable of influencing the decisions made by elected officials and bureaucrats. If the public is ignorant of state actions, the existence of government policies, and the actors responsible for policy implementation, voters may be incapable of influencing the decisions made by modern democratic states. If voter ignorance is the primary variable responsible for the state's autonomy, we should expect an inverse relationship between popular influence of politics and the number of regulatory decisions undertaken by government. For when states undertake a large number of decisions and regulatory actions, voters will become relatively more ignorant of politics and will have a more difficult time collecting information about public decisions.[20]

This form of state autonomy needn't be the result of any deliberate effort to mask public decisions from social awareness; it is simply a function of the fact that most voters are unaware of the majority of decisions that are being made by public actors, and that state autonomy is the default condition for most democratic political decisions. Rather than resulting from any conscious decision or deliberate design, state autonomy in democratic societies is an unintended effect of our ignorance of the modern social world.

Ignorance-induced autonomy is not, however, the only type of state autonomy that may occur. Indeed, public officials are constantly trying to anticipate how the public will react if it subsequently becomes better informed.[21] In some instances this threat may allow voters' preferences to dominate the policy process even though voters are unaware of elites' decisions. Although elites are constantly trying to anticipate public reactions, the threat of voter retaliation will only be effective if the effects of policy decisions are clear and easy to explain.[22] If policy decisions are complex, have delayed effects, or involve counterintuitive mechanisms, voters may not be able to identify the decisions and individuals responsible for policy outcomes. This indicates that certain public decisions may be difficult for voters to control because the causal linkages between policies and effects are often difficult to perceive.

When the causal relationships between policy decisions and outcomes are clear and direct, for example, as they are with tariff policy or welfare payments, the public will have less difficulty identifying those responsible for certain social conditions. Thus, depending upon the relationship between regulatory decisions and their effects, different levels of state autonomy may exist in different policy areas. Distributive policies where the causal effects of policies are clear and immediate may be easier for the public to control than issues where policy effects are less obvious and difficult to understand.

ELITE MANIPULATION OF PUBLIC OPINION

In addition to providing the underlying condition responsible for state autonomy in democratic societies, public ignorance may also allow political elites to manipulate public opinion and fabricate popular desires in ways that further enhance their autonomy. This claim is, for well-known methodological reasons, difficult to substantiate.[23] It is also the most interesting. For the mediated nature of modern politics, the fact that the electorate cannot directly observe legislative deliberations, bureaucratic regulations, or the effects of many public decisions makes it difficult for public opinion to emerge as anything but a reflection of elite interpretations.[24]

This indicates there may be two ways voter ignorance may enhance state autonomy. Aside from ensuring that voters are simply unaware of most public decisions, voters may fail to recognize that elected officials are popularizing crude and inaccurate explanations for politics that mask the actual calculations and social relationships that voters are trying to understand and control. However, the fictitious nature of the explanations political elites popularize may never be recognized due to voters' weak understanding of social causality and their ignorance of empirical information necessary to recognize the fictitious nature of the explanations public officials popularize. This indicates that there is a distinction between the public's understanding of politics, an understanding that is subject to distortions and elite manipulation, and the actual reality of political conflict.

While public officials or media elites may produce competing interpretations for political events, some of which are more plausible than others, the public is reliant upon elites to produce and disseminate interpretations for political events they cannot directly observe. Voters are hardly blank slates that can be induced to believe any interpretation; they exist in political cultures that make some explanations more plausible than others, and the explanations that are simple and cater to popular assumptions and understandings will be more likely to be adopted by the public.

This may, however, create situations where voters cannot control political decisions, not because they are unaware of political decisions or uninformed of information, but because they adopt misleading accounts of politics that obscure the causal relationships that are actually governing social relationships and political decisions. In such situations, voters may become aware of information and explanations, but state actors may still act autonomously because the explanations of political events voters adopt fail to identify the actors or decisions responsible certain social relationships or decisions. This process involves a distinction between the understanding of politics by the public and by elites who are competing to control various decisions and influence certain social conditions. While elites may have inaccurate understandings of social processes, often in ways that have significant consequences, it is important to recognize the bifurcated nature of the democratic political process, whereby voters adopt crude and incomplete accounts of politics, while elites struggle to influence complex decisions that are impossible to fully explain.

For the purposes of theory construction, *state* elites will be conceptually distinguished from *political* elites. State elites are defined as incumbent officials who staff the state's legislative, executive, or judicial positions. However, political elites may include groups who are unaffiliated with the state, elites who may be either (1) party elites or (2) mass-media personnel. The former category may include (1a) incumbent elected officials—a subset of the category "state elites," which would also include judges and bureaucrats—and (1b) nonincumbent candidates for elective office.

In case 1a, the state itself may enhance or diminish its own autonomy, depending on how public officials affect public opinion. As the nineteenth century mass media were explicitly partisan organs, the second category of political elites—media elites—can be subdivided into those who do the bidding of (2a) partisan incumbents and those who do the bidding of (2b) partisan nonincumbents; in case 2a, as in case 1a, the state can enhance or diminish its own autonomy, depending on which messages state elites transmit through the media to the public, and how easily such messages are adopted.

While the specific elites that disseminate the interpretations that the public is offered may change over time, public ignorance may allow elites to disseminate simple, but inaccurate, explanations for politics that may create the demands that come to be called public opinion. This process need not be deliberate or conspiratorial; it may simply be caused by the ease with which simple ideas can be understood. However, the power of elite interpretations is derived from the underlying condition of public ignorance, and the difficulties in collecting, and interpreting, political information independently of mediators of such information.

Insofar as politics involves complex issues, we should expect the public's ideas and interpretations to be grossly simplified, containing factual inaccuracies and mistaken views of causality. Even if there were no incentives for political elites to disseminate inaccurate interpretations, public ignorance makes it unlikely that voters will find nuanced or complicated explanations of politics persuasive. Although the opinions that political elites create may enhance or constrain state autonomy, the state's degree of responsiveness to such opinions will be incomprehensible if we overlook how the underlying condition of voter ignorance structures modern political conflict, and the states' corresponding tendency toward autonomy derived from this condition.

PUBLIC IGNORANCE AND REGULATORY CAPTURE

In addition to granting the state autonomy from society, public ignorance facilitates the capture of state actors by organized societal groups in ways that cannot be explained by traditional theories of regulatory capture.[25] Regulatory capture is typically explained as a collective action problem where voters rationally calculate that the benefits that would accrue from resisting regulatory capture are not worth the costs. Yet if voters do not know that the agencies in question exist, let alone the policies agencies are enacting or the costs imposed by these policies, organized social groups may capture the state due to low popular awareness of what state actors are doing, and not because voters are rationally calculating that the costs of opposing such policies outweigh the benefits.

Regulatory capture can be seen as a diminution of state autonomy—a ceding of state power to an organized faction of society. However, since my focus is on the state's autonomy from the *electorate,* regulatory capture is conceptualized as an *exercise* of state autonomy, even if public officials work to serve an organized societal group. The extent to which capture occurs, however, is always an empirical question. In some instances state actors may act in opposition to organized social groups' demands, while in other situations they may aid such groups at the expense of the larger society. I make no assumptions regarding the frequency of either of these outcomes but instead focus on how public ignorance grants states a degree of autonomy from popular control.

IDEOLOGY AND STATE ELITES

If public ignorance indicates voters are largely unaware of states' decisions, to explain why states embark on certain developmental trajectories, and to explain the factors that led to specific regulatory decisions, requires analyzing certain characteristics of state elites. Specifically, it is necessary to examine certain features of the ideas and ideological belief systems state elites use to make sense of modern societies. Elites use ideology due to their own ignorance of the social world, as ideology serves a useful organizing function for those who must deal with large numbers of complex issues that they cannot acquire expertise in.[26]

Given the critical role of ideas, both for the determination of specific elite worldviews and for the public's second-hand interpretations based upon these worldviews, it is necessary to recognize certain features of ideological belief systems.[27] Ideology can be conceptualized either as a "total" worldview or, in a narrower sense, as limited only to the specific policy positions espoused by an ideological belief system. I use the latter conception of ideology, and it is only in the Conclusion that I will turn to discuss the ramifications that specific historical transformations had for the general ethos of American political culture.

I use a very specific, and very limited, conception of political ideology. Instead of focusing on ideas' correspondence with a socioeconomic "structure" or individuals' material interests, I focus on the effects of the acts of "creative synthesis" produced by ideological belief systems, political parties' application of these belief systems to governance, and the subsequent transmission of ideas from political elites to the mass public.[28] I follow Converse and define belief systems as sets of ideas bound together by some form of functional interdependence.[29] Functional interdependence is conceived as ideologies' tendency to "bundle" issue positions together, such that if we know one position an ideologue holds we will have a high probability of success in predicting some other set of attitudes or positions. Political ideologies link multiple ideas together, creating a seemingly coherent system of logically related propositions that appear to be an internally coherent "package" of ideas and issue positions.

A critical effect of these packages is that they generate feelings of psychological constraint, where once the discrete elements of an ideological worldview are accepted the nascent ideologue feels compelled to accept a host of additional positions and associated propositions.[30] This indicates that ideology is not simply a reflection or rationalization of some underlying variable, such as an individual's "interests." For ideological constraint makes individuals feel that they cannot adopt individual components of an ideology on the basis of their correspondence with some underlying variable. Rather, once they have accepted a discrete element of the belief system they must accept the bundle of issue positions associated with the ideology in its entirety.[31]

Furthermore, the specific reasons why an ideology bundles certain issues together are not a simple consequence of the interests served by an ideology, nor are they a consequence of strictly logical principles. Rather, belief systems bundle ideas together on the basis of "quasi-logical" arguments developed by a certain type of intellectual, the miniscule fraction of any populace that is responsible for "creatively synthesizing" ideological belief systems into packages large numbers of people find credible.[32]

I make no claims regarding whether the individual positions and claims made by discrete elements of ideologies are distortions of individuals' "real" interests. Instead I follow Converse in suggesting there is little underlying logical coherence to the particular configuration of issue positions that ideologies assume at a given point.[33] What is critical for the successful transmission of an ideology is the *appearance* of coherence, and once it is recognized that ideology bundles issues together on the basis of quasi-logical assertion, the idea that elites' political beliefs are logically determined "collapses like a pricked balloon."[34]

In modern democracies, the result of this informational division of labor is a bifurcated political culture, with a tiny group of individuals creating the ideological belief systems that political elites and parties use to organize their perceptions and attitudes while the mass public remains largely "innocent" of ideology, exhibiting little understanding of why parties and elites adopt specific issue positions.[35] Since elites use ideological belief systems to organize their political ideas, the upper strata of modern societies are decisively influenced by the history of ideas.[36] However, the cultural process of ideological production is a degree removed from the mass public.[37] Since they are "innocent" of belief systems, mass publics rely upon information from social groups, charismatic leaders, and the tangible objects of the private sphere to organize the few political ideas and positions they do adopt.[38]

Furthermore, since there is little underlying logic organizing the disparate positions ideologies link together, the ideas espoused by social groups or classes in prior historical periods, or in different cultures, may appear paradoxical and confusing. It is specifically because ideology packages issue positions in ways that often appear illogical to culturally or temporally distant observers that it is essential to understand this characteristic of ideological belief systems. To avoid the impression that my analysis is elitist in any normative sense, it bears noting that the socialization of the leaders of mass opinion indicates they are as influenced by the long-dead philosophers who shape their worldviews as by the voters that mimic the positions of the officials they mistakenly believe they control.

Regardless of whatever normative implications may stem from this argument, recognizing the arbitrary bundling function of political ideologies is necessary for explaining why certain political innovations occur. For it is only by recognizing how ideological belief systems influence political elites, and how the arbitrary connections between ideologies' issue positions are created and transmitted, that we can explain why American political institutions were created when they were, and why certain innovations occurred at specific points.

To explain the origins of contemporary American political institutions, we must examine how voter ignorance grants states autonomy from the societies they govern, how ideology influences elite action and perceptions, and how the struggle for political power provides the motive force driving political innovations. We need to consider the interaction of these three variables, each of which is conditioned by the underlying condition of public ignorance, in order to explain the creation of the administrative institutions that are the focus of my analysis.

Chapter 3 Civil War Finance and the American State

Scholars of modern political development often argue that state formation is linked to the organizational and financial pressures associated with war. Military conflict is believed to impose a quasi-evolutionary selection pressure on the population of states, rewarding those states that successfully extract resources and build bureaucratic institutions necessary to prevail in war with other states. These developments facilitated an expansion of state power, as new institutional arrangements were necessary to collect, and successfully deploy, the resources necessary for prolonged military operations.[1]

In Europe, the military revolution of the sixteenth and seventeenth centuries led to innovations such as the use of gunpowder weapons, massed infantry, and new naval forces. Despite important differences between European and American state formation, the American Civil War stimulated the expansion of American state authority in ways that resembled the European experience. Aside from creating a professional military and imposing new forms of taxation, developmental pressures focused on the financial instruments used by the Treasury Department to fund the Northern war effort.[2]

This chapter examines how two of the Treasury Department's financing strategies—the creation of the "greenback" paper currency and the national banking system—stimulated American state formation.[3] While the Treasury Department acquired novel forms of authority during the Civil War, before the war federal bureaucracies had not functioned as regulatory agencies but were used to generate revenue and reward party loyalists with offices. In this sense the antebellum American state resembled absolutist Europe, where bureaucratic offices were often sold as a means of generating revenue and were not employed as centers of regulatory expertise.

The American state would, however, emerge from the Civil War with new capacities to manipulate national economic conditions, capacities that would inaugurate the beginning of a shift toward a state that was federal, regulatory, and bureaucratic. In this chapter I examine three aspects of the federal government's strategy for financing the Civil War. First, I consider how the federal government issued greenback currency and created the national banking system to fund the Northern war effort. These financial instruments unintentionally helped establish federal control over the money supply, a basic feature of modern central banks, and created a novel form of state capacity.

Second, I examine Eastern financiers' preferences, particularly those of New York banks associated with the New York Clearing House Association, regarding the federal government's funding strategies. This discussion is intended to determine how financial groups influenced Civil War finance, and whether the government's financial decisions were made in response to their demands. Aside from documenting how powerful bankers viewed the Northern government's funding operations, a close examination of financiers' preferences is necessary to understand how voter ignorance influenced the Democrats' shift to supporting inflationary currency policy in the elections following the Civil War. The Democrats surged into electoral contention by making specific, and largely fictitious, claims about Eastern financial groups' influence over Civil War finance policy. Thus, before I examine how voter ignorance influenced these elections, I will analyze the Treasury Department's Civil War funding operations.

Third, in this chapter I examine how certain politicians and Treasury bureaucrats believed voters were only dimly aware of the methods used to finance the Civil War. Documenting voter ignorance of finance policy, and the preferences of Eastern financiers, helps explain the specific decisions made to finance the Northern war effort. However, public ignorance of Civil War finance decisions would influence the elections that immediately followed the war. Accordingly, this chapter's discussion of public ignorance provides the basis for the next chapter's examination of elite manipulation of public opinion in the postwar elections.

In discussing the ideological assumptions that influence public actors' decisions regarding Civil War finance, bankers' opposition to these decisions because they would harm their material interests, and the public's general unawareness of these decisions and conflicts, the chapter depicts a political environment in which ideological political elites, powerful economic actors, and ignorant voters interact in ways that ensure public decisions are granted autonomy from popular awareness or control. Although later chapters focus on different policies and decisions, the general depiction of the interaction between ideological public officials, powerful economic groups, and ignorant voters is replicated in subsequent chapters.

At the outset of the Civil War, the federal government faced distinct challenges to raising the financial, military, and organizational resources necessary to prosecute the war. The particular course of antebellum financial conflict, the ideological assumptions of the Democratic and Whig parties, and the displacement of economic conflicts by concerns associated with slavery, had limited federal authority in ways that limited its capacity to raise revenue and fund the Northern war effort. Lacking a circulating national currency and facing states hostile to federal centralization, the antebellum Treasury assumed few central-banking functions.[4]

Nor did the various military bureaucracies function as centers of expertise; the Departments of State, War, and the Navy simply did not possess the expertise or capacity to wage protracted war. The Post Office possessed an immense patronage, and the Interior Department focused on service functions such as the sale of public lands, negotiations with Native Americans, and issuing patents. While the Treasury Department enjoyed a degree of independence at various points, such as when retiring the public debt accumulated during the War of 1812, Jackson's removal of Secretaries Louis McLane and William Duane expanded presidential influence over Treasury policy, and the Independent Treasury system limited the Treasury Department's influence over the financial system.[5]

Lacking a professionalized bureaucracy and relying on the states to field and equip its armed forces, the federal government entered the Civil War lacking the organizational capacity necessary for sustained military operations.[6] Lincoln's initial appointments did little to harness executive expertise. Although the Treasury Department was critical for raising revenue to prosecute the Northern war effort, when Lincoln appointed Ohio Republican Salmon Chase as treasury secretary, bankers complained that Chase lacked the experience and humility necessary to conduct funding operations in concert with their demands.[7]

On July 4, 1861, Chase outlined his strategy for financing the Civil War. He initially sought a total of $320 million, of which $240 million would be derived from loans and $80 million from taxation and tariffs.[8] As the war had curtailed investment opportunities, many banks' reserves were swollen with bullion from mines in California and Nevada, and Chase believed that financiers in Boston, New York, and Philadelphia would willingly purchase federal loans.[9] In this context, government bonds were attractive investments, and across the East Coast there was "a strong desire on the part of capitalists here to give liberal aid to the Government at this time."[10]

Given its position as a major financial center of the American economy, the federal government found itself reliant upon New York capital to fund the war effort. Yet New York's role in supporting the Northern war effort was initially a strained alliance. With the exception of certain New York manufacturers, the close relationships that New York's financial and merchant elites enjoyed with Southern cotton interests had caused them to oppose the Republican Party.[11] Despite the importance of New York financial elites in funding the Northern war effort, their influence over the Treasury's funding operations would be as tenuous as their influence over secession and the antebellum Republican Party, and they would find themselves regularly antagonized by Chase's decisions.[12] As the economic actors most directly influenced by the Treasury Department's actions, New York financial elites found themselves struggling with the material implications of Chase's decisions, decisions that most voters were unaware of.

Chase had the authority to issue loans bearing various rates of interest, interest-bearing currency, and "demand notes," currency that bore no interest and could be used to pay public dues.[13] Chase, however, initially opposed creating a national currency, believing "immeasurable evils" would result from creating a currency not secured by specie.[14] Such opposition was rooted in his ideological assumptions regarding monetary policy, and his specific distaste toward paper currency. Although Congress granted Chase discretion in setting interest rates on a hundred million dollars in loans to foreign and domestic banks, he was uncomfortable with such discretion and asked that future loans leave "this matter altogether to the better judgment of Congress."[15] Chase specifically requested that Congress limit the Treasury's authority over future loan issues, stating that "whatever discretion it may be thought prudent to give [the treasury secretary] . . . in other respects, the rate of interest [should] be limited by law."[16]

Reluctant to print paper currency and uncomfortable with assuming discretion over loan negotiations and interest rates, Chase further restricted his finance operations through his interpretation of the Independent Treasury Act of 1846, which required banks to conduct their transactions with the government in specie.[17] Although many financiers assumed Chase would ignore this statute and accept bankers' checks as payment for the loans, he insisted that the banks transport tons of bullion from Eastern cities to Washington.

The impracticality of this decision was the initial indication that Chase would be a difficult partner for New York banks. Members of the New York Clearing House Association, a group of banks that facilitated interbank lending operations, urged Chase not to "compel our Banks to advance coin," instead hoping the treasury secretary would draw specie "only as actually needed for daily disbursements, which would not cripple [the banks]."[18]

As demanding that the banks pay specie for government loans would strip banks of their bullion reserves, Chase's adherence to the Independent Treasury Act of 1846 seemed designed "to kill the banks by inches and not at one blow."[19] Funding negotiations between the banks and the Treasury rapidly deteriorated, and a "factious feeling . . . vaguely apparent for some days" soon hardened into "a determination manifested upon the part of the Associated Banks . . . [to] obtain control of . . . financial matters."[20] Despite their concerns, Eastern banks agreed to receive $50 million of Treasury notes bearing 7.3 percent interest, and left open the option of receiving two additional installments of $50 million.

Although Chase had opposed issuing demand notes and was uneasy with his latitude over loan negotiations, he reluctantly accepted the discretion Congress granted him, noting: "It is only to guard against a possible exigency that I am willing to have the discretion given me."[21] Granting the Treasury unique wartime powers was hardly unprecedented; prior conflicts had led to similar powers. For example, Treasury Secretary William Crawford asked for congressional authorization to use the government surplus to retire the public debt incurred from the War of 1812.[22]

Yet instead of enjoying their support, Chase's actions were antagonizing powerful Eastern bankers. Early in January of 1862, James Gallatin and members of the New York Clearing House Association met Chase and members of the House Ways and Means Committee and the Senate Finance Committee to urge Chase to ignore the Independent Treasury Act, use the state banks as depositories for government funds, levy taxes for revenue, and accept market prices for federal bonds.[23]

Chase bluntly rejected Gallatin's demands, replying that "it is not the business of the Secretary of the Treasury to receive an ultimatum, but to declare one if necessary."[24] Unwilling to sell government bonds at depreciated prices, bankers refused to market federal bonds, and by December of 1861 dwindling bullion reserves forced New York banks to suspend specie payments. Other banks soon followed, and when the Treasury refused to redeem its own demand notes in coin, America was off the gold standard.

With New York bankers opposing Chase's funding strategy, Congress began exploring alternatives that would minimize the government's reliance on New York bankers. Chase began using financiers such as Jay Cooke and Henry Clews to sell bonds directly to the public to circumvent bankers' leverage over his finance operations. In addition to such bond sales, Chase's annual report of 1861 had also proposed additional revenue options, such as the creation of a national banking system that would require state banks to secure their notes with federal bonds and impose a 10 percent tax on state banknotes to force them into federal incorporation.[25]

Chase's proposal for a national banking system was greeted with uniform opposition from Eastern bankers. George Coe promptly informed Chase that a national banking system would "hit [the banks] like a bombshell."[26] As Chase reiterated his recommendations for a national banking system, New York bankers complained that they had expected "a more friendly and favorable recognition of what they had done."[27] Other bankers, such as R. W. Latham and John E. Williams, observed that Chase's plan "does not and cannot meet the approbation of the business men of the country," warning him that the "radical change" proposed by the national banking system would "make war on [finance]" and, if continued, would "destroy the Banking, commercial and mercantile interests of the country."[28] Since the national banking system would be costly for existing banks, the Eastern financial press urged that Chase's national banking proposal "be postponed to the calm consideration of a day of peace."[29]

While bankers criticized Chase's national banking proposal, the Treasury Department was running out of revenue options. Recognizing the national banking system "could not, with the State banks opposed to it, be passed through both Houses of Congress," Congressmen Elbridge Spaulding (R-NY) introduced an alternative funding bill that created a paper currency to pay government expenses.[30]

Just as they opposed Chase's national banking system, members of the New York Clearing House Association criticized the Spaulding proposal "in rather severe terms."[31] Both James Gallatin and George Coe complained that even the national banking system was "less objectionable, than the issue of a government paper by the government."[32] Others argued that "no worse measure could be devised than the issue of circulating notes, notes which cannot be converted into coin at the pleasure of the holders."[33] Claiming that under a regime of "bonds and notes . . . the entire mercantile community must come to utter ruin," some bankers bitterly asked whether New York's "commercial supremacy [was] . . . passing away as a consequence of [their] patriotism."[34]

Despite such complaints, the suspension of specie payments put many banks in violation of their charters, and a growing number of bankers were endorsing "an irredeemable government currency" specifically because they wanted to use government paper as a reserve for their own notes.[35] Dissociating themselves from the New York Clearing House Association, "various bankers and business men" claimed that the banks composing the New York Clearing House did not represent their views.[36] Some criticized Spaulding's proposal for not going far enough, suggesting that the "few leading minds, in connection with Chase, nerve up, and let the demand notes assume the place of specie in every particular."[37]

Some of Spaulding's correspondents bluntly called for the government to "issue $100,000,000 to $150,000,000 demand notes, and pay them out as the wants of the Government require; make them a *legal tender* in all transactions of business"; if the government "issue[d] one hundred and fifty millions Treasury notes legal tender," they said, "we will go on without any trouble. . . . There are not eight bank presidents that side with [Gallatin]. He is an odd fish—[and] has very little influence here."[38]

Bankers had straightforward economic reasons to endorse a new paper currency. Aside from legal questions regarding their reserve requirements, many recognized that if government bonds remained redeemable in gold but could be purchased with paper currency, banks could earn large profits by purchasing bonds with greenbacks that were certain to depreciate. Recognizing the appeal this had for banks that were "large holders of government securities and fancy stocks," conservative members of the New York Clearing House Association complained that those "unmindful of the ultimate evils of an inflated currency" were "pleased to see a further issue of legal tender notes that they might thereby realize . . . profit on these securities."[39]

Yet the New York Clearing House Association's criticisms were a minority position. Most Eastern bankers did not share these views; they wanted paper currency and they wanted its value to depreciate. Instead of opposing the greenbacks, Senator John Sherman (R-OH) observed: "[Eastern bankers] are the very men who now beg you for this measure of financial aid," and Spaulding similarly concluded that "bankers and other prominent citizens . . . [were] express[ing] themselves in favor of the legal tender bill . . . [and urging] its immediate passage."[40] Although Chase had opposed creating a paper currency in 1861, and while he still believed the creation of a paper currency was "full of danger," the creation of a legal tender currency had now "become a matter not merely of expediency, but of vital necessity."[41]

On the Senate floor, Sherman asked his colleagues to recognize what was "admitted by all," namely, that "very few members of this body are familiar with financial subjects."[42] Indeed, informed observers concluded that "the members [of both Houses] seemed to know very little . . . of [the bill's] details."[43] Sherman and Spaulding were attempting to explain the bill to a body composed of "people who . . . still thought that monetary policy was merely a matter of confining the Treasury's transactions to gold."[44] Recognizing that few senators understood the issues under consideration, Sherman asked the Senate to defer to these "recognized organ of financial opinion in this country" whose expertise was "worth more than that of any individual Senator."[45]

Aside from the opposition of certain bankers, the government's funding operations were generating political opposition from certain Democrats as well. Although the Radical Republicans and most of the Eastern banking community supported the greenbacks, George Pendleton (D-OH) and Clement Vallandigham (D-OH) led Democratic opposition to Spaulding's proposal.

Claiming the legal tender measure marked a departure from the Tenth Amendment, Pendleton claimed: "Not only . . . was such a law never passed, but such a law was never voted on, never proposed, never introduced, never recommended by any Department of the Government; [or] . . . seriously entertained in debate in either branch of Congress."[46] Aside from his constitutional objections, Pendleton expressed Jacksonian skepticism of paper money and criticized the measure because it would produce those "manifold dangers which follow inevitably, closely in the wake of an illegal, unsound, and depreciated Government paper currency."[47]

Pendleton's denunciations were echoed by Vallandigham, who claimed that the greenbacks violated "the plainest principles of finance, the commonest maxims of political economy," and declared that "this bold, but ill-advised and most hazardous experiment of forcing a paper currency upon the people ought to be met by the Representatives of the people with unanimous and emphatic condemnation."[48]

While Pendleton and Vallandigham's arguments focused on economic and constitutional questions regarding paper currency, their opposition to the greenbacks was also clearly tied to their opposition to the Civil War. Pendleton and Vallandigham represented the "peace" and "copperhead" wings of the Democratic Party that opposed continuation of the Civil War and expressed traditional Democratic opposition to paper currency, indicating their economic and political interests were mutually reinforcing positions.[49]

However, as Pendleton and Vallandigham led Democratic opposition to the greenbacks, Republicans, in particular members of the Radical faction of the Republican Party, denounced the Democrats' attacks. Frequently Republicans drew attention to public support for the greenbacks, claiming: "The sentiment of the nation approaches unanimity in favor of this legal tender clause," and asserted the American people's "rightful authority . . . to control their currency."[50] Others pointed to popular support for the wartime measure, arguing that "no act of legislation of this Government was ever hailed with as much delight throughout the whole length and breadth of this Union, by every class of people, without any exception," as the legal tender bill.[51]

Despite such claims, Chase's bond agents who were selling the loans across the United States were reporting a different view of public opinion. Bond agents said that the public exhibited "total ignorance of financial and currency questions," and they complained of having "to explain to so many ignorant people the whys and wherefores" of government finance.[52] The complexity of Chase's bond and currency operations, and the immense distance separating the decisions made in Washington from the country, made Republicans worry that it would be difficult for their justifications of the governments' funding operations to "reach . . . popular understanding."[53]

Chase's Treasury agents were not alone in their view of public opinion. Members of the New York Clearing House Association complained they had facilitated the government's financial demands so skillfully that the public was "utterly unconscious of any unusual demand upon their resources, and are not alive to the duties and dangers which surround them."[54] In the Midwest, it was reported that "Mr. Chase's scheme, so far as it is known here, meets with disfavor from all but the wild cat bankers," because of a belief "whether well founded or not" prevalent among "the great mass of the loyal people of the North West" that the banks were "under the influence of foreign capitalists."[55]

Indeed, some observers believed that knowledge of basic issues associated with secession remained unclear. After assuming administrative command over Kentucky, James Garfield found that the region's inhabitants "had not the slightest understanding of the issues of the war that had intruded into their valley. Some had supported the South only because Confederate recruiters had told them the Yankees were coming to murder them all, but 'who or what the Yankees were, they had no idea.'"[56] In addition to criticizing the economically backward characteristics of Southern society, Northern soldiers reported that many Southerners were ignorant of basic facts about the Civil War. For example, one Connecticut private reported that the North Carolinians he encountered were unaware that the South had attacked Fort Sumter.[57]

Yet despite opposition from some Eastern bankers, and tepid popular awareness, the legal tender measure passed Congress on February 25, 1862. By the end of 1862, the federal government had issued bonds and paper currency to finance the conflict, and state banks had suspended specie payments and were using greenbacks to secure their notes. This led Chase to worry that inflation of paper currency had become inevitable, threatening to leave the government's finances to "be tost [sic] helplessly . . . by conflicting gusts of opinion, until the inevitable wreck."[58]

Chase believed these problems would be eliminated by transferring control over certain banking functions from state to federal authorities. Chase began reiterating his proposals for a national banking system that would curtail potentially inflationary emissions of state banknotes and limit the interest owed on the public debt.[59] Under Chase's plan, national bank charters would be issued when five or more individuals provided the comptroller of the currency with either $30,000 or money equaling one-third of their capital in federal bonds.[60] National banks would receive national bank notes amounting to 90 percent of the market value of the bonds; 25 percent of these notes were required to be held by the bank as a reserve, and their total volume was restricted to $300 million to limit inflation.[61]

Despite the national banking system's unpopularity when initially proposed in 1861, Chase's annual report of 1862 reiterated his demands for creating a national banking system. Like Chase, Sherman had become convinced that, in his words, "it was indispensable to create a demand for our bonds" and that "the best way was to make them the basis of our banking system."[62] Both Chase and Sherman believed that a national banking system would limit the inflation of state banks' currency and create a market for the federal bonds that would be required as a reserve for national banknotes.[63]

Regardless of how crucial Chase believed the national banking system was for the war effort, Chase's suggestions were "not received with favor or anything like favor," either by bankers or by Congress, and Chase openly admitted: "[Bankers] "look with disfavor on the plan proposed in my report."[64] The *Merchants' Magazine and Commercial Review* reported that the financial community considered the national banking system "wholly unwelcome"; Chase's annual report had "failed to allay the public inquietude in relation to the government resources" and had further alienated banks from the treasury secretary.[65] The *New York Times* decried the "rank injustice of oppressive legislation" to compel state banks "to transfer their allegiance from the State by which they were created, to the legislative and bureaucratic authorities at Washington."[66]

Hardly endorsing the national banking system, bankers simply "wished to be left alone, with greenbacks continued in use as a generous source of [their] reserves."[67] Under the proposed national banking system, banks would have to sell their state bonds to purchase federal securities. This would cause the prices of these bonds to decline and impose losses on the banks.[68] State bankers were complaining that they could not see how they would "derive any particular advantage from Mr. Chase's plan."[69]

Nor did bankers welcome their ability to issue national banknotes under the national banking system. John Williams, president of New York's Metropolitan Bank, recognized that bankers were "satisfied with [the greenbacks]," which they considered "vastly superior . . . to this, so called, National Currency."[70] Williams believed that greenbacks "are, in fact, the best [currency], and it is next to a fraud on the people to issue the national bank notes."[71] Although state bankers endorsed the creation of greenbacks, there was "a wider and stronger opposition felt to [Chase's] proposition to replace the present bank note currency, by one of uniform character and value, secured by [government] bonds," opposition that had emerged specifically because the national banking system "threaten[ed] some of the profits of the banking interest."[72]

Opposition was not limited to the Eastern banking community. Since many Midwestern banks issued a higher proportion of notes relative to demand deposits than Eastern city banks, the proposed tax on banknotes was especially harmful to their business and appeared designed to force them into federal incorporation.[73] Ohio bankers complained that Chase had "decided upon the destruction of the country banks," as the banknote tax was simply "too much for [them] to carry."[74] Others complained that federal taxes on their notes "[would] be so great as to compel the winding up of every country bank in Ohio."[75]

Financiers' opposition to the national banking system was adamant, and for good reason. The government was "attempting to ram the new system down their throats, a system whose features they did not like and in which they saw little profit for themselves."[76] Many doubted whether "capitalists could be induced to invest in any system of banking" that was subject to the "whims of every party which might happen to come into power."[77] Members of the New York Clearing House complained: "The salvation of the nation, under Providence, was through [the initial loans] of the banks. Without their generous action the flag of a conspiracy maturing for a generation would have floated over its capitol. But what has been the response to that action? It has been this, and the finger of the historian will point to it with amazement, that while the ink was yet undried the same pen that was drawing from us these millions was coldly and deliberately drafting the plan for our destruction."[78] With Chase trying "to cram the National Banking System down the throats of old Bankers," it appeared that a "war is going on between Chase and our men of wealth."[79]

In addition to condemning the national banking system, some bankers, such as Gallatin, worried about the power the treasury secretary was accumulating over financial markets. Gallatin complained that the treasury secretary was acquiring "overwhelming . . . power," allowing him to make decisions that, in Gallatin's words, "can make wages high or low; he can raise prices or depress them; and he can advance or put down values of property, in his discretion, by the course which he has it in his power to adopt in funding his loans, issuing his currencies, disposing of his deposits and making his disbursements."[80]

In the course of financing the Northern war effort, the treasury secretary had acquired discretion to market loans and issue currency, powers that allowed him to manipulate the volume of money circulating in the American economy. While Chase had no intention of using such authority to regulate financial markets, some expected "a general howl from our hard currency friends at the bare mention of a bank or institution having so much power."[81]

Aside from bankers' opposition, Congress too was hostile to the introduction of Chase's national banking system.[82] Legislative debate deteriorated into open declarations of Chase's incompetence, and prominent Republicans who had supported creating the greenbacks, such as Spaulding and Justin Morrill, opposed the national banking system. Recognizing that state banks would gain little from the national banking system, congressmen complained that the measure would "uproot all the State banks issuing currency which now exist . . . in order to make room for funding United States bonds."[83] Sherman "had his say in the Senate, and silence . . . ensued," leaving newspapers to conclude that there was "very little chance" for the passage of the national banking system.[84]

Despite such opposition, Chase remained adamant that the national bank system was essential for the war effort: "No reduction in the volume of national issues, under these circumstances, can work material benefit to the circulation; for every such reduction merely makes room for fresh corporations issues, which are not always or even generally restricted to the amount of United States notes withdrawn. Thus the issues of the State corporations create a constantly increasing excess in the volume of currency as compared with the requirements of actual transactions; and this excess works progressive depreciation."[85] If the national banking system was to be implemented, however, Chase had to generate congressional support for a measure that was deeply unpopular among the financial community. To do so, he began trying to manipulate congressional perceptions of public opinion by using his access to newspapers to publish laudatory editorials claiming that the public was demanding the national banking system.

This strategy assumed that Congress had little information about popular reactions, and that the public was unaware of what Chase was doing. Chase's reluctance to use government-issued paper currency to finance the Civil War, opposition based upon his political ideology, provided the justification for the national banking system. Bankers opposed the national banking system because it threatened their economic interests, and voter ignorance of politics allowed certain public officials to manipulate the policy process to achieve their objectives. The ideological commitments of political elites influenced their policy options, the material commitments of economic elites led them to oppose these efforts, and voter ignorance ensured that this process was conducted autonomously from popular awareness or control. The elites responsible for this process *assumed* that the electorate was unaware of what was occurring, for had Chase believed that the public was informed, he would never have believed that his strategy could be effective.

To produce supportive editorials Chase enlisted Jay and Henry Cooke, the Philadelphia bankers whose extensive contacts with various newspapers had helped them advertise and market Chase's loan sales. Chase advised Henry Cooke "to use [the] . . . advertising fund freely in behalf of the bank bill, getting editors of leading papers enlisted."[86] Chase also personally told certain newspaper editors, such as Horace Greeley of the *New York Tribune*: "All . . . [the bill] needs is vigorous support from the influential press for a few days or perhaps weeks," and then the measure would pass.[87]

Soon editorials supporting the national banking system appeared in leading newspapers; they were "freshened daily" and distributed to congressmen each morning.[88] Within a month Henry Cooke was reporting that his "'medicine' [was] having its [desired] effect."[89] With newspaper editorials endorsing the national banking system, Chase began claiming that "a strong public opinion, in favor of a uniform currency . . . and [supporting] the National Banking System . . . [had] developed itself," and he applauded the press's "all powerful effects."[90]

Seeking to reinforce the impression Chase and Cooke were creating through the press, in Senate debate Sherman began claiming: "[The national banking system] has steadily gained in favor with all classes of our citizens," a sentiment that was bolstered by Chase's assertion that popular demands for taxing state banknotes had become "too strong to be resisted."[91] Although Sherman admitted that the national banking system "ran counter to the local interests of those engaged in the business of banking," he claimed that the measure's "adoption [was] demanded by the people."[92]

When these public pronouncements were combined with the Cookes' editorials, there appeared to be growing pressure to support the legislation. Henry Cooke reported that opponents of the measure were commenting: "What a . . . change in popular sentiment! Everybody seems to be going in for the Bank bill—I guess we'll have to go [for] it!"[93] The Cookes had clear reasons to support the national banking system; if banks were compelled to purchase federal bonds, this would create another market for the federal bonds the Cookes were selling.

Yet the appearance of popular support for the national banking system was largely a product of the Cooke publicity machine. Although Chase and Sherman claimed public opinion demanded the measure, Treasury officials were reporting to Chase that the public exhibited "almost heathen darkness" regarding government funding operations.[94] Although the Cookes' editorials claimed voters were demanding the national banking system, the Cookes' correspondents were reporting that voters had difficulty monitoring congressional deliberations due to the great "depravations . . . [and] the great scarcity and age of news," which in turn made it difficult to "make an impression politically or financially" upon public opinion.[95]

Chase's correspondents echoed this assessment, complaining that many newspaper editors were unaware of their decisions and their ramifications. One correspondent informed Chase, "I need not tell you that 49 out of fifty political editors are as ignorant as asses on all questions of political economy—in fact on all questions except the claptrap of sectarian party politics."[96] A bond agent reported to Jay Cooke that voters appeared to "let the [government] mind its own business. . . . They figure . . . out when Congress is not sitting, but when in session they are in the dark. Fact is, when one considers this vast area, it is easy to see how states were carried out of the union before the people knew it."[97] Since the public seemed confused by the Treasury's funding operations, some agents concluded: "It matters little what they say outside of the limited circle of . . . the great commercial cities."[98] However, Treasury officials were hardly obeying the demands of the great commercial cities either, for in these cities opposition to the national banking system "had been continuous from the outset."[99]

While Chase and Sherman were claiming that the public was demanding the creation of the national banking system, after the Civil War radical agrarian organizations such as the Grange, the Greenback Party, and the Populists would claim that the national banking system was passed in the interests of powerful Eastern financiers to the detriment of American producers. Populist literature like Susan Emery's *Seven Financial Conspiracies Which Have Enslaved the American People* asserted that the national banking system was merely one of the conspiracies imposed upon the American people.[100]

Yet powerful bankers had *opposed* the national banking system. The New York Clearing House Association was initially so opposed to the creation of the national banking system that it refused to allow national banks to join its association.[101] Yet voters appeared unaware of such details. Chase complained that voter ignorance hampered his ability to enlist public opinion to support his preferred policies and would ensure that "we have not time to produce through the people the desired effect upon the present congress."[102] Even when people were aware that Congress was debating war finance, Jay Cooke complained the legislation's complexity made "the people . . . confused and confounded worse than they were at Babel."[103] Even certain bankers who would be materially affected by the measure complained they were unaware of its stipulations.[104]

Despite Sherman's claims on the Senate floor and in spite of the impressions created by the Cookes' editorials, the public was not in fact demanding the national banking system. Chase, Sherman, and the Cookes manufactured the appearance of popular support to secure congressional approval for a measure that financiers opposed and most people had never heard of. Chase had manipulated congressional perceptions so effectively that he found himself implementing policies autonomously from popular preferences, if we can even speak of the public's having preferences at all, for the electorate did not appear to have been aware of the measure's implementation.

Chase and others had concluded that the Treasury Department's funding operations were simply not understood. Despite weak popular awareness, Chase's endorsement of the national banking system had alienated members of his own party. Radical Republicans, such as Thaddeus Stevens (R-PA), who endorsed the greenbacks were reported to be "the most powerful enemy of the bill," and other Radical Republicans complained of the national banking system that it "makes two classes of money—one for the banks and brokers, and another for the people. It discriminates between the rights of different classes of creditors, allowing the rich capitalist to demand gold, and compelling the ordinary lender of money on individual security to receive notes which the government had purposely discredited."[105]

Despite such opposition the measure passed with a comfortable margin in the House and a bare majority in the Senate.[106] The national banking system was ultimately implemented by a small group of officials surrounding Chase and the Treasury Department. Reflecting on their role in creating the national banking system, Henry Cooke told his brother that they had "contributed more than any other living men" to the bill's passage.[107] Prior to the publication of their editorials, the national banking system "had been repudiated by the House and was without a sponsor in the Senate," leaving the measure "virtually dead and buried."[108] It was revived, Cooke wrote, only when he "induced Sherman to take hold of it, and we went to work with the newspapers."[109] Sherman's support had been so pivotal that Chase conceded "without reservation" that Sherman deserved "full credit" for the bill's passage.[110]

While the Treasury Department had expanded its authority to finance the Civil War, Chase and others within the department were not impressed with popular awareness of their actions. Sherman, Chase, and the Cookes had claimed that the public was demanding the national banking system even though they were convinced that there was little popular support or awareness of the measure.

By the conclusion of the Civil War the Treasury Department had resorted to funding methods that also allowed the Treasury to influence national economic conditions. The creation of the national banking system and the issuance of greenbacks had expanded American state authority over the national economy. By printing greenbacks and selling loans, the federal government could manipulate the amount of currency in circulation. As Hugh McCulloch, Chase's successor as treasury secretary, observed, this constituted "the first time the Government [had] undertaken judiciously to 'regulate the currency,'" a power that was all the more remarkable because there had "never been any great enthusiasm for the bill" that created the greenbacks in the first place.[111] With the treasury secretary able to "bring all circulation under national control," he could "now, to a large extent, control . . . the finances of the country."[112]

Furthermore, since the interest rates on the interest-bearing Treasury notes were "left to him to fix," the treasury secretary could manipulate the interest rates of government loans without congressional oversight. As dissident voices such as Gallatin recognized, this left "pretty much everything to [the treasury secretary's] discretion."[113] Yet this transformation had been inaugurated largely without the support of powerful Eastern financial groups. Chase had been widely criticized by Eastern financial interests and had relied upon the House of Cooke to partially neutralize hostility from New York financiers. Yet as the *Merchants' Magazine and Commercial Review* complained, the decision to grant the treasury secretary such authority over financial markets was a "mode of reasoning [that] is very extraordinary."[114]

Hardly a deliberate or planned decision, the treasury secretary's new discretion over the interest rates on government bonds, and his control over the money supply, had emerged as an unintended consequence of the funding strategies used to prosecute the Civil War. Yet since many Eastern financiers were uneasy with the treasury secretary's power over financial markets, and there was little congressional support for the Treasury Department's actions, there was no guarantee that this form of bureaucratic authority would be retained after the war.

The Treasury Department's authority over financial markets was structured by public actors' ideological assumptions regarding which monetary policies were appropriate, and by the reactions of financiers who were confronted with

the material effects of these policy decisions. These actors, however, were reacting to policies that were being implemented autonomously from popular control simply because voters were ignorant of politics. Recognizing the public's
ignorance, Chase and the Cookes manipulated newspaper coverage of finance
policy to mislead members of Congress regarding the state of public opinion
and secure their preferred policies. But these policy decisions and calculations
were premised on the assumption that the public was unaware of how the
Treasury Department was funding the war effort.

Of course the Treasury Department's expanding authority was hardly the
only case of bureaucratic development in American government during the
Civil War. For example, in 1862 the Department of Agriculture was created as
a bureau without cabinet status.[115] However, the Department of Agriculture
was not created as a *regulatory* agency; it was instead intended to promote
agricultural interests and development in ways that did not call for regulating
national economic conditions.[116] Rather than assuming novel administrative
regulatory functions, the department engaged in seed distribution, crop ex-
perimentation, the collection and distribution of various agricultural statis-
tics, and other activities previously exercised by the Patent Office.[117] In short,
although the Department of Agriculture expanded state authority, it did not
represent a departure from antebellum forms of government.

Despite expanding central state power, throughout the war Treasury officials were convinced that the public was only dimly aware of their decisions. It
is unclear, however, whether popular unawareness of Northern funding strategies was politically consequential. The public's ignorance of Chase's funding
strategies would only become politically important during the elections following the Civil War, a topic explored in the following chapter. However,
the expansion of regulatory authority following the war was closely associated
with the reintroduction of monetary policy as a topic of national political contention, and with the beginning of a broader shift within the ideology of the
Democratic Party. This would entail a reversal of the Democrats' traditional
"hard" monetary positions, and the adoption of inflationary currency policy
by certain Midwestern Democrats.

Although the Jacksonian Democrats had associated opposition to monopoly with defense of the gold standard, certain Midwestern Democrats would
reverse their traditional monetary positions and begin demanding payment of
the public debt in paper currency. In an attempt to distance themselves from
associations with rebellion and secession, Ohio Democrats George Pendleton

and Clement Vallandigham, the Democrats who had led opposition to the greenbacks during the Civil War, would popularize currency inflation in their attempt to seize the Democratic presidential nomination of 1868.

To do so, these two Democrats made a series of fictitious claims regarding their prior monetary positions and those of rival economic and political groups as well. This electoral strategy assumed that the electorate was poorly informed of what had transpired during the Civil War, for had voters been aware of the positions taken by political parties, politicians, and economic groups during the war, they would have recognized that these Democrats were making fictitious claims that had little relationship to the actual positions taken by Eastern bankers or the Republican Party.

Despite their reliance upon such fictions, the currency issue nearly allowed Pendleton to capture the presidential nomination of 1868, thereby demonstrating that inflation was a powerful electioneering platform. This had effects beyond specific questions regarding monetary policy. Since many of the political issues associated with slavery had been destroyed by the Civil War, a powerful justification for helping commit the Democratic Party to restricting federal authority had been removed. This novel political environment established a new terrain for the creation of the American regulatory state, eventually forcing certain Republicans to endorse bureaucratic delegation to remove certain policy issues from popular influence.

Chapter 4 George Pendleton and Mass Opinion

By the end of the Civil War, the federal government had extended its influence over the American financial system, and the creation of the greenbacks allowed direct control of the volume of currency in circulation. Through its discretion over federal loans and the greenbacks, the Treasury Department could manipulate the money supply and influence macroeconomic conditions. While similar powers had existed before, for example within the Bank of the United States' control over state bank currency and in the Treasury Department's prior issues of interest-bearing currency, the Treasury Department had assumed novel powers in the course of financing the Civil War.

There was no guarantee, however, that these powers would survive the conclusion of the Civil War. The institutionalization of such authority would require a partisan innovation: the adoption of currency inflation by the Democratic Party and the reintroduction of monetary policy as a national political issue. Although the Radical Republicans had been the strongest supporters of the greenbacks, after the war the Midwestern congressional Democrats that had led congressional opposition to the greenbacks adopted inflationary currency policy as a topic of national debate.

Oddly, the Democratic leaders of the inflationary greenback movement were George Pendleton and Clement Vallandigham, the Democrats who had led opposition to the greenbacks when they were initially introduced. Their adoption of currency inflation would have significant ramifications for the issues that consumed postbellum politics, the development of parties' financial policy platforms, and the Democrats' evolving stance toward federal authority. The Democrats' ideological shift would have implications for the development of bureaucratic authority in the Treasury Department, as Republicans explored ways to resist popular demands for currency inflation that the Democrats' unleashed.

The specific way the currency issue emerged, and the fact that Pendleton and Vallandigham took a leading role in demanding inflation, indicates that the public had a tenuous grasp of politics. Pendleton and Vallandigham made a series of fictitious claims regarding the Republicans' financial positions, bankers' preferences, and their own positions on the currency question. Public ignorance of finance policy ensured that the public failed to recognize that these statements were fictions intended to accomplish the personal political goals of certain politicians. However, these fictions allowed some Democrats to adopt policy demands they had previously opposed, and led voters to believe that if they endorsed currency inflation they should support the Democratic Party.

The Democrats' adoption of inflationary monetary policy led the Republican Party into an increasingly unpopular position: defending deflationary monetary policies and the gold standard, positions traditionally associated with the antebellum Democrats. To explain how this occurred requires examining the electoral pressures facing the Democratic Party in the immediate postbellum period, and Pendleton and Vallandigham's manipulation of public opinion in their attempts to secure the Democratic presidential nomination of 1868. Despite Pendleton's fictitious claims regarding monetary policy, his inflationary campaign marked the beginning of the Democratic Party's endorsement of federal monetary activism and the Republican Party's corresponding turn toward defending the gold standard.

This new partisan configuration would eventually force the Republicans to adopt an institutional innovation—namely, empowering the Treasury Department with autonomous discretionary powers, an expansion of bureaucratic authority with implications for American state formation extending beyond the context of postbellum finance policy. Yet instead of seeking to translate popular demands into policy, the Treasury Department was empowered to insulate monetary policy from popular influence. To explain this sequence of events and the interaction between political elites, voter ignorance, the Democrats' ideological shift, and the Republicans' subsequent institutional innovation, we must examine the postbellum electoral environment confronting the Democrats, and how the Ohio gubernatorial election of 1867 influenced the presidential election of 1868.

This chapter proceeds in two stages. The first section examines how Hugh McCulloch, Chase's successor as treasury secretary, began withdrawing greenbacks from circulation following the end of the Civil War. In the second section, I examine how Ohio Democrat George Pendleton realized that greenback inflation could be used as a campaign issue in the Ohio gubernatorial election of 1867 to make him the frontrunner for the Democratic presidential nomination of 1868. In his attempt to become the frontrunner for the Democratic presidential nomination, Pendleton made a series of fictitious claims regarding the positions of various political and economic groups, and also about his own history on the financial issue. By capitalizing on voter ignorance of finance policy, he reintroduced monetary policy as a topic of political contention and created the perception that the Democrats were the natural supporters of currency inflation.

Although the destruction of slavery made it inevitable that economic issues would reenter politics, Pendleton and Vallandigham ensured that monetary policy, and not other issues such as the tariff, would dominate political debate. In addition, the particular configuration of positions the parties assumed on financial issues was reversed, with the Democrats increasingly calling for inflationary policies, while the Republicans endorsed the gold standard. Monetary policy was a particularly helpful policy for encouraging state expansion and development, a topic I address at various points in subsequent chapters.

However, the parties' evolving monetary positions were conditioned by voter ignorance of Civil War finance policy and by the opportunities such ignorance created for elites to manipulate public opinion. As the Treasury Department's commitment to the gold standard created an opportunity for the Democrats to attribute economic hardship to the Republicans' policies, they were able to manipulate public opinion and popularize grossly simplified accounts of monetary policy. The public's resulting opposition to contracting the money supply would eventually lead certain Republicans to endorse bureaucratic delegation to isolate monetary policy from public opinion, a decision with important implications for American state authority but one that cannot be separated from Republicans' ideological commitment to the gold standard. Yet this sequence of events was initiated when Pendleton popularized fictions in his attempt to secure the Democratic presidential nomination of 1868, fictions whose power over public opinion was derived from voter ignorance of finance policy.

At the conclusion of the Civil War, Chase's successor as treasury secretary, Hugh McCulloch, immediately began efforts to withdraw greenbacks from circulation.[1] McCulloch had served as president of the Bank of Indiana and had been appointed comptroller of the currency in the Treasury Department in 1863. During the Civil War he had criticized the national banking system and stated that the greenbacks were a necessary, but unconstitutional, measure.[2] With the cessation of hostilities he began efforts to remove the greenbacks from circulation and reinstate the gold standard.

McCulloch's actions were influenced by his constitutional concerns, and because he worried that the greenbacks created the opportunity for the politicization of monetary policy, a deplorable situation, as "few things would be more injurious to business."[3] McCulloch worried that the existence of a paper currency created the potential for reunifying the Southern and Midwestern wings of the Democratic Party on an economic issue—monetary policy—a sectional alliance that could threaten the Republican Party. He was "greatly alarmed" that monetary issues could lead to a coalition between Southern and Northern Democrats, and he urged the "leader[s] and creator[s] of public sentiment not to encourage this idea."[4]

To avoid these potential problems McCulloch sought to retire the compound interest notes and use bond sales to withdraw one to two hundred million dollars in greenbacks.[5] He recognized that the aggregate volume of currency would exercise a critical role over macroeconomic growth, yet the Treasury Department lacked metrics to determine just how much currency could safely be retired. Without such information, McCulloch recognized that the optimal amount of greenbacks to retire, and the timing of their reduction, could not "be estimated with any degree of accuracy."[6] Despite recognizing such uncertainty, he requested congressional approval to sell bonds bearing up to 6 percent interest that would be used to remove greenbacks from circulation at his discretion.[7]

Business reaction to currency contraction was mixed. Eastern bankers generally endorsed specie resumption and currency contraction.[8] Having purchased government bonds, banks wanted their bonds repaid in gold, and not in depreciated paper currency. However, the Eastern financial community did not exhibit any homogenous position on McCulloch's policies. Although some New York financiers endorsed McCulloch's contraction, others worried that the reduction of the currency would occur "too early and be pressed with too much vigor."[9]

Furthermore, although Jay Cooke had helped the Treasury neutralize the power of New York banks during the war, he was a vocal critic of McCulloch's contraction, and for good reason: he feared his European bond sales would be damaged by elimination of the gold premium the greenbacks had created.[10] Thus, although Cooke supported the gold standard, he did not approve of McCulloch's actions. Cooke advised that "the least said about [specie resumption] the better," specifically because, he wrote his brother, Henry, "it is the premium on gold that enables us to sell the 5–20's. If purchasers of 5–20's supposed that we will get back to specie payments within a year or two they would not touch them at present prices."[11] As McCulloch proceeded with his contraction of the currency, Cooke told his brother: "Totally disagree in the conclusions to which Mr. Chase and others come concerning the resumption of specie payments. There can be no such thing as a resumption until the 1862 loans, abroad, and other loans over there are taken care of. Otherwise the drain from Europe would swamp us in a month. And there can be no such thing as a resumption until the de-centralization system of redemption of national bank notes is adopted."[12] Given such opposition, McCulloch's contraction of the money supply was clearly not being directed by the House of Cooke.

Regardless of their reactions to McCulloch's specific policies, bankers were becoming concerned at the treasury secretary's power over financial markets. Since the secretary was manipulating the various forms of currency in circulation, one of Ohio senator John Sherman's correspondents complained: "The Secretary of the Treasury . . . has practically become an anti-Bank man. He seems to think that, being a Minister of Finance, he *must* 'financier;'—that, being a Physician, he must *practice,* whether he have a patient or no—What need [is there for] the Secretary to meddle with the price of gold, with the abundance or non-abundance of the currency, and thereby attempt to forestall and regulate the 'supply and demand'?"[13] This particular banker observed: "[It is McCulloch's] attempt to regulate and limit the 'supply and demand,' instead of letting the inevitable laws of trade and of 'supply and demand' regulate the *price,* that causes commotion, fear, alarm, distress, and may, if not let alone soon enough, bring disaster and ruin."[14] These criticisms went beyond the specific policies McCulloch sought; they reveal that the Treasury Department's regulation of the money supply was novel and upsetting for some bankers, despite their support for the objective—the resumption of the gold standard—that McCulloch sought to accomplish.

With the treasury secretary able to manipulate the money supply, the Treasury Department was able to influence general macroeconomic conditions, and this ensured that "the general shape of financial affairs in our country may depend in a great measure on the action which may be taken by the Secretary of the Treasury or by Congress."[15] Yet aside from their skepticism about these new tools for influencing the economy, both Jay Cooke and the Cincinnati Chamber of Commerce noted that there was "unquestionably reason to hesitate about giving [one] man large discretionary power in the administration of an important bureau."[16]

Not all members of the Republican Party shared these concerns, however, and some expressed support for delegating power to the treasury secretary. Elbridge Spaulding (R-NY) complained that leaving Congress in control of finance policy would leave businessmen "under constant apprehensions" that Congress would implement "some scheme . . . which [would] derange monetary affairs, and upset all their business calculations."[17] Spaulding endorsed a measure introduced by Samuel Morrill (R-VT) that allowed the treasury secretary freedom to determine the volume of currency and loans because there was "no doubt [he would] use his discretionary power prudently."[18]

Echoing Spaulding's concerns regarding congressional control of monetary policy, Edward Atkinson, who would later join the ranks of "liberal reform" intellectuals, informed McCulloch that "a large section of the Republicans" existed who "desire[d] to see financial and all revenue questions separated from party issues," and suggested that if this faction gained power within the Republican Party, McCulloch could "almost dictate the future policy" of the Treasury Department.[19]

Since McCulloch had been contracting the money supply without congressional approval, a measure was introduced endorsing McCulloch's contraction, but also limiting the volume of currency the treasury secretary could remove from circulation. The measure stipulated that only $10 million of greenbacks could be retired within six months of the act's passage, with no more than $4 million retired in each following month.[20] As this would limit the treasury secretary's range of action, McCulloch complained: "[It was] not what I wanted," because he believed "there would be months in which much more than four millions could be withdrawn without affecting the market;

and other months when the withdrawal of a much smaller amount would cause considerable stringency."[21]

Despite the limitations placed upon McCulloch's actions, the treasury secretary was operating in ways that were fundamentally different from the Treasury Department's actions prior to the Civil War. Recognizing the novelty of this authority, Senator Sherman, one of McCulloch's vocal congressional critics, complained that Congress was considering granting

> the Secretary of the Treasury greater powers than have ever been conferred since the foundation of this Government upon any Secretary of the Treasury. Our loan laws heretofore have generally been confined to the negotiation of a single loan, limited in amount. As the war progressed the difficulties of the country became greater, and we were more in the habit of removing the limitations on the power of the Secretary of the Treasury; but generally the power conferred was confined to a particular loan then in the market. This bill, however, is more general in its terms. This bill authorizes the Secretary of the Treasury to sell any character of bonds without limit, except as to the rate of interest. . . . The power conferred on the Secretary of the Treasury is absolute.[22]

Sherman's concerns were not limited to the loans the treasury secretary was issuing. Sherman was also critical of the secretary's ability to influence the volume of currency in circulation, complaining that by giving the treasury secretary the "power to reduce the currency," the measure was granting "a power that has not heretofore been granted to any Secretary of the Treasury."[23] Sherman believed the measure was unique because the amount of currency in circulation "heretofore has been fixed and limited by law," and not left to the treasury secretary's discretion.[24]

Furthermore, Sherman worried that delegation of such authority to an executive official could initiate an uncontrollable trend. He observed: "We are now about to confer upon the Secretary of the Treasury powers that we cannot in the nature of things recall. It is true we may repeal this law next year, but we know very well that when these large powers are granted they are very seldom recalled; they are made the precedents of further grants of power and are very rarely recalled."[25] To bolster his position, Sherman drew attention to the financial community's criticism of this form of the treasury secretary's authority. Instead of endorsing the expansion of bureaucratic capacity or removing control of the currency from elected officials, Sherman noted, "some of the best business men of the country" were complaining of "the uncertainty as to the policy to be adopted by the Government."[26] In his mind these problems were compounded by the treasury secretary's discretion, as "the will or whim of the Secretary of the Treasury might destroy all the men of the country who are compelled to go into debt to carry on their business."[27] Sherman concluded: "I do not think it wise now to place in the power of the Secretary of the Treasury or any mortal man this absolute and extreme control over the currency of the country. *We have never done it before.*"[28]

Echoing Sherman's concerns, the financial press complained that the treasury secretary could "make laws . . . to force the people of the United States at his bidding, to increase their production, to cease their speculation, to diminish their extravagance."[29] The *Commercial and Financial Chronicle* warned: "A greater power, a more absolute control, over the growth, the enterprise and the activity of a free people was never enjoyed by any executive than is now vested in the Treasury."[30] McCulloch had secured legislation "empowering him to issue other evidences of debt at his discretion," and some complained: "A power so tremendous has seldom, if ever before been lodged in the hands of a minister."[31]

Sherman's observations and McCulloch's recognition that the treasury secretary's bond sales, when combined with a national currency whose value was not tied to the gold standard, constituted a new set of powers indicate that the treasury secretary was exercising a novel form of authority that contemporaries did not see as a continuation of existing institutions. This is not to suggest that this was the first time the federal government had taken positive action or the first time the treasury department had intervened in the economy. Ever since the publication of Oscar and Mary Flug Handlins' *Commonwealth* and Louis Hartz's *Economic Policy,* scholars such as Brian Balogh, Richard John, William Novak, and Jerry Mashaw have documented numerous cases of government action in the antebellum republic, especially at the state and local levels. These examples are frequently used to claim that continuity existed in forms of government authority during the nineteenth century. In Mashaw's words, arguments that a new type of state authority was created in the late nineteenth century are "simply wrong."[32]

Despite recognizing the numerous cases of antebellum action and administration, especially at the state and local levels, nineteenth-century observers such as Sherman and McCulloch clearly believed that the treasury secretary was exercising new forms of authority that had not existed before the Civil War. McCulloch's method of action was described as "novel," and Sherman suggested that McCulloch was acting in a way that "was never enjoyed" by prior treasury secretaries. If there had been continuity in these officials' actions, it is unclear why so many were claiming that the Treasury Department was exercising new forms of authority.

Indeed, the novelty of McCulloch's actions, and the fact that his actions were a departure from prior forms of executive action, are precisely what many representatives and members of the business community were criticizing. Interestingly, the heart of such opposition did not come from the Democrats, many of whom supported the treasury secretary's efforts to retire the greenbacks from circulation. Rather, in the late 1860s McCulloch's strongest opponents were Republicans, certain Radical Republicans in particular. While every Democrat but one supported McCulloch's contraction, House Republicans divided 56 to 53 in favor of the measure, with "the heart of the opposition" coming from the "most ultra" of the Radical Republicans.[33]

With certain Republicans opposing his contraction of the currency, McCulloch's annual report of 1866 complained of not being "sustained by corresponding legislation," with the result being that "little progress has been made since [1865] . . . towards specie payments."[34] Dissatisfied with congressional limitations upon his authority, McCulloch recommended contraction increase from four million to six million dollars each month for the remainder of 1866, and then an increase to ten million per month in 1867.[35]

At this point certain Republicans began worrying that McCulloch had created an opportunity for the Democrats to use financial issues in the approaching gubernatorial elections.[36] Despite having little direct relevance for national politics, gubernatorial elections in states such as Ohio and Pennsylvania were used to reveal information about various platforms and candidates' popularity, and thereby influenced the parties' decisions regarding the candidates they nominated and platforms they proposed in the following year's presidential elections.[37]

Reflecting upon concerns that the Democrats could use economic issues to influence the approaching gubernatorial and presidential elections, Sherman reported that certain Republicans were "keenly [aware of] the danger of our financial position."[38] The *Nation* noted that prior to the war it was difficult to see how "that the great curse of the Old World—the division of society into classes—was likely to befall us here or affect American politics."[39] Yet economic conflict was threatening to spill into the political arena, and once "classes [are] formed, the growth and development and appearance in politics of class feeling is a matter of course."[40]

The Republicans' prospects further deteriorated when the country slipped into a recession that coincided with McCulloch's contraction.[41] Even with

congressional limitations upon the amount of currency he could retire, Mc-
Culloch contracted the money supply by 7 percent each year in 1865–1868,
and an 8 percent decline in the price level accompanied the contraction during this period.[42] Yet McCulloch remained convinced that contraction should
proceed, even though he worried that the "want of capital and credit, the
dullness of trade throughout the country," coupled with "the general failure
of the wheat and corn crops last year," could inhibit his efforts to reduce the
public debt.[43]

McCulloch had created an opportunity for the Democrats to attribute the
recession to the Treasury's financial policies, and hence the Republican Party.
Recognizing the opportunity this had created, and hoping that they could
use financial issues to win the Ohio gubernatorial contest of 1867 and thereby
control the subsequent presidential nomination, the Ohio Democrats Vallandigham and Pendleton decided to take advantage of this situation and try
to "shift attention to the finances" to create a political issue they could use to
return to national prominence.[44]

However, the nature of the Republicans' financial policies, the Democrats'
traditional monetary positions, and Pendleton and Vallandigham's prior financial positions created several problems. Specifically, McCulloch's efforts
to resume the gold standard echoed the traditional positions of the Democratic Party; the Democrats had endorsed McCulloch's contraction in 1866,
and both Pendleton and Vallandigham had opposed the greenbacks when they
were initially created. If the Democrats were going to use financial issues in the
approaching elections, they would have to endorse currency inflation, a policy
they had opposed throughout the antebellum period.

The Ohio election of 1867 coincided with a wave of agrarian radicalism that
swept across the United States and led to the creation of agrarian organizations, such as the Patrons of Husbandry, or the Grange, that would eventually
culminate in the creation of the Populist Party.[45] The creation of these organizations meant that politicians had new opportunities to appeal to voters on
the basis of economic issues and concerns. The specific form that these appeals
would assume was initially unclear, however, and the individuals who were
leading efforts to organize agrarians, such as Oliver Kelley, cofounder of the
Grange, found it difficult to inform voters of new political issues.

As a clerk in the Department of Agriculture, Kelley toured the South in
1866 to report on the condition of agriculture.[46] Although some argue that
rural Americans exhibited clearly articulated ideas about education, temperance, the family, and the state's role in mediating between conflicting forms of

nationalism and ethnocultural identity, Kelley's Southern tour impressed on him that agrarians were often unaware of basic knowledge immediately bearing on their economic interests.[47]

For example, despite its "vital interest" to farmers, Kelley complained to William Saunders, cofounder of the Grange, that 90 percent of farmers were "totally ignorant" of scientific agriculture.[48] Kelley complained that combating prejudice against scientific farming was difficult. Farmers, while mostly literate, did not read agricultural newspapers, and agricultural fairs seeking to disseminate scientific knowledge and foster a sense of corporate community had to resort to "Horse Races and numerous side shows" if they were to "bring the farmers out in any number."[49]

These challenges to organizing agrarians influenced the organizational structure the Grange adopted. Initially a nonpolitical fraternal organization, the Grange offered its members agricultural goods at discounted prices and lobbied for developing improved transportation routes to lower the costs of moving agrarian products to markets. Although Kelley hoped the Grange would combat agrarian isolation and offer various forms of economic assistance, he believed that novel methods were necessary to make the Grange appealing. He recommended the Grange mimic the secrecy and status ranks of the Freemasons because "the secrecy would lend an interest and peculiar fascination . . . [while] the material for manufacturing new degrees to keep up the interest would be inexhaustible."[50]

The informational challenges Kelley confronted in his efforts to organize the Grange would influence the trajectory of monetary issues in postbellum elections, and would also influence certain Democrats' attempts to use currency inflation as a political issue in postwar elections. Despite the Democrats' antebellum opposition to paper currency, currency inflation had several proponents before the Civil War. In the 1840s the writer Edward Kellogg had published arguments claiming inflationary monetary policy could help American labor.[51] Denying state banks had constitutional authority to issue currency, Kellogg's *Labor and Other Capital* endorsed congressional regulation of the money supply, ideas subsequently adopted in the late 1860s by the National Labor Union and labor leaders such as William Sylvis.[52]

Although the antebellum Democrats' support for the gold standard ensured that Kellogg's ideas remained obscure, in the face of the Democrats' postwar electoral defeats Pendleton realized that currency inflation was "tailor-made" for his electoral interests.[53] By endorsing currency inflation to help pay the principal of the public debt, he hoped to use financial issues in the Ohio gubernatorial election of 1867 to help him become the frontrunner for the Democratic presidential nomination in 1868.[54]

Pendleton enlisted Clement Vallandigham and Washington McLean, editor of the Cincinnati *Enquirer,* to help popularize his campaign message.[55] Pendleton began attributing the recession to McCulloch's contraction, and claimed that McCulloch's contraction and the creation of the national banking system were plots by Eastern bankers and Radical Republicans to enrich themselves at the expense of Western producers. Despite believing that financial issues "were beyond the understanding of most ordinary voters," Pendleton, Vallandigham, and McLean began popularizing currency inflation as a panacea for the recession.[56]

If Pendleton and Vallandigham were going to use currency inflation as a campaign issue, however, they faced several problems. Specifically, both Pendleton and Vallandigham had been vocal *opponents* of the greenbacks, which the Radical Republicans had *supported,* and both Pendleton and Vallandigham had *endorsed* McCulloch's contraction as recently as 1866; as late as January 20, 1867, McLean's *Enquirer* had endorsed specie payments and greenback contraction.[57]

Furthermore, Pendleton and Vallandigham had been vocal *critics* of the greenbacks when they were originally created. Such opposition was influenced by the greenbacks' role in supporting the Northern war effort. Vallandigham had been imprisoned in 1863 for his speeches claiming that the Lincoln administration misled voters regarding the war's objectives.[58] Opposition to the Civil War had been expressed in opposition to the North's funding for the war, and in 1862 Vallandigham had attacked the greenbacks and tried to appeal to "hundreds of farmers" by comparing "Democratic rule [to] a $5 gold piece the Republican by a greenback . . . to indicate what the country was coming to."[59]

Yet in 1867 Pendleton and Vallandigham's prior positions were irrelevant. Pendleton had been McClellan's vice-presidential nominee during the Democrats' unsuccessful 1864 campaign, and his political career now hung in the balance. By May of 1867, in what has been described as "among the most puzzling phenomena of American history," Pendleton, Vallandigham, and McLean's *Enquirer* reversed their earlier opposition to paper currency and began demanding that a "few hundred millions of legal tenders . . . [be] poured into the channels of trade."[60] Although Pendleton had denounced the greenbacks when they were initially created, and despite having endorsed McCulloch's contraction, he began claiming that "the condition of the country could bear an increase in the currency. . . . Every interest . . . would be advanced by the stimulating effect of an enlarged currency."[61] By attacking Eastern financial interests for engineering McCulloch's financial policies, Pendleton catered to voters' dislike of powerful economic groups and simultaneously offered a simple explanation for the causes of the recession.

Speaking in thirty counties across the Midwest, Pendleton was "favorably received," and Republicans quickly began complaining that currency inflation was looking "plausible to the masses."[62] Concerned Republicans worried that "a change in public opinion [is] going on" and, in many sections of the country, complained that there was a "steady increasing intention" to pay the interest on the bonds in greenbacks and not gold.[63] With speeches displaying his "accustomed energy and earnestness," Vallandigham canvassed "every section" of the Midwest, addressing "between seventy and eighty meetings."[64] Soon thereafter inflationary demands "rapidly began to grow in the Middle West."[65]

Pendleton's campaigning had "evoked a strongly favorable popular response," and currency contraction was now reported to have "excited a strong popular opposition."[66] Nor were these complaints limited to popular support for inflation, as Republicans noted that even businessmen were complaining of currency shortages, leading some to conclude that "repudiation will find . . . much favor with the voters of the North West."[67]

Prior to Pendleton's electioneering, both Republicans and Democrats had predicted the Ohio election would "go as usual," and some Republicans had expressed confidence that even their suffrage amendment would pass.[68] But now voters were reportedly expressing "general distrust in the Bonds and Currency," and McCulloch's policies and the national banking system were reported to be "very unpopular with the masses" and were being "denounced everywhere."[69] Financial questions seemed to be "all absorbing now," and the currency issue appeared to be "attracting more attention than the amendment to the constitution."[70]

Ohio Democrats claimed that currency contraction and the national banking system were attempts by "New England Radical manufacturers . . . to destroy our Western enterprises."[71] Democrats claimed that the Radical Republicans were seeking to "create a bonded aristocracy in this country"[72] and had become bitter "because they [saw] no hope of the success of the bondholders' ticket except by the appliance of the party lash to poor men whose interest [lay] with greenbacks and Pendleton."[73] Aside from attacking Radical Republicans, Jay Cooke was denounced as the architect of McCulloch's contraction.[74]

Although inflationary demands were gaining popular support, these demands were hardly spontaneous expressions of popular discontent, and some
noted that the parties' financial positions had "no natural unity."[75] Rather,
it took Pendleton, McLean, and Vallandigham to lead the public to believe
that the recession was "*naturally* related to McCulloch's policy of contraction"
and then popularize this argument with fictitious claims about the positions
of bankers and the Republican Party, such that voters concluded that if they
wanted inflationary currency policy *they should support the Democrats.*[76]

Yet there was no reason why demands for currency inflation should have
resulted in support for the Democratic Party. Pendleton and Vallandigham
had led congressional *opposition* to the greenbacks' creation, and opposition
to paper currency had been associated with the Democratic Party ever since
Jackson's veto of the recharter of the Second Bank of the United States. Furthermore, the economic and political groups that Pendleton was blaming for
McCulloch's contraction and for creating the national banking system, groups
such as the Radical Republicans, Eastern bankers, and Jay Cooke, had actually
endorsed the greenbacks and opposed the creation of the national banking
system.

Despite Pendleton's claims, the Radical Republicans had actually been the
most vocal *opponents* of the national banking system and ardent *supporters* of
the greenbacks. Prominent Radicals, such as Benjamin Wade (R-OH), Benjamin Butler (R-MA), Thaddeus Stevens (R-PA), and William Kelley (R-PA),
were vocal opponents of the national banking system and McCulloch's contraction. Similarly, while Pendleton was claiming that Jay Cooke was directing McCulloch's contraction, Cooke was actually demanding that McCulloch
cease contracting the greenbacks because the shrinking gold premium was
damaging his European bond sales.[77]

Nor were other Eastern bankers supporting the Republican's financial policy; the Eastern bankers Pendleton claimed supported the national banking
system had actually been its strongest opponents. Prominent New York bankers, such as James Gallatin, J. E. Williams, George Coe, and the New York
Clearing House Association, had condemned the national banking system as
a "mongrel, bastard thing is to be nursed and petted in to a worse than useless
life, only to die a more than disgraceful death."[78]

In fact, Pendleton's positions were nearly identical to those of the bankers he
claimed he was attacking. The New York Clearing House Association had criticized the national banking system for allowing bonds to be used as a reserve
for the national banknotes and complained that this would impose unneces-

sary costs upon the government.[79] Indeed, Bray Hammond has concluded that the similarities between postbellum inflationists, such as Pendleton, and the bankers they attacked were so apparent that the inflationists "might have got from Wall Street the greenback doctrine they were soon advocating."[80] Far from being designed by Eastern financiers, the national banking system had been created despite their opposition, and the New York Clearing House Association had initially refused to admit national banks into its association.[81] Furthermore, despite Pendleton's claims, the greenbacks had actually been created with support from the Eastern financiers Pendleton was claiming were their strongest opponents.

It was not even clear that currency contraction was actually occurring. Although a total of $72,018,846 of greenbacks had been removed from circulation by 1868, this reduction was offset by a corresponding increase in national banknotes, which approached their limit of $300 million by September 30, 1868.[82] The $114,806,565 increase in national bank notes offset the greenback contraction, and after the increases in the national bank notes and the decreases in the compound interest notes are calculated into the money supply, the total reduction in the volume of currency was a mere $45,493,129, a figure so insignificant that some wondered whether "it might well be asked what all the commotion was about."[83]

This was not lost on McCulloch, who recognized that the actual contraction of currency was so negligible that "no one outside of the department would have known that what was called contraction was going on but for the monthly published statements of the condition of the treasury."[84] Hardly a reaction to actual changes in the money supply, it was, McCulloch complained, "an unreasonable apprehension of what might be the effect of this contraction, rather than what it was, that raised the outcry against it."[85]

Finally, it had been Pendleton and Vallandigham, not the Radical Republicans, who had opposed the greenbacks when they were initially created. Vallandigham had attacked the greenbacks as being "cheap in material, easy of issue, worked by steam, signed by machinery," and had warned that "there will be no end to the legions of paper devils which shall pour forth from the loins of the [Treasury] Secretary" if the government issued a paper currency.[86] Pendleton's attacks on the greenbacks had been so eloquent that he had "settled forever" any questions regarding their constitutionality.[87]

Despite such inaccuracies, exasperated Republicans complained that in 1864 Ohio Democrats "spoke of greenbacks as 'Lincoln skins' . . . and said . . . that the greenbacks were practically worthless."[88] Yet the public did not appear to

remember these claims, and popular comprehension of Civil War finance policy seemed so shallow that Chase complained: "There are few who understand
what my work [as treasury secretary] was."[89] Similarly, although Sherman had
played an important role in Civil War finance policy, his correspondents confessed that their inquiries regarding his opinions on finance policy were made
"without knowing . . . what your views are upon the subject."[90]

Although Republicans recognized Pendleton had ensured public opinion
was "against us," they also complained that "the mass of the common people
can not and do not comprehend the reason of the depreciation of the [cur-
rency] . . . and no power of argument or exposition can stop them."[91] Always
attentive to public opinion, Jay Cooke complained the Democrats' mobilization of public opinion had created a "nation of croakers," forcing him to re-
double his efforts "to draw the public mind away from this gloomy and unjust
view of our condition."[92]

Similarly, Eastern Democrats appalled at the popularity of inflationary doctrines complained that the public had "little information . . . of what is going
on in the great centers of the nation," due to the "dependence of the rural districts on local press for miserably selected information."[93] Even greenback inflationists, such as Peter Cooper, cofounder of the American Industrial League
and future Greenback Party presidential nominee, believed in the "necessity
of increased effort to awaken and instruct public sentiment on . . . [financial]
subjects."[94]

Yet for Pendleton the inaccuracies of his claims were irrelevant. His political
career hung in the balance, and his campaign message had popular appeal. In
the contentious election of 1867 the Democrats won control of Ohio's state
legislature, elected Alan Thurman to succeed Wade in the Senate, and defeated
the suffrage amendment by thirty-eight thousand votes. Although Republican
Rutherford Hayes was elected governor by a slim margin, the Democrats had
seized control of Ohio, a state whose electoral votes were essential for presidential elections, and had performed well in other swing states, such as Pennsylvania, as well.[95] Appalled at their reverses, many Republicans attributed
their defeat to Pendleton's electioneering, leaving some Republicans concluding: "There will have to be some turn taken in our present financial policy or
we are all gone up, next year. . . . A few more turns of McCulloch's contraction
screw will give us a monetary panic that will eclipse 1840. An issue of fifty
millions of Legal Tenders would balance up our financial books and stop the
continued cry of a stringent money market by all our businessmen."[96] Many
were attributing the Ohio election outcome to financial issues and economic

discontent, and it appeared that "the people almost to a man . . . are opposed to the policy of Secretary McCulloch."[97] Reflecting on the political condition of the country and the recent elections, one Republican complained of being "quite discouraged at the prospect before us as a people . . . I 'am in the fog,' if not quite in the 'slough of despond.'"[98]

Before the Ohio election of 1867 voters exhibited "little interest" in economic issues, but now it was reported that economic and financial questions had become the chief topics of discussion.[99] Republicans worried that the financial issue was where "our greatest troubles are embraced," and they concluded that the Democrats' manipulation of economic antagonism ensured that unless they found some way to counteract Midwestern Democrats' inflationary demands "the next election will sweep our party out of existence."[100]

Acutely aware of inflation's popularity, some Republicans began considering adopting Pendleton's position as "the only feasible plan . . . to keep our hold with the People."[101] Deteriorating economic conditions had left manufacturers and merchants "perfectly prostrate," and with "times getting harder every day" the public was attributing these conditions to McCulloch's contraction of the currency.[102] Despite believing that the causes of the financial stringency "were numerous . . . the single cause of contraction was adroitly seized by the inflationists . . . and they so manipulated the subject that public opinion was strongly excited."[103] Similarly, the financial press was concluding the Republican losses were merely "a matter of dollars and cents."[104] Having "entrusted . . . McCulloch . . . with extraordinary powers," the people had also concluded the Republican Party was "responsible for the mismanagement of the finances."[105]

Lamenting the malleability of public opinion, Schuyler Colfax, soon to be the Republican vice-presidential nominee, complained that the Republicans were "weakened by finance almost as much as suffrage,"[106] and he noted that public support for greenback inflation had become "strong and almost resistless."[107] Sherman complained that Pendleton's campaigning had convinced so many voters to oppose contraction that Congress began considering limiting McCulloch's power over the money supply.[108] Those who endorsed resumption claimed that "not one [congressmen] in ten has any clear ideas of the financial problem," a problem magnified by the "stolid ignorance and sneering indifference . . . among many members who boasted . . . that they did not understand finances and did not want to."[109]

With both parties looking to the approaching presidential contest, it was apparent that "much feeling has been created amongst the people" by

Pendleton's arguments, and some were now concluding that agrarian states would vote Democratic in 1868, "no matter who may be the Republican Candidate for President."[110]

Because gubernatorial elections were used to gauge public opinion for the approaching presidential election, Radical Republicans, such as Butler and Wade, who had been considered as plausible candidates prior to the Ohio contest were eliminated from contention.[111] Consequently, the 1867 elections weakened the Republican faction most amenable to inflation and strengthened the inflationary Midwestern Democrats.[112] In this context Republicans concluded that Ulysses S. Grant's nomination was now critical, for he was the "one man that . . . can beat this repudiation platform."[113] The Democrats' manipulation of economic antagonism had "fixed the candidate for President . . . universally on Grant,"[114] and it seemed "as if [a] command had been given," and "nothing in the world" would now allow the Republicans to support any other nominee.[115]

We recall that in the Ohio gubernatorial election of 1867 George Pendleton manipulated voter ignorance of Civil War finance policy in an attempt to become the Democratic presidential nominee for the election of 1868. Aside from influencing the approaching presidential contest, Pendleton unwittingly initiated a shift in popular assumptions regarding government. Prior to the Civil War, federal action was associated with the Whigs and their electoral constituency. Pendleton's Ohio campaign began to reverse this association, and popular demands increasingly focused on using the state to enlist finance policy to achieve egalitarian economic ends.

The timing of this association was hardly accidental. State power had emancipated African Americans; Pendleton was merely suggesting that these powers be extended to aid others. In this sense the Radical Republicans' endorsement of currency inflation was not a coincidence, for this group of Republicans had endorsed using the powers of the federal government to destroy slavery—it took little to extend such powers to aid other disadvantaged groups as well.[116]

Despite his long-standing support for the gold standard, a combination of electoral pressures and his personal interests led Pendleton to endorse the currency issue that had initially been advanced by the Radical Republicans. Indeed, it is not even clear that Pendleton believed in the ideas he was popularizing. Once he had emerged as the frontrunner for the Democratic presidential nomination, he privately told Eastern Democrats, whose support was necessary to secure the presidential nomination, that he had "specially guarded against any . . . inference" that he supported inflation.[117] Although his opponents complained he had created popular support for inflation, Pendleton was privately disassociating himself from these demands, assuring Eastern Democrats that he was "not a Repudiator."[118]

One might view Pendleton as an effective opinion leader who helped voters realize that inflation was a solution to their economic problems. However, focusing on the interests served by the economic policy Pendleton adopted overlooks the *partisan* innovation he introduced. Pendleton had manipulated perceptions regarding which party supported inflationary monetary policy, creating the impression that the Democrats were natural advocates of paper currency. Had voters been informed of the parties' financial positions, and had they understood what had happened during the funding of the Civil War, this impression would not have seemed obvious.

In fact, Pendleton practically ensured that voters would not receive the inflationary policies they were increasingly endorsing, for the Democratic Party was poorly suited to serve as a vehicle for currency inflation. Not only did the Democrats' ideological tradition oppose paper currency, the opposition of the anti-inflationary Eastern faction of the Democratic Party would have to be overcome before currency inflation was accepted as part of the Democrats' party platform. This transition would not occur until after the election of 1896 had resulted in the nomination of Bryan and the adoption of free silver.

The Democrats' adoption of the currency issue was, in part, a function of the disorganized state of the Republican Party's economic positions. Before the Civil War the Republican Party had exhibited little agreement on economic policies. The Republicans' amalgamation of antislavery and Free Soil Democrats, Whigs, Know-Nothings, and abolitionists ensured that the party exhibited little homogeneity on issues extending beyond slavery.[119] After the Radical Republicans were increasingly marginalized within the Republican Party, the Republicans began to turn against monetary activism in particular and the exercise of federal power in general. While this turn led them to adopt economic positions that were increasingly unpopular, reinforcing the perception that the Republicans were tools of hated Eastern bankers, this set of associations had little relationship to the actual history of either political party.

Yet it is also critical to recognize how voter ignorance structured this process. The realization that the institutional arrangements used to finance the Civil War had been implemented in the absence of popular awareness is crucial to understanding why Pendleton's message was effective in the first place.

Had the electorate understood the financial policies implemented during the war, or had they been cognizant of the positions of Eastern bankers, rival parties, and politicians, they would have realized that Pendleton was making a series of fictitious claims designed to secure the presidential nomination of 1868 and little else. For Pendleton had been the most vocal opponent of paper currency, and the very economic organizations and parties he attacked had been espousing the positions he had adopted.

Pendleton had tested the viability of a pro-inflationary platform for the Democratic Party, and the Democrats' success in the Ohio election revealed that voters were receptive to this message. While this outcome had implications for the platforms and candidates that the parties nominated in the approaching presidential election, Pendleton's electoral strategy was predicated upon the assumption that voters had little understanding of Civil War finance policy. Voter ignorance of Pendleton's prior positions, and those of the Radical Republicans and Eastern financiers, provided the underlying condition that made Pendleton's electoral strategy viable in the first place.

Despite the inaccuracies Pendleton was popularizing, the financial issue had effects beyond the elections of 1867 and 1868. Specifically, the Midwestern Democrats had assumed control of the currency issue, and the Republicans were increasingly associated with defending the gold standard. Part of this was due to the Radical Republicans' losses and the resulting elimination of the pro-inflationary wing of the Republican Party. However, the parties' platforms in 1868 would create a clear distinction between the parties on the currency issue, and they placed the Republicans on the unpopular side of the issue.

Pendleton had introduced two innovations with important implications for postbellum politics and American institutional development. First, he had demonstrated that the Democrats could use currency issues to attack the Republican Party, and that they could do so by adopting the inflationary policies they had opposed throughout the antebellum period. Second, the reintroduction of monetary policy as a topic of political contention would facilitate the growth of bureaucratic authority in ways that other issues could not.

Of course it is likely that the development of the American industrial economy, and its increasing integration and exposure to market prices, made it inevitable that political conflict would return to focus on the economic issues that had dominated the second party system. There was little reason, however, to think that monetary policy would emerge as the principal economic topic when it did, and more specifically, that the parties would assume the specific positions that they did.

Although the reintroduction of monetary policy as a topic of political contention marked a return to one of the salient issues that dominated the second party system, changes in the American economy, especially in the transportation infrastructure, made it much more plausible that, absent Pendleton's actions, the Democrats would have been principally focused on the tariff as an electoral issue immediately following the Civil War.

Prior to the war the tariff was sustained by a coalition of Midwestern and Eastern political and economic interests. Midwestern wheat and corn producers, and associated agricultural industries, received federal aid for internal improvements to compensate for the losses imposed by protected goods. By the 1860s, however, the development of the railroad infrastructure had decreased the Midwest's reliance upon federal aid for internal improvements, causing a convergence of Southern and Midwestern political interests.[120]

In this new economic context it would have been more plausible for the Democrats to focus on tariff reform than on monetary policy. Tariff reform would not have required a complete reversal of the policies the Democrats had traditionally supported, and it would have been plausible given the context of America's changing transportation infrastructure. Unlike the tariff, monetary policy required the Democrats to reverse their prior opposition to paper currency, a reversal that fractured the party due to opposition from Eastern Democrats aligned with Eastern financiers who endorsed the gold standard.

Monetary policy was hardly the inevitable product underlying economic forces. It had taken Pendleton and his allies to raise the salience of monetary policy rather than other economic issues, such as the tariff, that were equally plausible topics of political contention. For Pendleton to do this *effectively* required voters to be ignorant of the actual history of financial conflict during the Civil War. Had voters been informed of the financial positions Pendleton and various economic and political groups had taken during the war, they would have found his electioneering to be far less persuasive, if not duplicitous. In this sense, voter ignorance influenced the policies that emerged in the postwar electoral context, and allowed politicians to adopt policy programs to advance their personal political interests in ways that prevented voters from receiving the policies they sought.

Chapter 5 The Election of 1868

While the Ohio election of 1867 did not directly involve national political debates, the election influenced both parties' calculations regarding the policies and candidates they would endorse in the presidential election of 1868.[1] The Ohio election had increased the salience of the currency issue and caused a shift in the parties' financial platforms, as the Republicans were increasingly defending the gold standard while the Democrats became more amenable to currency inflation.

These positions marked the beginning of the public's association of the Republican Party with Eastern "money power" and support for the gold standard, associations that would be maintained for decades. Conversely, the Democrats, and social movements and third parties such as the Greenback Party, the Grange, the Farmers' Alliance, and the Populists that emerged in the 1870s and 1880s, would eventually adopt greenback doctrines that had previously been associated with the Whigs and the Radical Republicans.

Aside from structuring postbellum economic debates, these shifting partisan positions would lead to institutional transformations that would alter the nature of the American state. These institutional innovations are discussed in later chapters; this chapter examines how the Ohio election of 1867 influenced national politics, the presidential election of 1868, and the evolving monetary positions of the Democratic Party.

This chapter's discussion of the parties' shifting monetary positions is necessary for explaining the subsequent incarnation of inflationary monetary policy, namely the rise of the free silver issue, and for explaining why certain Republicans endorsed bureaucratic delegation to insulate monetary policy from popular control. Unlike other chapters, this chapter examines the parties' shifting monetary positions during the election of 1868, and does not focus on explaining how voter ignorance influenced politics.

The chapter begins with a brief discussion of the origins of the Republican Party, certain components of its ideology, and its antagonistic relationship with New York's financial groups.[2] This discussion is used to help demonstrate how odd the Democrats' appropriation of the greenback issue was, a discussion that helps illustrate how conflict over monetary influenced the restructuring of party ideologies.

After discussing the Whigs and Democrats during the second party system, I consider the shifting Democratic and Republican parties' monetary positions during the presidential election of 1868. In addition to discussing elite Democrats' views on the financial issue, I foreshadow the Republicans' endorsement of bureaucracy by presenting evidence that Republicans recognized that their support of the gold standard was increasingly unpopular.

The disintegration of the Whigs following Winfield Scott's defeat in 1852 and then the rise of the Republican Party in the election of 1854 led to the solidifying of the Republicans' ideological program in the election of 1856. The Republican Party united disparate political groups, including Free Soilers, Know-Nothings, Nativists, Whigs, and certain Democrats, an amalgamation that led to the Republicans exhibiting little coherence on economic issues aside from slavery.[3]

Recognizing that the disparate groups in their coalition disagreed on the economic issues that had dominated the second party system, the Republicans focused on deploying their "master symbol," their claims that the Southern "slave power" was engaged in a conspiracy to use the federal government to extend slavery into the free states.[4] While Republicans ranging from Lincoln to Seward espoused the slave power conspiracy theory, the original creator of this conspiratorial narrative had been Lincoln's treasury secretary, Salmon Chase.[5]

By attacking the slave power and glorifying free labor, the Republicans reconfigured their understanding of republicanism, ignoring its traditional anticommercialism to valorize the dignity of labor, while also minimizing traditional republican concerns regarding centralized political power.[6] Despite minimizing the Republicans' associations with elitism that had plagued both the Federalists and the Whigs, this new conception of republicanism was subsequently assimilated and further developed by populist forces that became antithetical to the Republican Party.[7]

As the Republicans glorified free labor and distanced themselves from elitist associations, the affinity between the Republican Party and Eastern commercial and banking interests was initially tenuous at best; this was especially true of the Republicans' relationship with New York City's economic elites. This was largely due to the unique ties between New York and Southern cotton interests, an association that initially generated widespread hostility toward the Republican Party.

During the 1850s New York's influx of immigrants and the city's relationship with Southern cotton interests ensured that New York City was dominated by the Democrats, and by the 1860s this was "overwhelmingly so."[8] During the Civil War, however, New York banks had purchased federal bonds, creating a clear rationale for them to support efforts to pay the public debt in gold, thereby linking these banks with the Republican Party. This relationship was not due to financial groups' capture of the Republican Party but was a consequence of the federal government's Civil War funding operations, which many members of the New York Clearing House Association had opposed.

Aside from the shifting relationship between the interests of New York banks and the Republican Party, the Ohio Democrats' adoption of the "Pendleton Plan," and the weakening of the Radical faction of the Republican Party, had reconfigured the parties' positions on financial issues. The 1867 elections had eliminated Radicals such as Butler, Wade, and Chase from contention, weakening the Republican faction most amenable to paper currency while shifting ownership of the financial issue to Midwestern Democrats.[9]

The financial issue had helped resurrect Democratic electoral fortunes, leading unnerved Republicans to complain that financial issues had become salient "as never before."[10] As the presidential election approached, Republicans observed that the currency issue was "the all absorbing one" and noted that even businessmen were complaining of a shortage of money.[11] The economic logic of the Democrats' electoral appeals appeared relatively straightforward. For most voters, economic hardship was manifested in the scarcity of money, and Pendleton's demands that the government print money catered to this understanding. Acutely aware of the issue's growing popularity, Republicans found "the people almost to a man . . . [appeared] opposed to the policy of Secretary McCulloch."[12]

Although certain Democrats worried that their new financial position might cause them to "lose some of their monied men," it was clear they would "undoubtedly gain largely with the mass of the people."[13] Recognizing that "much feeling has been created amongst the people" by the Democrats' inflationary arguments, some Republicans worried that the approaching presidential election was lost, "no matter who may be the Republican Candidate for President."[14] "The people," it seemed, were "a fickle crowd."[15]

Paradoxically, although the Radical Republicans had been the most ardent supporters of the greenbacks and Pendleton had criticized paper currency mere months before the Ohio election of 1867, monetary policy had become the Republicans' "chief liability."[16] Voter ignorance had helped Pendleton portray himself as an ardent greenbacker, even though his calls to pay the public debt in greenbacks were inconsistent with his former positions and the traditional positions of the Democratic Party. Nevertheless, the resulting support for Pendleton's plan to pay the public debt in greenbacks began influencing the political calculations of elites in both parties.

Aside from altering the parties' monetary positions, the Democrats' appropriation of the currency issue influenced the Republican presidential nominees for 1868, leading some Republicans to conclude that there was "but one man that . . . can beat this repudiation platform, and that man is Grant."[17] Grant hoped that his nomination would encourage the Democrats to focus on economic issues, thereby displacing the sectional conflicts that had given rise to the Civil War. Grant realized that if he became the Republican candidate, the Democratic Party might be "forced to adopt a new platform," perhaps leading to a nominee who would "disappoint the Copperhead element of their party."[18] Grant saw this as "a great point gained if nothing more is accomplished" by his candidacy.[19]

Initially it appeared this was exactly how the Democrats would proceed. In the months preceding the Democratic national convention, twelve state conventions endorsed Pendleton and his inflationary agenda.[20] The Midwest seemed to be acting as "a unit" for Pendleton, whose popularity was so striking that "nothing similar to it has been seen since the days of Jackson."[21] These comparisons were, in a sense, appropriate. Like Jackson, Pendleton was mobilizing voters with antielitist attacks on banks. Historians such as Sean Wilentz have described the Jacksonian Democrats as having articulated "radical critiques" of the American economic system, yet this critique had associated paper currency with the opponents of agrarians and labor.[22] This association led antebellum Democrats to conclude that "it was *natural* . . . [to support] the *hard-money,* antibank position."[23] Pendleton, however, had reversed the policies the Democrats endorsed to achieve their ends. Although early in 1868 he was commending the Ohio Democrats' "unwavering fidelity to principle," before the Civil War the Democrats had endorsed specie payments and not paper currency.[24]

Capitalizing on voter ignorance to make his specious claims about sectional demands and the preferences of Republicans and Eastern bankers, Pendleton was now claiming that paper currency and inflation would aid Democratic voters. Although some recognized that these ideas were "inconsistent" with the Democrats' prior positions, few seemed to notice.[25] This posed a conundrum for Republicans, who faced a public failure of memory, the intuitive appeal of Pendleton's new platform, and voters who were unaware of which policies the parties had favored during the Civil War.

Facing the approaching presidential election, Republicans complained that during the war Democrats had declared the greenbacks to be "quite worthless" yet now sought to use them to inflate the currency and pay the public debt.[26] Pendleton had helped create the perception that the Republicans had "no financial policy except high interest, untaxed bonds, and gold for the bond holder with double taxation and depreciated shin plasters for the people."[27] As the presidential election neared, Republicans worried that voters facing economic hardship would "*feel* their sufferings and think any change will bring relief. So we [Republicans] are put at once on the defensive, and are obliged to resist the conviction [among] . . . all the discontented that the dominant party is the cause of their want."[28] Popular discontent over economic conditions was hardly novel, nor was it unusual for voters to retrospectively punish the incumbent party for hard times. What was novel was that popular cries for economic relief were being expressed in demands for currency inflation, not for the resumption of specie payments, and that these demands for relief were now assuming that the Democrats were the natural vehicle for inflationary monetary policy.

Although the Republican Party had faced Democratic opposition when they created the greenbacks, Republicans complained that voters were now "humbugged by that jesuitical cry of 'gold for bondholders and rags for the people,' sufficiently to lose us the Presidential election."[29] The New York Chamber of Commerce stated, "The popular mind has become debauched and demoralized by specious pleading and seductive address, artfully directed to the insatiable love of money in the human heart."[30] Thus, several years after the conclusion of the Civil War alarmed Republicans were complaining: "It is rather an alarming circumstance that half the voters in the free states of Pennsylvania and Ohio, after four years of warfare for the preservation of the nation's unity can be induced under any kind of pressure to vote for the very men who have either been in open rebellion or assured sympathies with those who have!"[31] However, unless the GOP managed to "take away the biggest of the Copperheads thunders," the Democrats' new monetary program made them more appealing, ensuring that in future elections "they [would] be hard to beat."[32] Aware of the unpopularity of the gold standard, some Republicans concluded that any failure to converge on the Pendleton Plan would be "a very suicidal policy," and would risk "endangering the very existence of [the Republican] party,"[33] especially in "rural districts" populated by "thrifty farmers—well-to-do tradesmen and mechanics," as these districts made up "most of our strength."[34]

With "the tide of error & insane clamor for paper money rising higher & higher,"[35] there was "a change in public opinion going on . . . in regard to the payment of the public debt in Treasury notes, and taxing the Government bonds," and "if the vote was taken today on either proposition, the entire copperhead party and at least one half of the Republicans . . . would vote for it."[36] Hard times demanded an explanation, and with "times getting harder every day, everybody is ready to attribute it to the contraction policy of Secretary McCulloch."[37] Given the unpopularity of McCulloch's policies, some concluded: "The whole question [of the finances] is to be dodged" in order to counteract the "uneasiness in the public mind."[38] The end of the Civil War left the Republicans without campaign issues: "What issue have we on which to face the people . . . can [we] win the election without an issue? . . . [Do we] suppose that the common people—plow men and artisans are in favor of the present rate of interest on 5–20 bonds; or will consent to pay them in gold while the greenbacks are worth but 70 cents?"[39] One response to this situation was to attack inflationary Democrats on nationalist, moral, and religious rather than economic grounds. In an effort to redefine the economic debate, the Republicans began denouncing inflation as "repudiation," and they tried to mobilize religious and nationalist animosity against inflation even though they had initially justified the greenbacks on nationalist terms.[40] The 1868 Republican platform denounced "repudiation" and called for repaying the public debt in specie.[41]

Republican opposition to currency inflation marked the beginning of a more general trend in conservative ideology similar to the Democratic reversal Pendleton had initiated. The Republicans who had been Whigs had endorsed an activist orientation toward government economic action, part of which involved support for paper currency.[42] The Democrats, however, had appropriated the Whigs' monetary position, albeit with a different justification for why paper currency was necessary, how it should be used, and which interests it would serve. Once the Democrats changed sides on the issue, Republicans observed that "what the masses of one party favor, the other will assuredly oppose *right or wrong*."[43]

Yet this put the Republicans on the unpopular side of the issue. Although Whig pamphleteers, such as Henry Carey, had defended paper currency against antebellum Democrats, the Republicans now began to reverse the policies they had endorsed. The greenbacks and the rhetoric used to justify them had been strongly endorsed by the Radical Republicans, but in 1868 the Republican Party "repudiated its own radical handiwork" and started identifying paper currency and inflation with rebellion and repudiation.[44]

This reversal was forced upon Republicans as a consequence of Pendleton's attempt to secure the nomination of 1868. By claiming that "the Secretary of the Treasury . . . can tell when [money] flows too fast and strong; and [when] the [currency] expansion should cease," Pendleton was demanding the federal action to aid the Democrats' electoral coalition.[45] While this required the Democratic Party to jettison support for the gold standard, currency inflation fostered administrative development in ways that other issues could not. Although various workingmen's parties preceding Pendleton had endorsed such policies as the limitation of the workday, public education, suffrage expansion, and the elimination of debtor prisons, these policies, much like the tariff, required little administrative expertise.[46]

Forced to denounce inflation, some Republicans called for reversing the economic positions they had inherited from the Whigs. Some Republicans now believed that "our 'paper money' and high tariff policy was utterly wrong," and that "our whole Whig platform of privileged legislation was founded on a mistake."[47] Although the Republicans originally justified the greenbacks as a nationalist measure, they were now portraying paper money as unpatriotic and immoral.[48] Given the Republicans' Protestant constituency, it is little surprise that Republican attacks contained religious overtones. Democrats complained that "whole Protestant . . . religious organizations" were requiring their members to endorse the Republican platform or face expulsion, ensuring that Protestant Republicans now "took the lead" in attacking the Democrats' monetary positions.[49]

Oddly, the Republicans found themselves allied with the very New York bankers who had opposed them before the Civil War, and who had opposed Chase's methods for financing the conflict. The Republicans had no desire to "cut [their] own throats to protect a class of Shylocks who will spend their money and influence to . . . elect the copperhead ticket," but following Pendleton and the Democrats' changing monetary positions, that is exactly what they were doing.[50]

However, Pendleton still faced opposition from Eastern Democrats who wondered how voters could endorse his demands for "thinly veiled repudiation."[51] Yet since he was only committed to his new policy position insofar as it aided his political interests, once he had emerged as the frontrunner for the presidential nomination he and his supporters quietly informed certain Eastern Democrats that they were not committed to their financial policies.

After Pendleton's ally Washington McLean met with Samuel Tilden, the Democrats' New York party chairman, McLean was reported to have "expressed himself very much pleased and satisfied with [the] interview[s]," and after private conversations, Horatio Seymour, governor of New York and hard-money partisan, admonished Pendleton's antagonists, claiming that "the fact that [Pendleton] thought a class of Bonds were payable in 'greenbacks' does not commit him for inflation nor does it make him an opponent of specie payment."[52]

Eastern Democrats balked at the opportunity Pendleton had created for them, however. The Eastern and Western factions of the Democratic Party disagreed on monetary issues, and despite the popularity of greenback inflation in the Midwest, Eastern Democrats like Tilden sought to focus on racial animosity and the restoration of the Southern states to the Union.[53] Tilden argued that one advantage to avoiding economic issues was that if prosperity returned, the issues "may disappear while we are discussing them" or could "be . . . adopted by the other side"—problems that did not exist with racial animosity and Southern restoration.[54]

While Francis Blair, the Democrats' eventual vice-presidential nominee, also expressed opposition to "idle . . . talk of bonds, greenbacks, gold, the public faith and the public credit"[55] from the outset of the Democratic convention, it was clear that Pendleton had considerable support, especially in the Midwest. Pendleton received 105 votes on the first ballot, and on the eighth ballot he came within two votes of a majority of 158. But New York had sixty-six votes, and his supporters recognized that if Pendleton were defeated these votes would go to Governor Seymour despite the "formidable and constantly increasing outside pressure for Pendleton."[56]

While Seymour eventually seized the nomination, the *New York Times* reported that Pendleton and his supporters had managed to control "the platform, if they do not have the candidate."[57] Although both the presidential and the vice-presidential nominees were hard-money men, the Democratic platform "went after the bondholders hammer and tongs with out-and-out greenback planks."[58] This created a degree of confusion, however, and since the Democratic nominees endorsed resumption while their platform endorsed inflation, the platform appeared to be "a strange piece of joinery."[59]

Recognizing the popular appeal of greenbacks, Seymour made ambiguous statements on the financial question.[60] Although the Republicans hoped to neutralize the Democrats' appeal on economic issues by mobilizing Protestant religious animus against paper currency, they still faced the problem of race. To counteract the Democrats' racist appeals, Republicans claimed that Blair's vice-presidential acceptance letter had endorsed the Democrats' launching a second civil war.[61] Although Blair had served in the Union Army, Republicans charged that he "was on the rampage" and sought to "inaugurate a little rebellion of his own."[62]

On economic questions, the Republicans denounced Pendleton's "ridiculous and wasteful policy" and claimed that it would lead to economic catastrophe.[63] As the campaign progressed, the Republicans used several campaign messages that they tailored according to sectional requirements, denouncing Eastern Democrats for endorsing "repudiation" while at the same time claiming that August Belmont's position as head of the National Committee indicated that the Democrats were agents of the Rothschilds.[64]

Grant wound up carrying the election of 1868 by a thin margin. At the conclusion of the campaign, several things were apparent to both parties. Economic issues appeared to have been overpowered by the Republicans' invocation of the war, and through such devices as their campaign against Blair. Republicans worried that in future campaigns,

the financial questions are to be the most important. The close contest in the great central states, with the odds in favor of your party as the result of the mistakes of the Democracy will doubtless indicate the necessity of great wisdom on the part of the incoming administration in meeting these questions. I look for wide spread disaster as the result of an attempt to return to *specie* payments. In the west, we have too *little currency*. So in the South. The contest upon the finances will be kept up. Money is growing scarcer and the rate of interest increasing. Our eastern friends are draining us of our wealth, and property is fast going from one class to another. I look for great public discontent and dissatisfaction on the part of the people unless a more equal and liberty policy is to be pursued.[65]

Recognizing the difficulties facing the Republican Party, John Sherman bluntly told Henry Cooke, brother of financier Jay Cooke: "I like your object, specie payments, but the real difficulty is that the great body of the people don't want specie payments."[66] Cognizant that the Republicans' monetary positions were increasingly unpopular, Sherman urged the need "to get the truth into the popular mind before the next campaign begins."[67] However, "so much ignorance prevails among the people generally on these most interesting subjects" that it was difficult "to enlighten the masses of the people on a subject which so intimately concerns their best interests."[68] While Sherman was convinced that resumption "will endanger the popularity of any man or administration that is compelled to adopt it," he maintained that "specie payments must be resumed."[69]

The Republicans had become identified as the agents of Eastern bondholders and bankers, even though these groups had endorsed the creation of the greenbacks and had opposed their contraction. Republicans complained of the public's "contented ignorance and indifference," and the "slush of false opinion in financial subjects" across the country.[70] In those areas of the country "where people yearn for information,"[71] as one Republican put it, another Republican noted: "It is to be deplored that so much ignorance prevails among the people generally on [financial] subjects."[72] But some Republicans thought popular economic education was hopeless; the Democrats had energized a "strong effort to further inflate . . . the amount of currency," ensuring that public opinion was arrayed against efforts to resume the gold standard.[73]

Immediately after the Civil War, Secretary McCulloch assumed that both parties would support resumption. Now, however, he complained of the "decided and overwhelming public sentiment in favor of [the greenbacks] being continued in circulation as a part of the financial policy of the Government."[74] Recognizing that the public was increasingly receptive to inflation, the Republicans quickly sought to remove financial issues from popular debate after Grant's victory.

The Republicans were galvanized into action when Andrew Johnson issued a statement on the financial issue in his final days in office. In a closing message, Johnson repudiated his prior support for McCulloch's policies and endorsed paying the national debt in greenbacks.[75] By supporting the Pendleton Plan, Johnson ensured a swift Republican reaction. On December 14, 1868, the Republicans homogeneously opposed a measure simply reiterating Johnson's message. In this vote, all 133 opposing votes were cast by Republicans, three Eastern Democrats voted with the Republicans, and all but one of the thirty-six votes supporting the president were Democratic. Similar action was taken three days later in the Senate, which by a margin of 43–6 condemned the financial doctrines espoused by the president.[76]

Besides their opposition to Johnson, immediately after the election the Republicans introduced legislation designed to remove the financial issue from popular discussion or influence. Chairman Robert Schenck of the House Ways and Means Committee introduced the Public Credit Act of 1869, which required payment of the public debt in specie unless otherwise stated by law. The measure passed largely on party lines, and by ensuring that the public debt would be paid in specie Republicans hoped the greenback issue would be eliminated as a topic of political contention.

Although the Public Credit Act appeared to neutralize the greenback issue, Republicans were facing a new and unsettling situation. Both parties were aware of currency inflation's popularity, and Sherman privately lamented that the Republicans had "no policy" on the financial issue.[77] Republicans who had clear political reasons to denounce inflation's popularity and the "ignorance" of those endorsing it, and Eastern Democrats who maintained support for the gold standard, such as Samuel Tilden, complained that the public possessed "little knowledge in these respects."[78]

However, the complexity of financial issues was confusing other political elites as well as the public; Sherman admitted that the "intrinsic difficulties of the subjects referred to us" were responsible for "the great diversity of opinion that exists in all parts of the country as to the proper measures adopted."[79] The diversity of opinion was aggravated by a diversity of interests. Sherman acknowledged: "In the agricultural districts . . . money is so scarce that any contraction of the currency would operate most injuriously upon the agricultural and mechanical interests."[80] One congressman asked: "Has any person seen a farmer or mechanic who complains of a redundancy of money? The complaints that have reached my ear are precisely the reverse."[81]

Hardly the result of interest-group pressure, the Republican adoption of hard-money economic policies had been the result of the defeat of the Radical Republicans and the corresponding adoption of the currency position by a faction of Midwestern Democrats. Although the Republicans had justified the greenbacks on nationalist grounds during the Civil War, inflation and paper currency whose value was not backed by gold were now denounced as "repudiation" and indicative of loose business morals.

Despite the Democrats' continued opposition to economic privilege and corporate monopolies, their claims that the Republicans were the tools of moneyed interests were fictional, but these fictions seemed persuasive given the parties' evolving positions on the currency question. Recognizing that the Republicans had themselves reversed their positions on the currency issue, one Democratic senator complained: "Those who forced . . . depreciated paper . . . upon the country are now its deadliest foes."[82] Yet this reversal was mirrored by the increasing willingness of Democrats to adopt currency inflation, a policy that they had opposed during the second party system.

This shift in one aspect of the Democratic Party's ideology was not the result of economic groups seeking to extend their ideological hegemony over Americans, nor was it a simple reaction to the economic interests of the Democratic Party's electoral coalition. Rather, this shift was inaugurated by Pendleton's efforts to accomplish mundane personal objectives, which had led to the demonstration that monetary policy could be an effective tool for winning elections. Hardly the result of any larger ideological objective or program, this shift was produced by a political logic that was a degree removed from economic groups' interests and demands.

In addition to influencing the elections of 1867 and 1868, Pendleton's endorsement of inflationary monetary policy inadvertently began eroding the Democrats' opposition to federal authority. While Pendleton's electioneering started to reverse the traditional hostility of Democrats toward paper currency, in their reversal they assumed that the federal government would become more involved in the national economy. This was never overtly stated in the elections of 1867 or 1868; it was simply an assumption necessitated by the Democrats' policy demands.

This reversal could have left things as they were before the Civil War, with the Whigs developing into the Republican Party and then adopting the Democrats' antebellum suspicion of federal authority. However, the Democrats' commitment to restricting federal authority had been driven by their fear that federal power could undermine slavery. Similarly, the Republicans' opposition to slavery had been limited by the "federal consensus," the constitutional understanding that relegated slavery to the states, not to the federal government.[83] Postbellum Republicans had no similar anchor for their positions; and the intellectual doctrines, such as Social Darwinism and classical political economy, that could have served a similar ideological function were poorly suited to mass consumption.

Although the Whigs had absorbed the Federalists' association with economic and cultural elitism, the Republicans initially avoided this association through their egalitarian attacks on the Southern "slave power" aristocracy. The Republicans had shifted attention from fears of corruption and concentrated political power to the threats posed by concentrated economic power. Pendleton had refocused these fears away from the Southern slave power to the economic elites of the emerging industrial order, and because the Civil War had deposed the slave power, the Republicans had no clear way to counter these appeals.

A final barrier remained between the Democrats' new view of the appropriate relationship between the economy and the state: opposition to *bureaucracy* as a vehicle for policy activism. The Democrats, though, were not responsible for the initial expansions of bureaucratic authority. Rather, certain Republicans would conclude that the Democrats' populist appeals required empowering executive bureaucrats with new forms of authority, authority that became a template for subsequent economic interventions. The initial impetus for the Republicans' turn toward bureaucracy, however, was their attempt to use unelected officials to resist populist economic appeals that were being adopted by the Democratic Party.

Although the initial expansion of the American state's bureaucratic regulatory institutions was conditioned by public opinion, the bureaucratic institutions that the Republicans empowered were not created to respond to popular demands; they were created to resist the policies that the American public was endorsing. In this sense the institutional innovations that marked the origins of the new American state were conditioned by public opinion but were not expressions of the public will.

Although initially focused on demands to pay the public debt in greenbacks, conflicts over monetary policy intensified with demands for the free coinage of silver that emerged in the mid-1870s and culminated in the nomination of William Jennings Bryan in 1896, an election that marked the final turning point in the Democrats' endorsement of federal economic intervention. This transition was influenced by the Democrats' adoption of policy demands made by the Populist Party and its conspiracy theory regarding the actors responsible for the "demonetization" of the silver dollar. Explaining the conflicts over free silver, and the political decisions responsible for introducing this issue into American political debate, is the aim of the next chapter.

Chapter 6 The Crime of 1873

The elections of 1867 and 1868 had reintroduced monetary issues into political debate and associated the Democratic Party with currency inflation. However, financial issues would eventually dominate national politics with the free silver issue, which was deeply associated with the Populist Party and William Jennings Bryan's candidacy in the election of 1896. Although various bimetallic groups and the Populists endorsed the free coinage of silver before Bryan's candidacy, the Democrats' adoption of free silver in 1896 solidified their new willingness to use federal power to intervene in American economic life.

The silver issue captivated the popular imagination for reasons largely unrelated to its economic rationale. Part of free silver's popularity was attributable to the conspiracy theory, and allegations of political corruption, surrounding silver's demonetization.[1] Specifically, the Populists and various bimetallic groups preceding them claimed that European bankers bribed public officials to eliminate bimetallism to protect the value of their gold-bearing bonds.

The Populists claimed that the Coinage Act of 1873, the legislation which demonetized silver and which they denounced as the "Crime of '73," was merely one instance where shadowy and corrupt economic elites had influenced American politics, and they were convinced that similar conspiracies had influenced other important chapters of American history.[2] These claims were adopted by Bryan, who, despite losing the election of 1896, captivated the popular imagination with one of the most memorable convention speeches in American history.[3]

Bryan actually added little that was original to demands for the free coinage of silver or to the conspiratorial claims regarding the Coinage Act of 1873. Rather, he adopted most of his ideas from the Populists, who had been influenced by minor third parties, such as the American Bimetallic League and the American Bimetallic Party.[4] Recognizing his debt to these organizations, Bryan's retrospective of the 1896 election, *The First Battle,* noted the importance of silver advocates such as A. J. Warner (D-OH), John P. Jones (R-NV), and William Stewart (R-NV). Bryan claimed that Jones's speeches were the most "complete and comprehensive" defense of free silver ever offered, and he also commended Stewart:

> [He has attended] every National conference where the subject was under consideration, and has devoted all his energies to the restoration of the bimetallic standard. I had frequent occasion to visit the United States Senate during the prolonged struggle which ended in the unconditional repeal of the Sherman [silver purchase] law, and I shall never forget the earnestness with which he pleaded against the passage of that act. Not only has he availed himself of every opportunity offered by his official position, but he has been constant in his work outside of the Senate, having for more than a year past been connected with the Silver Knight and National Watchman, a paper published at Washington and devoted to the restoration of the money of the Constitution.[5]

In his role as executive director of both the American Bimetallic League and the American Bimetallic Party, Stewart helped print and distribute *Coin's Financial School,* a book that was so widely read that Bryan claimed that nothing else had "produced so great an effect" in exposing the public to the critical monetary issues of the day.[6] Indeed, Bryan claimed the American Bimetallic League's pamphlets were the "first thing" he had read regarding the silver issue.[7]

While the silver issue was central to the election of 1896 and influenced the ideology of the Democratic Party, the politics of silver is also relevant for general issues involving popular comprehension of democratic politics. Specifically, scholars have argued the Populists' conspiratorial view of the silver issue exhibited paranoid tendencies with little relationship to actual political events.[8] Perhaps the best-known proponent of this view is Richard Hofstadter, whose famous essay "The Paranoid Style in American Politics" criticized the Populists' paranoid view of American history.[9] Indeed, assessing the accuracy of the claims surrounding the silver issue, and the role of conspiratorial myths in the American political imagination, has been a central topic in the historiography of American populism.

A second set of studies, however, argues that there was a conspiracy to demonetize silver, yet still maintains that the Populists' portrayal of events was wildly inaccurate. Instead of attributing the Coinage Act to scheming creditors, Paul O'Leary, Allen Weinstein, and Walter Nugent argue that congressmen and Treasury Department bureaucrats demonetized silver because they realized that collapsing silver prices would threaten the gold standard by making silver attractive to monetary inflationists.[10] Despite recognizing a secretive effort to demonetize silver, these studies argue that this conspiracy—if we can call it that—was led by public officials such as Senator John Sherman (R-OH), Treasury Secretary George Boutwell, and Director of the Mint Henry Linderman, and did not involve Eastern or European bankers.[11]

Despite offering different accounts of the calculations surrounding monetary politics during this period, nearly all studies share Hofstadter's conclusion that the Populists erred when they claimed that bankers bribed public officials.[12] In the absence of evidence of banker influence over silver's demonetization, the Populists are often seen as part of an embarrassing chapter of American history best forgotten if they did not foreshadow McCarthyism and other episodes of political hysteria.[13] With little evidence of bankers' involvement in silver's demonetization, studies of this period bluntly conclude: "There was no 'Crime of '73.'"[14]

Three issues are at stake in our understanding of the silver issue. First, since the silver issue completed the Democrats' turn toward federal monetary activism, it is important for our understanding of the ideological development of the Democratic Party. As free silver was the most important issue in the election of 1896, an election that was a turning point in the Democrats' transition to contemporary liberalism, it is critical to understand the forces responsible for silver's demonetization. The elimination of the silver dollar as a legal tender currency provided the underlying condition necessary for free silver to become a political issue in the first place. As the Democrats' monetary activism caused a reaction among Republicans who sought to empower bureaucratic authority to combat inflationary demands by removing monetary policy from popular control, the silver issue influenced both popular electoral politics and the trajectory of American state formation.

Second, aside from influencing these aspects of American political history, the silver issue has more general ramifications for our understanding of public opinion and rationality, and by extension for our evaluation of the Populists' paranoid tendencies. If the public adopted an inaccurate conspiracy theory regarding one of the most salient issues of the nineteenth century, a conspiracy theory that was persuasive because it tapped into paranoid tendencies exhibited by mass political movements, this chapter of American history may have more general implications for our evaluation of popular understanding of democratic politics.

Third, since our conclusions regarding the rationality of public opinion are based upon academic studies' accounts of what actually happened with silver policy, the free silver issue also has implications for our conception of elite understanding of democratic politics. As the studies that followed Hofstadter's famous essay provide an alternative, nonconspiratorial explanation for the Coinage Act, the silver issue offers an opportunity to evaluate the accuracy of elite conceptions of politics, and by extension may help illustrate some of the general difficulties associated with efforts to accurately reconstruct past political events.

Unfortunately, the misunderstanding surrounding the silver issue is far greater than has been recognized. Although Pulitzer Prize–winning books such as Hofstadter's *Age of Reform* and Irwin Unger's *Greenback Era* argue that there is no evidence supporting the Populists' claims, there really was a Crime of '73—a scheme involving a banker who bribed the official who wrote the Coinage Act of 1873. This chapter presents evidence that William Ralston, president of The Bank of California, paid thousands of dollars to Director of the Mint Henry Linderman to influence the Coinage Act of 1873. Ralston's involvement in the Coinage Act's passage, and his payments to Linderman, demonstrate that the measure the Populists decried as the Crime of '73 was actually influenced by a banker's bribery, indicating that the Populists' central suspicions were more accurate than has been recognized.

Although the Populists blamed the wrong bankers and officials for the Crime of '73, Ralston's involvement in the Coinage Act vindicates the Populists' central suspicions. Accordingly, it raises important questions concerning our understanding of this period in American politics and—perhaps more crucially—challenges accepted notions of democratic accountability. Furthermore, Ralston's involvement in the Coinage Act demonstrates that important studies by Hofstadter, Unger, and Milton Friedman and Anna Schwartz were unaware of basic facts involving the interests and methods used to pass legislation that created one of the most salient political conflicts of the late nineteenth century. The errors in these studies—particularly the claim that the Populists were obsessed with imaginary grievances—indicate that scholars' attempts to reconstruct the history of democratic politics may generate interpretations that mislead and obstruct more than they clarify and reveal.

Finally, understanding the actual forces involved in the passage of the Coinage Act of 1873 may influence our understanding of why the conspiratorial account of silver's demonetization was popularized. For some of the legislators that helped Ralston pass the Coinage Act would deny their involvement in its passage, or would blame Eastern and European bankers for a bill *they* had supported. One of Ralston's allies, Nevada Republican William Stewart, became a prominent leader of the free silver movement and attacked the legislation he had helped Ralston pass, an act of duplicity that was hidden by widespread public ignorance of what had occurred.

To clarify these misunderstandings and to reveal the impact that silver policy had upon American politics requires explanation of two events: the demonetization of the silver dollar in the Coinage Act of 1873, and the claims made by the free silver movement in the 1870s and 1880s that were subsequently adopted by the Populists and William Jennings Bryan. It is difficult, however, to make sense of these events without recognizing how public ignorance enhanced certain state elites' autonomy and facilitated manipulation of public opinion. Although the silver issue attracted widespread media scrutiny and popular attention, the individuals responsible for eliminating bimetallism managed to elude popular detection and deflected popular attention from their role in the Coinage Act's passage.

Although the Populists and many other nineteenth century Americans correctly suspected that banking interests influenced the Coinage Act, they blamed the wrong bankers for the act's passage. Furthermore, the errors in subsequent studies that were unaware of Ralston's role in the Coinage Act have bleak implications for our ability to reconstruct and understand critical political events. While public confusion over the complexities of monetary policy is understandable, political elites' confusion is indicative of the general problems social complexity poses for democratic politics.

To illustrate how the silver issue exemplifies general epistemological challenges facing democratic politics requires analyzing the passage of the Coinage Act of 1873, the legislation that the Populists denounced as the Crime of '73.

For it is only by revealing how bribery influenced the Coinage Act that we can assess the accuracy of the Populists' claims and attempt to offer a more accurate explanation of certain critical historical events. Furthermore, documenting Ralston's involvement in the Coinage Act will help us to understand how political calculations and misinformation not only influenced the Democrats' ideological development but also marred subsequent studies of the Populists and this period of American history more generally.

Up until the early 1870s finance policy had focused on issues involving the greenbacks and the public debt. Although the silver issue would captivate the public's imagination and dominate the election of 1896, in the early 1870s silver played little role in finance policy because the amount of silver contained in the silver dollar was worth roughly $1.04 in gold, making it more profitable to melt silver dollars into bullion than to use them as currency. Consequently, silver was rarely used for domestic transactions and was largely irrelevant for monetary policy.[15]

Although the Public Credit Act of 1869 eliminated the threat of greenback inflation by stipulating the public debt be paid in specie, it did not specify which kind of specie the public debt had to be paid in. If the silver dollar became worth less than a dollar in gold the public debt could be repaid in depreciated silver dollars, and it would also become profitable to exchange silver dollars for gold at the Treasury. This would cause silver to drive other currency from circulation, and it would become impossible to accumulate the gold reserve necessary for specie resumption, as any gold held by the Treasury would be exchanged for silver coinage. Furthermore, if America retained bimetallism, collapsing silver prices could make it difficult to sell the loans needed to accumulate a gold reserve because financiers would worry that government bonds would be redeemed in depreciated silver dollars, not in gold.

So long as the silver bullion in the silver dollar remained worth more than a dollar in gold these concerns were irrelevant for finance policy. However, in the early 1870s massive silver discoveries in California and Nevada coincided with several European countries' decisions to demonetize their silver currency, indicating that an unprecedented volume of silver bullion would soon enter silver markets.

These developments were first noted in 1867 when Henry Linderman,[16] who at the time was director of the Philadelphia Mint, recognized that technological advances in mining indicated that American silver production "will be carried on . . . to an extent hitherto unknown."[17] Linderman would play a critical role in subsequent political decisions involving silver, and his expertise in coinage, and extensive contacts with bankers, granted him unique influence over monetary legislation. Although Linderman was no longer director of the Philadelphia Mint when he wrote the Coinage Act of 1873 but was instead employed in a series of temporary assignments for the Treasury Department, he played a critical role in writing the Coinage Act and was more important than any other actor in silver policy in the 1870s.

Aside from Linderman, several other officials were aware of silver's impending depreciation. Both Senator John Sherman and New Yorker Samuel Ruggles had been alerted to Europe's impending demonetization of silver while attending the Paris monetary convention of 1867, where several European officials discussed demonetizing silver and adopting an international monetary standard. Ruggles reported to Sherman that the convention's "object, among others, [was] to agree, if possible, on a common unit of money for the use of the civilized world," and that the conference participants had agreed to "adopting as . . . [a monetary] unit the . . . French five franc piece of gold."[18] As the demonetization of European silver currency would force large amounts of silver bullion onto currency markets, Sherman recognized that European demonetization would influence the price ratio between silver and gold, and hence would influence American finance policy.[19]

In addition to these public officials, certain private actors were closely monitoring developments in silver markets. Perhaps the most important of them was William C. Ralston, president of The Bank of California, who was monitoring silver prices and assessing how political decisions could influence the vast business empire he had built from his control of the Comstock silver mines.[20] Known for his lavish parties and affable manners, Ralston controlled a vast network of business enterprises that were dependent upon The Bank of California, which was in turn dependent upon ore from the Comstock mines.

Ralston's Comstock investments included the Ophir Gold and Silver Mining Company, the Gould and Curry, and Savage mines, and the Union Mill and Mining Company, which processed most of the Comstock ore.[21] Ralston's control over the Union Mill and Mining Company allowed him to control the processing of ore critical for any Comstock mine. By refusing to process ore from certain mines and by manipulating the prices he charged others, Ralston exercised control over the Comstock mines and acquired many other mines at bargain prices.[22]

Ralston's influence over the Comstock mines allowed him to invest in business ventures throughout California. Ralston was involved in the Pacific and

Mission Woolen Mills of San Francisco, the Pacific Sugar Refinery, the Buena Vista Vinicultural Society, the Virginia and Truckee Railroad, stagecoach companies, and the Spring Valley Water Company, which provided San Francisco with water.[23] Ralston also spent huge sums on various cultural projects in his attempt to develop San Francisco's international renown, financing the San Francisco Opera House and constructing the extravagant Palace Hotel.

However, Ralston's empire depended upon the success of The Bank of California, which was in turn dependent upon the value of the Comstock silver mines. The stability of Ralston's bank, and his financial empire more generally, was constantly an issue because Ralston's extensive business investments left him perpetually overextended. Lacking the self-control of a Rockefeller or a Morgan, Ralston invested in various unprofitable enterprises; spent extravagantly in the opulent Palace Hotel; was swindled out of huge sums in a diamond hoax; and used various bookkeeping gimmicks to mask his risky investments.

Given The Bank of California's precarious position throughout the early 1870s, Ralston's concerns regarding the stock value of the Comstock mines were hardly misplaced. Anything threatening the value of Comstock mining stock could trigger a run on The Bank of California. In this context, a flood of European silver into America could have had dramatic effects on the value of the Comstock mines, and hence on Ralston's precarious business empire. As Linderman warned Ralston in 1872, if European countries demonetized their silver currency "the countries maintaining the double standard [would] be overrun with silver bullion," a development which would make "a serious decline in price unavoidable."[24]

These concerns were heightened when Germany's demonetization of silver set off a chain reaction among countries anxious to avoid exchanging their gold for other countries' demonetized silver currency.[25] Lacking any international agreement protecting bimetallism, American silver producers would face serious losses if America became a dumping ground for Europe's demonetized silver.[26] Because The Bank of California and the Comstock were "almost totally interdependent" during this period, if America remained on a bimetallic standard after Europe demonetized silver, Ralston would face serious declines in the value of his Comstock holdings.[27]

If The Bank of California had been operated by a conservative financier, this would have been less of a threat. But Ralston was unorthodox to a fault, and by the early 1870s he was so overextended that there was serious doubt over his ability to prevent a run on his bank. As any deterioration in silver prices would influence his banking and mining interests, he was closely monitoring international bullion trends and was formulating policies to protect his financial interests. Conferring with Linderman and Deputy Comptroller of the Currency John Jay Knox, Ralston began working "hard and astutely" to avoid the dangers facing The Bank of California.[28]

To protect Ralston's business empire it was essential to demonetize America's silver currency, as this would prevent European silver bullion from flooding American silver markets and depressing the value of domestic silver mines. Demonetizing silver, however, would limit the domestic market for bullion produced by the Comstock mines. To create a new market for Comstock silver Ralston sought to create a commercial coin, the trade dollar, intended for export to Asian currency markets, which he hoped would replace the Mexican silver dollar favored by the Chinese.[29] Given California's proximity to China and the cheaper cost of shipping trade dollars to China from the West Coast, Ralston would enjoy a monopoly over the production of trade dollars, creating a profitable outlet for his bullion despite the domestic demonetization of silver.

Finally, Ralston sought to eliminate the coinage charge the Treasury Department placed upon bullion that was converted into coin. The Bank of California functioned as an intermediary for refining bullion produced by Western mines that was brought to the U.S. Mint in San Francisco and converted into coin. Ralston hoped that reducing the refining fee would increase the profitability of his Comstock mines, which produced large amounts of both gold and silver, while also having the government pay for the conversion of his silver bullion into trade dollars.

Given his extensive contacts with the Treasury Department bureaucrats and congressmen who would control the revision of the coinage statutes, Ralston was well positioned to influence legislation to protect his interests. Perhaps most critical was his relationship with Linderman, then director of the Philadelphia Mint and subsequently director of the mint in the Treasury Department.[30] Ralston was introduced to Linderman in 1869 in San Francisco, and it was apparent that "the two men liked each other at once."[31] Linderman was responsible for revising the coinage statutes and would be Ralston's key conduit for influencing coinage legislation.

Working with Linderman, Ralston soon began to secure Treasury policies advantageous to the Bank of California. However, Ralston's relationship with Linderman would prove to be mutually profitable. Ralston paid Linderman thousands of dollars in exchange for influencing coinage legislation in ways that aided The Bank of California. Although the Populists have been criticized for their conspiratorial claims that bribery was associated with the revision of the coinage statutes, Ralston's relationship with Linderman appears to vindicate their suspicions.

In addition to his dealings with Linderman, Ralston cultivated contacts with a loose coalition of public officials. Ralston corresponded with John Jay Knox, deputy comptroller of the currency in the Treasury Department, who would write the first draft of the Coinage Act of 1873 with Linderman's assistance. In 1869 Knox had assured Ralston that his position in the Treasury Department meant he could "very likely be of service here."[32] Besides Linderman and Knox, Ralston maintained contacts with certain Western congressmen from California and Nevada, such as Aaron Sargent, Eugene Casserly, and William Stewart. These representatives were attentive to Ralston's interests due to The Bank of California's importance for their state's economy, and because of their shared benefits from Ralston's largesse. However, a loose coalition of shared interests linked these representatives' actions, and the amount of coordination between them is unclear.

The first revision of the coinage statutes was initiated in response to the Public Credit Act of 1869. Since the Public Credit Act stipulated that government bonds had to be redeemed in specie, Treasury Secretary Boutwell recognized that developments in silver markets had implications for the public credit. Boutwell dispatched Linderman to examine Western mints and report on conditions relevant for revisions of the coinage statutes.

Finding Linderman's suggestions "intelligent" and conducted in a "business-like manner," Boutwell thanked him for furnishing his "views upon other kindred topics which [were] valuable to the Department."[33] As the Treasury Department began to revise the coinage statutes, Boutwell told Linderman: "Confer with me in reference to your report, and other subjects referred to in your letter."[34] Using information from Linderman's report, Linderman and Knox began consolidating the coinage statutes and making revisions to eliminate the bimetallic standard.

Although most Americans were unaware of how developments in silver markets would influence finance policy, certain elites realized that silver prices were about to collapse, and they were working to limit silver's potential as an inflationary alternative to the greenbacks.[35] While Boutwell and Sherman sought to demonetize silver for political reasons, Ralston began using his contacts in the Treasury Department to manipulate the revisions in ways he hoped would be advantageous to The Bank of California.

The initial revision occurred after Boutwell asked Knox to confer with monetary experts to standardize the coinage statutes.[36] Given Knox's connections with Ralston, it was hardly surprising that Linderman, Ralston, and Louis Garnett, manager of Ralston's San Francisco Assaying and Refining Works, "were among those consulted" by Knox.[37] As the initial draft of the Coinage Act was being formulated, Ralston was helping Treasury Department bureaucrats revise the coinage statutes in ways that were helpful to The Bank of California.[38]

Knox made a number of suggestions that appeared to merely rationalize the existing coinage statutes but incorporated recommendations made by Linderman, Garnett, and Ralston. In the opening gambit to initiate Ralston's plan, Linderman complained of the effects of the coinage charge: "On comparison, and especially at San Francisco, . . . the expense of coinage are much greater than abroad, and hence our metallic product commands a higher price in foreign countries than can be realized by its coinage at home."[39] Linderman claimed that the coinage charge encouraged the exportation of American bullion and recommended the charge "should be abrogated altogether," calling for a "return to our uniform practice prior to 1853, which was to coin [bullion] without charge, not only as an expedient for encouraging coinage, but as being more consistent with the theory of money as a universal standard of value."[40]

Knox's revised statutes initially retained silver as a legal tender, reduced the weight of the silver dollar from 412.5 to 384 grains, and limited its legal tender status to five dollars except for payment of duties on imports.[41] Knox noted that, prior to the revision, the currency statutes authorized bimetallism.[42] However, after he had consulted with Linderman, Knox's bill eliminated the silver dollar completely, ensuring "the present gold dollar piece . . . [was] made the dollar unit . . . and the silver dollar piece [was] discontinued," thus demonetizing silver.[43]

In addition to removing the coinage charge and demonetizing silver, Ralston had Louis Garnett, manager of his San Francisco Assaying and Refining Works, recommend the creation of the 420-grain trade dollar Ralston hoped would replace the Mexican silver dollar widely used in China.[44] Using Garnett's suggestions, Knox's initial draft of the Coinage Act recommended the creation of a silver coin for export. But Knox was careful to say, "If however such a coin is authorized it should be issued only as a *commercial dollar,* not as a standard unit of account and of the exact value of the *Mexican dollar which is the favorite for circulation* in China and Japan."[45]

Although demonetizing silver would prevent European bullion from flooding American markets, the trade dollar would create an export market for Ralston's Comstock silver, and eliminating the coinage charge would maximize the profitability of producing the trade dollar. The Coinage Act appeared to merely rationalize existing coinage statutes, but Linderman was in close consultation with Ralston regarding the measure's stipulations and was relaying Ralston's suggestions to Knox as he drafted the measure. When the Coinage Act was introduced to Congress, Ralston's influence would extend beyond Linderman and Knox to a coalition of Western congressmen from California and Nevada who would protect the measure from harmful amendments.

When a draft of the Coinage Act was introduced to Congress, however, it met strident opposition. Prominent senators, such as John Sherman, and certain Eastern representatives opposed reducing the coinage charge. Linderman complained to Ralston that both William Kelley (R-PA), chairman of the Coinage Committee, and Sherman (R-OH) were "disposed to delay," which forced him to have "a plain talk" with Kelley in which Linderman "showed him the impossibility of sustaining the present rate of expenditures at [Philadelphia] and the advantages to be [had] by the passage of the Bill."[46]

As the Coinage Act faced "some apathy in the House and a quiet opposition from [Philadelphia]," Linderman asked Ralston to use his influence with Western congressmen to stimulate support for the measure. Linderman urged Ralston: "Write to all your members in the House particularly Sargent and Axtell asking them to give special attention to the Mint Bill in the House" so as to "work up some enthusiasm and interest in the House in order to insure early action by the committee on coinage."[47]

Ralston also enlisted the support of Nevada senator William M. Stewart and California senator Eugene Casserly. Ralston had been associated with Stewart ever since The Bank of California became involved in the Comstock holdings. Before becoming a Nevada senator, Stewart was known as one of the "most eminent and affluent of the Comstock lawyers," and had been involved with Ralston since the 1860s.[48]

This relationship occasionally verged on questionable financial transactions. For example, upon his election to the Senate in 1869, Stewart sold his Virginia City mansion to Charles DeLong, his law partner and a "one time California miner who knew Billy [Ralston]."[49] Once in the Senate, Stewart immediately had DeLong appointed to be America's minister to Japan; DeLong promptly vacated the Stewart residence, selling the house to Ralston's brother, Andrew, who "paid DeLong $10,000 for the once Stewart property."[50] Although this specific transaction would not meet a formal definition of bribery, it does indicate that Ralston was involved in questionable financial dealings with certain political figures.

Ralston and The Bank of California also helped finance Stewart's election campaigns, and Stewart in turn helped Ralston with legislation that influenced his financial operations and recommended senators he believed deserved Ralston's support.[51] Other Western representatives, such as Senator Casserly, also worked with Stewart to secure Treasury appointees favorably disposed to Ralston's banking operations.[52]

Western congressmen had several reasons for assisting Ralston. Many believed the Coinage Act would benefit Western states. As Stewart recognized, eliminating the Treasury's charge would make San Francisco "a city of exchange" for bullion normally shipped East for conversion into coin.[53] Because the measure would aid Western bullion interests at the expense of their sectional competitors, Stewart closely monitored the Coinage Act to prevent any effort to reinstate the coinage charge. In one instance when Sherman attempted to reinstate the coinage charge Senator Henry Wilson (R-MA) was "dragged up . . . at the last moment by Stewart" to defeat Sherman's amendment by a single vote.[54]

In addition to protecting the Coinage Act from amendments harmful to Ralston's interests, Stewart was keeping Ralston informed of Linderman's influence over legislative proceedings. As the Coinage Act moved through Congress, Stewart assured Ralston: "Linderman is at work on your matters in good earnest and I feel confident of results this session."[55] Given Stewart's involvement with Ralston, it was not surprising that Ralston was assured that "Stewart and others of the 'faithful'" were working to protect Ralston and The Bank of California.[56] As the thousands of miles separating Linderman from Ralston made direct oversight of his actions impossible, Ralston was using Western representatives to provide information about Linderman's actions on his behalf.

Introduced in the Senate in April 1870, the coinage bill was referred to the Finance Committee on April 28 and submitted to the House on June 25, 1870.[57] Although the initial draft eliminated the coinage charge, Sherman introduced an amendment reinstating the coinage charge, leaving Ralston's congressional allies complaining that "Linderman and his boasted influence with . . . Sherman were not here."[58] Cornelius Cole protested that the amendment was "exceedingly oppressive . . . to the people of the Pacific coast" and claimed: "The people of the Pacific coast are . . . with wonderful unanimity, against this charge."[59]

Despite Linderman's efforts, Sherman was not persuaded and complained that Western senators were asking for "the people of the United States [to] . . . pay the entire cost of the Mint."[60] He noted: "[If the] persons who are interested in this question are not satisfied with the very large benefits that are conferred on their particular region by the terms of this bill I do not think it is wise for the people of the United States to assume . . . the expense of coinage."[61] He concluded that "only the officers of the mint at San Francisco, who desire to enlarge their business at the expense of the people of the United States," were in favor of removing the charge, and "that is all there is of it."[62]

Since eliminating the coinage charge was a key component of Ralston's plan, Sherman was attacked by nearly every member of Ralston's congressional coalition. Stewart denounced the coinage charge as "a discriminating and unjust tax against the producer of gold."[63] Similarly, some mistakenly denied that the measure would have inequitable sectional effects, instead claiming: "It is a mistake to suppose that this bill, as it was originally framed, is for the particular benefit of the people of the Pacific coast."[64] Instead of benefiting the West, senators argued, the measure "was framed by persons who do not reside upon that coast and are not in any way interested in its affairs."[65]

Despite such opposition, both Sherman and Justin Morrill remained opposed to eliminating the coinage charge. Recognizing "a majority of the Senators . . . [to] be controlled by the opinions of the two Senators [Sherman and Morrill] . . . rather than by the merits or the demerits of the question," Casserly attempted to counteract Sherman's and Morrill's opposition.[66] The "complex questions" posed by the coinage charge, Casserly argued, were "questions which we had not been able to examine for ourselves" and compelled senators to follow "the experienced and competent leaders of committees who had given special study to the subject"; since it was "impossible for any of us to examine personally all the subjects . . . that come before us," members of Congress would be forced to "act upon some such theory."[67]

Realizing Sherman and Morrill were opposing a component of Ralston's plan, Casserly presented the "testimony of an extremely well-informed and capable gentleman in San Francisco," William Garnett, manager of Ralston's San Francisco Assaying and Refining Works, and read his recommendations into the *Congressional Globe*.[68]

Despite Casserly's efforts, Morrill and Sherman were not cooperating. Morrill dismissed Western representatives' arguments: "The idea that mere speculators go to San Francisco to buy up gold . . . in consequence of this coinage tax, is utterly preposterous."[69] Since the justifications for repealing the coinage charge were incoherent, and since "no Senators except those from that section of the country [the West] have appeared in opposition to this so-called tax, . . . the Senators from the pacific coast seem to . . . believe they have some interest in abolishing this seigniorage charge."[70] Because he did not understand that these representatives were acting at Ralston's behest, Morrill confessed: "[I am] unable to see how it is going to benefit the Pacific coast or the miners."[71]

Regardless of Ralston's efforts, Sherman and Morrill reinstated the coinage charge. Ralston's coalition was once again mobilized into action. William Huntington, cashier of Henry Cooke's First National Bank, reported: "[I have seen] Sherman and . . . Kelley the Chairman of the Committee on Coinage, and a number of other members, and think that the matter is now in *good shape*."[72] Linderman complained there was "some difficulty in getting action on the Mint Bill by the coinage committee of the House";[73] the measure faced "local pressure, from [Philadelphia]," which, when taken in conjunction with the fact that "Sherman, Morrill, [and] Fenton . . . undoubtedly wanted the Bill smothered to death," indicated that efforts to reduce the coinage charge were in trouble.[74]

While they would subsequently be blamed for the Coinage Act's passage, Eastern bankers opposed the measure because they believed it would drive business to the West Coast. Eastern representatives complained that the measure would grant Ralston's assaying operations a monopoly over refining silver coinage, leaving Linderman complaining: "The New York folks, through Mason, of the Assay office, are stirring up the question of cheap refining claiming to be able to do it at rates much below S.F."[75]

The principal cause of this complaint was that The Bank of California would be placed in a highly advantageous position. Since The Bank of California dealt with more refining than any other U.S. bank, Ralston would benefit from a repeal of the coinage charge. Nonetheless, as Eastern bankers pointed out the advantage that would be gained by The Bank of California, Linderman complained to Ralston: "Seligman or some such man grossly misrepresented matters about 'the repeal of the coinage charge for the benefit of the Bank of California, to enable them to avoid paying about $90,000 per annum into the U.S. treasury.'"[76] While Linderman denounced this "misrepresentation," he would subsequently assure Ralston: "There will be a saving to . . . [The Bank of California] of $90,000 per annum on account of reduction of coinage charges," the exact amount Seligman had quoted when he denounced the Coinage Act.[77]

Despite Eastern bankers' opposition and complaints from senators such as Sherman, Linderman was confident enough to tell Ralston: "We have the matter well in hand."[78] Western representatives such as Casserly, Stewart, and Stevens supported their efforts, and Linderman could report of Alan Thurman (D-OH): "[He] is strong with us for a free coinage"; Thurman in turn had "impressed [General] Morgan of Ohio with the importance of a free coinage."[79] Linderman also claimed: "Mr. Randall of [Pennsylvania] who has much influence in the House was thoroughly posted and assured me of a solid Democratic vote," and Secretary Boutwell "strongly favors a free coinage, and is very pleased with the results of the present refining system."[80]

Yet Sherman's opposition to reducing the coinage charge remained problematic. Even after Casserly "had quite a talk with John Sherman," Sherman still "refused decidedly" to endorse Ralston's plan, opposition that persisted after additional lobbying from William Huntington, cashier of Cooke's First National Bank.[81] The House of Cooke, with its history of intimate ties to Sherman, was unable to persuade him to endorse reducing the coinage charge. Even after the measure passed the House in 1871, Ralston's congressional allies complained they had faced "the determined opposition by Sherman and the whole finance committee of the Senate."[82]

While Ralston was using questionable methods to influence Linderman, Linderman believed "money will not be required" to assure the measure's passage.[83] Linderman felt it was only necessary "to urge the matter *officially* if possible, on the necessities of the service and the importance of cheap refining and a free coinage for the financial and industrial interests of the country."[84]

Although he believed bribing congressmen was unnecessary, Linderman noted that he was "not able to give my services without compensation."[85] Since Linderman's contemporaries claimed to be "shocked at the suggestion that the Director [of the Mint was] . . . bribed," and since scholars such as Milton Friedman claim that "no allegation of bribery has ever been . . . documented . . . against any individual member of Congress or government official in connection with the passage of the Coinage Act of 1873,"[86] it is worth quoting Linderman's letter to Ralston at length:

For my services and expense here, including anything that may be required in coming to Washington, off and on, or New York and until 30th of June next, you will please send me thirty five hundred dollars—on recipt hereof. I suppose you will desire to have me attend to these matters and the pushing of the Mint Bill next session say up to Sept 1, 1872—13 months, which will carry us to the expiration of your present refining contract and by which time, I hope and firmly believe you will have all matters pertaining to refining and coinage in good shape. If so, I will make no engagement nor enter into any business which would interfere with the service indicated. I am willing to do so for the sum of Five Thousand dollars payable January 1st 1872.[87]

Although existing accounts of silver's demonetization conclude that Linderman "broke no laws" when revising the coinage statutes, he was clearly receiving bribes to aid the Bank of California.[88] As he was enabling Ralston to directly influence coinage legislation, Ralston, probably referring to a prior conversation they had in San Francisco, assured him: "As I said *then, we will take care of you,*" promptly sending Linderman a check for $3,500.[89]

Recognizing the value of the services Linderman was rendering, Ralston further noted: "We leave all our interests in your hands appertaining to the coinage charge question . . . we concur in all you suggest as to further compensation . . . and all other matters of this nature, and will depend on you *solely* to carry out and *do* the *needful.*"[90] The original check that Ralston sent Linderman remains in Ralston's manuscript collection (see figure 1).[91]

Although clearly Ralston was paying Linderman, it is also apparent that Ralston's bribe did not cause the passage of a measure that otherwise would not have passed. Nor was Ralston bribing a majority of representatives. His

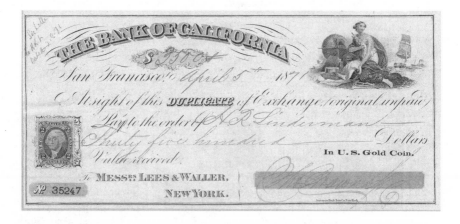

Figure 1. Ralston's bribe. (William Chapman Ralston Correspondence, BANC MSS 77/88 c, the Bancroft Library, University of California, Berkeley.)

bribe focused on influencing Linderman, who was writing the measure and was in charge of explaining the bill to elected officials who had little understanding of what was occurring. Although there is a range of influence the bribe could have had, it is likely that it functioned as a form of "insurance" to help increase the probability that Linderman would be attentive to Ralston's interests.

While it is unlikely that the bribe made Linderman do something he opposed, it is unlikely that Ralston would have bribed Linderman had he not received something in return, nor would he have had to bribe Linderman if the measure's passage was a foregone conclusion. There were three aspects of the measure that interested Ralston: the repeal of the coinage charge, the creation of the trade dollar, and silver's demonetization. The reduction of the coinage charge was not influential enough to have consumed Ralston's time or money, leaving the creation of the trade dollar and demonetization as the only aspects of the bill that could have interested him. These two enterprises, however, were mutually dependent. Ralston could have left the trade dollar a legal tender, yet he explicitly opposed doing so. He endorsed demonetizing the trade dollar for the same reason that led him to endorse demonetization—namely, if America retained bimetallism, large amounts of demonetized European silver would flood American silver markets for conversion into gold.

Indeed, we can only explain the trade dollar's inclusion in the Coinage Act by recognizing Ralston's opposition to bimetallism. The trade dollar was necessary to create an international market for Ralston's silver that would exist after the elimination of the domestic market for silver coinage. Since Ralston's proximity to China lowered his transportation costs for shipping trade dollars to Asia, The Bank of California would enjoy a virtual monopoly over producing trade dollars. Thus the Coinage Act would have prevented America from becoming a dumping ground for demonetized European silver coinage while simultaneously creating an international market that Ralston would control.

As the Coinage Act moved through Congress, it was apparent that few representatives understood why the act was being introduced, and fewer understood Ralston's influence over the measure. Since most members of Congress had no factual information about which interests were endorsing the measure and how it would influence different interests, congressional debate focused on the repeal of the coinage charge, a relatively minor aspect of the measure that would have far less influence on finance policy than silver's demonetization. While some representatives, such as Sherman, understood the measure would protect the gold standard from the expected decline in silver prices, few realized Ralston was manipulating congressional proceedings through Knox, Linderman, and representatives such as Stewart.

Given that Linderman was collecting bribes from Ralston, he had ample reason for concealing his relationship with The Bank of California. Yet Ralston's congressional coalition had also played a critical role in the measure's passage. As the Coinage Act moved through congress, Linderman assured Ralston: "It is hardly necessary to say that all the Pacific Coast men have done their duty. . . . I have been on the alert all the time and know all that has been going on. Let them continue consistently in the good work and I have no doubt whatever of full success the next session."[92] However, just as Ralston's legislative allies were masking their motives for supporting the Coinage Act, officials such as Sherman and Boutwell—who were not operating at Ralston's behest but sought to demonetize silver for political reasons—were similarly guarded because they worried that silver would emerge as an inflationary alternative to the greenbacks.[93] The refusal of Sherman and others to explain the bill's effects to all representatives, as well as their recognition that silver prices were about to collapse, indicates that some realized silver's inflationary potential and were taking actions to prevent silver from emerging as an inflationary alternative to the greenbacks.

Yet since those who understood the Coinage Act's ramifications were either concealing their motives or simply not explaining the measure's intended effects, silver's demonetization appeared to be an irrelevant detail in a technical revision of the coinage statutes. Lacking specialized knowledge regarding bullion trends, most representatives voted for the measure "ignorant of the facts," unaware that they were protecting the gold standard from the impending decline in silver prices, and never realizing that the Coinage Act had been deeply influenced by Ralston's efforts to protect his bank.[94]

The underlying condition that facilitated this sequence of events was widespread ignorance of specialized information regarding silver bullion trends. Recognizing that his power over Congress was derived from his expertise and specialized knowledge, Linderman told Ralston: "[You] would be astonished at the general want of knowledge on this subject, not half a dozen men in Congress know anything about bullion manipulations."[95] As Linderman was steering the bill past representatives who had little understanding of what was occurring, Ralston was assured: "Anything that uses the words bullion, assaying, refining, appears to be a perfectly unfathomable mystery to most people, and unless you were to undertake to explain these things yourself you can scarcely credit the blunders and stupidity of people generally."[96] Given the

Coinage Act's complexity, legislators were deferring to Linderman's expertise, and this allowed Ralston to focus his resources on Linderman and not on a larger number of representatives.

Only Linderman and a handful of others perceived the deflationary consequences of the measure, leaving Congress debating a bill few understood. Those who did understand the measure were simply choosing not to explain it. William Kelley (R-PA) admonished his colleagues to "examine the bill and look into the facts of the cases," complaining that comments from James Garfield (R-OH) had "illustrated how little the most industrious and capable members of the House understand about the facts in question."[97]

Garfield, who was typically well informed regarding financial issues, confessed to having "not looked at the general scope of this bill enough to have formed any judgment about it," an admission echoed by others who openly admitted they had "not been able to give much attention to this bill, except while it was being read."[98] In the absence of information necessary to understand the measure's effects, and unaware that a California banker was bribing the official who was revising the coinage statutes, few representatives understood what was transpiring.

When the coinage bill was referred back to the House in January 1872, Kelley reported: "[The bill has] received as careful attention as I have ever known a committee to bestow upon any measure . . . the committee proceeded with great deliberation to go over the bill, not only section by section, but line by line, and word by word."[99] Despite such scrutiny, when House debate began on January 13, 1872, there was "little discussion" of the fact that the measure ended bimetallism.[100] The bill was referred to the Senate on May 29, 1872, where it languished for six months.

While the bill was delayed in committee, Germany and the Latin Monetary Union announced the demonetization of their silver currency. In addition to threatening the public credit, demonetized European silver threatened American silver producers, who, if America remained on the bimetallic standard, would soon find their markets overrun with European silver. Unless immediate action were taken, Linderman warned Ralston: "The countries maintaining the double standard will be overrun with silver bullion," a situation making "a serious decline in price in unavoidable," which "we must prevent, by timely agitation and proper measures."[101]

Indeed, Ralston complained that Germany had "demonetized about $350,000,000 of silver which must take the form of Bullion and pass into the markets of the world," and that as a consequence there "[is] no market now open to us that we are advised of, to which shipments can be made without the possibility of a loss."[102] European demonetization was hastening the collapse of silver prices, and Ralston observed that "the prospects for silver . . . are in no way encouraging."[103]

These concerns were also influencing policy makers. In December 1872 James Pollock, director of the Philadelphia Mint, warned Secretary Boutwell of additional price declines brought about, he said, by "the very large increase in silver deposits . . . [which] have largely increased during the past ten or twelve months" and were "caused by the still larger production of silver in the different mining regions of our country."[104] This view was shared by Linderman, who, upon returning to Washington after another visit to the Comstock mines, warned Boutwell that new silver discoveries meant that "a further increase in [the volume of silver was] quite certain," a development he believed rendered "the future value of silver as compared with gold . . . a matter of national importance."[105]

A confluence of factors, "all tending to an excess of supply over demand for silver, and its consequent depreciation," indicated that "the gradual but eventually certain adoption of the gold standard and consequent demonetization of silver by all commercial nations" had become a foregone conclusion.[106] If the silver dollar became worth less than a dollar in gold, it would be profitable to exchange silver dollars for gold at the Treasury, leaving the government holding depreciated silver and stripping the Treasury of the gold reserve necessary to resume specie payments.

Linderman would claim that he had demonetized silver to protect the gold standard and the public debt, subsequently defending the Coinage Act by suggesting that if silver remained legal tender the value of government bonds would depreciate "proportionally with the decline in the value of silver; and all attempts to fund obligations at lower rates of interest would no doubt . . . [have failed], as it would have been impossible . . . to have sold at par in gold, public securities legally payable in silver dollars of 412 ½ grains."[107] In his correspondence with Ralston, however, Linderman admitted that these claims were designed to draw attention away from the fact that he was protecting Ralston's interests.

By the end of 1872 silver's premium had disappeared, and after filing a report for the Treasury Department in 1872, Linderman informed Boutwell that silver could now profitably be exchanged for gold in the Treasury.[108] Deteriorating silver prices were threatening "the whole edifice of specie resumption and protection of the public credit."[109] Unless silver was demonetized, the

Treasury's gold reserves would be depleted and exchanged for depreciating silver.[110] As this would make resuming the gold standard impossible, certain elites concluded it was essential to end bimetallism. Reacting to the information in Linderman's reports, Boutwell and Sherman began to take immediate steps to demonetize silver "before their expert and specialized information became public knowledge" and before the coinage of silver currency "became attractive to monetary inflationists."[111]

Boutwell's annual report for 1872 recognized that over the past decade silver prices had "depreciated about 3 per cent. as compared with gold, and its use as currency [had] been discontinued by Germany and some other countries."[112] Silver had begun to threaten the stability of the public credit: "As the depreciation of silver is likely to continue, it is impossible to issue coin redeemable in gold without ultimate loss to the Government; for when the difference becomes considerable holders will present the silver for redemption and leave it in the hands of the Government to be disposed of subsequently at a loss."[113] However, Boutwell was concerned that deteriorating silver prices would threaten the Treasury's solvency. With Boutwell "recognizing the dangers of inaction under these circumstances," he urged Congress to pass the Coinage Act.[114] Sherman invited Boutwell and Linderman to testify before the Senate Finance Committee to discuss how the declining silver premium would influence resumption.[115] Four days later, Boutwell gave Sherman a draft of the Coinage Act, leaving the 420-grain trade dollar the only silver coin in the act.[116]

By providing an international market for Ralston's silver, Linderman believed the trade dollar would arrest the decline in the price of silver. He argued that the trade dollar's "great importance" was due to the "large and increasing silver production and the depreciation which that precious metal [was] undergoing."[117] Facing declining silver prices, the trade dollar would, he said, give "some relief to our mining industries from the serious decline and further apparent depreciation in the value of silver."[118] As bullion prices continued to "show a gradual and continued decline in the price of silver bullion," he believed that "the successful introduction of the trade dollar in the Oriental markets is to us a matter of great importance."[119]

Although Linderman publicly claimed that the trade dollar was intended to support silver prices, it was crucial for Ralston's financial interests. The Coinage Act granted Ralston and The Bank of California a monopoly over the production of the trade dollar, a privilege potentially so profitable that Linderman believed that if the coin was "favorably received in China it [would] prove the most important economic event for California that [had] yet happened."[120] As the trade dollar was not legal tender for more than five dollars, it would not threaten the gold standard.[121]

On January 7, 1873, Sherman introduced a draft of the Coinage Act that eliminated the 384-grain silver dollar from the bill, effectively demonetizing the domestic silver dollar. Instead of explaining this change, he claimed that the bill provided for a new silver dollar that was "the precise equivalent of the five-franc piece" and "contains the same number of grams of silver" as the franc.[122] Since the French five-franc piece contained 384 grains of silver, Sherman gave the impression that the Coinage Act covered both coins. Rather than revealing that he had removed the 384-grain domestic silver dollar from the measure, he claimed that the bill was *identical* to the legislation Congress had passed two years prior that included *both* 384-grain and 420-grain coins.[123]

Moreover, Sherman did not explain "the essential reason for [his] actions—the expected market downturn in silver."[124] Instead he "left the distinct impression among his Senate colleagues that the revised coinage bill . . . now contained both the 384 grain and 420 grain silver dollars."[125] However, since most congressmen were unaware that silver prices were about to collapse, and that this would influence finance policy, congressional debate focused on retiring coins whose weight had been eroded and on removing the eagle from the back of coins.[126]

When Casserly pointed out that the bill called for raising the amount of silver contained in the silver dollar, Sherman claimed that this change was intended to bring the dollar into parity with the French franc and suggested that the New York Chamber of Commerce had requested the alteration.[127] Sherman maintained that the trade dollar had been introduced at the behest of California voters to provide, as he put it in his reply to Casserly, a "coin which is exactly interchangeable with the English shilling and the five-franc piece of France; that is, a five-franc piece of France will be the exact equivalent of a dollar of the United States in our silver coinage. . . . I must confess I do not think it is very important; but I think the Senator ought to be willing to defer in these matters to the practical knowledge of the officers who have charge of this branch of the Government service. I will say that Mr. Linderman, whom the Senator must know, has suggested this as being a convenient mode of promoting international coinage."[128] Although dropping the 384-grain coin from the measure demonetized silver, Sherman had done so at the behest of Linderman, openly claiming that these changes had been made in response to suggestions made by mint officials. Sherman noted: "I do not like myself to break in upon this plan, or to change it in the slightest degree, but prefer to leave it to the proper officers of the Mint. Indeed I would be perfectly willing to leave the whole thing to the officers of the Mint rather than to fix it by law."[129]

Neither Boutwell nor Linderman wanted the trade dollar to be legal tender. Sherman allowed the coin to be legal tender for five dollars to placate Samuel Hooper.[130] With this amendment, the bill passed the Senate without further discussion, and President Grant signed the bill into law on February 12, 1873. Yet eight months after signing the Coinage Act, Grant was asking why "silver is not already coming into the market," indicating that he did not understand the measure he had signed.[131]

Although the Coinage Act demonetized silver, and although Ralston had used his influence with Linderman, Stewart, and others to protect his banking and financial interests, few understood what had happened. The day the Coinage Act passed Congress, Garfield noted in his diary that Congress had merely "considered a few odds and ends of appropriations," even though the economic effects of demonetization would deeply influence political conflicts for the next thirty years.[132]

While the Coinage Act had accomplished most of Ralston's objectives, it retained a small coinage charge. Casserly complained to Ralston that he had "tried to strike it out, but could not," and while Casserly reported "our friends from the [Pacific] Coast seemed to think it best to let it go," he told Ralston: "[I will] never rest satisfied however until I see the whole thing kicked out of the statute book."[133] Yet even with the retention of a small coinage charge, Linderman assured Ralston: "[The measure] cannot but prove beneficial to the country and the mining interest especially, and I trust that directly or indirectly you will share in it."[134] Far from complaining that the Coinage Act's demonetization of silver would harm his bank, following the Coinage Act's passage Ralston assured Treasury Secretary Benjamin Bristow: "*We appreciate* what you have had done for this coast most fully."[135]

Hardly drafted at the behest of Eastern financiers or by elected officials seeking to protect the public credit, William Ralston "could claim the major part of the credit" for the Coinage Act's passage.[136] Henry Linderman had served as the principal conduit for Ralston's influence, and Linderman's receptivity to Ralston's interests was due to the thousands of dollars he was paid in exchange for influencing the measure. Reflecting on Ralston's role in passing the Coinage Act, Linderman remarked: "If it had not been for us (yourself Garnett and myself) this measure never would have come to fruition. It had not the least chance. Never in the history of legislation was a measure more carefully and persistently guarded than this coinage bill by me and of course I could not have been there without some friends behind me."[137] Unbeknownst to most legislators or the public, Linderman, Ralston, and a loose coalition of Western representatives such as William Stewart and Eugene Casserly had helped pass legislation designed to aid Ralston and The Bank of California. In addition to the backing of Ralston's allies, the measure had been supported by certain representatives, such as Sherman, who recognized that continuation of bimetallism would threaten efforts to resume the gold standard.

Yet it is also clear that none of this was apparent and that few outside Ralston's small group of allies understood what had occurred. Nor did Linderman fail to recognize the power such secrecy conferred. He assured Ralston: "It will never of course be known to the outside world what labor this measure has taken, nor will the mining interest ever likely know that they owe the reduction of the coinage charge primarily to you."[138] Wielding his expertise among representatives who did not understand his actions or what the Coinage Act stipulated, and enjoying ignorance-derived autonomy from the public, Linderman had implemented legislation that would set the terms of political debate for decades.

Since few representatives understood what the Coinage Act had done, it was a foregone conclusion that the public was unaware of the measure's ramifications. As the Coinage Act moved through Congress there was "nearly [a] total absence of public notice of it," and public commentators believed there could be "no dispute" that it was "common knowledge" that the Coinage Act "was not understood by the people."[139] As the public "had no notice" of the Coinage Act's ramifications for finance policy, silver's demonetization was "an unexpected stab in the dark, unseen until too late to be avoided."[140] Those subsequently seeking to mobilize public opinion behind bimetallism found that the public was "without opinions and without any special knowledge" of the legislation responsible for silver's demonetization.[141]

Yet certain officials understood the measure and how silver price trends would influence finance policy if bimetallism were retained. As Linderman reported, silver prices continued their "further depreciation"; this trend, he said, was "what I have expected for some time past, and will no doubt be accelerated when Germany shall commence exporting silver, as must soon be the case under the operations of their new coinage law."[142] While certain experts in the Treasury Department and in Congress had closely monitored the Coinage Act's progress, "most others did not," and as a result the measure "was not understood by the Congress which passed it."[143]

Linderman repeatedly invoked the accuracy of his predictions. In his annual report of 1873 he observed that since 1863 "the large annual production of [silver] from the mines in the United States and Mexico" had caused silver prices to decline by about "5 ½ cents per ounce, or 4 ½ %," leading him to conclude: "It is evident that Congress acted wisely in establishing gold as the sole standard of value."[144] The following year, he observed that silver prices "exhibited a declining tendency" that would continue, he wrote, so long as "the mines of the United States and Mexico continue to yield so largely."[145]

Given silver's continued depreciation, Linderman concluded: "The action of our Secretary of the Treasury was a good shot of policy."[146] Instead of aiding Eastern banks, Linderman assured Ralston that "the next two or three years [look] to be somewhat rough for the Atlantic coast, financially speaking."[147] Although Eastern financiers would subsequently be blamed for the Coinage Act's passage, it was apparent to those who understood what the measure was supposed to accomplish that the Coinage Act "came very close to being what the West wanted."[148]

Unbeknownst to voters, media elites, and most public officials, silver had been demonetized to protect Ralston's business empire, and by public officials seeking to protect the gold standard and the public debt.[149] Voter ignorance of silver price trends, and widespread failure to recognize how these trends would influence monetary policy, allowed implementation of a law that few were aware of or understood. The Coinage Act's complexity, and the fact that one had to understand international price trends and the ramifications these trends would have for finance policy, made it difficult for nonspecialists to understand what was occurring.

Given the Coinage Act's deflationary implications, there would have been far more resistance to demonetization had the Coinage Act been understood. Those officials who understood the act's deflationary consequences, such as Sherman, refused to explain the consequences in congressional debate because they knew the unpopularity of their actions and wanted to shield the measure from popular scrutiny and attention.

The autonomy of Ralston's coalition and officials such as Sherman was derived from popular unawareness of congressional action and the public's failure to recognize that trends in silver prices had important ramifications for monetary policy. Contemporaries recognized that the Coinage Act had been passed before "the great mass of the citizens . . . had yet to learn even the meaning of the word *demonetization*."[150] Such ignorance allowed Ralston's coalition to take actions that would subsequently become deeply unpopular. While some of Ralston's allies, such as Casserly, may not even have understood the Coinage Act's consequences, Sherman certainly did. His refusal to explain the act to other representatives indicates that he recognized that an informed public would have opposed his actions. Had voters realized that silver prices were about to collapse and that the domestic silver dollar was being eliminated as a legal currency, the Coinage Act would have been much more difficult to pass.

However, unlike Pendleton's adoption of greenback inflation in 1867, which had involved the popularization of fictions that the public found credible, the autonomy of Ralston's legislative coalition and officials such as Sherman was derived from simple popular unawareness of what was occurring, and from the public's failure to observe silver price trends and then properly interpret what these trends meant for finance policy. In this sense, elected officials' autonomy was due to the public's simple unawareness of the officials' actions, and to the fact that even most members of Congress did not understand the implications of the bill they were considering.

The public should hardly be blamed for this. The coinage revisions were complex and difficult to understand, and the officials who realized what the Coinage Act would accomplish deliberately refrained from explaining its implications. Instead, they simply claimed the measure was necessary to rationalize outdated coinage statutes and had few implications for monetary policy. As they lacked specialized knowledge and the ability to interpret the implications of such knowledge for finance policy, it was difficult for voters or public officials to understand what was occurring.

Similarly, many representatives, including Ralston's legislative allies, failed to predict how outraged voters would become once they understood silver had been demonetized. Even though these officials had incentives to predict how voters would respond if they subsequently became informed, voters' potential preferences did not constrain the officials who voted to pass the Coinage Act.[151]

The public's failure to identify the officials and interests responsible for the Coinage Act was reflected in the Populists' claims that the measure was part of a broader conspiracy. Although the Populists were denounced for their paranoid and conspiratorial tendencies, their suspicions were more accurate than has been recognized. This is not to suggest that their suspicions were correct; the Populists blamed the wrong officials and bankers for the Coinage Act's passage. Nor were these errors trivial, for they allowed Ralston's allies to elude detection or punishment.

Despite such errors, the Populists' suspicions that bankers and bribery had influenced the Coinage Act were relatively more accurate than the assertions of historians and social scientists denying that any conspiracy existed. Studies by Richard Hofstadter and Irwin Unger never recognized Ralston's involvement in the Coinage Act, denied the existence of any conspiracy, and denounced the Populists for endorsing conspiracy theories. Subsequent studies by Allen Weinstein, Milton Friedman, and Anna Schwartz echoed these claims, and if these arguments were accepted, the Populists' allegations appeared to be the products of paranoid cranks.

This is not to harangue studies for overlooking facts that were concealed in an obscure manuscript collection.[152] Rather, the errors in the existing historiography help illustrate the epistemological problems confronting democratic politics, and they indicate that even commentators with ample time, resources, primary sources, and strong incentives to accurately reconstruct prior events may still fail to understand the forces influencing politics. How are voters, or anyone else for that matter, supposed to know where to look, and what to pay attention to, when political actors' calculations are complex and concealed?

While the Populists' claims were more accurate than has been recognized, the Populists incorrectly attributed the Coinage Act to Eastern bankers. This oversight was not a random mistake; it was a perception that some of Ralston's congressional allies cultivated either by never explaining what had happened or by echoing the inaccuracies in the initial media coverage of the act. By failing to explain what had occurred, Ralston's allies escaped blame for the act's passage.

Although most of Ralston's allies simply never admitted to having any role in the Coinage Act, one of them, William Stewart, would join the free silver movement and help lead popular denunciation of the alleged European banking conspiracy behind the act's passage. Although Stewart was the only member of Ralston's coalition who became active in the free silver movement, he became executive director of the American Bimetallic Party and the American Bimetallic League, and he edited the *Silver Knight-Watchman*. Stewart's involvement in these organizations indicates that the leaders of bimetallic social movements failed to understand the interests responsible for a bill that captivated popular attention, was denounced by countless public orators, and dominated the election of 1896.

Before the initial explosion of free silver agitation in the late 1870s, however, the gold standard would be threatened by one final effort by greenback inflationists. The Panic of 1873 would lead to a Democratic majority in the House, an event that caused a corresponding reaction by certain Republicans, specifically Ohio senator John Sherman, who drafted legislation to prevent implementation of inflationary legislation. Sherman would draft a measure, the Specie Resumption Act, that delegated authority to the Treasury Department and allowed the treasury secretary to issue loans and retire greenbacks at his discretion.

In doing so, Sherman did not deliberately or consciously try to create a new form of state authority; he was simply attempting to isolate financial issues from popular influence and accomplish short-term political objectives. However, delegation of control of the money supply to the treasury secretary was a critical moment in American state formation, marking a turn away from the exercise of authority by state legislatures and judges, toward a state where independent policy authority was exercised by federal agencies.

Chapter 7 Discretion and the
Treasury Department

Although the Public Credit Act of 1869 and the Coinage Act of 1873 removed inflation from the political agenda, in 1873 a banking panic swept across the country, catapulting monetary issues back into public debate. Bank failures were initially concentrated away from the Eastern seaboard, but after the panic destroyed the Northern Pacific Railroad and the House of Cooke, a deep economic depression spread across the country.[1]

Aside from its economic impact, the Panic of 1873 had important political implications for the Republican Party and the development of the Treasury Department's authority. Specifically, the Panic of 1873 led to devastating losses by Republicans in the midterm election of 1874 and their loss of the House for the first time since the Civil War. The losses were attributed to popular dissatisfaction with Republican economic policies, and especially to Grant's veto of an inflationary currency bill. Hardly the result of elite manipulation of public opinion, the elections of 1874 were interpreted as a mandate opposing the Republicans' economic policies, leading many to predict a Democratic victory in the approaching presidential election of 1876.

This chapter explains how the Republican defeat in the congressional elections of 1874 led certain Republicans to empower the Treasury Department with new forms of authority. The chapter focuses more specifically on the passage of the Specie Resumption Act of 1875, legislation that institutionalized powers that had initially emerged in the Treasury Department during the Civil War. As the Democrats and some Midwestern Republicans were increasingly receptive to currency inflation, delegation of monetary policy to the Treasury Department was an attempt by Republicans such as John Sherman (R-OH) and George Edmunds (R-VT) to insulate monetary policy from popular influence and minimize its influence over the presidential election of 1876.

Delegation of policy authority was not part of a coherent, or deliberate, state-building project; the Treasury Department was given novel powers in order to achieve short-term political goals and resist the popular demands that were threatening the Republicans' electoral prospects. The Republicans' decision to delegate authority to the Treasury Department, however, was an implicit recognition that the policy objective the Republicans sought, resumption of the gold standard, had become so unpopular that it threatened their electoral prospects. In this sense, the expansion of the Treasury's bureaucratic capacity was not intended to fulfill popular demands, nor was it an attempt to implement policies the public was demanding. Rather, the Treasury Department had been empowered to accomplish distinctly unpopular policy objectives.

Despite being intended to accomplish short-term political objectives, this institutional innovation unintentionally created a new template for the American state, and the powers granted to the Treasury Department were retained and then replicated in subsequent agencies. Although empowerment of the Treasury Department was, in a sense, a reaction to popular pressures for currency inflation, the bureaucratic powers the Treasury Department was granted were used to prevent implementation of policies the public was demanding.

Following the Panic of 1873, the midterm elections of 1874 were disastrous for the Republican Party. In what was described as a "genuine tidal wave," the Republicans lost control of the House for the first time since the Civil War.[2] Equally worrisome, this popular reaction was widely attributed to voter dissatisfaction with economic conditions in general and the Republicans' financial positions in particular. In the South, where it seemed that "all are in debt or need," voters were increasingly receptive to inflation.[3] Republicans who supported the gold standard were attacked for having "misapprehended the wishes of the great mass of the people of the West" and for acting "against the will of the people."[4]

Many issues contributed to the 1874 defeat of the Republicans, but across the country their monetary positions played a key role.[5] Although the Republicans still narrowly controlled the Senate, the election gave the Democrats a sixty-seat majority in the House. When the lame-duck Republican Congress convened in December 1874, the incoming Democratic majority appeared poised to pass inflationary legislation. Aside from their policy objections, Republicans worried that monetary policy might become an issue in the approaching presidential election of 1876, and since defending the gold standard was increasingly unpopular, finance policy could become a liability for the Republican Party.[6]

These fears were hardly misplaced. Public opposition to contracting the greenbacks had been apparent ever since the Ohio Democrats had conceptually linked financial crises and currency contraction. The Democrats' resurgence in the 1874 midterm election led hard-money Republicans to conclude: "A large portion and perhaps a majority of our people [demand] more paper money," a view echoed by others who recognized that "a large number of more than ordinary able men really believe in cutting loose altogether from a gold standard."[7]

Specie resumption's unpopularity was apparent to hard-money Democrats as well. Manton Marble, editor of the *New York World,* complained that "the hindrances in the way of currency reform are . . . the ignorance of the people which will be long in enlightening, shared by the . . . ignorance of politicians who are rarely willing to run counter to popular . . . opinions."[8] Despite their objections, Eastern Democrats agreed with inflationary Democrats who asserted: "90 out of every 100 voters in the United States favor the greenback policy [of inflation], and if we could get that question submitted to them, pure and simple, it would carry the whole country New York and New England included."[9] Reflecting on the unpopularity of specie resumption, the New York Committee of Commerce dourly noted: "The popular will has been opposed to congressional action in the direction" they desired.[10]

Reflecting on the inflationary measures proposed in the prior congressional sessions and the general tenor of public opinion, Treasury Secretary Benjamin Bristow decried the "undefined and incoherent desire for some sort of change . . . the chief . . . [result of which] is that the party in power will always be held responsible for hard times."[11] The problem, it appeared to some, was that "when working men are out of work, they—or the ignorant many then lay the blame on the govt.—and want *any* change for the sake of change."[12]

This more general conception of what was happening—the politicization of monetary policy—led to an explicit move to formalize the last Republican reaction to the popularity of inflation: removing monetary policy from popular influence. Reflecting upon the problems posed by the politicization of monetary policy, Secretary Bristow's annual Treasury report of 1874 admitted: "The opinions entertained and expressed by public men and communities of people . . . must be accepted as one of the factors of the financial problem."[13] The volume of circulating currency had become "controlled by the legislative will and . . . party exigencies," a condition Bristow found "objectionable in the highest degree."[14]

Bristow's annual report recommended immediate steps toward resumption, including repealing the legal tender status of the greenbacks, funding them through a long-term bond, and redeeming fractional, or small-denomination, greenbacks with silver coinage.[15] Congressional reaction to Bristow's recommendations, however, revealed that politicization was not solely a matter of partisanship. In the House, Bristow's report was attacked by Republicans William Kelley and Benjamin Butler, who "exhibited their inflation doctrines in full blast," and who were in turn denounced by hard-money Republicans, such as James Garfield and Henry Dawes.[16] The Republican Party had degenerated into "hopeless division on the question of the currency," and some worried it would be impossible to field a unified ticket in the approaching presidential election.[17]

In the midst of a deteriorating political situation and deeply concerned that the incoming Democratic majority would implement inflationary legislation, Republicans concluded it was essential to take steps toward resumption of the gold standard. Yet the magnitude of the Republicans' 1874 defeat indicated that resumption remained deeply unpopular, leading the financial press to conclude that Congress would take no action on financial questions, and there would "be no rash legislation either as to the contraction of the currency or for the disturbance of business by any crude financial experiments."[18]

As the Democratic victory in the 1874 midterm elections was interpreted as a mandate supporting inflation,[19] several Republicans began drafting a resumption measure out of committee and "away from the glare of publicity."[20] Principally written by Sherman, the resulting legislation, the Specie Resumption Act, granted the treasury secretary the authority to issue bonds to accumulate a gold reserve, coin recently demonetized silver currency to retire "fractional" greenbacks, and take actions to resume specie payments by January 1, 1879.[21]

While the Specie Resumption Act was critical for resumption of the gold standard, the measure had implications for state power that extended beyond monetary policy. By granting the treasury secretary "a wide discretion for delay and for method of action" to accomplish resumption, the measure expanded the Treasury's authority, a shift that powerful economic groups and electoral groups opposed.[22]

Although the election of 1874 was interpreted as evidence that the public endorsed inflation, the Specie Resumption Act sought to accomplish the opposite objective: resumption of the gold standard. Despite this, the Specie Resumption Act was not intended to placate Eastern financiers who endorsed the Republican's policy objective. Despite endorsing resumption, the *Commercial and Financial Chronicle* complained: "[The] principle of Congressional responsibility, obvious as it is, seems to have been unaccountably lost sight of in too much of our monetary legislation since the war."[23] Instead of welcoming delegation to the Treasury Department, the *Commercial and Financial Chronicle* noted: "Congress . . . cannot, as seems to have been supposed, devolve upon the Secretary of the Treasury the burden and the sole responsibility of making practical provision for reaching specie payments."[24]

Indeed, there is little evidence that business groups were responsible for, or even aware of, the measure when Sherman introduced it.[25] In the weeks prior to the Specie Resumption Act's introduction, conservative Eastern financial journals such as the *Financier* and the *Commercial and Financial Chronicle* pleaded for "stability and quiet" on the currency question, and expressed the hope that "Congress would stop legislating on the currency."[26] Various senators complained that the Republican caucus responsible for the Resumption Act had deliberately *excluded* the business community from their deliberations. Thomas Bayard (D-DE) urged delay in order to give "an opportunity . . . [for] the intelligent business sense of the country [to] learn what the proposed measure [was], and not only to learn what it [was], but make some accommodation of their affairs to the result."[27]

That, however, would have been difficult, as many business groups observed: "It is quite as impossible now as it was before the passage of the bill to determine whether it will turn out to be a measure of inflation or not."[28] Senator Adlai Stevenson (D-IL) demanded the bill be delayed so he could "have an opportunity of knowing what the business sentiment of the country [was] upon the great subject of the finances of the country," and Stevenson suggested that it was doubtful "whether the business men of the country in the great centers of this wide domain [could] themselves tell what its precise operation [would] be."[29] Stevenson also claimed that the business community remained divided on the Resumption Act because "business men differ in regard to what the exact needs of the country are in relation to a system of finance."[30] Stevenson claimed: "[I cannot] vote now knowingly on this bill; and if you were to force me to vote to-day I should not exactly know how to vote. I have not had time either to consider it or to know its probable operation."[31]

Nor could the public have understood the measure, given its sudden appearance and the lack of congressional debate.[32] Although Republican advocates of the gold standard had reason to claim that the public endorsed their actions, many openly recognized the Resumption Act's unpopularity. Despite such opposition, requests for delay and deliberation went unheeded, and under Sherman's guidance the bill was submitted for a roll-call vote hours after its introduction. The Resumption Act passed along straight party lines in the Senate and, after an abrupt period of contention, passed the House on January 14, 1875.

Hardly drafted at the behest of powerful bankers who endorsed the gold standard, the Resumption Act had some of its harshest critics in conservative financial groups who endorsed resumption. Sherman openly admitted: "The resumption act was generally received with disfavor by those who wished the immediate resumption of specie payments."[33] Hard-money businessmen "were openly contemptuous of the new legislation" and bitterly complained that the Resumption Act was a measure that "popular opinion has neither demanded nor accepted as final."[34]

Complaining that the Resumption Act had inflicted "losses, which [were] estimated at 10 millions of dollars," the financial press was being "assured by leading bankers and financiers of . . . [New York City] that the effect of the Congressional determination to interfere with the currency [was] checking enterprise, that it [was] causing failures in various ways."[35] Criticizing the tactics used to pass the measure, the *New York Times* derisively observed: "The humor of this transaction deserves to be fully appreciated."[36]

Aside from the measure's short-term effects, the Eastern business community complained that the Resumption Act granted the treasury secretary "dangerous and unlimited powers . . . too complicated and too risky to be dealt with by vague legislation, or to be confided by Congress to one man."[37] Criticizing the expansion of the Treasury's authority, the *Commercial and Financial*

Chronicle noted: "We have always contended that the Treasury should possess as little discretionary control as possible over the volume of the currency."[38]

Despite writing the Specie Resumption Act, in 1866 and 1867 Sherman had been a strong critic of Treasury Secretary Hugh McCulloch's use of discretion to withdraw greenbacks from circulation. Sherman had demanded Congress strip McCulloch of his discretion over the greenbacks and "restore the legislature their power over the currency," stating that control over the money supply was "a power too important to be delegated to any single officer of the government."[39] In 1866 Sherman recognized that discretionary authority was "a power that has not heretofore been granted to any Secretary of the Treasury," arguing it was *not* "wise . . . to place in the power of the Secretary of the Treasury or any mortal man this absolute and extreme control over the currency of the country."[40]

Sherman's opposition to delegation, however, had occurred *before* George Pendleton had popularized greenback inflation, and before the Republican Party had become wracked by sectional divisions over the currency issue. By 1875 the situation had deteriorated, and facing the possibility of party disintegration on the eve of a presidential election, Sherman used the Resumption Act to empower the Treasury Department with the discretionary authority he had formerly opposed.[41]

The critical second section of the Resumption Act granted the treasury secretary the power to issue loans and manipulate the money supply at his discretion, and in doing so, institutionalized discretionary authority in the Treasury Department. By delegating control of the money supply to the treasury secretary, Sherman not only took concrete steps toward resumption but also ensured that the financial issue was removed from legislative debate in the months before the election of 1876.

Indeed, one of the reasons Republican representatives supported the Resumption Act was specifically because they were looking for a way to remove the financial issue from discussion prior to the election of 1876. Yet unlike the Public Credit Act of 1869, when Congress simply ordered the treasury secretary to redeem greenbacks in specie, the Resumption Act of 1875 had significant ramifications for American state formation, as discretionary bureaucratic authority would subsequently be applied to other agencies.

Sherman was not alone in recognizing the utility of bureaucratic delegation. One of Secretary Bristow's correspondents noted: "Any commercial nation, which successfully maintains specie payment . . . habitually resort to a great central agency for regulating international exchanges"; France, Great Britain, and Germany all possessed "institutions [that] are enabled to exert a constant influence upon all the treasure in their respective countries, and in the commercial world—They regulate the supply of treasure through exchanges."[42] In the United States, there had traditionally been "the lack of such machinery," but perhaps it was, in the correspondent's words, "necessary (now proper perhaps) to establish such an institution in this nation," and instead of having to design a new institution it appeared, he continued, that "the United States Treasury can perform these functions."[43]

If Congress took no action toward resuming the gold standard, another correspondent told Bristow, "it may be necessary for you to exercise powers not generally supposed to exist" in order to "protect the public honor against the risk of violation."[44] The salience of financial conflicts and the Republicans' unpopular financial positions had forced Sherman to delegate discretionary authority to the Treasury Department. Delegation allowed implementation of the Republicans' preferred policies while simultaneously removing financial issues from congressional debate, thereby minimizing the issue before the approaching presidential election.

While delegation was intended to counteract popular inflationary pressures, this form of bureaucratic authority was not created in response to the demands of economic groups who endorsed the gold standard. Instead of endorsing the Resumption Act, Eastern financiers complained that Congress "[was] entirely disregarded by the business community in its calculations."[45] Rather than reflecting the demands of powerful financiers or public opinion, the Resumption Act was the "product of distinctly political forces."[46] Under pressure to provide a unified Republican financial position prior to the 1876 presidential nominations, Sherman had drafted a measure that "was at heart political in origin, as isolated from public opinion as any political event can be where universal male suffrage prevails."[47]

In a deteriorating electoral situation, and concerned that finance policy would influence the approaching presidential contest, certain Republicans used the Specie Resumption Act to remove finance policy from congressional discussion. Intended to help the Treasury Department accumulate the gold reserve necessary to redeem greenbacks and resume the gold standard, the Specie Resumption Act passed even though the congressional elections of 1874 were widely interpreted as a mandate supporting inflation.

By granting the Treasury Secretary discretion to market loans and accumulate a gold reserve, the Specie Resumption Act institutionalized a form of authority that prior treasury secretaries, such as Hugh McCulloch, had exercised. Although the act altered the Treasury Department's authority over the money supply, it was not part of any deliberate state-building project. Rather, it was a response to the unpopularity of the gold standard and political problems the currency issue posed for the Republican Party.

Despite granting the Treasury Department new forms of authority, it was apparent that the Specie Resumption Act was widely unpopular. Indeed, the election of 1874 was generally interpreted as an expression of public support for currency inflation, and Sherman and many other Republicans openly recognized the unpopularity of the act's objective—resumption of the gold standard. Yet it was specifically because their preferred financial policies had become unpopular that certain Republicans concluded that delegation of authority was necessary. Sherman's delegation of power to the Treasury Department was a consequence of his concern that public opinion threatened the rationality of monetary policy.

Sherman's decision to quietly draft the measure, introduce it, and demand a sudden roll-call vote with almost no time for debate and discussion was part of his recognition that he needed to pass the measure quickly and before media attention could focus on explaining the measure's effects. The Specie Resumption Act's sudden introduction led representatives to complain that their constituents could not even know that the measure was under consideration, nor was the business community given time to assess how the act would influence economic conditions.

While voter ignorance granted Sherman autonomy to draft and implement the Specie Resumption Act, it is clear that had voters been aware of the measure they would have opposed it. The elections of 1874 were interpreted as indicating public disapproval of Republican economic policies. Despite popular inattentiveness, the Treasury was granted authority that it would subsequently use to market bonds and accumulate the gold reserve necessary for resumption of the gold standard in 1879.

In a pattern that would be repeated in other policy areas, such as railroad regulation, conservatives who worried that the public was endorsing irrational policies turned to bureaucracy as a way of minimizing the influence of popular demands. This form of autonomy was not simply a case were popular unawareness allowed the autonomous implementation of certain policies that the public did not understand, nor was it a case where elites manipulated public opinion to generate popular acquiescence or endorsement of a specific course of action. Rather, certain political elites had concluded that the public's ignorance of economic theory had led them to endorse irrational policies, and rival policy makers were catering to these public preferences. In this context, certain conservatives realized that delegating authority to bureaucracies offered a short-term solution to the political problems posed by the unpopularity of their preferred policies, and thereby ensured that policy decisions would enjoy a degree of insulation from public opinion. Delegation of authority to unelected officials was, however, an implicit admission that the Republicans' preferred policies were unpopular.

The fact that the election of 1874 was interpreted as a public rejection of the Republicans' monetary policies, and also representatives' complaints that the Specie Resumption Act was introduced so suddenly that they did not have time to read it, indicates that this measure passed with scant public awareness. Yet public ignorance did not ensure that powerful financial interests were responsible for the act either. Financial elites were critical of the act specifically because of the power it granted the Treasury Department, indicating that the measure was not drafted at the behest of Eastern financial elites.

Thus, rather than being a response to powerful financial groups or public opinion, the empowerment of the Treasury Department was a short-term reaction to a hostile political environment and was intended to insulate the Republicans from electoral retribution. The Treasury Department was granted discretion over the money supply not as part of a deliberate state-building project but as a consequence of certain Republicans' attempts to resume the gold standard and minimize the salience of financial issues in the presidential election of 1876.

Despite the unpopularity of resumption, both parties converged on nearly identical anti-inflationary monetary platforms in the election of 1876. As both parties' nominees, Republican Rutherford Hayes and Democrat Samuel Tilden, endorsed the gold standard, voters had no opportunity to select a party that endorsed currency inflation. This policy convergence rendered the outcome of the election of 1876 irrelevant for monetary policy; America was going to resume the gold standard regardless of which party won.

This policy convergence was produced by the interpretations that party elites gave to certain local elections, particularly the Ohio gubernatorial election of 1875. While local elections had little direct impact on national politics, they were used as barometers for public opinion and influenced the policies and candidates nominated in the approaching presidential election. Thus, despite focusing on local issues, the Ohio election of 1875 is critical for understanding the presidential election of 1876, as the Ohio election caused both parties to adopt identical monetary positions. As this convergence institutionalized the authority the Specie Resumption Act had granted the Treasury Department, the Ohio election of 1875 was a turning point in postbellum monetary policy that had important implications for broader patterns in American political development.

Given its influence over the specific policies and candidates the parties nominated in 1876, and for broader shifts in American political development, it is noteworthy that the Ohio election was deeply influenced by elite manipulation of public opinion. The victorious candidate, Ohio Republican Rutherford Hayes, won the Ohio election by manipulating voter ignorance and exploiting anti-Catholic religious animus. Although Hayes was a relatively unknown national political figure, his victory in the Ohio election threw him into contention for the Republican presidential nomination, which he subsequently won. The next chapter examines how Hayes manipulated voter ignorance to win the Ohio election and explains how this election influenced not only the subsequent presidential election but also the development of American state capacity.

Chapter 8 The Ohio Gubernatorial Election of 1875

Although the Specie Resumption Act delegated authority to the Treasury Department, many Republicans worried that they faced certain defeat in the gubernatorial contests of 1875, especially in critical swing states like Ohio and Pennsylvania. Despite being local elections, gubernatorial contests were critical because they were used as barometers for public opinion and influenced the policies and candidates selected in the approaching presidential election. Many predicted that Democratic victories in the 1875 elections would cause both parties to nominate inflationary candidates in the presidential election of 1876.

Due to Ohio's large agrarian population, prior support for greenback inflation, and large number of electoral votes, both parties were particularly focused on the state's gubernatorial election of 1875. Many Democrats believed that if they carried Ohio a Western inflationist would secure their presidential nomination, while a Republican victory in Ohio would practically guarantee that New York governor and hard-money advocate Samuel Tilden would become the Democratic nominee.[1] Similarly, Republicans believed that a Democratic victory in Ohio would strengthen inflationist Republican presidential nominees, while a Democratic defeat would make a hard-money nominee possible.[2]

This chapter examines the Ohio gubernatorial election of 1875 and focuses on how the Republicans managed to win this election despite the unpopularity of their financial positions. The chapter explains how Rutherford B. Hayes exploited voter ignorance and mobilized religious animus to become a dark-horse candidate for the Republican presidential nomination of 1876. Specifically, it examines how Hayes and the Ohio Republicans made fictitious claims that the gubernatorial election would determine whether Catholic religious instruction would be imposed upon Ohio's public schools. The Republicans claimed that the Geghan bill, a measure passed by the Ohio legislature in 1874, imposed Catholicism on Ohio's schools, even though the Geghan bill had nothing to do with Ohio's public schools. In making this claim, Hayes manipulated voters' understanding of what the election would influence, and his subsequent victory in the Ohio election led him to become a viable presidential candidate for the Republican Party.

After discussing how Hayes manipulated voter ignorance, the chapter concludes with a discussion of the national implications of Hayes's victory, arguing that the Republican victory in the Ohio election led both parties to nominate presidential candidates that endorsed the gold standard in the election of 1876. This ensured that America would resume the gold standard regardless of which party was victorious in 1876. By influencing the platforms and candidates the parties nominated in the subsequent presidential election, Hayes's Ohio victory had broader implications for American politics, ensuring that the United States resumed the gold standard and that the Treasury Department would retain the authority it was granted by the Specie Resumption Act.

Aside from influencing these specific issues in American political development, the Ohio election of 1875 is interesting because it is a particularly unlikely venue for political elites to have manipulated public opinion. Specifically, since the Ohio election turned on a simple factual question regarding local legislation—whether a bill passed in the prior Ohio state legislature required Catholic religious instruction in Ohio's public schools—and did not require voters to evaluate complex regulatory policy or make predictions regarding the effects of parties' policies, it should have been relatively easy for the Ohio electorate to become politically informed and discern truthful claims from fictions.

If, however, elites were able to manipulate voter ignorance in this election, elite manipulation of public opinion may be even more prevalent, and more powerful, when politics involves distant political decisions with delayed effects and counterintuitive causal mechanisms. For these reasons, the Ohio election of 1875 is a particularly interesting illustration of how political elites may be able to convince voters to accept misleading causal narratives, even in contexts where it should be relatively easy for voters to become informed.

Following their defeat in the congressional elections of 1874 and the passage of the Specie Resumption Act in 1875, the Republicans faced local elections that posed serious questions about their viability in the approaching presidential election of 1876. The Ohio gubernatorial election of 1875 in particular was critical, as the outcome would influence the parties' nominees and platforms in the next year's presidential election. However, deteriorating economic conditions and the unpopularity of the gold standard initially made the Ohio election's outcome appear to be a foregone conclusion, and the Democrats seemed poised to carry the state by a comfortable margin.

Ohio Republicans vacillated between nominating Alfonso Taft and Rutherford B. Hayes. Hayes initially refused the nomination out of deference to Taft's candidacy, and due to serious doubts regarding the Republicans' prospects.[3] Taft, however, was ultimately rejected because of his role in the Cincinnati "Bible war," in which, as a state Supreme Court justice, he ruled in favor of removing the Bible from public schools.[4] Hayes, despite his initial reluctance to enter the election, realized that victory in Ohio in 1875 could make him a contender for the presidential nomination in 1876.[5] Recognizing that the Ohio election offered him an opportunity to reenter national politics, he agreed to accept the Republican gubernatorial nomination.

Even though he hoped to use Ohio election to become a contender for the presidential nomination, Hayes recognized that the Republicans' economic policies were deeply unpopular. He observed that large numbers of "debtors and speculators" in Ohio endorsed currency inflation, and that in parts of Ohio "the tariff and finances [were] controlling subjects."[6] Despite knowing the unpopularity of the Republicans' policy positions, he refused to alter his positions, noting: "At any rate, we are right."[7]

In the context of the approaching presidential election, many Republicans recognized that the Ohio election had implications beyond the selection of Ohio's next governor. Treasury Secretary Benjamin Bristow worried: "I don't know what is to become of us" if the Democrats were to carry Ohio, and complained: "I have not much faith in the good sense of 'the people,' and I believe that the election of some Copperhead as President would be almost sure to follow."[8] Given its influence over the approaching presidential contest, the Ohio gubernatorial campaign of 1875 "became the most closely watched state contest since the Lincoln-Douglas campaign of 1858."[9]

Republicans who recognized the gubernatorial election's importance noted that "everything turned on Ohio"; the Ohio election had become "the pivotal point" for the approaching presidential contest.[10] A Democratic victory would strengthen the odds for inflationary presidential candidates, while a Republican victory would solidify support for the Specie Resumption Act and hard-money presidential nominees. Although the election was "local in its character," observers were noting: "[Its outcome] may yet have far reaching consequences."[11] With both parties divided, on the eve of the Ohio contest it appeared, as Bristow put it, that "the financial question . . . must be the controlling one in our next national contest."[12]

Initial indications were discouraging for the Republicans.[13] The Democrats nominated inflationist Allen Thurman, and across the Midwest they claimed: "The whole people are opposed to the infamous Sherman resumption bill," and even members of the business community worried that specie resumption "would be ruinous to all industries and cannot be carried out."[14] Recognizing the Specie Resumption Act's unpopularity among voters and businessmen alike, one Republican newspaper complained: "We do not understand . . . [how] the Republican party of Ohio was foolish and impolite enough . . . to place itself in antagonism to the interests of nine-tenths of the business men of Ohio and the West."[15]

Keenly aware of the unpopularity of the gold standard, John Sherman concluded: "the people were not quite prepared for any measure looking to resumption."[16] Even the strongest proponents of resumption were forced to admit: "Inflation has no terrors for the . . . majority of the people of the Great West."[17] Meanwhile, Democrats attacked the Republicans for being beholden to "banks . . . gold worshippers and usurers."[18] In both Pennsylvania and Ohio "strong and influential Republicans . . . looked upon the financial plank adopted by their party as a fraud."[19]

Across the Midwest economic conditions also conspired against the Republicans. Many worried: "The great destruction of the crops and the . . . hard times which are ahead of us will lose us a great many voters."[20] Public opinion seemed to be arrayed against currency contraction; as a correspondent told Sherman: "[It is] hard for men who are in debt to learn in reference to a public question except as they suppose it will affect them in their own business."[21] Democrats were "surprised to find leading Republicans engaged in the iron business who pronounced in favor of our platform and ticket."[22] Others concluded: "[Governor] Allen may be elected in consequence of the hard times with the miners."[23]

The combination of economic hardship and unpopular Republican financial policies prompted large defections among Republican constituencies. Hayes wrote of the "people carried off by the cry of hard times to be relieved by inflation."[24] In certain areas, one of his correspondents commented, "along the lines of Rail Roads among the working men, there seems to be a settled determination to vote against [the Republicans]."[25] Concerned Republicans reported: "The condition of the laboring men and businesses in the large manufacturing districts is fearful and will have more influence at the ballot box than everything else combined."[26]

After their initial optimism regarding the election, Ohio Democrats became concerned when Republicans began drawing attention to legislation enacted by the most recent Democratic state legislature. The Republicans began focusing on the Democratic legislature's passage of the Geghan bill, drafted by a Catholic tobacconist who was involved in Ohio politics, which allowed Catholic priests to offer religious services in Ohio jails and mental asylums.[27]

The Geghan bill was initially uncontroversial, and prominent Republicans openly admitted: "The Geghan law . . . is harmless."[28] Yet Republicans recognized that the Geghan bill could be used in the gubernatorial election, and they were soon claiming that it mandated Catholic religious instruction in Ohio's public schools. This claim was incendiary, and it was also completely false. The Geghan bill had nothing to do with Ohio's public schools. Nevertheless, in an effort to mobilize religious animus and deflect attention from economic issues, Hayes accepted the Republican nomination and joined other Republicans who were claiming that the Geghan bill diverted public funds to support Catholic religious instruction in Ohio's public school system.[29]

In his private correspondence Hayes noted that the Geghan bill would be central for the campaign. Following his nomination, he explained that his electoral strategy would claim: "A division of the school fund is agitated and demanded by the same power and upon the same grounds, by which and on which the passage of the Geghan Bill was demanded. . . . I think the interesting point is *to rebuke the Democracy by a defeat for subserviency to Roman Catholic demands.*"[30]

But the Republicans' claim that the Geghan bill influenced the public schools was wholly fictitious. The bill did not deal with Ohio's school system at all; it was strictly limited to religious instruction in the penal system and public asylums. The Republicans were in a dire electoral environment, however, and Hayes wanted to become a presidential nominee. This led him and the Republicans to make false claims about the Geghan bill that catered to voters' religious prejudices and focused attention away from the Republicans' unpopular economic positions.

For Hayes, the accuracy of his claims about the Geghan bill were irrelevant. Ohio's election was occurring in the midst of an economic recession, the Specie Resumption Act was unpopular, and Hayes understood that if he could somehow win Ohio's governorship he would become a frontrunner for the Republican presidential nomination of 1876. Despite his service in the Civil War, he was a local Ohio lawyer and had been an unremarkable congressman. In the context of a hostile electoral environment, Hayes realized that if he could successfully manipulate the public's understanding of what the Geghan bill stipulated, he could inject himself back into national politics. In this context the Geghan bill was a godsend for Hayes and the Republican Party, offering them a way to divert public attention away from economic issues and toward religious antagonisms.[31]

Ever since its origins as a political organization, the Republican Party had drawn electoral support from evangelical and pietistic Protestant sects. This gave the Republican electoral coalition a religious dimension that could be activated during elections. Conveniently, Ohio Republicans could remind voters that in the 1850s Ohio's Catholics had indeed sought public funding for Catholic instruction in parochial schools.[32] Given nineteenth-century Protestants' animus toward Catholics, the Geghan bill could be used to create a powerful religious issue, and Ohio Republicans quickly moved to connect the bill with Roman Catholics and the Democratic Party.

Meeting in Columbus on June 2, the Ohio Republican platform included a hard-money plank and declared opposition to any "division of the school-fund."[33] Attacking the Democrats' association with Catholics, the platform endorsed separation of church and state, and opposed sectarian legislation.[34] Although the Republican platform also discussed African American civil rights, tariffs, military pensions, and presidential term limits, during the convention "the cheering . . . was longest and loudest, when . . . the opening speech touched on the school question, [and] the Geghan law."[35]

Despite hoping the Geghan bill would deflect attention away from economic issues, the Ohio Republicans were manufacturing public opinion from whole cloth. The Republicans' claim that the Geghan bill was a Catholic attempt to impose religious instruction on the public schools was pure fiction.

Voters were being manipulated into believing that the election focused on this issue, but it had no basis in fact; it was an issue designed to satisfy little else besides Hayes's personal desire to become president.

Indeed, this entire process required voters to remain ignorant of what the Geghan bill stipulated. Had voters been informed of the basic facts about this legislation, information that Democratic newspapers were printing and attempting to popularize, they would have realized that the Republicans were campaigning on a fictitious issue that simply did not exist. The Ohio election was rife with ignorance and misinformation, and even certain Republicans, such as James G. Blaine, failed to understand Hayes's actions. Not recognizing that Hayes's anti-Catholic attacks were an attempt to manipulate public opinion, Blaine wrote to Ohio Republicans: "[The public school issue has been] forced upon you," and "those who would abolish the non-sectarian public school necessarily [need] ignorance—and ignorance is [as powerful as] intolerance and bigotry."[36] Blaine may have been trying to preemptively combat rumors that he had received Catholic education, but it is likely that his statements reveal that he simply did not understand Hayes's electoral strategy.

Yet despite the falsehoods that were influencing public opinion, the Republicans' interpretation of the Geghan bill had resonance and quickly became the central focus of the campaign.[37] Revealing the effectiveness of the Republican's campaign message, one voter confided in Hayes: "I am as you are awire [sic] a true republican; I have not voted with the party or with eany [sic] party for four years. To vote with the democrt [sic] party is voting the roman catholicks [sic] in to [sic] power and the destruction of our public schools is shure [sic] to follow. You can depend on me I will do all in my power to secure to you a shure [sic] election."[38] Pleased with the public's reaction to his interpretation of the Geghan bill, Hayes observed: "The Catholic question is . . . interesting the people very much. This seems to be thus far almost wholly favorable."[39] Other Republicans agreed: "[The Catholic issue makes] the prospects . . . brighter. The school and Catholic question are the questions in our county. We have but 100 Catholic voters, all Democrats of course, all in one corner and can afford to work these points up and are doing our best."[40]

Exasperated Democrats tried to counteract the Republicans' statements by printing the actual wording of the bill in newspapers, and pointed out that the Geghan bill did not deal with local schools.[41] One newspaper stated: "Any one who has ever read the bill knows that it contains no allusions of that kind [i.e., dealing with the public schools] . . . the idea that this bill forebodes anything of the kind is preposterous."[42] Indeed, the laws creating the public school system, and the Ohio Constitution, which maintained a strict division between church and state, and had been enacted by a Democratic legislature.

The Democrats tried to counteract the Republican charges by adopting a resolution in their platform supporting a strict division between church and state. They denounced the Republican platform as "an insult to the intelligence of the people of Ohio, and a base appeal to sectarian prejudices," and attacked the national banking system and the Specie Resumption Act for causing "general bankruptcy and ruin."[43]

On the campaign stump, George Pendleton criticized the Republicans for their "cruel and wicked effort to excite the most baleful passions of the human heart for mere partisan purposes."[44] The irony of the situation was not lost on Pendleton. Having himself manipulated popular understanding of monetary policy in Ohio's gubernatorial contest of 1867, he now realized that Hayes was destroying the final hopes of inflationary monetary policy. Recognizing the severity of the situation, and the ramifications the Ohio election had for the approaching presidential contest, Pendleton claimed that the Republicans "fear to risk the fight on these [economic] questions, they seek to make an issue which is no issue, and to drive you from considerations of interest by appeals to prejudice or bigotry or honest difference in religion . . . who commenced this agitation? asks General Hayes in his first speech. He did—his party did—no one else thought of it."[45] Ohio Democrats recognized that the Republicans' electoral strategy indicated that they "acknowledge[d] their defeat on the currency issue" and had resorted to fostering religious antagonism "to arouse the prejudices of the people and thus divert the public mind."[46]

Republican papers countered by claiming that the Geghan bill would result in the presence of "altars, then, wax candles, holy water, incense, wafers, and all the rest of the paraphernalia of the Roman Catholic church . . . in our State institutions . . . [opening] up all our public institutions to the wrangling of sects and mak[ing] of them a denominational battle ground."[47] One Republican journalist, purporting to have met "our strawberry blonde friend" Geghan on a train, reported how Geghan's "face lighted up with glee" when discussing the bill.[48] Republican newspapers published reports from Cincinnati's *Catholic Telegraph* claiming to show Catholic priests had demanded the Democrats pass the bill, as well as excerpts from one of Geghan's letters allegedly claiming that the Catholics had "a prior claim upon the Democratic party in Ohio."[49]

The Republicans also used the Geghan bill to appeal to Protestant Germans who had "bolted" from the Republican Party in 1872 in favor of the Liberal Republicans.[50] Charles Francis Adams Jr., a prominent Liberal Republican, concluded: "The weapon with which to kill [the Democrats] is the German vote; it is the only effective weapon at hand."[51] Republicans had to balance appealing to Germans with anti-Catholic rhetoric and repelling them on other issues, like temperance, often associated with such attacks.[52]

Initially it was unclear whether Germans would support the Republicans, and many feared that a temperance plank would drive them to the Democrats.[53] Temperance organizers assured Hayes: "[You will] receive the votes of all Germans who are Republicans if the [temperance] issue is not made."[54]

After smothering the temperance issue, the Republicans began to mobilize Germans with anti-Catholic appeals. William McKinley, Canton lawyer and future president, noted: "[My] district contains a large Catholic population which is thoroughly democratic, a large protestant german element that hitherto have been mainly democratic, they hate the catholics—their votes we must get."[55] Hayes was similarly told: "All that will be necessary to make . . . the Liberal [Germans] . . . support certain will be a strong avowal by you upon the Catholic question."[56] Republicans printed anti-Catholic speeches in German and used prominent Liberal Republicans, such as Carl Schurz, as speakers.[57] By July Germans who had voted the Liberal Republican ticket in 1872 had returned to the Republican fold.[58]

Although economic issues still favored the Democrats, ethnic and religious appeals began to overpower them. Expressing surprise that "many Democrats were present on all occasions" to hear Republican speakers, Edward Noyes, one of Treasury Secretary Bristow's confidants, reported: "[The Catholic issue is] the one which gives us our great gains."[59] While some voters were unclear about Hayes's financial positions well into the campaign, they understood his attitude toward Catholics, and as the campaign progressed the outpouring of anti-Catholic sentiment became overwhelming.[60]

Recognizing the power of their anti-Catholic appeals, Hayes urged his fellow Republicans: "[We] must not let the Catholic question drop out of sight. If [the Democrats] do not speak of it, we must attack them for their silence. If they discuss it, or refer to it, they can't help getting into trouble."[61] Catholic priests added further fuel to Republican demagoguery by staging public rallies defending the Geghan bill. The combined effects were disastrous for Ohio Democrats. Recognizing the deteriorating electoral situation, an adviser to the incumbent Democratic governor William Allen pessimistically noted:

I must confess to a good deal of uneasiness for our success, this fall, owing to the aggressive prominence the Catholic Church seems disposed to give to itself just now. The Geghan bill, the letter of Geghan, the editorials of the Catholic Telegraph in reference to that measure, the conferring of Archbishop McClosky, and the demonstration here, yesterday, including the speech of Bishop McQuaid, are creating a feeling that will give the state to the Republicans by an overwhelming majority. As things now look to me, we shall lose this city, and you may judge from that, how the state is likely to go. This is no sudden . . . scare. The mutterings of the storm that is coming are very audible. I can breathe in the atmosphere about me [*sic*] coming defeat. The Republicans are cock sure of success. They . . . [say they] shall sweep the state as with a whirlwind. It will be worse than Know Nothing times. Secret societies are being formed, and the state will be full of them before fall. And the idea that animates them will override all party considerations. Democrats will be as numerous in these societies as they were in the Know Nothing days. The insolence of the Catholic press, the claims put forth that the Democratic party owes its success to its Catholic voters, and the charge that few or no native Americans belong to the Democratic Party, are driving our American born into these secret anti-Catholic societies. Believe me when I tell you there is hell in the near future. It is long since I have seen such fixedness of . . . opposition to anything, as you may discern by conversing with American born Democrats and Republicans, against the pretensions of the Catholic Church. No other sect parades its strength, nor thrusts itself so before the public as the Catholic. All of which goes to convince the persons, who are going into these secret societies, that the Church is not so much striving for the cause of Christ and true piety, as for civil and political power. Now, there is no use trying to reason this feeling down. You are too well read not to know that that is impossible. . . . And [the Republicans] have no more doubt of sweeping the state than they are of the sun rising on the 2nd Tuesday of October. Remember they are out of meat, and this Catholicism is a perfect godsend to them. And the unfortunate matter about it is, that the Catholic Priests and Catholic papers are playing directly into the hands of the Republican party. They are furnishing the Republican press and leaders with ammunition with which to overthrow the Democratic party, not only in Ohio, but in the United States.

I am sorry this conflict is coming just now. I was in hopes that it might be deferred until after the Presidential election of 1876. But the Catholic leaders will not permit, and the Republican leaders are the most willing souls in the world, to accommodate them. And so my dear Governor, you are to be slaughtered, and with you the Democratic Party of Ohio, and not unlikely of other states.

The political atmosphere is growing heavy and oppressive under the [burden] of the Catholic leaders. I feel it here very sensibly, and the letters we are getting from the Country tell us it is felt everywhere. Such is our fix—a damned hard one. To have the cup of victory dashed from our lips just as we were going to taste it, is not a subject for tame contemplation. I don't give it even one half as bad as it is. And nobody to blame but the Priests![62]

Public opinion had polarized along religious lines. In Findlay, Ohio, Hayes reported seeing "many Republicans from the country. Without exception they were most interested in the [Geghan issue]."[63] The Democrats' fears regarding the salience of anti-Catholic electioneering were well founded. In an election that drew the largest turnout in Ohio history, the Republicans won a slim majority of 5,544.

The Democrats' failure to win in Ohio, an inflationist state with a large agrarian population, made the ramifications for finance policy straightforward. Prior to the Ohio election public opinion appeared adamantly opposed to specie resumption, and both parties recognized that the Ohio election would influence the candidates and platforms in the approaching presidential election. The Republicans, however, had overpowered popular opposition on economic issues, and although the Ohio Republicans' electoral strategy was itself an admission of the unpopularity of their financial policies, "jubilant conservatives talked as if resumption were assured."[64] Despite recognizing inflation's popularity, Republicans concluded: "We [are now] thoroughly committed to specie resumption on the first of January 1879."[65] Eastern Democrats similarly concluded: "You can bury the rag baby it is dead."[66] This point was not lost on Ohio Democrats, who concluded: "[Our] side of the financial issues . . . did not make a vote, and all we lost, and they were not a few, was on the *church* question."[67]

Seeking to emulate the Ohio strategy, President Grant endorsed a constitutional amendment banning support for religious schools, in an attempt "to stimulate a ground swell of opinion" opposing Catholics and their Democratic allies.[68] The *New York Sun* felt that Grant was attempting to mobilize "Protestant prejudice . . . in a political crusade against the Catholic church, and thereby carry the presidential election."[69]

Some Republicans concluded that if the House refused to ratify Grant's proposed amendment, it would create "an issue which [would] destroy all chance of Democratic success in the fall."[70] Grant received numerous letters from correspondents saying that his constitutional amendment was "offered none too soon."[71] Grant, however, was focusing attention on the Catholic "issue" to help the Republicans in the approaching presidential election, even though the issue had been used to aid Hayes's presidential ambitions and little else. As it turned out, Hayes's actions and his resulting nomination in the presidential election of 1876 would have additional consequences for monetary policy, and for broader shifts in American state formation.

While the election made Hayes Ohio's governor, the election had national political implications. Although Ohio Republicans were convinced that the public opposed their preferred financial policies, some Democrats mistakenly interpreted the Ohio election outcome as indicating that the public now opposed inflation.[72] However, Republicans who understood the tactics that were employed to carry the Ohio election reported: "[We do] not share in the general belief that the inflation doctrines are overthrown."[73]

Prior to the Ohio election, many speculated that a Democratic victory would result in an inflationary Midwestern presidential nominee such as Thomas Hendricks. If the Republicans carried the state, however, it was predicted that New York governor Samuel Tilden, a hard-money advocate, would be the Democratic nominee.[74] These forecasts were uncannily accurate, not simply because some Democrats misinterpreted the Ohio election as a negative verdict on inflation, but because the Democrats realized that the Republicans could neutralize their financial positions at the national level just as they had in Ohio.

The Republicans' success in Ohio, the birthplace of greenback inflation, indicated that the Democrats could not count on the Midwest in the approaching presidential election. If the Midwest could not be counted on, New York's electoral votes, always important in any presidential election, now became even more critical than they normally were. At the Democratic convention in St. Louis, William Dorsheimer, lieutenant governor of New York and a close Tilden ally, reminded delegates that if the Democrats won the South and New York, they could still carry the presidential contest. Dorsheimer's announcement "was like an electric shock to the convention and sent a thrill through the entire assemblage. . . . From that moment there was no doubt of the result."[75] Since victory in New York was now crucial, and since "no one could carry New York on a soft-money platform," Tilden secured the Democratic nomination.[76]

This delighted Eastern Democrats, who were critical of the Republican Party for failing to resume the gold standard fast enough. Manton Marble of the *New York World* happily wrote: "[Tilden] has had a large commercial experience, is extremely well-informed in the English part of the literature of economic and financial subjects, [and] has an undoubted faculty of reasoning upon them."[77]

Meanwhile, Southerners were eager to nominate whoever they thought could remove the Republicans from power, so Tilden's disagreements with their monetary positions were not deemed important enough to oppose his nomination.[78] One Southerner claiming to "reflect the sentiments of the very large proportion of the conservatives of Virginia," reported: "In spite of the differences of views on the currency question . . . we are willing to put in abeyance convictions of right to secure a large, more essential present benefit [i.e., Tilden's election], if we shall be permitted so to do."[79]

Hayes's Ohio victory convinced Democrats that they could not rely on financial issues to carry the Midwest in the upcoming presidential contest. This led the Democrats to adopt a strategy focused on carrying the South and New York. As New York's electoral votes were critical for this strategy, the Democrats nominated Governor Tilden as their candidate, minimized financial issues, and focused their campaign on government reform and sectional reconciliation.[80]

Despite opposition from Southern and Midwestern Democrats, Tilden and the Eastern faction of the Democratic Party forced the 1876 convention to support hard money.[81] Although the Democrats denounced the Republicans' "financial imbecility and immorality," their platform merely questioned the date that the Resumption Act set for specie resumption.[82]

Tilden's confidants were divided regarding the attention they should give financial issues in the campaign. Despite recognizing that monetary policy would be a major issue after the election, many did not think it should be a major campaign, because neither party could afford to aggravate its organization's "festering divisions" on the issue.[83] Some still urged Tilden to make a public statement on finances to try to shift public opinion in favor of hard money.[84] Others, such as David Wells, advised Tilden to refrain from taking a public stance on financial issues because the "masses won't comprehend it," and instead advised Tilden to "stick to the great principles and do not connect yourself against contraction."[85]

While recognizing that the bloody shirt would be prominent in 1876, Democrats worried that the Catholic school question was "one of the weightiest," as the anti-Catholic prejudices of Americans were such that "they [could] be made to believe almost anything."[86] The Ohio election had caused both parties to oppose currency inflation despite recognizing the gold standard's unpopularity. Had Hayes lost the Ohio election, the Midwest could have been counted on to support an inflationary Democratic ticket and the Republicans may have been forced to either nominate an inflationary candidate or promise some sort of compromise on the specie resumption.

The Republicans initially oscillated between nominating Blaine and Hayes; some worried that Blaine's Catholic education would cost Republican votes.[87] When Blaine was implicated in a railroad corruption case, the nomination went to Hayes. Prior to the Ohio election Hayes was a marginal political figure who was described as being "competent but unspectacular."[88] He had been a Civil War officer with little involvement in national politics, serving as Ohio's governor and as a congressman. Hayes's victory in Ohio, however, had transformed him into a viable candidate for the Republican presidential nomination of 1876.

Hayes's emergence as a presidential candidate cannot be explained without recognizing his manipulation of voter ignorance in the Ohio election of 1875. Indeed, Hayes's 1875 campaign assumed that voters were so poorly informed that he could campaign on an issue, the threat of Catholic religious instruction in Ohio's public schools, which did not actually exist. Had voters been minimally informed, had they simply understood that the Geghan bill did not involve Ohio's public schools, they would have realized that Hayes was campaigning on a fictitious issue.

Voter ignorance of what the Geghan bill actually stipulated allowed Hayes and the Republicans to lead voters to believe the election had implications for Catholic religious instruction in Ohio's public schools. Yet this claim had no correspondence to reality, and the principal reason the Ohio Republicans were propagating this claim was because they recognized the need to distract popular attention from their unpopular economic policies.

Despite the fictitious nature of the Republican claims, the salience of the Catholic issue compromised voters' control over other issue dimensions, leading to the election of a party and candidate who would have been defeated had the election had focused on economic issues alone. Hayes and the Ohio Republicans had not, however, merely manipulated the issue dimensions that voters evaluated during the election.[89] Rather, their manipulation of voter ignorance had created an issue where none actually existed.

Just as many had predicted, the Ohio election had national implications. Hayes's victory in Ohio led both parties to nominate financially conservative candidates and platforms. The fact that both parties had taken "sound" currency positions removed financial topics from the campaign and meant that voters had "no real opportunity to register their attitude on the financial issue."[90] Midwestern Republicans happily noted that this guaranteed that financial issues would "scarcely appear" in the 1876 presidential election, ensuring that the Republican Party would be "united, resolute and aggressive" in the approaching contest.[91]

Hard-money advocates happily reported: "[We are] already victorious," because regardless of the election's outcome, "[we have] captured the candidates of both parties and . . . we are destined to have a good honest hard money president unless Peter Cooper [the Greenback Party candidate] shall be elected."[92] Hayes's victory in Ohio, a victory that was produced by manipulation of public ignorance, had rendered the outcome of the presidential election irrelevant for the course of monetary policy, marking a turning point in postbellum finance policy after which "there would never again be a serious threat of paper inflation."[93]

Although the Ohio election of 1875 was a particularly interesting case of elite manipulation of public opinion, the Ohio election influenced the candidates and platforms that the parties nominated in 1876, and just as some had predicted, Hayes secured the Republican nomination. Aside from influencing the candidates and policies appearing in the presidential election of 1876, Hayes's nomination and eventual victory had larger implications for institutional development. In the case of the Treasury Department, once Hayes became president he nominated John Sherman to be treasury secretary, and under Sherman's guidance the Treasury Department used the power granted by the Specie Resumption Act to accumulate a gold reserve and resume the gold standard. This solidified the discretion the Treasury Department enjoyed over the money supply, and ensured that the country pursued a conservative finance policy.

This sequence of events was initiated by the Ohio election of 1875, and by Hayes's manipulation of public ignorance and voters' anti-Catholic prejudices. Hayes's manipulation of public opinion, however, was not conducted upon a public devoid of information that merely provided a tabula rasa for fact-free interpretations. The Ohio electorate was immersed in a political culture exhibiting its own history, prejudices, and biases. Instead of crafting public opinion from a blank slate, Hayes activated voters' cultural biases through an electoral campaign filled with fictitious information. Doing so allowed him to defeat the Ohio Democrats and throw himself into contention for the Republican presidential nomination, political events with significant implications for American politics despite being initiated by Hayes's promotion of a self-serving political illusion.

Although the Ohio election of 1875 was determined by illusions and fictions produced by elites for their own purposes, the outcome of this election had significant effects upon politics. Hayes's Ohio victory led him to become the Republican presidential nominee, and after the contested election of 1876 was settled in his favor, he became president. The particular way the election of 1876 was settled, however, inadvertently influenced another policy area that influenced American state formation, railroad regulation, and the creation of the Interstate Commerce Commission (ICC), the independent commission which regulated the American railroad industry and which marked a continued expansion of bureaucratic authority.

Traditional explanations for the origins of railroad regulation suggest that different industries and organized groups, such as powerful railroads, Pennsylvania's independent oil producers, and New York shippers, led efforts to regulate the railroads. Such explanations focus on the economic advantages industries sought, for example the lower transportation costs shippers would receive, or the railroads' hope to stabilize their rate structures and legalize their pooling agreements. Various economic groups' preferences are often used to explain political outcomes and policy decisions, offering reductionist explanations of this period of American state formation.

Despite offering detailed descriptions of economic groups' preferences, the next chapter argues against these studies and instead suggests that railroad regulation was influenced by political conditions surrounding the contested election of 1876. The election of 1876's outcome was thrown into controversy when the Republicans claimed to have carried Southern states that the Democrats appeared to have won. Hayes eventually became president through a bargain struck between with certain Southern Democrats involving Republican promises to support federal railroad subsidies to Southern Democrats who agreed to endorse Hayes's bid to the presidency.

This bargain, which became known as the "Compromise of 1877," collapsed after Hayes became president, and it was never fully consummated. Once Hayes had become president he simply refused to deliver the railroad subsidies Southern Democrats had been promised in exchange for supporting his candidacy. The political forces unleashed by the collapse of the Compromise of 1877 caused Texas Democrat John Reagan, whose congressional district would have gained access to a transcontinental railroad route had Hayes fulfilled his end of the compromise, to introduce railroad regulation into the congressional agenda. Reagan's power as chairman of the Interstate Commerce Committee ensured that railroad regulation had a powerful ally in the House.

Although the collapse of the Compromise of 1877 led Reagan to champion railroad regulation, he never sought to create a regulatory commission; he simply wanted to outlaw certain railroad practices, such as charging different prices for shipping goods based upon the distance the goods were transported. Reagan's explicit opposition to creating a regulatory commission creates a second question regarding how railroad regulation would influence administrative development. For it is unclear how Reagan's efforts unintentionally resulted in the creation of an independent regulatory agency.

The creation of an independent regulatory commission would be introduced by a faction of liberal reformers loosely allied with the Republican Party, eventually culminating in the creation of the ICC. Much like Sherman's delegation of authority to the Treasury Department, the ICC was not created as a response to popular demands or social groups' preferences. Rather, this institutional innovation was a conservative reaction to the popularity of congressional regulation of the railroads. Liberal reformers hoped an independent commission would help inform the public of railroad policy because they worried that the public was poorly informed of critical issues associated with railroad economics.

Hardly a response to public opinion or social groups' demands, the ICC, as the next chapter argues, was created as a result of the collapse of the Compromise of 1877 and the subsequent efforts of certain liberal reformers who hoped bureaucracy could help inform voters of the complex decisions that were increasingly the subject of the state's regulatory operations. The following chapter focuses on explaining how these two groups of actors interacted to produce an institutional innovation that was subsequently replicated in other policy spheres.

Chapter 9 The Compromise of 1877 and Railroad Regulation

The gubernatorial elections of 1875 led both parties to minimize the monetary issue in the presidential election of 1876. Since both parties' candidates endorsed the gold standard, the outcome of the election of 1876 was irrelevant for finance policy. As the Specie Resumption Act granted the treasury secretary discretion to sell loans to resume the gold standard, even if an inflationary congressional majority had been elected, it would have faced a conservative treasury secretary empowered with authority to sell bonds and accumulate a bullion reserve necessary for resumption of the gold standard.

Besides influencing monetary policy, the election of 1876 led to novel developments in railroad regulation, setting in motion forces that would culminate in the creation of the Interstate Commerce Commission (ICC) in 1887. As America's first independent regulatory commission, the ICC has traditionally been seen as marking the origins of the American regulatory state. While the ICC initially exercised limited and contested powers, subsequent conflicts focused on defining the nature of its authority, not on the legitimacy of the administrative organization itself.

To explain the ramifications that railroad regulation had for American state formation, we must explain two events: first, how the contested election of 1876 caused Texas Democrat John Reagan to adopt railroad regulation, and, second, how Reagan's bill caused a reaction among the liberal reformer faction of the Republican Party, who sought to temper Reagan's bill by creating a bureaucratic commission to regulate the railroad industry. While forces unleashed by the contested election of 1876 provided the proximate cause for the introduction of Reagan's bill, liberal reformers' justifications for creating a regulatory commission were influenced by their pessimistic views of public opinion, and by their hopes that an expert agency could make rational decisions and disseminate information to help inform voters of railroad policy.

The combination of Reagan's actions and liberal reformers' reaction to Reagan's efforts culminated in the creation of the ICC, spreading bureaucratic regulatory authority beyond monetary policy and the Treasury Department. However, the contradictory forces driving this administrative expansion, and the disparate objectives Reagan and liberal reformers sought to accomplish, were poorly understood at the time.

Indeed, although the Compromise of 1877 is typically believed to have ended Reconstruction, the fact that the Compromise of 1877 involved anything other than the removal of federal troops from the South was not understood until the publication of C. Vann Woodward's *Reunion and Reaction: The Compromise of 1877 and the End of Reconstruction* in 1954.[1] If scholars attempting to reconstruct prior historical events did not know that the Compromise of 1877 involved promises of federal aid to railroads until three-quarters of a century after the fact, it is unrealistic to expect nineteenth-century voters to have understood what the Compromise of 1877 involved, or how it influenced other policy areas and debates.

Although few nineteenth-century Americans understood how vague promises regarding the subsidization of railroads influenced the Compromise of 1877, similar misunderstanding existed with liberal reformers' justifications for creating a regulatory commission. Liberal reformers endorsed creating a regulatory commission, and drafted legislation that was introduced as a substitute for Reagan's bill, because they hoped bureaucratic experts would publicize impartial information to help inform the public of complicated economic issues associated with railroad regulation.

In this sense voter ignorance influenced both the forces that placed railroad regulation on the congressional agenda and the calculations that led liberal reformers to endorse creating a regulatory commission. Without recognizing how the Compromise of 1877 was poorly understood, and without focusing on liberal reformers' concerns about public opinion, we cannot explain the timing of Reagan's bill or the specific reason liberal reformers proposed using a bureaucratic commission to regulate the railroads.

Before analyzing these issues and explaining their ramifications for American state formation, we need to examine how the Compromise of 1877 influenced Reagan, a Texas Democrat, to introduce regulatory legislation in 1878 that eventually culminated in the creation of the ICC. Although many argue Reagan was appealing to agrarian hatred of the railroads, his bill was associated with his efforts to use the Compromise of 1877 to deliver federal assistance to the Texas and Pacific Railroad and stimulate his congressional district's economy. By focusing on the forces unleashed by the Compromise of 1877, I argue that Reagan sought political objectives that were not directly related to electoral pressures or the demands of populist social movements.

Hayes's refusal to actually deliver railroad subsidies to the South has led some to argue the Compromise of 1877 never constituted any concrete political bargain.[2] Instead of questioning such studies, my argument is premised on Hayes's failure to consummate the Compromise of 1877; for it was precisely the collapse of the compromise that led Reagan to introduce his bill. The collapse of the compromise shattered Southern Democrats' hopes to secure railroad subsidies to their districts, and it was this unexpected development that induced Reagan to introduce his bill in a desperate effort to aid Thomas Scott's collapsing railroad empire. Accordingly, railroad regulation was not a response to the demands of powerful railroads, shippers, or outraged agrarians; rather, the Reagan bill was a reaction to political pressures associated with the collapse of the Compromise of 1877.

Although Reagan's bill was an attempt to aid Scott's faltering railroad empire, it shifted the locus of regulatory authority from the states, where agrarian efforts had previously been focused, to Congress, thereby altering the level of government that would exercise regulatory authority over the railroad industry. While Reagan opposed creating a commission, he created the underlying condition, assumption of federal responsibility for regulating the railroads, that made regulation by federal commission possible.

To explain how the election of 1876 influenced American state formation, it is necessary to examine the methods used to settle the contested election of 1876 that made Hayes president. It is only by explaining how the Republican Party settled the contested election of 1876 that we can explain why Reagan adopted railroad regulation when he did, and why the Reagan bill assumed its specific form. However, the bill's popularity convinced certain liberal reform-ers, Charles Francis Adams Jr. in particular, that the public endorsed irrational methods for regulating the railroads. These liberal reformers reacted to the popularity of Reagan's bill by endorsing the creation of a regulatory com-mission, which they hoped would disseminate expert information to educate voters and avoid implementing the more radical elements of the bill. The ultimate product of their reaction to Reagan's bill was to create a regulatory commission, the ICC, thereby completing the state-building project Reagan inadvertently began.

Despite influencing American state formation, the public was unaware both of the calculations constituting the Compromise of 1877 and of those produced by the collapse of the compromise. Regardless of how poorly the public understood the forces influencing American politics, various political elites' decisions were influencing the trajectory of American state formation, and a form of authority that initially emerged in the Treasury Department was being applied to other areas of the American economy.

Although Hayes and Tilden adopted similar positions on a range of policies during the election of 1876, the contest generated intense popular engagement and high turnout levels.[3] During the election campaign, Hayes and Tilden adopted similar financial positions, portrayed themselves as reform candidates opposed to the Grant administration's corruption, and promised minimal fed-eral involvement in Southern affairs.[4]

Believing that success in the Midwest could not be assured, the Demo-crats focused on carrying the South and New York. The initial election returns seemed to vindicate this strategy, as the Democrats unexpectedly carried Indi-ana, New York, and what initially appeared to be the Solid South. Despite ap-pearing to have lost the election, Hayes used Republican-controlled returning boards in Florida, South Carolina, and Louisiana to claim he had carried these states, which the Democrats appear to have won.

Since the Twelfth Amendment was ambiguous regarding which branch of Congress was responsible for counting the electoral ballots, and since the Democrats controlled the House and the Republicans controlled the Senate, each party declared that the branch of Congress it controlled had the consti-tutional authority to count the contested ballots.[5]

The two parties fought each other to a standstill that was broken only after they agreed to the creation of a commission to count the contested ballots. Composed of five representatives, five senators, and five Supreme Court justices, the commission initially contained seven Democrats and seven Republicans, with David Davis, an Illinois Independent, holding the balance of power. After Davis was elected to the Senate, however, he was replaced with a Republican, giving the Republicans a single-vote majority on the commission.

Despite having a majority control of the electoral commission, the Republicans needed to prevent the Democratic House from delaying the commission's count of the electoral ballots. To prevent delay by the House Democrats, the Republicans began trying to split the Democrats by promising to appoint certain Southern Democrats to patronage-rich cabinet posts, such as the Post Office, and by offering federal subsidies to extend the Texas and Pacific Railroad into Southern Democrats' congressional districts if they supported Hayes.

One of the Southern Democrats who took "a leading part" in assisting Hayes during the Compromise of 1877 was John Reagan, the Texas Democrat who would introduce railroad regulatory legislation in 1878 and became a key leader of efforts to regulate the railroads.[6] Although nearly a decade would pass between the introduction of Reagan's bill and the creation of the ICC in 1887, efforts to regulate the railroads represented the "first attempt" to exercise "systematic oversight" over the American national economy.[7] Since the creation of the ICC has been described as "a founding moment" in the development of the American regulatory state, and since Reagan's bill was critical for leading to the passage of the Interstate Commerce Act, understanding how the Compromise of 1877 influenced railroad regulation is crucial to understanding broader shifts in American political development.[8]

Generally, scholars have attributed railroad regulation to popular demands or the industry-specific efforts of organized economic groups. Some argue that popular opposition toward industrialization and railroads' use of price discrimination led voters to demand regulation to secure lower transportation costs and combat monopolization.[9] Organized agrarian groups are often believed to have been critical for this process, and although groups such as the Grange initially endorsed subsidizing railroad development, after the Panic of 1873 agrarians increasingly focused on regulating, and not on promoting, railroads.

Others, however, argue that railroad regulation was not a response to public opinion or agrarian outrage but was instead the result of organized economic groups' demands. These explanations disagree regarding which economic groups were critical; some emphasize the role of powerful railroads, while others focus on shippers, merchants, or independent oil producers.[10] Instead of seeing regulation as a response to popular pressures, these studies argue that organized economic interests sought to use regulation to advance their specific interests.

A third set of studies accepts elements of these interpretations but suggests the ICC was the product of political conflicts a degree removed from social demands.[11] Despite recognizing that public support for regulating the railroad industry was mounting in response to pressures associated with industrialization, Stephen Skowronek argues that railroad regulation was not merely a functional response to social groups' demands and cannot simply be attributed to pluralist pressures. Similarly, Scott James argues that railroad regulation was the product of strategic partisan electoral calculations that often overrode median party preferences and social groups' demands.[12]

Despite the important contributions of these studies, there is considerable uncertainty regarding why railroad regulation was introduced onto the legislative agenda in the late 1870s. For example, Lee Benson's analysis of New York shippers' efforts to influence regulation concludes: "No implication is intended that . . . national railroad regulation was the product of their creation."[13] Similarly, after suggesting that powerful railroads were vocal supporters of federal regulation, Gabriel Kolko admits that regulation was not "deliberately initiated by the railroads."[14] Although Scott James offers an extensive analysis of the railroad issue, his analysis begins in 1884 and thus does not examine the origins of the railroad issue in the late 1870s.

It is also unclear why certain actors decided to champion regulation when they did. Although John Reagan was among the most important advocates of railroad regulation, Benson concludes that Reagan's motives are still "not clear."[15] Similarly, Reagan's biographer notes that it was so "strange" that an ex-advocate of Confederate states' rights would endorse centralization of federal regulatory authority that Reagan's actions "puzzled his opponents."[16] Nor did Reagan do much to clarify his motives; his autobiography devotes a mere three pages to discussing railroad regulation, even though this issue consumed nearly a decade of his legislative career.[17]

Although Reagan is often depicted as an agent of agrarian grievances against the railroads, this chapter argues that Reagan adopted railroad regulation as a consequence of political forces unleashed by the collapse of the Compromise of 1877, and in his attempts to aid Thomas Scott's railroads in order to give his congressional district access to a transcontinental railroad. While Reagan's bill was intended to support Scott's railroad empire, popular support for the measure led Reagan to champion regulation long after the pressures that drove him to introduce his bill had subsided.

Despite its origins in the collapse of the Compromise of 1877, the Reagan bill had broader ramifications for larger shifts in American state formation. Although the bill had few implications for administrative development, its popularity generated a reaction among members of the liberal reform faction of the Republican Party that was concerned about the American public's increasingly populist demands. Believing that the public was endorsing irrational economic policies, liberal reformers such as Charles Francis Adams Jr., head of the Massachusetts Railroad Commission, drafted legislation to create an independent regulatory commission despite opposition from Reagan and his supporters.

When Reagan's bill was altered to create an independent commission, the form of bureaucratic authority that John Sherman initially delegated to the Treasury Department was applied to the railroad industry. Although popular animus focused on railroads' use of price discrimination, namely, the practice of charging different shippers different prices based upon the distance goods were shipped, the ICC would use its discretion to make *exemptions* for railroads, thereby allowing them to continue to engage in price discrimination. This was done despite liberal reformers' recognition that the public opposed both the creation of a bureaucratic commission and the specific objective, granting railroads exemptions that allowed them to continue to engage in price discrimination, which the ICC used its discretion to accomplish.

Thus while Reagan shifted the locus of regulatory authority from the states to the federal government, Adams and liberal reformers shifted regulatory authority from Congress and the courts to an unelected commission, completing the state-building project Reagan had unintentionally begun. To explain how the collapse of the Compromise of 1877 influenced this process, we must examine why the Compromise of 1877 led Reagan to ally himself with the interests of Scott's railroad empire. It is only by establishing why Reagan sought to protect Scott's railroads that we can explain why Reagan's bill took the form that it did.

Recognizing that the outcome of the presidential election would depend upon the forces they could muster, Hayes and certain Republicans established a coalition of newspaper editors, public officials, and railroad executives to support his candidacy. Hayes enlisted Republican editors from the Western Associated Press, including Murat Halsted, proprietor of the Cincinnati *Commercial,* and Joseph Medill of the *Chicago Tribune,* as well as Ohio's former secretary of state William Henry Smith. Hayes also began contacting Senators John Sherman and James Garfield, General Henry Van Ness Boynton, and former treasury secretary Benjamin Bristow, who were allied with the reform wing of the Republican Party and were opposed by "Stalwarts," such as James G. Blaine and Roscoe Conkling.

Although vague threats were made by certain Northern Democrats to use armed militias to seat Tilden, Southerners were not anxious to resort to force, and certain Southern Democrats began maneuvering to secure the benefits the Republicans were offering.[18] Southern Democrats tempted by the compromise were led by Andrew J. Kellar, editor of the Memphis *Avalanche,* and were opposed by states-rights advocates, such as Isham G. Harris.[19]

The compromise that emerged had both political and economic components. One economic aspect of the Republican plan involved Hayes's endorsing federal subsidies to extend Scott's Texas and Pacific Railroad into Southern Democrats' districts. Scott, who was also president of the Pennsylvania Railroad, was working with Grenville Dodge, former Union general, former congressman, ex-president of the Union Pacific, and close Grant associate, but he was facing serious challenges from competing railroads.[20]

Powerful competitors were challenging both the Texas and Pacific Railroad and the Pennsylvania Railroad. In the West, the Texas and Pacific was engaged in a long-standing conflict with Collis P. Huntington's Central Pacific and Southern Pacific Railroads, which were allied with Jay Gould and Sidney Dillon's Union Pacific Railroad.[21] Huntington and Scott were struggling over control of transcontinental lines from California to the South, as the creation of a competing railroad route could undermine Huntington's monopoly over railroad lines to the West Coast.[22]

Huntington hoped the Central Pacific would secure "a handsome business in both passengers and freight" by constructing a second transcontinental route from San Diego to Fort Yuma, Colorado.[23] Huntington was warned by one of his correspondents, however, that the "strong competition for the freight business from New York to points in New Mexico and Arizona by the different railroads extending into Southern Colorado" made it critical for the Central Pacific reach the Colorado River in order to "turn the business to our line."[24]

In addition to competition from Huntington, in the East Scott's Pennsylvania Railroad was often embroiled in conflicts with the Erie and New York Central Railroads over cartel agreements with Standard Oil.[25] These railroads were fighting for control over shipping oil from the "oil region" in northwest Pennsylvania, to refineries in New York, Philadelphia, Cleveland, and Pittsburgh.[26] The oil region was the center of American oil extraction, and transporting costs to refining centers was a critical component of American oil producers' competitiveness.

Scott and the Pennsylvania Railroad had been embroiled in conflicts with railroads like the Atlantic and Great Western Railroad ever since the oil region became the center of American oil production.[27] As Standard Oil emerged and consolidated its power over the American oil industry, the railroads shipping Standard Oil's crude from the oil region to refineries along the East Coast began competing for Standard Oil's business.

Competition among the railroads led to price wars, as each railroad attempted to offer competitive rates to gain a greater share of Standard Oil's crude. These price wars led Scott to try to limit competition among the railroads by creating the South Improvement Company, a railroad cartel consisting of the Erie, New York Central, and Pennsylvania railroads, which set prices and freight volumes to prevent rate wars and establish advantageous shipping prices for the railroads.

While the prices set by the South Improvement Company were higher than those that would have prevailed under unrestricted competition, Standard Oil was willing to pay high shipping costs so long as the railroad cartel charged competing oil producers rates higher than those they charged Standard Oil.[28] Imposition of high transportation prices on competing oil producers was a central component of Standard Oil's strategy for controlling the oil industry, as raising rivals' shipping costs granted Standard Oil a competitive edge relative to independent oil producers.

Given the volume of oil Standard Oil shipped via the Erie and the New York Central, and Standard Oil's provision of the specialized tank cars these railroads used to transport its oil, John D. Rockefeller maintained cordial relationships with both of these railroads.[29] Yet Rockefeller did not maintain a cordial relationship with Scott, because the specific route the Pennsylvania Railroad took through Pennsylvania gave the Pennsylvania Railroad incentives to violate Standard Oil's cartel agreements and ship oil from independent oil producers.

Facing Huntington's Central Pacific and Southern Pacific railroads in the West and Standard Oil and the Erie and New York Central railroads in the East, Scott found himself facing powerful, and hostile, alliances. When the contested election of 1876 presented Scott with an opportunity to advance his interests, he mobilized his formidable lobbying apparatus to try to use the contested election to aid his railroads. By using federal subsidies to help finance construction to connect the Texas and Pacific's lines in Texas to the

Pennsylvania Railroad's Eastern lines through St. Louis, and to complete the Texas and Pacific's line east from Texas to meet the Central Pacific's line that was being built east toward Texas, Scott hoped the contested election could help him create a transcontinental route that would compete with Huntington's Central Pacific.

Scott's political leverage, however, was not derived from his economic power. Nor were the Republicans sympathetic to Scott for any abstract reasons regarding notions of economic development or from any desire to strengthen the American state. Scott's railroad empire was actually weak in comparison with Huntington's railroads and was near financial collapse. Instead of being derived from his economic power, the political influence Scott wielded was derived from the location of his railroad lines, and the resulting benefits he could offer Southern representatives and the Republicans who wanted to influence them. Since the Texas and Pacific's lines extended across Texas, Scott's railroad was useful to Republicans looking for ways to splinter certain Southern Democrats.

Recognizing that the Texas and Pacific could be used for their political purposes, Republicans began indicating they would endorse subsidies extending the Texas and Pacific into Southern representatives' districts if the electoral commission were allowed to count the contested electoral ballots for Hayes. By January of 1877, certain Republican newspapers reported that some Democrats had begun to "talk a great deal about a 'compromise' of the Presidential question."[30] As Scott and Huntington struggled over Western railroad routes, the electoral commission began counting the contested ballots for Hayes. On February 18, 1877, outraged House Democrats met to discuss the commission's counting of the electoral ballots.

At this meeting, certain Democrats, including Texas representative John Reagan, began shifting their positions on the electoral controversy. Reagan had previously opposed any effort to declare Hayes president and had accused the Republican-controlled Louisiana returning boards that had counted their ballots for Hayes of committing "fraudulent and illegal acts."[31] Yet during the February 18 caucus Reagan began demanding the electoral ballots be counted "without dilatory opposition."[32] As this would make Hayes president, Reagan was endorsing Hayes's bid for the presidency.

Reagan's reversal was a consequence of the Republicans' bargain with the Texas and Pacific Railroad. Hayes and other Republicans were supporting federal subsidies for it in exchange for Southern Democrats' acquiescence in the electoral commission's counting of the electoral ballots, overtures that were particularly appealing for Reagan given his district's proximity to the Texas and Pacific's proposed transcontinental route.

Reagan had struggled for years to bring railroads to his congressional district. His hometown of Palestine lay at the junction of the International, Huston, and Great Northern railroads, which connected to the Texas and Pacific lines in Marshall. Reagan's support for securing charters for the International Railroad and the Huston and Great Northern Railroad had led to accusations during his 1874 Senate candidacy of his being a "prominent lobbyist and lawyer for railroad rings."[33] Although Reagan would become closely associated with railroad regulation, instead of being a consistent opponent of the railroads, it has been noted that before he introduced his regulatory bill Reagan was "paradoxically" seen by some as "a foe and some as a friend" of the railroads.[34]

Reagan sought aid for the Texas and Pacific because the parallelogram of the Texas and Pacific's lines connecting Fort Worth, Sherman, Marshall, and Texarkana, constituting "the best railway property in the state of Texas," would have connected Reagan's district to a transcontinental route.[35] If Scott could connect the Texas and Pacific's lines to St. Louis via Vinita, the Pennsylvania Railroad would be connected with the Texas and Pacific, establishing a transcontinental route running through Reagan's district.[36] If the International and Great Northern railroads could be connected to a transcontinental route, the port of Galveston would have access to shipping to both coasts, further stimulating the economy both of Reagan's district and of Texas more generally.[37]

In January 1877, Reagan received a letter from Guy Bryan, Hayes's Kenyon College friend and Texas confidant, assuring him: "I trust that you will get a branch from the Pacific road to our coast, if not, then lop off all branches, and place all intersecting or connecting roads on an equality, with prorating privileges."[38] Despite many Democrats' concerns that the Republicans had outmaneuvered them and controlled a majority of the electoral commission, Bryan told Reagan: "'The Commission' if it settles the impending crisis successfully may be well," as, given the circumstances they faced, Bryan believed it was "the best that could be done."[39] Congratulating Reagan on his efforts to aid his congressional district, Bryan wrote to Reagan: "[You have] won confidence of good men by your fidelity to the interests of Texas by your efforts to improve the coast of Texas."[40]

By May 1877 Huntington's correspondents warned him: "[We have learned] *confidentially* that President Hayes will favor subsidizing a Southern Pacific Rail Road," indicating "the fight promises to be active again."[41] Charles Crocker told Huntington it was essential to "build the Southern Pacific without any connection with St. Louis, or the Pennsylvania Railroad," because Scott was attempting to link the Texas and Pacific to the Pennsylvania's lines in St. Louis.[42] As the *Galveston Daily News* recognized, Huntington's line would not "operate for the benefit of the Pennsylvania road," making it critical for Huntington to prevent Scott from completing his rival transcontinental route.[43]

When reform-oriented Republicans heard rumors of Hayes's overtures, however, they were outraged. Carl Schurz urged Hayes to drop all reference to the "rather dangerous policy" of endorsing Southern internal improvements.[44] Hayes assured Schurz: "[Your opinion] impresses me very strongly," and he admitted that in his "anxiety to do something to promote the . . . South," he may have gone "too far."[45] Hayes told Schurz he had made "no 'overtures'" to the Democrats, and when accused of using railroad subsidies to support his candidacy, said to him: "Nothing will come of it," specifically because "the influence referred to," meaning the Texas and Pacific lobby, "is too small to control the large House majority."[46]

It was apparent to various Democrats and some reform-oriented Republicans that certain promises were being made to appeal to certain Southern Democrats. It is also clear, however, that the precise nature of these promises remains ambiguous. Certain Southern Democrats believed that they would receive railroad subsidies, but it remains unclear what Hayes's precise level of involvement was in the quid pro quo constituting the Compromise of 1877, and what specific guarantees were offered to Southern Democrats.

Although his inaugural address eliminated all reference to "internal improvements of a national character," Hayes seemed to endorse federal subsidization of Southern economic development when he stated: "[The South] needs and deserves the considerate care of the national government,"[47] leading Southern newspapers to lament the Democrats' paralyzing sectional divisions.[48]

Although a bargain had been struck between certain Republicans, the Texas and Pacific Railroad, and certain Southern Democrats, information about what this bargain involved was simply not being conveyed to the American public. While a president had been selected, few outside Washington understood how this had occurred. As politicians with knowledge of what happened complained that the truth was being "buried in dusty darkness," voters who didn't understand that the election had been settled, in part, by the promise of federal railroad subsidies were mistakenly concluding that the election involved "no cheat, or swindle, or fraud or double-dealing."[49] Recognizing that few understood what had occurred, both Henry Watterson and Abram Hewitt remarked: "The whole truth underlying the determinate incidents which led to the rejection of Tilden and the seating of Hayes will never be known."[50]

Those who understood what the compromise had required, such as Boynton, observed: "The real force at work here is small," and given the nature of the "work" they had performed, clearly their actions "can not be done before all eyes."[51] Although many Republicans were publicly claiming that Hayes had been lawfully elected, privately some admitted it was "an outrage . . . to put on Hayes" as president, yet they couldn't help but marvel at "what a piece of history it is too."[52] This particular "piece of history" involved a series of implied quid pro quos that were not entirely clear even to the elites who were being influenced by the bargains constituting the Compromise of 1877.

Although it is unlikely that Hayes ever fully understood what had happened, largely by his own unwillingness to directly involve himself in the compromise, Tilden's outmaneuvered Democratic allies complained: "Our leaders who led us into . . . [this] trap, shall insist, and boast of it as most exalted prudence, wisdom, and patriotism."[53] Certain newspapers had their suspicions, and the losing side of the conflict often made allusion to the corrupt powers Hayes and the Republicans had marshaled. Yet even had someone understood the calculations involved in the compromise, these calculations were so complicated that it was impossible to explain them to the public. It would take years of effort by one of America's most gifted historians to reconstruct the sequence of events that led to Hayes's inauguration.

It is tempting to see Hayes's actions as merely another "corrupt bargain" executed by an unscrupulous politician and devoid of democratic legitimacy. Yet it is not entirely clear that Hayes or the Republicans could have pursued any other course of action, and they were hardly alone in their extra-electoral machinations. As vague promises regarding railroad subsidies were being used to split the Southern Democrats, Tilden was resorting to simpler overtures. After the election was settled, it was revealed that Tilden's nephew, William T. Pelton, had promised direct payments of $80,000 and $20,000 to the South Carolina and Florida election boards.[54] The promises made by both candidates, and the forces they were willing to turn to, indicate that both candidates were resorting to methods of influence that they had repudiated during the election campaign.

Aside from making Hayes president, the Compromise of 1877 would influence railroad regulation, and hence broader shifts in American political development, in ways that are poorly understood. Although the compromise involved promises of railroad subsidies to Southern congressional districts, once Hayes became president the railroad subsidies that Republicans had promised never materialized. This caused Reagan to introduce legislation that would have aided Scott's railroads and penalized his competitors. The legislation Reagan introduced would lead to the creation of the ICC, America's first independent regulatory commission, transmitting the bureaucratic form of authority that had been adopted by the Treasury Department into another realm of American economic life.

To explain how this occurred, we need to explain how the collapse of the Compromise of 1877 tied Reagan to Scott's interests, and how Scott's conflicts with Standard Oil and the railroads composing its transportation cartel, provided the proximate cause for the introduction of Reagan's regulatory bill.

Although Hayes's alliance with Southern Democrats helped him secure the presidency, once Hayes was president he withdrew his support for subsidizing the Texas and Pacific, dashing Reagan's hopes of connecting his congressional district to a transcontinental railroad.[55] Hayes's refusal to honor the Compromise of 1877 was influenced by the failure of Southern Democrats to organize the House as they had promised, and by certain actions taken by the Central Pacific Railroad.

Collis Huntington had realized that federal subsidies would allow Scott to connect the Texas and Pacific's line from El Paso in West Texas to the parallelogram of roads connecting Fort Worth, Sherman, Marshall, and Texarkana, completing a route that would "prove a powerful competitor" to the Central and Southern Pacific railroads.[56]

Recognizing that Scott was threatening his monopoly over eastbound traffic, Huntington illegally extended his line east to Fort Yuma, bridged the Colorado River into Arizona, and then stopped all further construction.[57] Texas was not connected to this railroad line, and Huntington had no intention of extending his railroads farther east. Huntington had expanded his railroad into Southern California to prevent competing roads from drawing shipping business away from the ports he controlled in San Francisco, and completion of his Fort Yuma line ensured that there would be "no rapid construction" across Arizona to link Texas to California.[58]

Huntington had removed the principal justification for Scott's subsidy, and Hayes's reaction was to simply take no steps to deliver federal assistance to the Texas and Pacific Railroad. Realizing that Huntington was rendering his railroad irrelevant, Scott unsuccessfully tried to use Grenville Dodges's associate, Secretary of War George W. McCrary, to prevent completion of the Southern Pacific's line. Yet by December 1877 the compromise was collapsing, and despite placing Hayes in the presidency, the Southern Democrats' plan to deliver railroad developments for their districts "bore no fruit."[59]

As the Compromise of 1877 unraveled, Scott's allies complained: "[We are] losing any hope that we can be in hearty accord with the present administration."[60] In September 1877 the *Commercial and Financial Chronicle* reported that the Texas and Pacific was about to forfeit "immense" land grants in West Texas due to its failure to connect Fort Worth to Weatherford as stipulated by its charter, and in March 1878 the Texas and Pacific failed to sell bonds necessary to finance its line west from Fort Worth.[61] The situation was particularly dire because the Texas and Pacific's charter required it to connect Marshall, Texas, to the Southern Pacific's line at Fort Yuma or forfeit its land grants to the Southern Pacific.[62]

In January 1878, Congress voted against subsidizing Scott's railroads, a decision that the *Railroad Gazette* reported was a "death-blow to all hopes of a vote of Government aid, direct or indirect, to the Texas & Pacific."[63] Aside from damaging Scott's railroad, the collapse of the compromise was devastating for the Southern Democrats who had helped make Hayes president. Southern Democrats allied with Boynton, Smith, and Kellar "felt . . . outraged" at the turn of events.[64] Boynton complained that he simply "did not know what to say" and threatened to reveal Hayes's knowledge of the quid pro quo.[65] Boynton was restrained only after Bristow questioned whether it would be "a violation of propriety to speak of the matter publicly."[66]

While the Texas and Pacific struggled against Huntington's roads in the West, Scott's Pennsylvania Railroad was suddenly confronted with dire problems from Standard Oil, and the railroad comprising Standard Oil's railroad cartel, in the East. After consulting with Pennsylvania's independent oil producers, Scott allied the Pennsylvania Railroad with the Empire Transportation Company, a railroad company whose expansion into the oil refining business brought it into conflict with Standard Oil. As the Empire Transportation Company began expanding beyond railroads and into refining crude oil, this was seen as an attack on Standard Oil, and in August of 1877 the Pennsylvania Railroad began a price war with the Erie and New York Central railroads.

Scott had been involved with Standard Oil's railroad cartel agreements since 1871, when he created the South Improvement Company, a railroad cartel designed to stabilize railroad rates among the railroads shipping Standard Oil's petroleum.[67] Scott hoped the South Improvement Company could be used as an enforcement mechanism for the railroad cartel that was shipping Standard Oil's oil. By allocating a fixed volume of oil to the various railroads shipping

Standard Oil's crude, the South Improvement Company sought to create an enforcement mechanism to prevent rate wars and violations of cartel agreements. Popular outrage at the cartel, however, forced the South Improvement Company to be disbanded in 1872.

Shortly afterward, Standard Oil recognized that it could control the oil refining business by using the railroads to raise the transportation prices that the railroads charged competing oil refiners. Standard Oil ensured that the railroads would impose higher prices on competing oil refiners by paying them relatively high prices for transporting their oil, and extracting both rebates and drawbacks on oil the railroads carried from competing oil producers. For all these reasons, Standard Oil's business was highly profitable for the railroads.

While Standard Oil used the railroads to raise their rivals' shipping costs, it was also trying to "move shipments away from the Pennsylvania Railroad" to prevent Scott from shipping the oil of Pennsylvania's independent producers.[68] Standard Oil believed that there were greater advantages to establishing a cartel between the Erie and New York Central railroads that forced them to charge competing oil producers higher transportation rates than to instigating a price war with the Pennsylvania Railroad.[69]

Since nearly two-thirds of the Pennsylvania's traffic involved shipping Standard Oil's petroleum, there were "significant tensions" between the railroads that made up Standard Oil's transportation cartel, and between the railroads and Standard Oil. The railroad that "most frequently" broke the cartel agreements was the Pennsylvania Railroad, and the "most dramatic" breakdown of the cartel occurred during what became known as the Empire Rate War in 1876–1877.[70]

The conflict between the Pennsylvania Railroad and Standard Oil came at a particularly difficult time for Scott's railroad empire. As Huntington's railroads were undermining Scott's Texas and Pacific in the West, in July 1877 railroad strikes spread from the B & O Railroad in West Virginia to the Pennsylvania Railroad in Pittsburgh, forcing Scott to ask Hayes to use the U.S. Army to put down the strike.[71] As the Great Railroad Strike of 1877 festered, in August 1877 Scott allied himself with the Empire Transportation Company and Pennsylvania's independent oil producers in a bid to challenge Standard Oil's control of oil markets.[72] Scott "generally feared" Rockefeller and hoped his alliance with Pennsylvania's independent oil producers would be able to replace the oil that he had previously shipped for Standard Oil.[73]

By March 1877 Standard Oil recognized that the Empire Transportation Company and the Pennsylvania Railroad were threatening its control of oil refining and retaliated by shutting down refining operations in Philadelphia and Pittsburgh and completely stopping oil shipments on the Pennsylvania Railroad. Scott responded by cutting his rates, initiating a price war with the Erie and New York Central railroads, and soliciting oil shipments from Pennsylvania's independent oil producers.[74]

Scott's conflict with Standard Oil proved disastrous for the Pennsylvania Railroad. Pennsylvania's independent producers were unable to match the volume of oil the Pennsylvania Railroad had shipped for Standard Oil, and Scott incurred such "drastic losses" that he was compelled to rejoin the Standard Oil cartel.[75] In October 1877 Standard Oil forced the Pennsylvania Railroad to purchase the Empire Transportation Company, and acquired the Empire Transportation Company's pipelines, which could be used to avoid oil producers' reliance upon the railroads for shipping their products.

Standard Oil's victory over Scott shifted the balance of power among Standard Oil and the railroads composing its transportation cartel. Now instead of relying on a third party, such as the South Improvement Company, to regulate the allocation of traffic among the railroads, Standard Oil had established "itself as a policer of railroad rates."[76] By controlling the pipelines and railroads that shipped oil from the oil region, Standard Oil could dictate the volume and price of oil shipped on the railroads in its cartel. This left the railroads without any means of determining the volume of oil being carried, or prices being charged, by the other members of the railroad cartel, essentially preventing the railroads from access to the information they needed to determine the volume of crude oil Standard Oil was shipping on each railroad.

Having acquired this power, Standard Oil renegotiated its cartel agreement with the railroads, granting the Pennsylvania 47 percent of its oil shipments, the Erie and New York Central each 21 percent, and the B & O 11 percent. Standard Oil was granted its 10 percent rebate, guaranteeing that it would receive lower rates than its competitors.[77] Unfortunately for the railroads, these agreements were difficult to verify. Standard Oil frequently established shipping agreements that were never committed to paper, and since Standard Oil was policing the cartel, the railroads lacked any means of determining whether Standard Oil was abiding by their agreements.

By May 1878, the Pennsylvania Railroad realized that the Erie and New York Central were granting Standard Oil secret rebates, violating the terms of the cartel and forcing the Pennsylvania to reduce its rates. When Scott realized that the price reductions had not been made in consultation with the Pennsylvania Railroad, it became apparent that Standard Oil would negotiate secret rebates and drawbacks to undermine the Pennsylvania Railroad.

Scott had been outmaneuvered by Huntington, devastated by Standard Oil, and double-crossed by Hayes. With Huntington's Washington lobbyists gleefully reporting that Scott was "evidently alarmed" at the turn of events, Scott was clearly not dictating railroad policy from a position of strength.[78] Reportedly being "quite discouraged" by the prospects of further competition with Huntington and Standard Oil, Scott arrived in Washington on May 5, 1878, to try to muster congressional support for his roads.[79]

Scott sought several measures that would impose costs on his competitors. One measure introduced by Scott's allies, the Thurman bill, required the Union Pacific and Central Pacific railroads to allocate 25 percent of their profits to pay the interest on their government loans, leaving Huntington complaining that Scott sought to "derive advantage from an undesired collision" between the government and the Central Pacific Railroad.[80] The Thurman bill, however, was not the only measure introduced to aid Scott's roads, nor was Thurman the only legislator working at Scott's behest. One of the House Democrats working for Scott was John Reagan, whose interest in the Texas and Pacific was a result of the collapse of the Compromise of 1877.

Reagan had gambled that he could counteract his constituents' outrage for supporting Hayes by securing access to a transcontinental railroad. When the electoral commission declared the contested ballots for Hayes, Texans had expressed "great indignation," and the outcome was regarded as the "chief topic of discussion."[81] Yet when the compromise collapsed and Hayes refused to support federal subsidies for the Texas and Pacific, Reagan was left "under heavy fire" from constituents outraged by his apostasy, and he had no railroad to claim credit for.[82]

The collapse of the compromise provided the underlying condition that made Reagan sensitive to Scott's interests. Had Hayes supported federal subsidies to the Texas and Pacific, Reagan would have received his railroad and would have had no reason to introduce legislation to aid Scott. Yet once the compromise collapsed, the proximate cause for the introduction of Reagan's bill was the price war between the Pennsylvania Railroad, Standard Oil, and the Erie and New York Central railroads. A month and a half after the Pennsylvania Railroad lost the Empire Rate War and capitulated to Standard Oil, Reagan announced his intention to introduce a bill to regulate interstate commerce. The two events were closely linked, as Reagan's bill would have had beneficial effects for Scott's railroads.

On May 2, Reagan introduced his bill, denied that it intended pro rata regulation of rates, and asked that it be printed and distributed to members of Congress.[83] Scott arrived in Washington on May 5, and three days later Congress began debating the Reagan bill (H.R. 3547).[84] Reagan's bill outlawed rate discrimination on the basis of the distance traveled, forbade pooling, outlawed rebates to shippers, and placed enforcement authority in the judiciary, not a commission.[85] Critically, all of the Reagan bill's stipulations were only applicable to interstate trade.

It is important to remember that Standard Oil's business was highly profitable for the railroads. Despite demanding rebates and drawback, Standard Oil paid above-market rates to the railroads shipping its oil, provided the railroads with costly shipping containers which it insured, and guaranteed the railroads oil shipments at fixed prices regardless of business conditions or the price of oil. Standard Oil was willing to bear these costs because doing so ensured that the railroads imposed higher shipping costs on Standard Oil's competitors, thereby granting Standard Oil a competitive edge in the oil industry.

The profitability of Standard Oil's business for the railroads, the railroads' attempts to secure business from Standard Oil, and Scott's failed attempt to break Standard Oil's transportation cartel were critical for the timing and content of Reagan's bill. Specifically, since the bill applied only to interstate trade, it would have redirected Standard Oil's shipping away from the Erie and the New York Central and toward the Pennsylvania Railroad because the Pennsylvania Railroad did not cross state lines when shipping oil from the oil region to refining centers in Pittsburgh and Philadelphia (see figure 2).

The Pennsylvania Railroad was unique among the railroads serving the oil region because it shipped oil from the region to Philadelphia and Pittsburgh, a shipping corridor that did not cross state lines.[86] The critical difference between the Pennsylvania Railroad and the other railroads competing for Standard Oil's business in the oil region was that the Pennsylvania Railroad's shipping route did not cross state lines. Since the Erie and New York Central railroads had to cross state lines when transporting oil from the oil region to refineries in New York and Cleveland, the Reagan bill would have made the Pennsylvania Railroad the only railroad that could give rebates to Standard Oil. Given the profitability of Standard Oil's business for the railroads, this would have granted Scott a powerful advantage over competing railroads, effectively forcing Standard Oil's business onto Scott's Pennsylvania Railroad.

Recognizing that the Reagan bill would injure the Pennsylvania Railroad's competitors, Charles Sherrill, the Central Pacific's Washington lobbyist, complained to Huntington that the bill was "a put up job."[87] Huntington's correspondents complained: "*Scott* has every old political played *Bum* of the South

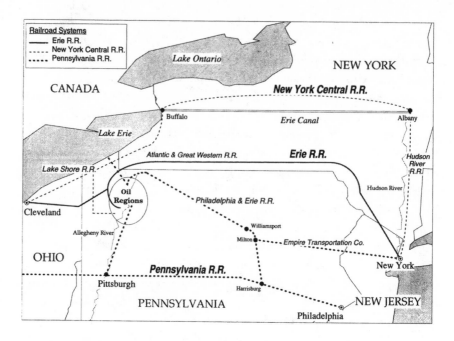

Figure 2. Map of the Pennsylvania Railroad and the oil region. (Elizabeth Granitz and Benjamin Klein, "Monopolization by 'Raising Rivals' Costs': The Standard Oil Case," *Journal of Law and Economics* 39, no. 1 (1996): 4, figure 1. Published by the University of Chicago Press.)

in his employ here."[88] Given the importance of the rebate system for its business it was hardly surprising that Standard Oil opposed Reagan's measure. Standard Oil's treasurer complained to Rockefeller that even some of Ohio's representatives "vote and work for this Regan [*sic*] Bill," indicating that Standard Oil was "without representation . . . in Washington."[89] Since the Reagan bill would have undermined Standard Oil's control over its railroad cartel, Standard Oil had clear reasons to oppose the measure.

Recognizing that the Reagan bill would drive Standard Oil's business away from its lines, George Blanchard, vice president of the Erie Railroad, complained that the Pennsylvania Railroad would be "exempt from the operations of this law."[90] Since the Pennsylvania Railroad did not cross state lines when shipping Standard Oil's oil, Blanchard pointed out, the Reagan bill "would not touch that railway" and would grant the Pennsylvania an advantage relative to the Erie and New York Central railroads.[91] Clearly Standard Oil, the

Central Pacific, Union Pacific, and New York Central railroads were not behind the "put up job" that Sherrill denounced.[92]

It was precisely for this reason that the Pennsylvania Railroad suddenly
found itself allied with the Pennsylvania Independent Oil Producers Union.
The Pennsylvania Independent Oil Producers Union recognized that the
Pennsylvania Railroad was "not averse to abandoning the rebate system, if
by so doing it [could] obtain greater or even an equal share of the business of
carrying petroleum."[93] Since the Pennsylvania Railroad was now supporting
an antirebate measure, the Pennsylvania Independent Oil Producers Union
recommended: "All appearance of special hostility to the railroads should be
avoided and it should be the effort to protect their true interests, and *particularly* those of the P[ennsylvania] R[ailroad]."[94]

It is not surprising that Reagan used previous legislation drafted by Pennsylvania independent oil producers as a model for his bill. His use of this legislation was not due to his concern for Pennsylvania's independent oil producers;
he had no reason for caring about this industry any more than he did any
other industries that were outside his district. Reagan's sympathy with Pennsylvania's independent oil producers was due to their sudden alliance with the
Pennsylvania Railroad to oppose Standard Oil and its railroad cartel, and the
fact that the legislation they had previously introduced had also been used to
combat Standard Oil.[95]

It is no coincidence that the earlier regulatory measures championed by
Pennsylvania representative John Hopkins had been influenced by the Reading Railroad's legal council to aid the Reading against Standard Oil. Hopkins
had faced opposition to his bill because the Interstate Commerce Committee
had included Standard Oil allies and an ineffective chairman.[96] After Reagan
was appointed chairman of the Interstate Commerce Committee, efforts to
penalize Standard Oil's railroad cartel were given new life because he was not
allied with Standard Oil.

While the Pennsylvania Railroad's attempts to break Standard Oil's transportation cartel explains the Reagan bill's antirebate clause, both the Texas and
Pacific Railroad and the Pennsylvania Railroad opposed price discrimination
as well. Scott's efforts to stabilize rate structures for railroads shipping oil from
the oil region led him to create the South Improvement Company in 1871, and
officers of the Texas and Pacific had clearly endorsed congressional regulation
of rates.[97]

Frank Bond, vice president of the Texas and Pacific, had written to the Senate Committee on Railroads in 1876 and pointed out that while the Central

Pacific and Southern Pacific railroads opposed rate regulation, the Texas and Pacific endorsed placing its "rates . . . under the control of Congress," as the Texas and Pacific would operate "open to all, upon equal terms, without discrimination against individuals, or localities."[98] Continuing with this line of argument, in January 1878 John Brown, vice president of the Texas and Pacific, complained to the House Committee on Pacific Railroads of the "enormous exactions and unjust and outrageous discriminations" the Central Pacific extracted from shippers "because there [was] no competing line."[99]

Unlike the situation with the Central Pacific, whose rates were "free . . . from the wholesome control of the National Legislature," Brown endorsed placing the Texas and Pacific's "rates . . . under the direct supervision and control of Congress; so that the farmer, the merchant, the manufacturer, the Government itself shall be free from the extortion and the power to extort of the existing monopoly."[100] Quoting Leland Stanford, president of the Central Pacific, Brown noted Stanford's opposition to completion of the Texas and Pacific's line to the West. Stanford argued: "Had Tom Scott built his road to the Pacific, he would have taken from us our best prospective traffic, and carried it East. He would have reached over to *our* borders, and carried away *our* trade. *Our* system . . . *discriminates in favor of California,* as against the East, and in favor of San Francisco."[101] In the Senate, Texas and Pacific ally Stanley Matthews (D-OH) proposed altering the Texas and Pacific's charter to outlaw "unjust discrimination in charges for freight or passengers" by railways connecting with the Texas and Pacific.[102] Matthews's bill endorsed "in unequivocal terms" congressional regulation of the Texas and Pacific's rates to guarantee investors minimal rates of return on Texas and Pacific's bonds.[103] Yet not all railroads shared the Texas and Pacific's willingness to allow congressional regulation of their rates, and Huntington claimed that rate regulation "is not one for which large legislative bodies are well adapted."[104]

While the antipooling clause was intended to prevent Standard Oil from creating cartels to oppose the Pennsylvania Railroad, Scott's railroads shared Reagan's opposition to regulation by commission.[105] Indeed, Reagan consistently opposed efforts to create a regulatory commission or delegate discretionary authority to a commission to rule on the fairness of railroad rate structures. The creation of a regulatory bureaucracy was simply never part of Reagan's efforts. Rather than being introduced in response to public opinion, Reagan's bill had been introduced to aid Scott's failing railroad empire due to pressures unleashed by the collapse of the Compromise of 1877 and the Pennsylvania Railroad's conflict with Standard Oil.

While some suggest that Reagan introduced his bill to preempt radical agrarian third parties from challenging his congressional seat, the Texas Greenbackers' 1878 platform focused on financial issues and never mentioned railroad regulation.[106] Nor was the Grange threatening Reagan's seat.[107] By 1876 the Grange's dwindling strength was centered in West Texas, and Granger theoreticians, such as David Cloud, opposed centralizing regulatory authority in the federal government.[108]

Furthermore, Reagan's principal congressional *opponents* were Southern and Western representatives who complained that by banning price discrimination Reagan's bill was "hostile to . . . the great agricultural interests of the West."[109] These representatives believed that the long distances to Chicago and New York and the competition their constituents faced from farmers on the East Coast indicated that eliminating price discrimination would harm their constituents. Given such opposition, some have concluded that agrarian demands "scarcely figured in [Reagan's] thoughts" and have suggested that "little basis exists" for depicting Reagan as a champion of agrarian interests.[110]

Nor was Scott's interest in Reagan's bill entirely masked from legislative debate. Edward Bragg (R-WI) claimed that the Scott-controlled Pennsylvania state legislature had ordered Pennsylvania's congressmen to support Reagan's bill, and he complained it was unrealistic to expect "Tom Scott's legislature to instruct their Representatives in this House to vote for a bill that is hostile to its interests."[111] Bragg further noted: "It has been announced upon this floor that this bill originated in Pennsylvania; Pennsylvania comes here crying for protection; her iron must be protected; her steel must be protected; her manufactures must be protected; her oil wells must be protected, and Tom Scott must be protected against competition from the New York Central Railroad, the New York and Erie Railroad, and the Canada roads, whose competition compels him to reduce his rates of freightage."[112] Bragg claimed that he would express "no disagreement" with Reagan that the measure would aid Western railroads: "The railroads leading from the great business centers of the West are protected under this bill against all competition either between themselves or with any adverse interest."[113] Since prohibiting price discrimination would limit competition between railroads, Bragg complained: "[The Reagan bill] protects one [railroad] against the other; Garrett against Scott and Scott against Garrett, and the representatives of Vanderbilt against both."[114] Bragg opposed the bill because, he said, "I do not propose to put it in the power of these railroad corporations to unite and make a schedule of rates which the law will protect and to make then a law which will punish any one of the roads which violates that law by carrying at a less rate. And that is the purpose of the bill, and, such being its purpose, it is directly in hostility and antagonism to the interests I represent; and I desire those people whom I represent to know when I oppose this bill I do not oppose it because it is a restriction upon railroad corporations, but I oppose it because I regard it as a fraud and a deception upon the people and really in the interest of the railroad instead of adverse to it."[115]

Reagan's antidiscrimination clause drew opposition from groups that endorsed other aspects of the bill. For example, the *Railroad Gazette,* which Reagan noted was "not at all unfriendly to railroads," sought to outlaw rebates but rejected banning price discrimination.[116] While the *Railroad Gazette* noted that demands for a pro rata law had been voiced "from the country districts . . . for years," in the New York legislature such a demand "was not heard at this late session."[117]

Yet the Reagan bill was not a response to public opinion or popular outrage against the railroads. Although the railroads were typically the targets of antimonopoly invective, instead of seeing any surge in popular interest in railroad regulation, Joseph Cannon (R-IL) complained: "I do not find that this bill has been generally discussed anywhere, nor is it generally known throughout the country that it is pending."[118] If his bill were a response to popular antirailroad sentiment Reagan surely would have drawn attention to it in the campaigns of 1878. Yet when addressing his district's Democratic convention in July 1878 he endorsed free coinage of silver, repeal of the Specie Resumption Act, and improvement of Texas harbors and rivers but never mentioned railroad regulation.[119]

While some recognized that Reagan's bill would aid Scott's railroads and undermine his competitors, Reagan was simply not explaining the reason he introduced his bill. The specific calculations associated with the Compromise of 1877 were too complicated to explain, and it simply would not have made political sense for him to reveal that his bill was intended to aid certain railroads at the expense of other powerful economic groups. Nor did he have any interest in admitting that he had helped make Hayes president by betraying his party in an effort to secure railroad subsidies that never materialized. When Reagan subsequently began depicting his bill as part of his war against monopoly, it was rhetorically more powerful to claim he was representing agrarian antimonopoly sentiment and that public opinion demanded his bill.

In fact, even had Reagan wanted to explain his actions it would have been impossible. The fact that he was trying to extract economic concessions from the collapse of a secretive political bargain, and the complex way he hoped his bill would influence his district and various railroads, ensured that the real motives and objectives driving his actions could never be publically explained.

It is critical to recognize that there was nothing deliberately conspiratorial about Reagan's actions. Reagan was hardly in control of the forces he was trying to influence, and he was trying to deal with actions and events that were impossible to have foreseen. Much like William Ralston's unsuccessful efforts to manage the forces that eventually destroyed The Bank of California, Reagan was attempting to navigate conditions established by other actors' decisions. The nature of the forces confronting him, and his reactions to these forces, were simply too complex for him to explain.

Such complexity was then exacerbated by the different responses that the Reagan bill would have for various economic groups in different areas of the country. Since the bill would have general effects upon shippers and other areas of the economy, once it was introduced various business groups began taking positions on the measure and denouncing their opponents. The New York Board of Trade and Transportation met in April 1878, and Francis Thurber's Committee on Railroad Transportation endorsed Reagan's bill, but it called for enforcement by independent commission, while Chauncey Depew, representing the New York Central Railroad, opposed the commission's creation.[120] Reagan's opposition to the commission that the New York Board of Trade and Transportation endorsed indicated that he was not simply acting at its behest even though it endorsed parts of his bill.[121]

However, the fact that Reagan was acting to aid Scott's railroads does not demonstrate that, as Gabriel Kolko argues, the railroad industry "positively welcomed" or "always supported" regulation.[122] Powerful railroads were vocal opponents of the Reagan bill, and both the Erie Railroad and the New York Central Railroad criticized Reagan's bill because it would undermine their position in Standard Oil's cartel. Similarly the Union Pacific, Central Pacific, and Southern Pacific railroads opposed creating a rival transcontinental route whose rates would be "subject to the unlimited regulation of Congress."[123] Hardly endorsing rate regulation, Huntington claimed that rate regulation was "inappropriate," and instead called for determination of rates by "that incessant regulator" of modern economic life, market competition.[124]

Indeed, Jay Gould of the Union Pacific reported to Huntington: "[We are] doing all we can to defeat the Reagan bill and agree . . . that there should be a systematic organization of the leading roads to defeat the measure [and] we will gladly cooperate in such a movement."[125] Similarly, the Baltimore and

Ohio Railroad and "four or five different roads" composing the trunk lines between Chicago and New York hoped the Pacific railroads would organize congressional opposition to Reagan's bill.[126]

As the railroad issue was debated in Congress and in the press, all of the participants denounced their opponents as agents of the railroads.[127] In Texas the *Galveston Daily News* reported that the Reagan bill's passage was "doubtful" because powerful corporations "[would] combine to defeat it."[128] The *Galveston Daily News* claimed that Roscoe Conkling would "smother" the Reagan bill because, it wrote, he "serves the great corporations."[129] Similarly, Senator Richard Coke (D-TX), former Texas governor and Reagan's ally, claimed that the railroads opposed Reagan's bill from the outset, but others would argue that instead of opposing Reagan's bill certain railroads "desired the measure passed."[130] Given the sheer number of railroads, shippers, oil producers, and other corporate interests that would be influenced by the Reagan bill, it was impossible to convey the complexity of the interests and rival positions surrounding the railroad issue.

Apart from influencing different economic groups immediate interests, the Reagan bill embodied new assumptions regarding state authority. Clarkson Potter (D-NY), chairman of the Committee on Pacific Railroads, claimed the transfer of regulatory authority from the states to the federal government was "a novelty; it is an innovation."[131] Potter noted that once Congress acquired the power to regulate railroads, "it must have power to regulate business as conducted by any of them."[132] Potter worried that "beginning then, by regulating the tariff on railways," Congress would be drawn into "regulating the prices and profits of every citizen."[133] For once such authority was extended over the railroad system, other representatives worried it "may be extended to other transactions."[134] Potter was hardly alone in his predictions. Bragg complained: "The very moment we adopt the precedent that Congress can so interfere, we have done that which is calculated to promote a general centralization of power in the Federal Government; this will become not a Government of confederated States but a government representing a centralized power."[135] Potter noted that the introduction of such authority by Reagan, an ex-Confederate, "show[ed] how things [were] changing politically as well as otherwise."[136]

Indeed, the fact that an ex-Confederate Democrat was endorsing centralization of federal authority drew confused reactions from Radical Republicans, such as Bragg, who declared: "[I am] astonished to see gentlemen representing what was originally the old State rights party coming in here to father a bill which assumes on the part of Congress power to go into all the States and regulate the business of private corporations."[137] The *Cincinnati Commercial* complained that the Democrats could not "consistently" support Reagan's bill given their traditional ideological positions and opposition to federal authority.[138] Reagan's actions "puzzled his opponents" because it seemed so "strange" for an ex-Confederate to endorse centralization of federal regulatory authority.[139]

Yet Reagan's actions are not puzzling once we recognize that the collapse of the Compromise of 1877 and his concern with Scott's railroads were critical for the introduction of his bill. Initiated by a failing railroad tycoon and an out-maneuvered Texas politician, the Reagan bill was setting into motion forces that would lead to the creation of America's first independent regulatory commission. As Charles Francis Adams Jr. recognized, Congress was considering legislation "designed to greatly change the relation of the government" to the railroad industry.[140] Such predictions proved to be accurate. When Benjamin Butler (R-MA) began calling for Congress to investigate Standard Oil's rebate structure, infuriated Standard Oil officials claimed that exercising such authority was "preposterous" and demanded to know "what possible jurisdiction has Congress" to investigate their business dealings.[141]

This is not to suggest that the railroads had previously been unregulated, or that there was no administrative oversight of the railroad industry. However, the postbellum railroad regulatory debate was proposing that the federal government assume regulatory authority over the railroad industry, and an independent bureaucratic commission was subsequently empowered with regulatory authority. Prior to the ICC's creation the individual states had regulated the railroads. There was significant diversity, however, in the nature of state-level railroad regulation, ranging from restrictions on railroad charters to administrative regulation of rate schedules, and it was not clear which type of regulatory regime would be implemented at the federal level. Indeed, the ICC would be created by the collision of two different logics, one advanced by the agrarian supporters of Reagan's bill, the other by liberal reformers who sought to use a regulatory commission to regulate the railroad industry. The product of these antagonistic forces was the creation of an administrative commission that Reagan opposed and had never intended to create.

While poorly understood at the time, the Reagan bill was not simply an inevitable result of industrialization, nor was it merely a product of agrarian outrage toward the railroads. Certainly industrialization was a background condition for the political conflicts occurring during this period, and by the mid-1870s public opinion had shifted against the railroads and their pricing practices. However, economic forces and public opinion cannot explain the timing of the Reagan bill's introduction, and they cannot explain why the Reagan bill took the specific form that it did.

Hardly a response to public opinion, the Reagan bill was introduced in reaction to the collapse of the Compromise of 1877, the pressures facing Scott's railroad empire, and the electoral goals of an outmaneuvered ex-Confederate politician. Reagan's involvement in the Compromise of 1877, the collapse of the compromise, and his failure to secure federal aid for his district in exchange for supporting Hayes led to the introduction of Reagan's bill. Had the Compromise of 1877 been fulfilled, Reagan would have received his railroad to the West, eliminating any reason for him to introduce legislation to aid Scott's railroads, and perhaps leaving him to focus on popular issues associated with improving Galveston's harbor or the free coinage of silver.[142]

This is not to draw too close a distinction between the forces unleashed by the collapse of the Compromise of 1877 and Reagan's electoral interests. Populist economic groups endorsed many of components of the Reagan bill, indicating that Reagan was not acting *against* his electoral interests. However, public opinion cannot explain why Reagan chose to adopt railroad regulation when he did, nor can it explain why the Reagan bill took the specific form that it did.

Given the complexity and secrecy surrounding the Compromise of 1877, the interests promoting the Reagan bill were as poorly understood as the forces that placed Hayes in the presidency. Instead of recognizing the complexity of the railroad industry, observed the *Railroad Gazette,* "the popular suspicion of railroad combination and consolidation is due to a misapprehension . . . of what actually does happen" in the industry.[143] Complaining that the public did not understand the railroad issue, Carl Schurz noted in 1879: "[My] hopes are not great" for the passage of "intelligent legislation . . . during the present session."[144] One of Schurz's correspondents suggested that the public's incomprehension extended beyond the railroad issue, for "masses of the people" exhibited an "utter lack of information on almost . . . every . . . public question relating to the conduct of the Government."[145]

While popular hostility toward the railroads was hardly new, popular opposition to the railroads indicates that even if Reagan had never adopted railroad regulation other legislators would have. Yet this does not mean that Reagan's actions were inconsequential. His adoption of railroad regulation was particularly important because Reagan was chairman of the Interstate Commerce

Committee, and, as Thomas Gilligan, William Marshall, and Barry Weingast note, played "the major role" in organizing support for his bill and influence regulatory legislation.[146]

However, the unique methods of railroad regulation proposed by the Reagan bill were also consequential. Indeed, several different regulatory methods had been proposed and introduced at the state and federal levels. For example, the 1874 Windom Report focused on how to lower transportation prices and recommended several methods for improving the American railroad industry. However, the Windom Report did not endorse *regulating* railroad rate structures to secure lower transportation prices but instead stated that it was "unanimously of the opinion" that cheap transportation should be secured "through *competition* . . . rather than by direct congressional regulation of existing lines."[147] Although Reagan also sought to enhance railroad competition, the Windom Report sought to accomplish this objective by using federally and state-owned canals and railroads to compete with private railroads to lower rates. As American railroad rates declined during the 1870s and 1880s, calls for government ownership of transportation that had been justified by high shipping prices would have provided an inadequate basis for regulatory efforts in the late 1870s.[148]

Furthermore, while the Windom Report endorsed government ownership of railroad lines, Reagan's bill called for congressional prohibition of price discrimination, outlawing rebating and pooling. This indicates that while the idea of regulating the railroads was not novel, Reagan was proposing regulatory methods that diverged from previous legislation. In short, there were diverse ways to regulate the railroads, as various methods, ranging from government ownership and operation, legislative prohibition of price discrimination, to commissions that determined the maximum rates railroads could charge, had been proposed at both the state and federal levels.[149] This indicates that there was nothing inevitable about the specific type of regulation Reagan proposed, a method that became especially consequential when it spurned liberal reformers to endorse creating a bureaucratic commission to blunt the implications of the Reagan bill.

Liberal reformers' efforts culminated with efforts to introduce a bureaucratic commission in legislation proposed as an alternative to the Reagan bill, an innovation that occurred despite Reagan's opposition to creating a commission. However, the particular way the Reagan bill spurned alternative legislation calling for the creation of a commission was critical for the timing of American state formation. The liberal reformers who endorsed a bureaucratic commission would not have been able to generate support for this regulatory method unless their proposal were introduced in response to a measure that, for all the misunderstanding surrounding it, became popular.

Despite his efforts, Reagan's attempts to prevent price discrimination through legislative prohibition would culminate in the creation of an institution he actively opposed: an independent commission armed with discretionary authority to determine the reasonableness of railroad rates. In the face of Reagan's opposition, this institutional innovation was introduced by the liberal reform faction of the Republican Party and was deeply influenced by the thinking of liberal reformer and railroad expert, Charles Francis Adams Jr.

Although Reagan shifted the locus of regulatory authority from the states to the federal government, he always insisted his bill left "no room" for creating a commission.[150] Such reluctance is not difficult to explain. Hardly introduced because Reagan endorsed administrative governance, his bill was a poorly understood short-term reaction to the collapse of the Compromise of 1877 and the difficulties facing Scott's railroads. Although his electoral interests led him to champion his regulatory bill after the forces surrounding the compromise collapsed, Reagan never intended to expand the state's *bureaucratic* authority.

Reagan's opposition to a commission poses a second series of questions for understanding how the railroad issue stimulated American state formation. For when the Interstate Commerce Act was finally passed in 1887, Congress did not pass Reagan's bill into law but instead created an independent commission to regulate the railroads and determine the reasonableness of their rates. The creation of an independent commission indicates that the forces that led Reagan to introduce and champion railroad regulation were not responsible for the administrative innovation that the railroad issue eventually generated.

To explain why a bureaucratic commission was created requires analyzing how certain liberal reformers reacted to the popularity of Reagan's bill, and how they sought to use a commission to improve the rationality of regulatory decisions while simultaneously seeking to inform public opinion. Two different logics governed the introduction of Reagan's bill and the subsequent efforts to create a bureaucratic commission. It took the liberal reform faction of the Republican Party and the efforts of railroad specialist and commissioner of the Massachusetts Railroad Commission, Charles Francis Adams Jr. to call for creating a commission as an alternative to the congressional oversight of the railroads that was proposed by Reagan's bill. Delegation of authority to an independent commission completed the transformation Reagan had initiated; Reagan had shifted regulatory authority from the states to the federal government, and Adams and other liberal reformers then began efforts to shift authority from Congress to an independent commission.

Steeped in the cultural life of Quincy and Boston, descended from a distinguished family, and a strong advocate of regulation by commissions, Adams has been criticized for his elitism, and there is some truth to this charge. However, Adams's justification for bureaucracy was more complicated than a simple desire to insulate politics from public opinion. Adams also hoped the commission would inform the public of complicated regulatory decisions that often confused political observers. In this sense, liberal reformers' views of public opinion, and their concern that poorly informed voters would lead representatives to implement irrational policies, fostered support for the legislation that eventually led to the creation of an independent regulatory commission.

Despite contributing critical ideas and influencing legislation, Adams was not solely responsible for shifting regulatory authority to an independent commission. The political coalition that shared Adams's ideas was the liberal reform faction of the Republican Party, a coalition of reformers who bolted from the Republican Party in 1872 and 1884, and who opposed corruption, the tariff, and currency inflation and endorsed civil service reform and the creation of an impartial administrative state.

The liberal reformers' education, exposure to certain political economists, and elite social background led them to endorse bureaucracy because they worried the public was poorly informed and legislators were susceptible to corruption.[151] Liberal reformers endorsed bureaucracy as a solution to the corruption that political parties fostered, and because they hoped impartial administrators could disseminate information that would help inform voters of the increasingly complex industrial market economy. In the paradoxical combination of ideological assumptions prevailing in Gilded Age America, bureaucracy was seen as a means to help inform voters of policy debates that reformers worried were controlled by corrupt legislators and the ignorant opinions of the American public.[152]

Chapter 10 Charles Francis Adams Jr.
and Bureaucracy

John Reagan's efforts to regulate the railroads sought to place clear statutory limits upon the railroads' behavior, yet called for little administrative expansion or oversight. By demanding that Congress outlaw pooling, rebating, and price discrimination based upon the length of the haul, Reagan altered the level of government exercising regulatory authority over the railroads. Despite placing railroad regulation on the congressional agenda, however, Reagan never sought to create a bureaucratic commission or foster administrative oversight over the railroad industry.

Although Reagan opposed expanding bureaucratic power over the railroads, the passage of the Interstate Commerce Act (ICA) in 1887 would create a regulatory commission empowered to rule on the reasonableness of railroad prices, and possessing discretion to grant railroads exemptions from the ICA's ban on price discrimination. Rather than emerging from Reagan's efforts or the social groups or legislators who endorsed Reagan's bill, creation of a regulatory commission was endorsed by certain Republicans and liberal reformers who sought to blunt the implications of Reagan's bill.

The creation of the Interstate Commerce Commission (ICC) inadvertently completed the state-building process that Reagan had begun. While Reagan shifted the locus of regulatory authority from the states to the federal government, liberal reformers reacting to the Reagan bill shifted government authority from Congress to a bureaucratic commission. These efforts culminated in the creation of the ICC, the federal regulatory commission that marked a turning point in the development of the American state. Organized with five commissioners serving six-year terms, and a nearly even partisan split between the commissioners, the ICC embodied an organizational form that was subsequently replicated in other administrative agencies, such as the Federal Trade Commission and the Securities and Exchange Commission.[1]

To explain why a regulatory commission was introduced to regulate the railroads, this chapter analyzes the ideas of liberal reformers, those of the railroad expert Charles Francis Adams Jr. in particular. The chapter focuses on analyzing liberal reformers' views of public opinion, their concerns that voters were ignorant of railroad economics, and their hopes that commissions would help disseminate information to inform the public. Indeed, one of the liberal reformers' key justifications for commissions was derived from their conviction that voters misunderstood aspects of the railroad industry and required expert and impartial information that they hoped commissions could provide. In this sense, broad concerns about knowledge and popular understanding of regulatory decisions were central to liberal reformers' ideas regarding the state's role as an agent of rational social development.

The role of liberal reformers in creating a new bureaucratic state has been discussed by a number of scholars, perhaps most extensively by William Nelson in *The Roots of American Bureaucracy, 1830–1900.*[2] Nelson argues that the liberal reform movement was a reaction against majoritarian thinking, and he suggests that liberal reformers sought to protect minority rights in the wake of the populist economic tendencies that emerged following the Civil War. Despite agreeing with much of Nelson's analysis, this chapter argues that liberal reformers were not simply focused on protecting minority rights but hoped to design institutions to prevent what they believed were irrational public demands from influencing political decisions.

The chapter begins by documenting how Reagan's opposition to creating a commission was based on his conviction that railroad regulation did not require expertise but could be dealt with through simple legislative prohibition. After discussing Reagan's opposition to bureaucracy, I examine liberal reformers' views of what they hoped independent commissions could accomplish, and how they hoped commissions would disseminate impartial information to inform the public. This chapter specifically focuses on the ideas of Charles Francis Adams Jr. regarding the railroad problem because Adams was among the most prominent railroad experts, and because he wrote some of the initial legislation introduced as a substitute for Reagan's bill.

In addition to discussing how Adams influenced legislation, this chapter examines his hopes that commissions would help educate voters, whose opinions he then hoped would prevent implementation of irrational or corrupt policies. Despite his initial hope that democratic politics could be rationalized by commissions' dissemination of information, Adams became skeptical of voters' capacity for rational political engagement, eventually dismissing the possibility of creating a rational public.

Despite this failure, the institutional form that Adams and other liberal reformers had introduced was retained, and this completed the state-building transformation Reagan had unintentionally begun. When Reagan's ideas collided with those of Adams and the liberal reform movement, the collision produced a new form of bureaucratic state authority that Reagan and his allies had never intended to create. Indeed, not only did agrarian antirailroad forces oppose creating a bureaucratic commission, they were also opposed to the exemptions on price discrimination that the ICC granted the railroads. Yet the creation of the ICC was no simple triumph for the liberal reformers who had called for its creation; one of their key justifications for a commission was to use bureaucratic experts to disseminate information to help educate the public, and it is clear that the liberal reformers were convinced that this effort to cultivate an informed public failed. Despite their failure to harness bureaucracy to create an informed public, these two groups interacted to produce a new form of bureaucratic authority that was subsequently replicated in other policy areas, marking a critical moment in the development of the American state.

The creation of the ICC has been identified as a key moment in American state formation, inaugurating a form of state authority that was increasingly federal, regulatory, and bureaucratic. This development was deeply influenced by the Reagan bill and the forces championing legislative prohibition of price discrimination, rebates, and pooling. Reagan and his allies were not, however, calling for creating a commission or bureaucratic regulation of the railroads.

Rather than emerging solely from Reagan's efforts, the ICC was produced through the collision of two different logics: first, Reagan's reaction to the collapse of the Compromise of 1877 and his short-term electoral calculations and appeals to agrarian animosity toward the railroads, and, second, liberal reformers' reaction to the opportunity Reagan's bill created to introduce a bureaucratic commission into the regulatory debate over the railroads. The institution created by these two sets of actors was a compromise that satisfied neither group and probably could not have been created by either set of actors acting in isolation.

Although the creation of the ICC completed the institutional transformation Reagan had initiated, he had never intended to create a commission to regulate the railroads.[3] Despite thinking it was "beyond doubt" that Congress should regulate railroad rates, he believed that legislative authority was "supreme and exclusive," and his bill "left little room" for bureaucratic experts.[4] Reagan's opposition to creating a commission indicates that neither he nor the coalition of interests that endorsed his bill was responsible for the *type* of bureaucratic state that emerged from the railroad regulatory debate.

While Reagan's bill sought to simply ban pooling, rebating, and price discrimination, in 1880 legislation was proposed recommending delegating authority to a regulatory commission. Two of the alternatives to the Reagan bill, the Henderson bill and the McLean bill, delegated regulatory authority to a bureaucratic commission. The Henderson bill was written by Charles Francis Adams Jr. and was denounced by forces ranging from the New York Chamber of Commerce to Reagan himself, who criticized the creation of a regulatory bureaucracy, as he did "not approve of the appointment of a commission as proposed by this bill."[5]

Rather than requiring "the knowledge and skill of an expert," Reagan declared, "common sense and common honesty" were all that was needed to prohibit price discrimination and pooling.[6] Yet he was not merely critical of the notion that the complexity of the railroad industry frustrated popular understanding of various regulatory strategies. Although one of the principal justifications for creating a commission was that it would effectively regulate the rates charged by railroad pools, he did not endorse curtailing railroad competition either.

His opposition to pooling and commissions led Reagan to denounce Standard Oil's "iniquitous proceedings,"[7] to attack Adams and Albert Fink, both of whom were calling for limiting competition among the railroads, as "the ablest representatives of the railroad interests," and to criticize efforts to reduce railroad competition.[8] While he thought pooling would be "to the convenience and advantage of the railroads," he believed it was "against the interests of the people in a commercial sense."[9]

It is important to note that Reagan's bill was not the only attempt to regulate the railroads during this period. Various state governments regulated the railroads, and numerous congressmen had endorsed regulatory legislation before Reagan introduced his bill, indicating that had he never adopted railroad regulation it is likely that other representatives would have. Regan's bill was notable, however, specifically because of Reagan's position as chairman of the Interstate Commerce Committee, and because it proposed methods for regulating the railroads that both curried favor with public opinion and expressed hostility toward commissions.

By the early 1880s the pressures that had caused Reagan to introduce his bill had dissipated. The Compromise of 1877 had collapsed, and Thomas Scott had suffered a nervous breakdown, leading to his loss of control over the Texas and Pacific Railroad. Although the original forces that led Reagan to introduce his bill had dissipated, the bill was popular, and his position as chairman of the Interstate Commerce Committee gave him a unique position to champion railroad legislation. This led him to continue to endorse regulation even though the pressures that originally led him to introduce his bill had subsided.

Indeed, popular distrust of the railroads was widespread, and after extensive congressional debate and the publication of the Hepburn Commission's report documenting railroad's use of secret rebates and drawbacks, even Reagan's opponents admitted the public endorsed *some* form of regulation. For example, while Thomas Henderson (R-IL) opposed the Reagan bill, he openly admitted there was "no doubt" that railroad regulation was now "demanded by the people,"[10] and railroad executives were often complaining of the "anti-railroad spirit which now prevails."[11]

The Reagan bill's popularity generated a reaction from liberal reform intellectuals and politicians that were influenced by thinkers such as Adams, E. L. Godkin, Charles Atkins, and David Wells, who found popular demands for railroad regulation unsettling.[12] Liberal reformers were associated with the Liberal Republicans' efforts to join with the Democrats in the election of 1872; they criticized corruption in the Grant administration, advocated tariff reform, sound monetary policy, and civil service reform. Despite being unsuccessful politicians, liberal reformers controlled periodicals such as the *Nation,* the *Atlantic,* and the *North American Review,* and their ideas reached the class of self-described "better men," Eastern elites who were displeased with American partisan politics.[13]

Although many liberal reformers hoped that the ideas circulated by their periodicals would help cultivate an informed public, some were more skeptical of the public's capacity for engagement in democratic politics. Their skepticism was, in part, due to the specific policies the public was endorsing. Popular support for currency inflation, railroad regulation, and the eight-hour work day, convinced liberal reformers that the public exhibited irrational policy preferences, and politicians' willingness to cater to these demands made them skeptical of parties and democratic politics more generally.

Dismayed by the direction of public opinion and party politics, some liberal reformers began exploring alternatives to reliance upon democratic institutions. One of their solutions was the use of regulatory commissions, an idea championed by Adams, who had served on the Massachusetts Railroad Commission since 1869, and whose writings on the railroads appeared in this commission's annual reports, the *Atlantic,* and the *North American Review.*[14]

Adams's ideas regarding the proper role of commissions were linked to his broader views of the role public opinion should play in democratic societies. Adams was convinced that the complexity of modern economies made it essential for voters to have access to educated and impartial opinion leadership.[15] Reflecting upon the public's need for, and elites' responsibility to provide, impartial information, in 1859 Adams asserted: "What this country needs, what it has not yet got . . . is a body of trained thinkers—men capable of directing public sentiment."[16]

Adams's views on the proper relationship between experts, public opinion, and government had been shaped by what he described as an "accidental epoch-marking" incident, his reading of John Stuart Mill's essay on Auguste Comte and positivism.[17] After the Civil War Adams had traveled to Europe, and although he felt that his intellect had been "lying fallow for nearly four years," he described being intellectually transformed by reading Mill's summary of Comte.[18] Adams claimed that Mill's monograph had "revolutionized in a single morning my whole mental attitude," and he had emerged "a changed intellectual and moral being."[19] Comte's ideas, as interpreted and summarized by Mill, provided Adams with a model for how to reform American government, and for the proper relationship between expertise and public opinion.

Critical to Adams's views of government were the relationship between public opinion, elected officials, and expert bureaucrats. Despite having at times proclaimed his faith in the "eventual supremacy of an enlightened public opinion," Adams concluded that popular analysis of railroad regulation "has not been remarkable for intelligence, and the currency question has hardly been more completely befogged in clouds of indifferent declamation, poor philosophy, and worse logic."[20] Adams believed that the public's understanding of both monetary and railroad policy was flawed. He saw that voters wanted low transportation prices, yet they opposed the rate discrimination that made low prices possible. In endorsing these positions, Adams complained: "The public calmly asks for an impossibility, and expects apparently some day to get it."[21] Adams concluded that voters had endorsed "thoroughly illogical" policy positions on the railroads, positions threatening the rationality of public decisions.[22]

Such misunderstanding was compounded by voters' misguided faith in elected officials' ability to satisfy their demands. Adams complained of the strong "desire of the man in the street to get things done and . . . disposed of," an attitude that in turn led to a "growing tendency to excessive legislation—to the everlasting issuing of new legislative edicts in which the supposed popular will is crystallized."[23] Yet he believed that popular demands for statutory enactments from the legislature were ineffective because of the complexity of the economic activities it sought to regulate.[24]

Since Adams had "never believed in" this form of governance, he claimed that he "failed to be in sympathy with the sturdy champions of the 'Dear Peepul.'"[25] However, poorly informed voters were influencing politics in ways that concerned Adams and other liberal reformers, as voters' superficial understanding of politics led them to elect officials that were ignorant, corrupt, and deserved "to be scorned."[26] In reaching these conclusions, Adams was skeptical that elected officials could effectively govern modern economies, and he worried that the complexity of the railroad industry practically ensured that the policies implemented by nonexperts would fail to accomplish the goals the public sought.

Adams believed legislators were susceptible to lobbying and corruption, and under the influence of an ill-informed public opinion, he worried that legislators would destabilize the railroad industry.[27] While legislatures "in many countries and in all conceivable forms" had regulated their railroads, he felt that all such attempts had "uniformly failed."[28] The "real difficulty," as he saw it, was Americans' intellectual "'superficiality' . . . we are too eager for immediate results."[29]

Given the challenges posed by the public's ignorance, and legislators' lack of expertise, Adams began exploring whether there were alternative methods for regulating the railroads. He initially opposed using commissions to regulate rates and instead endorsed state-owned railroads to compete alongside private roads to ensure a degree of public control over the railroads.[30] In his early writings he was skeptical of government efforts to regulate railroad prices and practices, as any attempt to "supervise and regulate the railroads . . . limit their profits . . . [and] fix maxima to their charges" would "reduce [the] industrial system to a chaos."[31]

While Adams initially opposed the use of commissions to regulate railroad rates, by 1878 he had reversed himself and concluded that any policy leaving railroads free to set their rates was "essentially wrong."[32] To prevent the "chaos" spawned by railroad competition, he endorsed regulated pools as the "only way" to rationalize the railroad industry, for he was convinced that the railroad system exhibited chaotic tendencies that were best addressed through the regulation of legalized railroad pools.[33]

While Adams never wavered in his commitment to bureaucracy, his views on bureaucracies' legitimate functions fluctuated. While working for the Massachusetts Railroad Commission, he had confined himself to collecting information, conducting voluntary conferences between the commission and railroads, and publishing information to inform legislative deliberations.[34] Yet when he wrote *Railroads: Their Origins and Their Problems* in 1878 he endorsed regulation of railroad pools' rates by commissioners, even though he believed this regulatory method was unpopular.[35] Given such opposition, Adams believed it was essential "to accustom the public mind to the idea that . . . the proper way to deal with them [railroad pools] may, perhaps, be through regulation and not through prohibition."[36]

In exploring the use of commissions to regulate railroad pools, Adams introduced a second innovation into the railroad regulatory debate. Reagan had shifted the locus of regulatory authority from the states to the federal government; Adams was now providing justifications for shifting regulatory authority from Congress to an independent commission. The objectives Adams and other liberal reformers sought diverged from Reagan's. Instead of simply prohibiting price discrimination, Adams believed that the commission would have to regulate the rates the railroads charged, determining whether price discrimination should be allowed in some instances and not others.

Adams openly recognized, however, that the public did not endorse this method of supervising the railroads. He was exercising a form of autonomy that was distinct from the manipulation of public opinion or implementation of a policy the public was simply unaware of. Adams believed that the public opposed bureaucratic regulation of legalized pools and simply wanted outright legislative prohibition of price discrimination. Since he felt that the public opposed both the institutions and the regulatory objectives he sought, Adams's actions cannot have been reflective of public opinion, and such public opposition was reflected in the fact that Reagan's legislative allies consistently preferred Reagan's bill to alternatives that included a commission.[37]

It is also apparent, however, that Adams and liberal reformers advocating a regulatory commission could not have successfully created a commission on their own. Advocacy for a commission could never have generated the popular support the Reagan bill enjoyed. In order for the liberal reformers to successfully create a commission, and thereby generate a shift in the nature of state authority, Reagan would have to place railroad regulation on the legislative agenda and organize enough support for his measure to threaten congressmen who wished a less radical measure. Reacting to the popularity of Reagan's bill, Adams used his expertise on the railroad issue to introduce a bureaucratic alternative to the bill that appealed to representatives anxious to halt the bill's momentum.

Although Adams hoped the commission would disseminate information and help increase the rationality of democratic politics, it is also apparent that for him the public's preferences had become a secondary concern. He was disillusioned with his work on the Massachusetts Railroad Commission, work which he complained had condemned him to a "fate to fill the ditch of state impotence,"[38] and which, he believed, "can accomplish no considerable results."[39] Instead of relying on state governments to oversee the railroads, he now hoped "a National Bureau" would be created to collect and publicize information pertinent to railroad regulation.[40]

Yet Adams did not explain why he preferred federal regulation to state-level oversight. Part of his resistance was because he believed that the state commissions were simply not effective. As it "now stands" with state-level regulation, he wrote to Carl Schurz, "we are all wasting our time."[41] Despite his frustration with his work on the Massachusetts Railroad Commission, and despite his opposition to legislative regulation of railroads, when the *New York Times* asked Adams for his views of the Reagan bill he claimed that his work with the Massachusetts commission had been "very gratifying" and commented that the "cheek" of railroad lawyers opposing the Reagan bill "takes my breath away."[42]

Adams's endorsement of the Reagan bill, a bill that Adams criticized both in his private correspondence and in his published writings, is not difficult to understand. He was a failed lawyer living in the shadow of his family's accomplishments. While he had gained some recognition for his writings on the railroads, he was a peripheral political figure; when compared to his family's prior accomplishments, he simply didn't measure up.

Yet Reagan had unexpectedly offered Adams an opportunity to influence national politics, and Adams had taken it. He admitted to Schurz: "I wish to shape a national policy," and the ideas presented in his book *Railroads* were "introduced to propose the way for it."[43] Yet Adams also recognized that the specific methods of regulation he endorsed, namely, commissions that would regulate legalized railroad pools, were unpopular. He was introducing a bureaucratic commission into the regulatory debate as a consequence of his personal drive to influence politics, rather than as consequence of pressures associated with industrial capitalism or popular demands for protection from the market economy.

In *Railroads* Adams identified three possible methods of regulation: commissions empowered with legislative and judicial powers as were found in England, partial state ownership as in Belgium, and state ownership of railroads as in Germany.[44] Yet he did not simply seek to apply European institutions to the American context.[45] He believed that commissions were a "distinctively American solution" to the railroad problem, and aside from Great Britain there was "little light . . . to be obtained from the experience of other countries."[46] Adams believed he was taking part in the creation of genuinely new political institutions: the decisions he was influencing regarding the railroads were providing, he wrote, "the foundations which are now to be laid" for subsequent policy decisions.[47] Instead of endorsing either laissez-faire or state ownership of the railroads, he hoped regulation would be performed "not by the State assuming directly the functions of industrialists, as the ordinary communist supposes, but by a more complete development and more confident reliance on the essential features of modern civilization, the sort of police power of public opinion that is, the operations of the great combinations of capital of the future have got to be carried on, not by the public as a body politic, but under a far stronger sense of responsibility to the public . . . than now."[48] Rather than seeking to create institutions that could ignore public opinion, Adams hoped commissions would educate voters, disseminating information and focusing popular attention, functioning as a "lens by means of which the otherwise scattered and powerless rays of public opinion could be concentrated to a focus and brought to bear upon any corporation."[49] By informing voters through their publications and dissemination of empirical information, he hoped commissions would enhance the rationality of public opinion and ensure that elected officials would implement rational policies.

Adams's recommendations mirrored certain recommendations later made by twentieth-century progressives. For example, Walter Lippmann closed the first chapter of *Public Opinion* by recommending that expert commissions disseminate information to help inform the public of the complex aspects of society that it could not directly observe.[50] Much like Adams, Lippmann hoped commissions would serve an informational function and help voters construct rational opinions. However, other progressives were critical of independent commissions.[51] Ironically, Herbert Croly, whose thinking had also been heavily influenced by Comte, denied that any conflict of interest existed between railroads and the communities they served, and noted: "Commissions, responsible as they are to an insistent and uninformed public opinion, and possessed as they inevitably become of the peculiar official point of view, inevitably drift or are driven to incessant, vexatious, and finally harmful interference."[52] Croly would embrace a more supportive role for bureaucratic governance in *Progressive Democracy*.[53] However, Croly's later conception of bureaucratic action was, in certain ways, the exact opposite of what liberal reformers such as Adams endorsed. In *Progressive Democracy* Croly did not endorse bureaucracy as an institutional counterweight to combat an irrational public: he believed public opinion would act to constrain and direct bureaucracy to prevent implementation of unpopular decisions.[54]

Such ambivalence toward commissions, and the conviction that bureaucracy would act in concert with popular demands, indicate that the initial turn toward regulatory administrative development preceded progressive analyses of American government. This indicates that the economic pressures and social conditions facing early twentieth-century America were not responsible for initially creating these new bureaucratic institutions, even if they were adapted, expanded, and empowered in the early twentieth century.[55]

Instead of attributing his institutional recommendations to economic developments or conditions, Adams ascribed them to his comparative institutional analysis and the intellectual history of economics. He believed that the "early school" of political economists left human nature "out of consideration"; the socialists' critiques were merely "the angry protests of human nature against the teachings of a philosophical system which ignored it."[56] Yet instead of endorsing the socialists' positions, he hoped bureaucratic commissions would help educate voters and enlist the public to aid the governmental process.

Adams often noted that the railroad problem was fundamentally one of knowledge, and his hope was that independent commissions would collect and disseminate information to educate Congress and public opinion. The experience of certain state railroad commissions, such as the Illinois commission's regulation of railroad rates, was instructive because it provided an institutional model for the use of bureaucratic commissions to apply general principles to specific cases.[57]

Despite Adams's hopes for reinvigorating popular democratic politics, by the 1870s his faith in public reason had been undermined. In 1878 Adams urged: "We have got to come back to a reliance on publicity and the force of public opinion," and he sought "to have as much intelligent discussion as possible" on questions of public policy, but he was privately pessimistic regarding the capacities of public opinion.[58] As early as 1869 he was complaining that in politics the "mass of men are always superficial," exhibiting a tendency to believe "the evidence of their own sense."[59] While the conclusions and interpretations generated by these impressions seemed simple and self-evident, the entire problem was that in politics "appearances are deceptive."[60]

By 1880 Adams was becoming increasingly skeptical of the public's engagement in politics. Worried that democratic politics was proving inadequate for modern economic problems, he complained that Americans lacked "even the first elements on which railroad discussion can be based."[61] Although Frank Dobbin argues that American industrial policy reflected a cultural consensus for allowing market prices to direct railroads' allocation decisions, neither the Reagan bill nor those supporting regulatory commissions wanted railroad competition to simply be determined by market forces.[62]

Despite his familiarity with classical political economy, Adams believed that the laws of supply and demand functioned imperfectly in the railroad industry.[63] Nor were railroad executives committed proponents of unhampered markets. For example, while he occasionally endorsed leaving railroad prices to be set by terms of competition, Collis Huntington was dependent upon federal subsidies and land grants to keep the Central Pacific Railroad operational. There was hardly a consensus among other railroads regarding the role of market forces, as the railroads were involved in extensive pooling agreements that sought to limit their exposure to market competition.

Although Adams was providing intellectual justification for delegation of authority to an administrative agency, he had not placed the railroad issue on the legislative agenda; he was reacting to a political situation that Reagan had helped create. Indeed, it is hardly surprising that Adams and Reagan sought to accomplish such contradictory objectives. While both Adams and Fink wanted to use a commission to regulate the prices charged by legalized pools,[64] Reagan's "principal object" was to *enhance* competition between the railroads in order to make pooling and collusive rate-setting impossible.[65] As Reagan believed that outlawing pooling would enhance competition among the railroads, he was clearly not using Adams's ideas to frame his legislation.[66]

Yet liberal reformers were hardly alone in their concerns regarding public attitudes toward the railroads. Legislative opponents of the Reagan bill complained that voters exhibited poorly informed opinions and mistaken views of the railroad industry. Henderson noted that the "general feeling" in New York and Pennsylvania was that price discrimination operated "in favor of the West," yet Western agrarians were making "many and loud complaints" that it harmed their interests.[67]

Adams's views of railroad regulation, public opinion, and commissions are important specifically because Adams influenced, and in some instances actually wrote, legislation that was introduced as alternatives to the Reagan bill. He was involved in writing the Henderson bill, and his writings influenced Shelby Cullom, the Illinois Republican who introduced the measure that eventually passed as an alternative to Reagan's bill and became the Interstate Commerce Act of 1887.[68]

From his time as governor of Illinois, Cullom was familiar with the Illinois state regulatory commission, agrarian opposition to the railroads, and the efforts of shippers and railroads to secure oversight by a commission whose decisions were subject to judicial review. Initially introduced in 1883, the Cullom bill passed the Senate in 1885 but was opposed by the House. The bill prohibited rebates and rate discrimination, and outlawed pooling. However, unlike the Reagan bill, the Cullom bill called for shifting authority to a regulatory commission.

The introduction of a regulatory commission was not simply an attempt by conservative business groups and Republican politicians to limit popular influence over regulatory policy. First, railroads did not simply homogenously endorse the Cullom bill or the regulatory objectives it sought to accomplish. For example, the Pennsylvania Railroad opposed the Cullom bill's prohibition on pooling; instead, it argued that pooling "ought to be legalized and encouraged."[69] The Cullom bill's opponents claimed that the same railroads that opposed Reagan's measure were also "seeking to defeat this bill."[70]

Although certain railroads opposed the Cullom bill's prohibition on pooling, other organized groups, such as the Minneapolis Board of Trade, opposed the bill's long-haul-short-haul clause and the "unnecessary and dangerous prerogative" of granting a commission an "almost autocratic power over the market," and claimed that the "very people who ought to derive most ben-efit from legislation of this general character—the farmers and wage-earners of the country—would be the first and greatest sufferers from its injurious effects."[71] The Minneapolis Board of Trade further complained that creating a commission in a sphere of legislation that was "now making its first tentative venture" would have effects that were difficult to predict and were likely to be "dangerous . . . to the interests of the distinctively agricultural sections of the country."[72]

Senator Richard Coke claimed that the Reagan bill was "being fought on every clause and section" by the railroads, with the "chief assaults" being made against the antipooling and antidiscrimination sections.[73] Yet in congressional debate Cullom tried to convey that, despite their opposition to the pooling and antidiscrimination sections, the railroads, as he put it, "take pains to ex-plain with more or less qualification that they approve the general scope of the bill, or, at least, that they do not seriously object to its other provisions. If the very able gentlemen who manage the railroads of the United States find only two points of serious attack in a measure which is intended to bring about, in many important particulars, a reversal of existing railway practices and methods of management, we have a right to assume that the bill is not, aside from the features which they specially criticize, unduly oppressive toward the railroads, or very far from right in its main provisions and regulations."[74] Al-though some state railroad commissions had the power to set maximum rates, these "strong" state commissions were not serving as examples for congres-sional legislation. Cullom believed that the experience of the Illinois com-mission demonstrated that the commission had "no practical power" over the railroads.[75] Simon Sterne noted that state railroad commissions possessed "no judicial powers," and instead of regulating rates, the commissions were "a mere perpetual committee of investigation to advise the Legislature . . . and to recommend remedies" for legislative action.[76]

Since many House Democrats opposed the creation of a regulatory com-mission, when the Cullom bill passed the Senate on January 14, 1887, it was described as a conservative alternative to the Reagan bill. Although the fourth section of the Cullom bill appeared to outlaw price discrimination, this sec-tion stipulated that railroads were permitted to engage in "reasonable" price discrimination that was based upon the proximity of other railways, canals, or competing transportation routes. Yet much hinged upon how the term "reasonable" was defined, and this was left to the discretion of the ICC. Although the ICC's determination of what constituted reasonable price discrimination depended upon whether goods were shipped "under substantially similar circumstances and conditions," the determination of what constituted such conditions was left to the discretion of the commission.[77]

This was hardly the first instance when commissions were empowered to regulate the railroads; certain state railroad commissions had already exercised such authority. For example, one of the strongest of the state commissions, the Illinois Railroad and Warehouse Commission, was created in 1871 and granted authority to rule on the reasonableness of price discrimination based upon the length of the haul and to fix the maximum rates the railroads could charge.

However, the Illinois Railroad and Warehouse Commission was hardly a simple response to agrarian outcry against the railroads. Agrarian organizations that endorsed regulating Illinois railroads, such as the Illinois State Farmers' Association, *opposed* creating this commission, and the most militant farmers were those who were most strongly opposed.[78] Furthermore, the ICC, unlike the Illinois commission, could not determine the maximum rate a railroad could charge but instead was granted discretion to determine whether a railroad's use of price discrimination was reasonable and would be permitted.

The ICC's discretion to rule on the reasonableness of price discrimination diverged from the authority enjoyed by previous federal agencies and commissions. Although the antebellum Treasury Department and Post Office exercised forms of discretion prior to the Civil War, such discretion was not used for *regulatory* purposes. For example, although the antebellum Treasury Department had discretion over the selection of the state banks to receive federal deposits, the Treasury did not use this authority to exercise central banking functions or implement a coherent monetary policy. Similarly, certain postal officials, such as Postmaster General John McLean, exercised discretion in Post Office appointments and in the bidding process used to determine mail delivery contracts.[79] However, the Post Office did not use its authority over the mail delivery system to regulate the American economy or improve market efficiency or fairness.

The legislators who were debating the railroad issue did not see their actions as extending an existing form of government but instead noted that the Cullom bill embodied a new form of state authority. Southern Democrats, such as John Morgan (D-AL), complained: "[T]he measure opens up the door to the interference of Congress with every regulation of trade and commerce" and predicted that it would "set in motion a doubtful and dangerous power which will soon become a factor of immense influence in the party politics of the Republic."[80] Morgan's language was not one stressing continuity; rather, his criticisms suggested that the ICC had initiated a new developmental trend that he worried would soon spread to other areas of the American economy.

Not only was such authority novel, efforts to create a regulatory commission were inspiring opposition from representatives who endorsed the Reagan bill and from economic groups who opposed the powers the commission would possess.[81] However, the introduction of a commission to regulate the railroads inadvertently completed the state-building project that Reagan had unintentionally begun. Rather than in response to popular preferences or the demands of organized agrarian groups, certain members of the Republican Party were endorsing delegation of authority, first in the Treasury Department and then in the ICC, in order to combat the influence of populist demands.

The specific configuration of ideas, policy preferences, and institutional recommendations espoused by Republicans and liberal reformers marked a novel development in American government. As Nancy Cohen has suggested: "The administrative mandate that liberal reformers divined marked a real departure not only from antebellum traditions of limited government but also from experiments with an active democratic state, which had been directed by Radical Republicans and subsequently had been taken up by a number of the postbellum social movements. Moreover, liberals laid the critical practical and ideological groundwork for the creation of a modern liberal democratic state wholly removed from democratic participation or accountability. Indeed, the liberal reform movement of the Gilded Age was both precursor and progenitor of the Progressive Era's administered democracy."[82] Cohen's argument requires qualification, however. For Adams and other liberal reformers did not simply want to remove railroad policy from popular influence, as John Sherman did. Rather, their wish was that commissioners would disseminate information to inform public opinion, which they hoped would operate through the electoral mechanism to encourage elected officials to implement rational policies.

Cohen's conclusions are perhaps most accurate for Sherman's efforts to minimize public influence over the Treasury Department's efforts to resume the gold standard. Indeed, Sherman never sought any larger political objective when he helped empower the Treasury Department; he simply hoped administrative discretion would ensure implementation of the Republican Party's increasingly unpopular monetary positions. Sherman had not sought to alter the nature of state authority, even though his comments in congressional debate over McCulloch's actions in 1867 revealed that he understood the gravity of what was occurring within the Treasury Department.

Other observers recognized the departure Sherman had inaugurated. As Sherman used discretion to sell loans and contract the money supply, liberal reformer Edward Atkinson wondered whether it was constitutional for "the Executive [to] accept a legislative function."[83] Yet instead of *criticizing* bureaucratic delegation, or offering a constitutional objection to executive assumption of legislative responsibilities, Atkinson *endorsed* Sherman's actions: "If such a wise discretion should be used . . . what a grand act it would be."[84] Convinced that the public had become "debauched by foolish theories and extravagant rhetoric," economic conservatives were exploring whether bureaucracy could be used to resist populist demands.[85]

While they were convinced that the public was poorly informed, liberal reformers were also convinced that transportation markets suffered from unique deficiencies, deficiencies that led them to endorse creation of a bureaucratic commission to implement rational regulations, a configuration of issue positions and institutional recommendations that appears illogical to twenty-first-century observers.[86]

Adams and Sherman had little sympathy for the public's demands, were dismissive of radical agrarians, and were seeking ways to accomplish conservative objectives. Sherman wanted to reinstate the gold standard, and Adams sought to legalize railroad pools. These policy objectives, however, were being used to justify empowering bureaucracies with independent policy authority, a form of institutional authority that Republicans would subsequently renounce. Although the elites responsible for this innovation never codified their justifications for this form of state authority into a coherent ideological worldview, a series of short-term calculations were responsible for bureaucratic innovations in the Treasury Department and the ICC.

Conservatives' responsibility for the initial cases of bureaucratic delegation in the Treasury Department and the ICC indicates that the American bureaucratic state cannot simply be explained as a functional response to economic developments or popular demands. This is not to deny that economic conditions and popular demands conditioned the issues that became topics of political contention, nor do I seek to deny that Sherman or various liberal reformers were reacting to the unpopularity of their preferred policies. However, the decision to delegate policy authority to the Treasury Department and the

ICC was a reaction *against* popular demands and was intended to fulfill policy objectives that were openly recognized to be deeply unpopular.

While the creative synthesis of these policy objectives and institutional recommendations had become accepted among certain intellectuals and a faction within the Republican Party, the ideological groups championing these reforms and the justifications given for the reforms appear illogical to present-day observers. Although Adams believed the necessity of a railroad commission was "obvious," there was little obvious about his institutional recommendations.[87] Despite the seemingly contradictory nature of these ideas, it is difficult to explain why liberal reformers endorsed independent commissions without recognizing how their pessimism regarding public opinion led them to endorse empowering executive agencies and bureaucratic commissions.

However, liberal reformers' concerns were hardly limited to the mass public; they believed that complex regulatory issues often confused other political elites as well. For example, when discussing the American railroad industry with Samuel Bowles, editor of the Springfield *Republican,* Charles Francis Adams Jr. complained that Bowles "knew just a little on the subject," and suggested that the railroad issue would be "much easier" to discuss if Bowles became better informed.[88] Similarly, when Francis Wayland III, Dean of Yale's Law School and son of the author of *Elements of Political Economy,* confessed that when it came to bimetallism "the majority of us are infants on this topic," he revealed that even other political elites found such issues difficult to understand.[89]

Adams's conviction that voters had little understanding of politics was critical for his institutional recommendations. Had Adams believed that voters were informed, he would not have believed that commissions were needed to inform the public. While certain liberal reformers hoped to cultivate an informed electorate, by the 1870s Adams was concluding that voter education was hopeless. He and other liberal reformers began exploring alternatives to mass politics, proposing voter disenfranchisement and the use of bureaucracies and independent commissions to rationalize politics.

Given the antidemocratic nature of these recommendations, there is a tendency to criticize liberal reformers for their elitism and subservience to corporate interests. There is considerable support for such charges. Yet despite serving as president of the Union Pacific Railroad, prior to the passage of the Interstate Commerce Act Adams was hardly a mere railroad apologist; he had simply become disillusioned with democratic politics. Reflecting on his personal efforts to influence American democracy, Adams noted: "In a democracy the true way is to despise your average man. They all like it. To be sure, it rather stands in one's way . . . but if you don't want what your [*sic*] after, it is all the same in the end. Perhaps you may ask, if I don't want the stakes why do I continue to play the game? And now you begin to talk—I really couldn't say."[90] Compared to the other members of his family and their accomplishments, Charles Francis Adams Jr. was of little consequence: he was a failed lawyer, he held an insignificant position on the Massachusetts Railroad Commission, and, while his writing brought him some degree of recognition, he had little influence over national politics.

Adams had, however, cultivated expertise on the railroad issue, and Reagan had created an opportunity for Adams to influence national politics. Reagan had shifted authority from the states to the federal government, and liberal reformers then began advocating for creating a commission. Liberal reformers contributed to this process by helping convince Republicans, through their writings, journals, and books, such as Adams's *Railroads: Their Origins and Problems,* to place regulatory authority in a commission, not in Congress. Although other, more broadly culturally inclined liberals such as Thomas Wentworth Higginson, Charles Eliot Norton, and James Russell Lowell retained their faith in educating public opinion, Adams and others had "ingeniously shifted the grounds of debate" and were developing intellectual justifications for the bureaucratic alternative to mass democracy.[91]

However, Adams believed the public had little understanding of commissions' regulatory decisions, and despite his conviction that the public endorsed some form of railroad regulation, he also believed that the public opposed the bureaucratic institutions he endorsed. This perception was hardly limited to Adams; other liberal reformers shared this conviction. As E. L. Godkin noted, Americans exhibited an almost instinctual opposition to "being instructed by any superior persons, or addressed with an air of authority based on special knowledge."[92] Yet it was precisely such expert and special knowledge that Adams, Godkin, and others hoped to enlist in a new empowered bureaucratic state. Although Adams hoped the ICC would disseminate information to inform the public, he became convinced the public had little understanding of the regulatory functions the ICC was performing.

When proposals for creating a commission were placed on the legislative agenda, Reagan wound up initiating a shift in state authority that he had never intended to introduce. He had never sought to create a bureaucratic commission; he simply could not control the alternative proposals being placed on the congressional agenda. Adams, liberal reformers, and various Republicans who sought to blunt the radicalism of the Reagan bill were responding to the political situation that Reagan had created, causing two different logics to interact to produce an institutional innovation that many of the original proponents of railroad regulation had never intended.

Reagan initially sought access to a transcontinental railroad and then subsequently attracted support from groups that endorsed his bill to advance their own interests. Adams did not share Reagan's objectives, nor did he appeal to the same social groups that endorsed Reagan's measure. Rather, Adams, like other liberal reformers, sought to build an administrative state to rationalize democratic politics. These two logics unintentionally produced a new institution for regulating the railroads, even though disparate objectives and interests influenced the individuals driving this process.

Despite appearing paradoxical to twenty-first century observers, the bureaucratic institutions that became ubiquitous features of American government were initially created by conservatives who were disillusioned with the popularity of populist economic policies. Instead of being created to fulfill popular demands and respond to public outrage toward industrialization, certain elites sought to use bureaucracy to minimize the influence of public opinion, and educate voters about the regulatory issues that were consuming democratic politics.

To identify this period as a pivotal moment in American state formation is not to deny the presence of regulation or bureaucratic agencies at the state and local levels, nor is it to suggest that these were the only bureaucratic innovations that were occurring at this time. However, the empowerment of the Treasury Department and the ICC marked the first time federal bureaucrats were empowered with discretion to regulate the market economy, and as the state began regulating the American economy additional bureaucracies acquired similar forms of authority.

The pressures leading to this bureaucratic expansion were distinct from those influencing European state formation. Instead of emerging in response to military pressures and war, the American regulatory state was created in response to pressures associated with mass democracy, party competition, and elites' attempts to deal with problems they attributed to an uninformed public. Although the Civil War clearly influenced American political development, the American state's expansion of bureaucratic regulatory capacity was due to pressures associated with elites and democracy, not war and international political competition.

Chapter 11 Free Silver and the Democratic Party

By the end of the 1880s the American state was exercising novel powers over monetary policy and the railroad industry. As the Treasury Department was taking steps to resume the gold standard, railroad regulation was emerging as a political issue, leading liberal reformers to endorse delegation to an independent commission. In 1876, however, a series of editorials introduced American voters to the silver issue, a policy that a decade later would captivate the public and a decade later still dominate the election of 1896.

By demanding inflationary monetary policy, free silver drew support from social groups that had previously demanded greenback inflation. However, when William Jennings Bryan demanded the free coinage of silver at the ratio of 16 to 1 in the election of 1896, the silver issue inadvertently influenced the ideological development of the Democratic Party.[1] As Michael Kazin has noted, when Bryan endorsed free silver he set the Democrats "on a course that led away from their laissez-faire past and toward the liberalism of the New Freedom, the New Deal, and the Great Society. To demand that the government control the money supply . . . was not quite a blueprint for a regulatory state. But the platform [of 1896] officially declared that Democrats were in favor of beginning to redistribute wealth and power in America. In rhetoric at least, the party has never gone back."[2]

Despite the importance of this shift, Bryan and the Democrats retained opposition to using the federal *bureaucracy* to satisfy popular demands, confining government activism either to state-level regulation or to federal-level legislation. Arguably, it was not until the New Deal that the Democrats endorsed applying the federal bureaucracy to solve American social problems and created the partisan landscape with which we are now familiar. This transformation, however, could only occur after the Democrats jettisoned their hostility toward federal activism, and despite the limits to the Democrats' newfound statism the partisan situation was novel.

Although the silver issue played a critical role in this transformation, Bryan added little that was original to demands for free silver. Rather, he adopted ideas and demands originally popularized by certain editorials and minor third parties, such as the American Bimetallic League and the American Bimetallic Party, organizations that popularized ideas that were subsequently adopted by the Populists.[3] These bimetallic organizations denounced silver's demonetization as the "Crime of '73," demanded the free coinage of silver at the ratio of 16 to 1, and published influential pamphlet literature, such as William "Coin" Harvey's *Coin's Financial School.*

The conspiratorial claims made by these organizations were initially presented in a series of newspaper articles published in 1876 by an editorialist named George Weston. Weston's editorials attributed the Panic of 1873 to silver's demonetization and claimed that bankers had bribed the officials who wrote the Coinage Act. Despite containing many inaccuracies, Weston's editorials generated popular outrage in inflationist states, such as Ohio, and in states with large silver interests, such as Nevada and California. Weston's claims would be adopted by various bimetallic organizations, politicians of both parties, and Bryan in the election of 1896.

Oddly, one of the most prominent leaders of the free silver movement was none other than William Stewart, the Nevada Republican who had helped William Ralston pass the Coinage Act of 1873. Although Stewart had defended the Coinage Act in legislative debate and kept Ralston apprised of Henry Linderman's actions on his behalf, Stewart would emerge as a vocal critic of the Crime of '73, and he became editor of the *Silver Knight* and the

Silver Knight-Watchman, newspapers that defended bimetallism and claimed that Eastern and European financiers had secretly demonetized silver to protect the value of their gold-bearing bonds.

It is important to note that although other members of Ralston's coalition also sought to mask their role in the Coinage Act and denied their part in the act's passage, Stewart was the only member of Ralston's legislative coalition to formally join bimetallic parties and organizations. Nor were Ralston's allies responsible for creating the free silver movement, which drew broad popular support and was led by individuals with no knowledge of Ralston's involvement in the Coinage Act.

This chapter examines the inaccurate myths that were created, and adopted by many Americans, regarding the Coinage Act's passage. Instead of suggesting that Ralston's allies created the free silver movement, I focus on how Stewart masked his associations with Ralston, denied his role in the Coinage Act, and used public ignorance to become prominent in a political movement that should have been denouncing him. Indeed, the fact that even political elites associated with the free silver movement did not realize that Stewart was involved in the very measure he was denouncing indicates that the political elites intimately involved in the politics of bimetallism and free silver failed to identify the actors who influenced this important issue.

As no one understood Ralston's role in the Coinage Act, or the interests his legislative coalition was trying to protect, the factual inaccuracies in the popular account of the Crime of '73 went unnoticed. Not only did this prevent the public from identifying and penalizing those responsible for the Coinage Act, it also allowed Ralston's legislative allies to avoid detection and enabled Stewart to become a leader of the social movement that was attacking a measure he had supported.

This chapter begins by analyzing the initial coverage of the silver issue and then examines how the publicity surrounding media analysis of silver's demonetization forced some of Ralston's legislative allies to deny responsibility for the measure and popularize claims they knew were inaccurate. As the initial media coverage of the Coinage Act reinforced popular stereotypes regarding Eastern and European bankers, the public adopted a simple explanation attributing the Panic of 1873, and the resulting recession, to these bankers. These claims were subsequently adopted by other political actors, and when adopted by Bryan during the election of 1896, they influenced the Democrats' turn toward federal economic activism.

However, the myths surrounding the Democratic Party's ideological transition appeared persuasive to a poorly informed public, even though critical political decisions had been influenced by interests that few understood. Despite all the media attention that focused on the Coinage Act and the politics of free silver, the misunderstanding and manipulation surrounding the act was never understood. Voters and political elites alike mistakenly believed that they understood a complex series of events, and the nature and magnitude of their errors were obscured by subsequent academic studies that offered their own flawed accounts of what had transpired.

The public was first alerted to silver's demonetization when the editorialist George Weston published several newspaper articles attributing the Panic of 1873 to silver's demonetization. Weston believed that the public had been unaware of what the Coinage Act accomplished. By September 1876 he had determined that silver had been demonetized "without the knowledge of the country," and, he wrote, it was "not certain that even now a majority of the people of the country know that it is so."[4] That demonetization elicited little attention was "shown by the entire absence of discussion, in and out of Congress"; any claims that it should have attracted voters' attention were irrelevant, since "it did not, as a matter of fact, and that is the end of it."[5]

Despite the absence of popular awareness or focused debate, Weston was convinced the measure would become deeply unpopular. Since public observers of all persuasions recognized greenback inflation's popularity, the Coinage Act's deflationary implications convinced Weston that the measure would eventually become contentious. "As selfish in its origin as it was surreptitious in the manner of its introduction," the Coinage Act, Weston wrote, "will be repealed when public attention is called to it."[6]

Weston's editorials recognized something that is obvious in retrospect. First, the representatives debating the measure simply had not understood its implications. Furthermore, aside from the legislation's complexity, the large number of individuals who were consulted made it difficult to determine who was responsible for the final version of the bill.[7] As Weston recognized that responsibility for the measure was "as indeterminable as the question whether the late Sultan of Turkey perished by suicide or assassination," he initially hesitated to attribute silver's demonetization to any group or individual.[8]

Weston was undeterred, however: "[We know] all that we need to know," he wrote, "and that is, what classes and interests, here and in Europe, profited by the falsifications, and who the men are who now insist that these falsifications shall remain uncorrected."[9] Yet the Coinage Act's ramifications for different groups' interests were not straightforward. Weston's narrative simply claimed that silver's demonetization was deflationary, and that this indicated that Eastern and European bankers were responsible for a measure that aided the Northeast at the expense of the West and the South.[10]

It is clear, however, that Weston, the public, various politicians, and subsequent academic studies misunderstood simple factual questions regarding which bankers and interests supported which policies. Nor did the silver issue initially generate predictable responses from rival economic and political groups. Hardly endorsing free silver as an alternative or supplement to greenback inflation, the 1876 Greenback Party platform opposed remonetizing silver, and greenback inflationists believed that "the people don't want it [silver coinage] beyond the amount required for change"; voters "prefer legal tenders to either gold or silver coin for the transactions of their own business."[11]

Initially there was no clear partisan division on the issue. The first advocates for silver coinage were certain Republicans who hoped to use fractional silver coinage to retire greenbacks. Silver's demonetization allowed the Treasury to exchange greenbacks for silver coins that could not circulate as legal tender, simultaneously reducing the volume of greenbacks and protecting the gold reserve necessary for resumption of the gold standard. While it seems obvious in retrospect that debtors and the Democrats would endorse free silver, this was not initially apparent at the time.

Weston was reinforcing popular preconceptions of bankers and sectional interests, but his narrative had erred in attributing the Coinage Act to Eastern and European financiers. Despite such errors, Weston's editorials stirred anger in agrarian states, such as Ohio, and in silver-producing states, such as California and Nevada. The reactions to Weston's editorials created distinct problems for some of Ralston's legislative allies, who suddenly found their constituents exploding in indignation over a bill that, unbeknownst to anyone, they had actually helped pass.

Reacting to this political environment, Ralston's congressional allies embarked upon a stunning, yet entirely comprehensible, course of action. Although they had helped secure the Coinage Act's passage, and although some of them fully understood that Ralston was paying Linderman to help the Bank of California, Ralston's allies either remained silent about the inaccuracies in Weston's editorials, actively denied any knowledge of the Coinage Act's passage, or began *echoing* Weston's claims that the Coinage Act was a criminal conspiracy executed by Eastern and European bankers.

The reasons for doing so were straightforward. So long as the public did not realize how Ralston had orchestrated support for the Coinage Act, and that Western representatives had helped him pass the act, Ralston's allies were safe from electoral retribution. This was simply because the inaccuracies in the causal story that voters adopted regarding the interests and representatives responsible for the measure did not identify the individuals and interests who were actually responsible for the Coinage Act's passage.

Ralston's allies could not simply ignore the silver issue, however. Ignoring it was impossible given the outrage surrounding the measure. But they could not try to inform the public, or explain why they had supported the measure, either. Any admission of involvement in the Coinage Act's passage would have been political suicide. A series of events beyond their control had left them few alternative courses of action, and had practically ensured that the politicians who could have explained what had actually occurred would never explain the causes of silver's demonetization.

It was also apparent, however, that the conspiracy theory that was being popularized was destined to make silver far more persuasive than greenback inflation. Soon after the publication of Weston's editorials, the silver issue "seized the public imagination" and was becoming a "popular craze threatening to sweep all before it."[12] These pressures were acute in states with large silver interests, such as Nevada, which was soon convulsed with outrage over the Crime of '73. Western representatives such as John P. Jones (R-NV) and Richard P. Bland (D-MO) began attacking silver's demonetization and embellished Weston's narrative.

Jones initially followed Weston in recognizing that few understood the Coinage Act's ramifications.[13] And he claimed—at first—that creditors had not played a critical role in drafting the act.[14] While Weston recognized that prominent European bankers, such as the Barings and the Rothschilds, had actually *opposed* silver's demonetization, Jones and others dropped such subtlety and began claiming that the Coinage Act had been drafted "in the interest of a few plutocrats in England and in Germany."[15]

Facing a difficult Senate contest against James G. Faire and Adolph Sutro, Jones used the silver issue to transform Nevada voters "into a passionate and issue-conscious electorate."[16] An opponent of the Hayes administration and allied with Roscoe Conkling's Stalwarts, Jones reveled in using the silver issue to embarrass Hayes's Midwestern Republican allies.[17] As Nevada plunged into recession, Jones began asserting that free silver "offered the promise of eventual relief."[18] He blamed silver's demonetization on Eastern bankers and claimed that creditors "did not care which metal was demonetized, provided money was made scarce and dear."[19] He charged that the Coinage Act "was a grave wrong on the people of the whole civilized globe and in the interests of a few plutocrats in England and Germany and in the certain interest of the whole pagan and barbarian world."[20]

Jones also claimed that remonetization would be an effective method of economic stabilization, contending that the Coinage Act had, in his words, tripled "the specie prices of everything we had and shall have to buy from China, Japan and the East Indies," a fact that he worried "wholly surpasses the understanding of men of plain minds."[21] While Jones asserted that he had always believed the Coinage Act had been "enacted in ignorance of the baleful effects" it had for the American economy, he continued to assail it as "one of those historical blunders that were worse than crimes."[22] After being reelected to the Senate in 1878, Jones became one of Nevada's most popular representatives, "an inconceivable achievement" that would have been difficult in the absence of the silver issue.[23]

While blaming Eastern and European financiers for silver's demonetization was politically effective, these claims were largely fictitious. Anticipating many of the themes that would dominate political debate for years, Thomas Ewing (D-OH) complained that silver had been demonetized "at the instance and for the benefit of European money kings," for after European bankers "had stricken down silver in Germany, they sent Mr. Ernest Loyd to the United States, and had our Congress demonetize it also."[24] These claims were often adopted by newspapers, which claimed that silver was demonetized by "the great money power—the worst legacy of the war—[which] intend[ed], by this scheme of forced resumption, to make gold the sole measure and payer of debts."[25]

Frequently the Rothschilds and their "bag man," Ernest Seyd, whose name was often given as Ernest Lloyd, were blamed for bribing American representatives to demonetize silver. Yet the Rothschilds had *opposed* silver's demonetization, a fact that had been recognized in Weston's original editorials, which had applauded the Rothschilds for being among the "practical financiers, who were unanimous *against* the . . . demonetization of silver."[26] Edmund de Rothschild actually told Treasury Secretary Benjamin Bristow: "It would be a great relief for the commercial world if the United States could extend their silver currency," as doing so would "facilitate the absorption of the great amount of silver now on hand" and would serve to "place the currency of the United States on a safer basis than the greenbacks."[27]

Claims that Ernest Seyd was the Rothschilds' "bag man," were simply fictional. Seyd was a British monetary expert who had written a book *endorsing* bimetallism.[28] Recognizing that inaccurate depictions of the Coinage Act were influencing public opinion, Republicans claimed: "[There is no] foundation for this absurd story . . . of the influence exerted by bankers and capitalists to control legislation at Washington . . . [even though] it is still being repeated by greenback orators," and they expressed the hope that these claims would "vanish into thin air when examined by the lights of truth."[29] Certain Republicans tried to point out that instead of obeying the demands of powerful financiers, since the Civil War monetary policy had been "made *in opposition* to the advice of the banking interest of the country."[30]

The popularized depictions of silver's demonetization contained some truth, however, and the Republicans' claims that nothing underhanded had occurred were inaccurate. A banker had deeply influenced the Coinage Act, and the measure's author had been bribed. Yet instead of being the work of European or Eastern financiers, it was William Ralston, a Western banker, who had used Linderman, the Coinage Act, and a coalition of Western representatives to try to aid the Bank of California. Since the public was relying upon newspaper editorials and politicians for information, and since no one understood what had actually occurred, none of this was apparent, and the wrong bankers and representatives were being blamed for a measure that was becoming increasingly unpopular. Voters confronted several competing explanations for what had happened, none of which was accurate, and none of which ensured the elected officials that had helped Ralston with the Coinage Act were penalized.

Yet it is difficult to see how it could be otherwise. Even if politicians had simply tried to explain what had actually happened, the complexity of the calculations and interests that had influenced the Coinage Act, and the fact that some of these calculations, such as those associated with the trade dollar, proved to be inaccurate, made the issue too complicated to explain. This ensured that the explanation that was offered would be a gross simplification and would reinforce popular preconceptions at the expense of explaining what had actually occurred.

Despite the falsehoods that were influencing public opinion, by the end of 1876 the silver issue became salient enough to warrant a congressional

investigation. Prominent economists and public officials were called to testify and explain the origins of the measure. Testifying before the committee
investigating issues relating to silver coinage, Linderman did everything he
could to mask his motives and predictions regarding the Coinage Act's effects.
When asked to explain why silver prices were collapsing, he tried to minimize
domestic factors: "First in importance was the demonetization of silver by the
German Empire; second, the limitation placed upon the coinage of full-tender
silver coins in France and by her monetary allies, and the action of the Nether-
lands in the same direction; the third point is the diminished export to India;
forth and last, the supposed or real increased production of silver, which, I
believe, has been exaggerated."[31] Yet as various officials began making similarly
misleading public statements, currency inflation on the basis of silver coinage,
not greenbacks, quickly developed. Despite the Greenback Party's initial opposition to the free coinage of silver, by September 1877, Ohio Greenbackers
were endorsing the free coinage of silver.[32] Free silver advocates believed that
"if the people of the East . . . could spare the time to read and compare the
arguments made for and against the free coinage of silver . . . it would not take
a week's time to restore the white metal to the place which it occupied . . . [be-
fore the] infamous legislative trick in 1873."[33] Indeed, such advocates believed
that the silver issue's "great importance demand[ed] that it should be brought
home with irresistible force to the understanding of the masses."[34]

Popular reactions to Weston's editorials were creating distinct problems for
the members of Ralston's legislative coalition. If their role in the Coinage Act's
passage had been exposed they would have been driven from office. However,
the initial newspaper coverage had framed the silver issue in a way that made
it impossible to explain that the measure was initially designed to help a California banker with extensive Nevada silver interests.

Ralston's coalition was safe from electoral retribution so long as the public remained unaware of their role in silver's demonetization. Yet this must have been
little solace to representatives whose constituents were exploding in indignation
over the Crime of '73. Although they had helped pass the Coinage Act and
understood that Ralston was using Linderman to influence the measure, Ralston's allies began echoing claims that a "crime" had been perpetrated upon the
American people, or denied that anything underhanded had occurred. By either
simply not contradicting the Weston editorials or actually reinforcing Weston's
inaccurate depiction of events, Ralston's legislative allies helped popularize an
explanation for the recession that was comprehensible, stimulated popular participation, and masked their responsibility for silver's demonetization.

While this allowed them to capitalize upon popular hostility to demonetization and avoid electoral accountability for what they had done, there had been no Eastern conspiracy, and Ernst Seyd was not the Rothschilds' "bag man." Rather, some of the representatives who were now criticizing the Crime of '73" had actually played a key role in the Coinage Act's passage; a course of action had been forced upon them by the inaccuracies in the initial newspaper coverage of the measure and the popular reactions these editorials had created.

In the face of rising popular opposition, Stewart and Eugene Casserly were not alone in their attempts to distance themselves from any responsibility for the Coinage Act. Once the public was denouncing the Crime of '73, Republicans who had helped demonetize silver simply to protect the gold standard, such as Sherman and Treasury Secretary George Boutwell, also began avoiding responsibility for the measure. Denying knowledge of collapsing silver prices, Sherman claimed that as the Coinage Act was being drafted, "no one then contemplated the enormous yield of silver from the mines, and the resulting fall in the market value of silver."[35] Sherman claimed: "We did not know that while we were acting . . . a silver dollar was worth over 3 per cent. more than a gold dollar, by changes of production and other causes that position would be reversed. If any man had then said to me that within twenty years, yea, within fifteen years after that time the silver dollar would only be worth 70 cents on the dollar, I would have thought him crazy. . . . [W]e did not foresee the great change in the value of silver bullion."[36]

Sherman would repeatedly deny that he understood that silver prices were about to collapse, even though Linderman repeatedly warned him of just that. Linderman had informed Sherman: "Rest assured . . . that the decline in silver value will continue until it reaches the gold value of our paper money."[37] Sherman had also received reports from British currency experts that echoed Linderman's predictions regarding the price of silver.[38] Despite his claims to the contrary, Sherman had clearly understood that silver prices were on the verge of collapse, and he had endorsed the Coinage Act because he recognized that it would help insulate the United States from the threat posed by silver's depreciation.

Just as Sherman denied that he understood how the Coinage Act would influence the public credit, Boutwell claimed that the Coinage Act was merely intended to correct "disordered" and "unsystematic" mint conditions, and rejected any suggestion that declining silver prices had influenced the legislation.[39] Linderman would also deny any knowledge of silver's impending depreciation, claiming that the Coinage Act had been introduced "before it became apparent that a serious decline in the value of silver was likely to take place," such that "this change [in the price of silver] in reality could have had no influence in determining the question."[40]

Yet Linderman, Sherman, and Boutwell were aware of silver's impending depreciation, and this recognition had played a significant role in their support for demonetization. Linderman's claims are the least credible. As early as 1872, Linderman reported: "[The silver price's] decline is what I have expected for some time past,"[41] and in 1875 he reported: that "[The] fall in the price of silver is as I have predicted for more than three years past."[42] Linderman's mint report of 1873 recognized that "a further increase in [the volume of silver was] quite certain," making it impossible that he did not recognize the ramifications of his actions.[43] Those familiar with Linderman's report of 1873 recognized that his predictions regarding silver prices were "fulfilled to the letter."[44]

Clearly Treasury officials were aware of silver's imminent decline, and given their reluctance to admit their motives, it is likely that they feared that if they explained their motives they would have drawn opposition from currency inflationists. Aside from the political concerns that influenced individuals such as Sherman and Boutwell, Ralston's allies had clear reasons for masking their motives from congress.

Although popular reactions to Weston's explanation for silver's demonetization were causing a clear pattern of obfuscation among certain public officials, Stewart's reactions to the emergence of the silver issue is particularly interesting. Although Stewart had defended the Coinage Act in congressional debate and had kept Ralston informed of Linderman's actions on his behalf, Stewart became an ardent bimetallist, edited influential free silver newspapers like the *Silver Knight* and the *Silver Knight-Watchman,* and was a prominent member of both the American Bimetallic League and the American Bimetallic Party, the organizations that published *Coin's Financial School* and other influential free silver literature.

Stewart was active in the initial meetings that organized prominent bimetallic organizations that defended free silver and attacked the Coinage Act. Speaking at the initial assembly of the American Bimetallic League in St. Louis in 1889, Stewart denounced the Coinage Act and claimed it was a fraud perpetrated by the world's governments.[45] The irony of Stewart addressing the American Bimetallic League is difficult to fully appreciate: Stewart had assisted Ralston with the Coinage Act and had been fully aware of Linderman's actions on Ralston's behalf. Despite his involvement with the act and his understanding of what had actually occurred, Stewart was celebrated by the very bimetallists who, had they understood the actors responsible for the Coinage Act of 1873, would have been denouncing him.

Yet since none of this was understood, Stewart was labeled "the original silver man" and, in the words of one of his biographers, was an ardent defender of bimetallism, "who since '73 has talked, slept, written, eaten, acted, voted and harangued the monstrous Crime of '73."[46] Subsequent historians who were unaware of the Ralston manuscripts had no reason to question Stewart's dedication to free silver and simply echoed these evaluations. For example, Richard Hofstadter described Stewart as "the silver Senator from Nevada," and Milton Friedman published an article on bimetallism in the *Journal of Political Economy* that began with a quote from Stewart denouncing silver's demonetization.[47]

It is important to note that most members of Ralston's coalition were no longer in public office by 1876. For example, Stewart left office in 1875 but, finding himself in dire financial straits, ran for reelection to the Senate in 1886. In the intervening period silver had emerged as a critical issue in Nevada and California. As early as 1878, the silver issue was being widely discussed in Western states, leading Stewart to recognize that silver had become "the major subject of current political discussion in Nevada."[48] Since it would have been impossible to ignore the issue, Stewart justified his return to politics by claiming: "My principal reason for deciding to become a candidate for the Senate was the act of John Sherman smuggling the silver dollar out of the list of coins in the Mint Act of '73, and I felt it my duty to return to the Senate and do what I could to rectify the crime which was clandestinely committed without my knowledge, or the knowledge of the American people, in the passage of that infamous mint law."[49] By the time Stewart was reelected to the Senate, free silver had become wildly popular in Nevada.[50] Due to his vocal adoption of the issue and his denunciations of the Crime of '73, Stewart's associates described him as a "stalwart champion" of free silver.[51]

Despite Stewart's dedication to free silver, not everyone was persuaded. Stewart's political opponents pointed out that "the great defender of silver" had voted in favor of the Coinage Act, which he now vocally denounced.[52] Stewart defended himself by claiming he had not understood the Coinage Act when he voted for it, and "had no knowledge of the change [in the monetary standards], but continued to suppose that the dollar of Jefferson and Hamilton was still recognized by the mint laws."[53]

Yet Stewart became such a vocal bimetallist that one of his biographers concluded that "it seems almost ludicrous that this ardent partisan for the free coinage of silver and the promotion of bimetallism should have been charged with negligence, or even collusion, in the passage of the [Coinage Act] of 1873."[54] Given his prominence in the subsequent free silver movement, charging Stewart with involvement in the Coinage Act's passage does not *seem* ludicrous, it *is* ludicrous, and yet this is exactly what had happened. For Stewart had been intimately involved in Ralston's efforts to pass the Coinage Act and had assured Ralston: "Linderman is at work on your matters in good earnest and I feel confident of results this session," revealing that he understood Ralston was supporting the measure and that Linderman was working at his behest.[55]

Yet Nevada voters were becoming outraged over silver's demonetization, and soon Stewart "began associating the gold standard with rich and powerful commercial and industrial interests, and silver with the masses,"[56] denouncing the Eastern "bondholding directory . . . [that had] deemed it necessary to demonetize the standard dollar and destroy its legal tender character."[57] He claimed that Jones had produced "the first impartial and philosophical exposition of the money question after the conspiracy to demonetize one of the precious metals was formed."[58] After Jones left Nevada politics in 1878, Stewart began "to establish himself as a leader of the silver forces . . . [and] hurried to fill the void left by Jones, and thus assure his reelection."[59]

Silver advocates began attempting to transform the silver issue from a sectional concern relevant to Western mining states into a national cause, demanding national solutions to what they claimed was a national problem.[60] Just as George Pendleton had not been responsible for creating the initial greenback doctrine but had popularized ideas that had originally been developed by others, Stewart popularized the silver issue to justify a federal response to economic discontent.[61] "It is the duty of Congress," he proclaimed, "to regulate the value of money so that neither the debtor nor the creditor can be robbed by violent contraction or expansion."[62] Stewart's message was emotionally appealing, global in scope, and benefited from details that seemed to lend it credibility.

Stewart had not, however, just "conveniently forgotten" his role in supporting the Coinage Act; his involvement had gone far beyond merely participating in congressional debate.[63] He had advised Ralston and clearly understood that Linderman was working at Ralston's behest. Despite coordinating with Ralston, Stewart's *Reminiscences* claimed: "If anybody . . . has patience to examine the debates between [Sherman] and myself it will be seen how he falsified his statements. It will be seen that the manipulators would take either gold or silver, or any other material, provided they could make money scarce and dear and property cheap, and thus enslave the masses and enrich the classes. If the selfish purposes of the fetish worshiper of the material upon which the Government stamps money could be exposed, the people might investigate the question and compel the Government to stamp money upon material which the unscrupulous could not monopolize."[64] While offering a detailed account of his accusations against Sherman, Stewart's *Reminiscences* are notable for the individuals who are *not* mentioned. Although Sherman is repeatedly denounced and John J. Knox is described as "a crafty, scheming, money-making individual," Stewart's autobiography never mentions either Ralston or Linderman.[65]

The reasons for such omissions are not difficult to understand. The Coinage Act had become deeply unpopular, and Stewart's extensive involvement with Ralston would have been politically disastrous. However, the public's ignorance of what had actually transpired, and the fact that even political actors and journalists such as Weston never understood Ralston's role in the measure or that he used certain Western representatives to help protect the Coinage Act, allowed Stewart to mask his role in the act's passage by simply echoing the myths that the public had adopted.

Deeply implicated in the measure he was now denouncing, Stewart was trying to focus attention away from anyone who could reveal his role in helping pass the Coinage Act. Thus he claimed it was "not surprising that New York City should be opposed to silver," specifically because "its business relations with the bondholding syndicate of Europe [were] exceedingly intimate."[66] New York banks, he said, "[are] either branches of European establishments or are so connected with the business of Europe as to be under the immediate influence of the bondholding directory," and as a consequence New York "apes foreign manners."[67]

There was no real reason to think that Ralston's role in the Coinage Act would ever be revealed. By 1875 the individuals who understood the forces that supported the act were either dead or committed to masking their involvement in the measure. Ralston died days following the collapse of the Bank of California in 1875, and Linderman suffered a fatal heart attack in 1879. The other legislators who had helped Ralston were just as committed to hiding the actors who influenced the Coinage Act, leaving Stewart free to say that he "was compelled in self-defense to investigate and expose the manner of the demonetization of silver and the tricks employed for that purpose."[68] Despite being deeply involved in the Coinage Act's passage, Stewart claimed that "there had been a conspiracy in the passage of the act which demonetized silver, and that its leader had been John Sherman."[69]

Nor was Stewart the only member of Ralston's coalition who was now attacking the Coinage Act. Other members of Ralston's coalition, such as Eugene Casserly and Aaron Sargent, were making similar claims. When the Coinage Act had retained a small coinage charge, Casserly complained to Ralston of having "tried to strike it out, but could not," reporting: "Our friends from the [Pacific] Coast seemed to think it best to let it go"; yet he promised Ralston: "[I will] never rest satisfied however until I see the whole thing kicked out of the statute book."[70] Despite his collusion with Ralston, and despite recognizing that Ralston was using a coalition of Western representatives to support the measure, Casserly began reiterating claims that Eastern and European bankers were responsible for the measure.

Although Linderman had urged Ralston, "Write to all your members in the House particularly Sargent and Axtell" to support the Coinage Act, Sargent was now denying that anything conspiratorial had occurred.[71] Indeed, although Sargent had written to Ralston: "I am watching for a chance to push the bill, believe I understand it, and will do *all* that I can,"[72] Sargent now stated that nothing underhanded had occurred: "I say there has been no fraud committed; I do not know of any fraud; and points are not gained by calling hard names. Fraud does not exist because a suspicion of it may exist in senators' minds. Let those who talk fraud show fraud. I know of no fraud in former legislation, and I admit none so far as myself is concerned, and I do not believe there was any on the part of congress . . . and it is a shame, an appeal of demagoguism to talk about fraud in any such connection as this."[73]

However, Sargent and Stewart were not the only representatives who knew far more about the Coinage Act than their public pronouncements indicated. Although John P. Jones chaired the legislative inquiry into silver's demonetization, he was probably far more aware of why silver had been demonetized than he ever revealed. Jones was clearly not involved in Ralston's efforts to influence the Coinage Act, as he was not a representative when the measure was moving through Congress. Yet he and Stewart jointly owned several silver mines, and Jones was also involved in questionable business dealings with both Bristow and Linderman. In one case when, Bristow ran short of money while treasury secretary, he was forced to call in investments that he had made through Jones. Jones wrote to Bristow: "Dr. Linderman has mentioned that in a letter to him you stated that your business affairs made it a necessity for you to realize the amount in my hands and I have accordingly made a draft on New York for $17,400, payable to him, and which, by his request, I enclose herewith. . . . Our business prospects are good and promise a prosperous and profitable season. I trust the enclosure will arrive in season to relieve you from inconvenience, and I assure you that it has been a great pleasure to me to return your talent with interest."[74] As resumption of the gold standard continued, Linderman assured Bristow: "We are getting the ship pretty well under way and need only stand firm and do our duty to come out with flying colors," and he also complained: "I am sorry that I have not control of the [amount] you gave our friend for investment as I could make an operation which would give you a large profit."[75]

The friend Linderman alluded to was Jones, who wrote to Bristow: "[I have been] deeply immersed in business of various kinds, so that my attention has been almost entirely diverted from affairs of state," and he had lost a considerable sum of money: "In regard to the matters in which you and I are interested I have to tell you that I lost a small amount but it will come out all right in the end."[76]

Because popular denunciations of the Crime of '73 exhibited such factual inaccuracies, it is difficult to see how these demands could have arisen as a simple reaction to economic conditions. The interpretations the public adopted had initially been framed both by journalists attempting to explain what had occurred and by the subsequent comments made by various politicians, including some who had helped Ralston pass the Coinage Act. The popular reactions to Weston's editorials had forced Ralston's legislative allies to either deny any conspiracy had existed or echo Weston's inaccurate claims.

By capitalizing on the popular outrage generated by Weston's editorials, and by attacking Eastern and European financiers in ways that fit popular stereotypes, Ralston's allies masked their responsibility for what had occurred and popularized an interpretation that became a source of popular support and power. The fact that these explanations were largely fictitious was, for Ralston's allies, irrelevant. The explanation was persuasive, appealed to voters' distrust of bankers and foreigners, and provided a simple prescription for how to end the recession, one that deflected attention away from their involvement in the Coinage Act.[77]

Yet since none of this was understood at the time, the debate that was occurring over the silver issue gave the appearance of a vibrant public dialogue on an important political issue. Noting the discussion the silver issue was attracting, some commentators concluded: "There never was a time in the history of the country when the average voter was so thoroughly informed as to the financial situation."[78] This impression was misleading, however, and instead of ensuring that voters were deliberating about the true nature of what had transpired, there was the illusion of popular comprehension where none actually existed. Had voters understood what had happened, they would have recognized that Ralston's allies were denying involvement in the passage of a measure they had been deeply associated with, and they would have found the popularized interpretations for what had occurred to be less persuasive.

It is important to emphasize that Ralston's coalition was not responsible for creating the free silver movement that emerged following Weston's editorials. The free silver movement would have emerged had Ralston's allies never mentioned a thing about silver. However, the passage of the Coinage Act, which Ralston's allies had been deeply involved in, had created the underlying condition, demonetization of the silver dollar, necessary for bimetallism to emerge as a political issue in the first place.

The irony of this situation was not lost on Stewart, who wrote a subsequent editorial in the Silver Knight-Watchman that revealed a degree of unease with what had occurred. After watching the country be consumed by the silver issue during the election of 1896, after watching Bryan's "Cross of Gold" convention speech, and after watching public opinion become captivated by falsehoods, Stewart noted: "We presume the perpetrators of the crime of 1873 can never be brought to punishment, except the sort that rankles in the soul and keeps criminals awake o' nights."[79] Although unrecognized by the *Silver Knight-Watchman*'s readers, or anyone unfamiliar with the Ralston manuscripts, Stewart was probably referring to himself.

Given his associations with Ralston and his knowledge of Linderman's actions, it is difficult to see how Stewart could have presided over mass political meetings, given impassioned political speeches, and accepted warm introductions from fellow bimetallists and not felt some degree of discomfort. Had anyone understood what had actually occurred, Stewart would have been denounced as a protagonist of the very "crime" he was now publically denouncing.

Yet it is also difficult to see what alternative course of action Ralston's allies could have pursued. The popular outrage generated by Weston's editorials made it impossible for the representatives of Nevada and California, both states with large silver-mining industries, to oppose bimetallism. Given the public's anger, it was hardly feasible for members of Ralston's coalition to admit to any involvement in the measure or to try to explain that they had mistakenly believed the Coinage Act would help their constituents. Yet their states' large silver interests ensured that they could not ignore the silver issue either. Since they couldn't explain their involvement in the measure's passage, explain that they had actually been supporting a measure they believed aided their constituents, or ignore the mounting outrage over the silver issue, Ralston's coalition were forced to popularize fictions and criticize a measure they had helped pass.

While this issue insulated Ralston's coalition from electoral retribution, the coalition's actions unintentionally wound up influencing the ideological development of the Democratic Party, and thus had broader ramifications for American political development. Weston's ideas were eventually taken up by various bimetallic organizations, the Populists, and then the Democratic Party. Once the Democrats adopted demands for the government to issue silver currency, these ideas stimulated a transformation in Americans' assumptions about the scope of government authority.

Just as the greenback issue had forced the parties to alter their monetary positions, a similar reversal was now occurring with silver, and something other than strict logic was organizing the parties' responses. Conservatives initially sought to use fractional silver currency to retire greenbacks, and greenback inflationists had initially opposed currency inflation on the basis of silver and not paper currency. As one newspaper recognized:

> In the East numbers of those who last year were in favor of a bi-metallic money standard are now contending that gold is the only proper basis. In the West the paper-money men are also dissatisfied with our monetary laws and, though heretofore . . . opposed to metallic money, are now quite willing—in fact, eager—to have silver and plenty of it. . . . So between the hard-money men of the East who are changing their bi-metallic ideas, and the greenback men of the West who are becoming hard-money men, it is difficult to tell exactly what ought or ought not be done. It was supposed that Hayes was a bi-metallic money man, while Secretary Sherman favors only gold. . . . But what is the meaning of this change in the sentiment of the East and the West? It may mean that the greenback party has seen the error of its ways and is willing to compromise with the hard-money men. But whatever the West means, it is certain there is an inconsistency in the logic of the East. The arguments that were good a year ago in favor of silver are equally good now.[80]

Despite such reversals in the policies that various groups believed advanced their interests, by the late 1870s the central tenets of the free silver position had been framed by the misconceptions contained in Weston's initial editorials, and various politicians, publicists, and bimetallic organizations were now transmitting these misconceptions to the public.

As popular outrage at the Crime of '73 mounted and the free silver movement gained strength, it became apparent that there had been a reversal in the
specific policies and general attitudes exhibited by the party's ideologies. Attacking those opposed to regulating financial markets, Stewart claimed: "The
suggestion that the government cannot regulate the volume of currency . . . is
in harmony with the goldite theory."[81]

The American Bimetallic League's first meeting occurred in St. Louis in
November 1889, and a subsequent meeting held in Washington, D.C., in February 1893 reiterated calls for action on behalf of silver.[82] Republican successes
in the congressional elections of 1894 were attributed to Grover Cleveland's
unpopular support for the gold standard, and the subsequent Democratic
losses in the elections of 1895 in Illinois, Kentucky, and Ohio solidified the
perception that the Democrats were doomed if they opposed free silver.[83]

By demanding that the federal government coin silver at the ratio of 16 to
1, there were increasing calls for using the state as a problem-solving instrument, and these demands were emanating from the Democratic Party that
before the Civil War had sought to limit the power of the federal government.
The Democrats' reversal was being mirrored by Republicans, who despite having inherited aspects of the Whigs' program of state-assisted industrialization,
were increasingly demanding nonintervention and the gold standard.

Although the Populists focused on a range of issues and grievances, and free
silver was hardly the most radical of their demands, monetary policy became
the "ideological centerpiece" of their appeals.[84] Given its widespread popular
appeal, and its relative moderation, free silver was, not surprisingly, the principal Populist policy absorbed by the Democratic Party.[85] However, since writers
and organizations that were unaffiliated with any major political party had set
the terms of the free silver issue, the issue was also the "least original" of the
Democrats' and Populists' ideas.[86]

Rather than being responsible for drafting the original ideas behind the
silver issue, Bryan had been introduced to the silver issue by reading *Coin's Financial School*.[87] He specifically singled out Stewart for having "devoted all his
energies" to the cause of free silver.[88] Having watched Stewart debate bimetallism in the Senate, Bryan claimed he would "never forget the earnestness" with
which Stewart denounced the Coinage Act of 1873, and commended Stewart
for his "constant . . . work outside the Senate" as editor of the *Silver Knight*
and the *National Watchman*.[89] As no one understood Ralston's allies' actions,
some of the very legislators who had helped Ralston were eluding popular de-

tection, and one of them was leading a social movement that was denouncing the measure he had helped Ralston pass.

By popularizing free silver as the solution to economic recession, George Weston introduced a powerful conspiracy theory into the debate over finance policy. Weston's conspiracy theory reinforced popular preconceptions regarding Eastern and European bankers, and after being espoused by other political actors, it helped extend the idea of using the state to aid the disadvantaged onto the national stage. While the Democrats retained their hostility to monopoly, by endorsing free silver, and the proactive federal actions required by these inflationary demands, the policies that were previously associated with hostility to centralized economic power were being reversed.

As the Democrats began to endorse expanding the state's role in the economy, the Republicans were backed into a politically uncomfortable position of opposing efforts to use the state to implement commonsense solutions to ordinary Americans' problems.[90] The Republicans' solution to the political problem this posed was to explore nondemocratic methods of resisting public opinion, first in monetary policy and then in railroad regulation. Although these institutions were later expanded, and adopted for different political purposes during the Progressive Era, their initial introduction was a short-term reaction to the electoral problems the Democratic Party's increasingly populist economic positions posed for the Republican Party.

It is important to emphasize that Ralston's coalition was not responsible for initiating or causing this sequence of events. Weston's editorials, the free silver movement, and the adoption of free silver by various political actors and parties would all have occurred regardless of Ralston's allies' actions. While the emergence of the free silver movement and the adoption of free silver by the Democratic Party were perhaps inevitable, Ralston and his allies had created the underlying condition, the elimination of bimetallism, that was necessary for political conflict over silver to occur in the first place. Thus while the congressmen in Ralston's loose coalition were not responsible for the emergence of the free silver issue or the free silver movement, they managed to elude popular detection due to voter ignorance of the actors responsible for the Coinage Act.

Indeed, perhaps the most interesting aspect of the silver issue is that the actors who influenced the Coinage Act were never identified by voters, the leaders of the free silver movement, or the principal academic studies of the period.[91] This is especially surprising because the silver issue was one of the most contentious and widely discussed policies of the nineteenth century. It generated sustained media coverage and popular discussion, and voters correctly identified the Coinage Act as the legislation responsible for ending bimetallism. Yet despite all the attention the act received, the public adopted a conspiracy theory that blamed European bankers, the Rothschilds, and Ernst Seyd for a scheme executed by the California banker William Ralston, Henry Linderman, and a loose coalition of Western representatives.

Furthermore, even the relatively informed political actors who were involved in the Coinage Act's passage and understood its ramifications, such as John Sherman, never suspected Ralston's role in the act. Given how poorly such officials understood what had occurred, it is difficult to criticize the public for misunderstanding the forces influencing the Coinage Act. Indeed, even elite political figures such as Sherman who understood the impending collapse of silver prices and endorsed silver's demonetization for simple political purposes never understood Linderman and Stewart's connection to Ralston, or Ralston's influence over the measure. If rival politicians, political parties, and media sources are necessary to alert democratic publics of important political decisions that voters cannot directly observe, the silver issue is a clear case where political elites lacked the information necessary to understand the sequence of events that had occurred.

Given the resulting misunderstanding of nearly all nineteenth-century observers, it is little surprise that the public found an inaccurate explanation persuasive, especially since it reinforced preconceptions about unpopular Eastern and European bankers. Instead of recognizing that a California banker, certain Western representatives, and Linderman had sought to use the Coinage Act to advance their interests, voters were mistakenly demanding an end to "British rule in our money matters."[92]

Nor was this entirely unrecognized. Nineteenth-century observers of all political persuasions complained that the public had simply not been aware of the Coinage Act's introduction and passage, and given the ignorance of the representatives who voted on the measure, it is difficult to see how it could have been otherwise. Regardless of which interests historians and political scientists have held responsible for the Coinage Act, it is clear that "very few people . . . understood" the forces responsible for the decisions concerning the act.[93]

However, the ignorance and misunderstandings surrounding the Coinage Act are hardly limited to nineteenth-century observers. One of the most interesting aspects of this chapter of American politics is that subsequent academic studies were, in a sense, *less* accurate than the fictions nineteenth-century voters adopted. When Richard Hofstadter attributed the myth of the Crime of '73 to tendencies prevalent among the paranoid and uneducated, he overlooked how his own interpretations were being influenced by myths espoused by long-dead politicians.[94] After concluding that bankers and bribery had not been associated with the Coinage Act's passage, Hofstadter dismissed the Populists for espousing the "paranoid style" of American politics, never realizing that Ralston's involvement in silver policy demonstrates that the Populists' suspicions were far more accurate than anyone realized. Subsequent scholars such as Milton Friedman, Anna Schwartz, Irwin Unger, and Allen Weinstein found no reason to doubt Hofstadter's conclusions, and their studies similarly failed to recognize the interests influencing this period of American politics.

Thus, although nineteenth-century Americans believed various fictions regarding silver policy, when scholars concluded the Populists were "obsessed with imaginary grievances," they failed to realize that the interpretations they offered were more mythic than those the Populists had espoused.[95] Oddly, these errors did not occur because Ralston's relationship with Linderman, or his involvement in the Coinage Act, was completely unknown. Both David Lavender's biography of Ralston and the coinage expert Robert Van Ryzin's subsequent *Crime of 1873* documented Ralston's relationship with Linderman. The fact that these important books have been overlooked indicates that even interested parties with strong incentives to learn about politics may simply not know where to look or what to pay attention to.

The errors in this period's historiography are indicative of the general problems facing democratic citizens' attempts to understand politics. For if academics possessing strong interest in the subject, ample resources, and free and open access to primary sources may fail to identify the actors responsible for important political decisions, it is little surprise that nineteenth-century voters adopted inaccurate explanations that concealed as much as they explained. Although the Coinage Act was widely discussed, the measure was attributed to the wrong bankers, and the resulting errors in attribution prevented the electorate from penalizing the officials responsible for one of the most salient political issues of the nineteenth century.

Chapter 12 The Conservative Origins of the American Regulatory State

The expansion of American state authority is often attributed to the economic, institutional, and intellectual innovations of the Progressive Era. Spurred by industrialization, the emergence of the modern firm, labor disputes, the Populist movement, the writings of intellectuals such as Herbert Croly, Walter Weyl, and Walter Lippmann, and the efforts of politicians such as Woodrow Wilson and Theodore Roosevelt, the American state is often seen emerging from the Progressive Era's economic environment, and the intellectual influence of German historicism and *Staatswissenschaft*.[1]

While these forces clearly stimulated the American state-building process, this chapter argues that the American state was initially created before these developments, and for reasons that were unrelated to the economic and intellectual forces that influenced progressive reformers. My chronology of this institutional development departs from the timing and variables that many argue generated a new form of politics that enlisted the state to serve social democratic ends. Hardly created to satisfy popular demands or to apply experimental knowledge to address modern social problems, the American regulatory state was initially created by the response of conservative political elites to electoral pressures and concerns regarding the rationality of public opinion. Despite being influenced by the ideological shifts occurring within the Democratic Party and by broad economic transformations within American society, the bureaucratic regulatory state was not created to satisfy popular demands for protection from market forces but was instead created to insulate policy from public opinion and to ensure implementation of policy decisions that political observers of all persuasions recognized were deeply unpopular.

This is not to deny popular hostility toward the American industrial order, nor do I wish to minimize the importance of economic developments such as the expansion of national markets, the development of transcontinental railroad infrastructure, the centralization of financial markets, and the commercial characteristics of American agrarian life. Indeed, the popular demands that arose in this new economic environment sought to enlist the state to combat the impersonal forces that were organizing the American economy, and these demands clearly *conditioned* the emergence of the American regulatory state. Despite recognizing that it was perhaps inevitable that there would be some political response to these new demands, I argue that the bureaucratic *form* the American state assumed was not initially a result of these pressures.

However, the political innovation that was created in this economic and social context, the empowerment of bureaucracies armed with discretionary authority over the national economy, was not intended to satisfy societal demands but instead was created to resist the policy demands that were becoming increasingly popular. Rather than emerging to fulfill popular desires, the bureaucratic innovations that culminated in a new American state were introduced to accomplish conservative policy objectives, resumption of the gold standard, and exemptions from the ICA's ban on railroad price discrimination.

Aside from seeking conservative policy objectives, the Republicans and liberal reformers who expanded the state's bureaucratic capacity hoped to insulate the Treasury Department and the ICC from public opinion, and in the case of railroad regulation, help educate voters about the complex forces that were transforming the American economy. In this sense the American state's bureaucratic regulatory characteristics were intended to limit public opinion's influence upon politics.

Despite arguing that the initial creation of the American state was a conservative reaction to public opinion, I do not seek to minimize how subsequent political and intellectual forces sought to employ this new state to serve social democratic ends. As an increasing number of Americans were trained in German universities and exposed to the teachings of intellectuals such as Gustav Schmoller and Adolph Wagner, new ideas were exploring the state's legitimate relationship to modern industrial problems.[2]

The *initial* empowerment of American bureaucratic institutions, however, was not a consequence of such influences. Rather, conservatives such as Charles Francis Adams Jr., David Wells, Edward Atkinson, E. L. Godkin, and John Sherman were championing novel institutional innovations to implement conservative policy decisions.[3] While German-educated economists, and organizations such as the American Economic Association, subsequently sought to enlist the state as an instrument of social democracy, federal bureaucracies were being empowered to accomplish conservative policy objectives.[4]

This chapter argues that the initial creation of federal bureaucratic regulatory capacity was a reaction by certain Republicans and liberal reformers to resist demands increasingly being made of American government. Although the public was calling for a more active government, the American state's *bureaucratic* characteristics were intended to resist implementation of these demands. In this sense the American state was created to fulfill unpopular policy objectives and to resist public opinion, and hence cannot simply be attributed to social demands and pressures. I do not, however, seek to minimize the impact that public opinion had upon elite actors but instead argue that these demands were precisely what led certain conservatives to endorse bureaucracy as a method of resisting popular demands they believed were irrational. Far from suggesting that the state was impervious to public opinion, I argue that popular pressures were not responsible for the bureaucratic institutions that were created, or the policies these bureaucracies implemented.

Ever since monetary policy was reintroduced into American politics, many Republicans had recognized the gold standard's unpopularity. Although they initially focused on greenback inflation, by the 1870s there were growing demands for the free coinage of silver. Yet despite demanding monetary expansion, silver inflationists did not initially seek to fulfill this policy objective bureaucratically. Indeed, George Weston's initial editorials opposed using the Treasury Department to manipulate the money supply. Weston complained that "investing the Secretary of the Treasury, or some other official, with the power to declare, authoritatively, how many silver greenbacks had left the country and to supply their place with an equal number of new ones" was problematic, as doing so would "invest the Secretary of the Treasury . . . with the power to refuse to issue new ones, or to fix the amount of the new coins at his will and pleasure. It would always be a matter of mere guess-work, based on probabilities more or less plausible. . . . A Secretary of the Treasury can guess what he pleases, or if he goes through the form of instituting a commission of subordinates to guess for him, or to relieve him from the responsibility of guessing, it is only the form of the thing which is changed and not the substance, as the selection of the guessers lies with him, and their tenure of office is only his caprice from day to day."[5] Weston concluded that if the treasury secretary were free to manipulate the money supply, "within wide limits" the secretary would possess the authority to manipulate national economic conditions.[6] Such concerns over enhancing the powers of bureaucracy were hardly limited to Weston's editorials; they were shared by other prominent free silverites as well. For example, although William Stewart was demanding silver's remonetization, he believed the Populists' Omaha platform's "proposal to give more power to the Federal Government" over the railroads and telegraphs was "folly," as this would merely empower politicians who were controlled by the "gold power."[7]

Such skepticism was not limited to monetary policy. Similar concerns existed with individual states' efforts to regulate the railroads. In states where Granger organization was extensive, such as Illinois, the creation of independent railroad commissions had been a result of conservative shippers' reactions *against* radical Grangers' demands.[8] But federal bureaucracies were not being empowered in response to powerful economic groups' demands either. Despite the policy disagreements between agrarians and Eastern financiers, Eastern financiers who endorsed the gold standard shared agrarian opposition to bureaucratic delegation.

Members of the Republican Party did not endorse delegation as a preferred policy response, however, and the expansion of bureaucratic capacity was in no way part of a deliberate state-building project. Rather, these actions were forced upon them as a response to popular dissatisfaction with their policy objectives. For example, in 1866 when Treasury Secretary Hugh McCulloch began initial attempts to withdraw greenbacks from circulation, Sherman *opposed* the Treasury's discretion over the money supply.[9] However, Sherman's opposition occurred *before* Pendleton popularized greenback inflation in 1867, and before the emergence of the free silver issue. In the absence of inflationary electoral pressures Sherman had no reason to endorse delegation, and he had opposed McCulloch's contraction of the currency because he feared the Treasury Department was operating in ways with few precedents.

Nor was Sherman quick to abandon his opposition to empowering the Treasury Department. As late as 1877 Sherman stated that legislation on the silver question was "one for Congress, and not for the Executive officers," even while noting: "We cannot but feel very solicitous upon a subject that if wrongly settled would render negatory all efforts at resumption."[10] In 1877 when Sherman was asked to explain the Treasury's course of action for resumption of the gold standard, he refused, replying that "nothing would so tend to disturb" his efforts to accomplish resumption "as unauthorized 'theses,' or dogma, by an executive officer upon a question purely legislative or judicial."[11]

Yet after public opinion had become captivated by greenback inflation and free silver, Sherman was forced to abandon his opposition to delegation and independent executive action. Specie resumption became his "one absorbing desire"; it was the goal that had consumed "the best energies of his life."[12] Despite having criticized McCulloch for his independent action immediately following the Civil War, Sherman's annual Treasury Department report for 1878 bluntly stated: "The means and manner of [achieving specie resumption] . . . are left largely to the discretion of the secretary."[13] Recognizing the utility of this form of authority, Sherman abandoned his earlier opposition to bureaucratic discretion, asserting that the treasury secretary enjoyed "discretion reposed by law in the Secretary of the Treasury, or in any head or subordinate of any department of the government," a form of authority that he claimed was part of the "custom of Congress to intrust to the Secretary of the Treasury specific powers over the currency, the public debt and the collection of the revenue."[14]

Sherman's interpretation of executive authority adopted elements of the Whig theory of the presidency, whereby the cabinet was to act with a degree of independence from the president.[15] Yet Sherman denied Whig assertions of legislative supremacy. In suggesting that the executive departments enjoyed a degree of independence from both the president and Congress, and in applying such independence to the regulation of national economic conditions, he had introduced an institutional innovation into American politics.[16]

While the Federalists had endorsed executive leadership and bureaucratic discretion, such powers were not intended to *regulate* markets. Although bureaucratic authority had existed at the state level and had been employed for regulatory purposes, the federal government had rarely used such authority. Similarly, Sherman never intended to use this form of authority to regulate the money supply; empowering the treasury secretary with discretion was intended to accomplish a strictly conservative goal, resumption of the gold standard.

Sherman, however, quickly realized the importance of retaining the Treasury Department's ability to influence financial markets and the money supply. His annual report for 1880 noted that the Treasury coin reserves granted the Treasury power to act to reassure markets: "In case of an adverse balance of trade or a sudden panic, or other unforeseen circumstances, the ample reserve of coin on hand becomes the sure safeguard of resumption, dispelling not only imaginary fears, but meeting any demand for coin that is likely to arise. In a supreme emergency, the power granted to sell bonds will supply any possible deficiency."[17] Maintenance of the gold standard required that the treasury secretary maintain coinage reserves to redeem notes that might be presented for redemption. Despite having little interest in actively regulating the money supply, Sherman sought to retain the secretary's ability to intervene in financial markets to defend specie resumption, ensuring that authority originally used to resume the gold standard was maintained even after this policy objective was realized.

While occurring amid fluctuating international monetary forces, this form of authority was a reaction to domestic electoral pressures that were themselves influenced by other political elites' interpretations regarding the causes of, and optimal responses to, economic distress, interpretations that Sherman and others believed were irrational views of monetary policy. However, unlike Treasury Secretary McCulloch, who had sought to reinstate the gold standard by permanently withdrawing greenbacks from circulation, Sherman sought to maintain circulation of the greenbacks, defend their value in gold, and preserve the Treasury Department's ability to redeem them. Doing so required the institutionalization of a new form of authority over the money supply, a form of authority that was described as representing a departure from the Treasury's prior actions.

Prior to the Civil War the potential for federal activism was limited by the disintegration of the Federalists, the Whigs' opposition to executive power, and the antebellum Democrats' hostility toward federal authority. Yet as Republicans recognized the unpopularity of their preferred policies, they endorsed bureaucratic delegation in order to remove certain policies from popular influence and because some hoped bureaucracies would disseminate expert information to help educate voters.

It is important to stress that this argument focuses on the *initial* creation of this form of state authority and does not extend to subsequent periods when populist social movements became less hostile to bureaucratic authority. In her study of the interaction between social movements and state authority,

Elizabeth Sanders argues that agrarians endorsed bureaucratic delegation as a compromise with other political actors' preferences. However, the Treasury Department's resumption of the gold standard was simply not a compromise with agrarians. Since the Treasury Department was defending the gold standard and opposing greenback inflation and bimetallism, there was no compromise position that would have satisfied currency inflationists.

Similarly, although agrarian populists acquiesced to bureaucracy *after* the passage of the ICA and endorsed empowering the ICC to regulate railroad rates, the bureaucratic form *initially* taken by the ICC was not a product of their demands. Like the Treasury Department's discretion over the money supply, the ICC's discretion was used to for distinctly unpopular purposes, namely, to *exempt* railroads from the ICA's prohibition on price discrimination. Given his opposition to creating a commission, after the ICA created a regulatory commission John Reagan was reported to have remarked, "in graceful Texan," that the ICA's creation of a bureaucratic commission "did not amount to a d——n, but Cullom could have that point."[18]

Despite Reagan's opposition to commissions, after the Treasury Department had demonstrated that discretion could be used to combat popular economic "heresies," leading this form of bureaucratic authority to subsequently be applied to other agencies. Thus, after currency inflation became a popular panacea for economic distress, voters began asking Congress, "Pass some act aiding us and controlling the Railroad," and such popular demands were increasingly spreading alongside a new form of state authority.[19]

Just as conservatives' support for the gold standard provided the basis for endorsing bureaucratic delegation in monetary policy, public opposition to railroads and price discrimination led liberal reformers to conclude that the public was endorsing irrational policies. Accordingly, liberal reformers introduced legislation to neutralize aspects of the Reagan bill and endorsed creating a regulatory commission empowered with discretion to determine whether instances of price discrimination were "reasonable." By allowing the ICC to determine the reasonableness of railroads' rates, the ICC acquired discretion despite *opposition* from Reagan and his supporters. Hence, the initial institutional form initially taken by the American regulatory state was the product of conservative forces.

It is critical to stress that although this form of state authority was created to serve conservative policy objectives, such authority was not intended to serve the interests of conservative groups.[20] Conservative financial groups had opposed granting the Treasury Department discretion, and powerful railroads criticized efforts to regulate their industry.[21] Rather than being created at the behest of powerful economic groups, these initial cases of bureaucratic delegation were generated by the particular configuration of conservative ideological positions and certain policy elites' reactions to popular economic demands.

Populist opposition to bureaucracy, the contradictory configuration of antistatism and statism by ideological groups that subsequently reversed both their specific issue positions and their general attitudes toward government, and the fact that those who held economic views that would currently be classified as "conservative" initially endorsed bureaucracy all make these transformations appear paradoxical to us today. The particular configurations of issue positions taken by various political elites seem as archaic as Adams's idea that bureaucracies could help inform voters and enhance democratic engagement.

His belief that the public did not understand the railroad problem has led some to dismiss Adams and other liberal reformers who shared his views as antidemocratic elitists, and there is some truth to this charge. However, one should not overlook the nature of the problems Adams recognized and tried to solve. He did not simply want to neutralize the power of public opinion; he hoped commissions would help educate the public about complex social forces that were increasingly the subject of American politics, and he hoped an informed public would pressure elected officials to implement rational policies.

Regardless of the interests bureaucracy was eventually used to serve, regulatory authority had shifted from the states to the federal government, and it was then transferred from legislative and judicial actors to bureaucracies. This transition occurred before intellectuals associated with the American Economic Association challenged laissez-faire, and before progressives such as Croly, Weyl, and many others began exploring how the state could be enlisted to serve social democratic ends. The American regulatory state was initially created by conservative ideological groups to serve policy objectives that these subsequent thinkers opposed.

It is important to note, however, that the form of state authority that emerged from postbellum political conflict was not simply endorsed by all progressive thinkers. While recognizing that many progressives endorsed bureaucracy, prominent progressives, such as Croly and Richard T. Ely, expressed skepticism toward regulating market prices by commission or bureau, and Ely believed government ownership of private industries was "eminently superior" to regulatory commissions.[22] Despite endorsing an activist national bureaucratic state in *Progressive Democracy*, Croly's *Promise of American Life* expressed reservations about independent commissions that were, in part, based upon his concern that they would elude control by an uninformed public opinion.[23]

Aside from concerns about the interaction between bureaucratic expertise and public opinion, as the American state acquired regulatory authority over the economy, some recognized difficulties in judging the effects of its regulatory operations. These problems were not apparent when Sherman used his discretion to sell loans to retire greenbacks from circulation. So long as the treasury secretary sought to resume the gold standard, the effects of the Treasury's policies could be determined by analyzing fluctuations in the gold premium. However, once the Treasury Department sought to determine the appropriate amount of currency to place in circulation, the nature of these calculations was altered because there was no similar method for assessing the effects of the Treasury Department's manipulations of the money supply.

A similar problem existed with regulating railroad rates. Two years after the ICC's passage, Adams recommended that the ICC divide traffic among the railroads at rates that it established to be "reasonable."[24] Thomas Cooley, the ICC's first chairman, identified this objective as the principal justification for the ICC's creation.[25] Yet implementing this rule proved to be far more complicated than was initially assumed. Given the different conditions associated with each railroad, the competing means of transportation unique to each locale, and various other considerations influencing the prices railroads charged, it was unclear how to determine a rate's reasonableness.

Indeed, although Richard White recognizes that the struggle to determine what constituted a reasonable rate became "the center" of political controversy over railroad regulation, it was difficult for the railroads themselves to know what rates they were charging shippers, since rates were determined though a decentralized process of bargaining among local freight agents and shippers.[26] Published rate schedules were often misleading, as the railroads frequently made confidential arrangements with shippers that were never publicized. Although the ICA required the railroads to send the ICC their shipping rates in an effort to increase the publicity of railroad rates, the ICC received between fourteen hundred and fifteen hundred rate schedules *each day*, indicating that there were significant difficulties in simply understanding existing rate structures.[27]

Aside from these difficulties, it remained unclear how to determine whether a rate was reasonable. This problem threatened regulatory decisions with irrationality. If regulators set rates lower than economic conditions demanded, resources would be inefficiently directed away from the railroad industry.[28] The problems associated with establishing a rational rate structure confounded voters and knowledgeable experts alike. Although Charles Francis Adams Jr. devoted himself to the study of the railroads and recognized "the heart of . . . [the railroad] problem was rates," it was clear that by the end of his life he had still "failed to work out the problem."[29]

One possible method for addressing this problem was offered by Henry Adams, the ICC's first statistician, who rejected the historicist tendency to simply reject laissez-faire and endorse reliance upon the state.[30] He viewed states' responsibilities to ensuring moral standards among businesses and endorsed government ownership of monopolies such that the state would set "price equals cost."[31] There were, however, difficulties associated with this form of regulation that had been recognized in congressional deliberation.

Testifying before Congress in 1879, Albert Fink had noted: "It is held by some that [railroad rates] . . . in order to be reasonable, must be made in exact proportion of the cost of the service performed; but then the question arises, 'What is the cost?' and this is a very difficult question to answer."[32] Although he studied the railroad industry with an intensity similar to that of Darwin studying evolution, in the end Fink simply "could find no uniform rule for rate making."[33]

Fink and Henry Adams were not alone in recognizing these problems. Although Commissioner Cooley defended the legitimacy of regulating corporate profits, he believed that, unlike calculations involving simpler issues such as supplying water to municipalities, the regulation of railroad rates "could only be mischievous."[34] As railroad rates had to remain flexible and adapt to "innumerable circumstances and contingencies, expected and unexpected," it was impossible for regulators to create a rate schedule derived from any fixed formula.[35]

These problems cannot simply be dismissed as ideological defenses of business interests, even if they were deployed for such purposes. The epistemological problems associated with regulating the market price mechanism lies at the heart of modern regulatory politics, and the intractability of these problems has led Stephen Skowronek to suggest that modern regulatory decisions are more political than scientific.[36] Yet regardless of how these decisions are evaluated, the creation of discretionary authority within the Treasury Department and ICC to intervene in, and manipulate, national economic conditions, was a transformational moment in American politics.

By claiming that the Treasury Department and the ICC's appropriation of bureaucratic discretion marked key turning points in American state formation, my analysis departs from the chronology of Skowronek's *Building a New American State*. According to Skowronek, until 1900 railroad regulation was not state building but "patchwork," a process by which existing institutions were applied in ways that did not result in novel institutional developments. In a key passage, Skowronek notes: "The problem with the Interstate Commerce Act was not that it served any one interest but that it ventured into inconsistency and ambiguity in failing to choose among the interests. Congress had not transformed the conflicts within society into a coherent regulatory policy but had merely translated those conflicts into governmental policy and shifted them to other institutions."[37] In this passage Skowronek's analysis shifts its focus from an institutional *innovation* to the *interests* served by the institutions that were created. Regardless of the effectiveness of the ICC's decisions upon the railroad industry, and regardless of which interests were advanced by the ICC's decisions, regulatory authority had been delegated to a federal regulatory commission. This shifted authority away from state and local governments, and within the federal government power was delegated to executive bureaucrats, an institutional template subsequently replicated in other agencies.

Regardless of the novelty of this innovation, there was widespread disagreement over how the ICC should regulate price discrimination. Commissioner Cooley noted that two interpretations had been given to the fourth section of the ICA, which granted the ICC discretion to determine whether railroads' price discrimination was reasonable. Some railroads hoped the ICC would permit most forms of long-haul-short-haul price discrimination, but Cooley believed that some thought that certain members of the House had intended a second position, expecting the ICC to prohibit price discrimination in a manner that was "imperative and absolute."[38] Cooley deviated from both of these stances, however, and instead endorsed a third position, concluding that the ICA only granted the ICC discretion to determine whether a railroad's price discrimination was reasonable.

How Cooley and the ICC would wield such power was critical. For example, when ruling on the Louisville and Nashville Railroad's petition to allow it to engage in price discrimination, Cooley explained that the ICC would exercise the "discretion [that] was left to the Commission in the matter of relaxing the rule when different circumstances and conditions rendered such relaxation in its judgment proper."[39] By using its discretion to grant railroads *exemptions* from the prohibition on price discrimination, the ICC blunted the more radical implications of legislation championed by agrarian interests.

Despite embodying a novel form of state authority, the ICC was not seek-ing to aggrandize its power or expand its organizational capacity. For example, the ICC refused to establish a uniform freight classification system or directly set railroad rates.[40] As Commissioner Augustus Schoonmaker noted, if the ICC attempted to directly set railroad rates, "it could do nothing else and would soon be overwhelmed."[41] Despite being a relatively modest exercise of authority, the ICC was allowing railroads to engage in price discrimination under conditions that it determined were reasonable.

It is important to note that the ICC was not the first case where bureau-crats intervened in markets or exercised discretion. At the state level, regula-tory commissions had regulated various aspects of intrastate railroads and had ruled on the maximum prices railroads could charge shippers. Nor was the ICC the first federal independent commission to wield discretion or draft administrative law; within the Treasury Department the Steamboat Inspection Service regulated steamboat safety and licensing, leading to the creation of a system of administrative law decades prior to the ICC's creation.[42]

Yet the Steamboat Inspection Service never sought to institute fair or rea-sonable levels of competition, it did not seek to regulate market prices, and it was never intended to have any larger implications for the rationality of transportation markets. In this sense the Steamboat Inspection Service did not exercise the form of authority the ICC possessed. Indeed, few nineteenth-century contemporaries viewed the ICC as a mere continuation of an existing form of state authority. Instead of seeing continuity between the ICC and prior forms of American government, the railroads subjected to the ICC's authority believed that the ICC's ability to rule on the reasonableness of price discrimination was "not only new, but novel."[43]

This form of authority had not been created to satisfy popular demands or populist policy preferences. Clearly the ICA had support from antimonopo-lists and shippers who hoped to secure lower transportation rates. However, the ICC used its discretion to *exempt* railroads from its prohibition on price discrimination. If we accept George Miller's claim that popular anger toward the railroads focused on price discrimination, if we accept the statements by Commissioners William Morrison, Augustus Schoonmaker, and Whealock Veazey that they believed eliminating price discrimination was the "great ob-ject" the ICA was intended to accomplish, and if we accept the claims made in the ICC's annual reports and in the national platforms of various agrar-ian organizations, the ICC was using its discretion to accomplish unpopular objectives.[44]

It is necessary to emphasize that popular attitudes toward the ICC's discretion were not constant or homogeneous. For example, years later in 1905 as the Hepburn Act was being drafted to give the ICC the power to set maximum railroad rates, Stanley Elkins observed that "the people" seemed convinced that "giving power to the Commission to make rates" was the best remedy for controlling the railroads.[45] I do not wish to challenge such claims, nor do I deny that such views of the ICC's authority helped legitimate the subsequent expansion of its authority. The setting of rates was not *initially* considered a legitimate exercise of the ICC's authority, however, and the ICC's commissioners maintained they would only rule on whether price discrimination was reasonable given the different competitive conditions facing specific railroads.[46]

Furthermore, despite its centrality to the ICC's regulatory functions, this principle was simply not widely understood. Although much of my analysis has focused on *voter* ignorance of politics, many *shippers* whose business interests were directly influenced by the ICC's decisions did not understand what the ICA stipulated or what the ICC was empowered to do. The incoming correspondence of the ICC is filled with letters from shippers demanding that the ICC prevent railroads from engaging in *any* form of price discrimination, indicating that important provisions of the ICA were not understood, even by those whose economic interests were directly influenced by the ICC's regulatory decisions. Their correspondence with the ICC reveals that shippers regularly did not understand that the ICC's jurisdiction was limited to interstate commerce and asked the ICC to intervene on their behalf to prevent cases of intrastate price discrimination.

Although the ICC was only empowered to rule on the reasonableness of interstate price discrimination, the ICC's commissioners believed this principle was not understood, even by shippers influenced by the ICC's decisions. As the ICC began issuing rulings on price discrimination, Commissioner Cooley complained that "every day" the commission's correspondence revealed "the prevalence in some quarters of a vague notion that power has been conferred upon it to interfere anywhere and for any reason satisfactory to itself in order to prevent what it may think is likely to be harmful."[47] Instead of operating in this manner, Cooley believed, the commission "must find its authority in the law, and not in its own ideas of right or policy."[48] Yet it was not clear this was possible. For it was not apparent that the ICC could establish a rational basis for determination of what constituted a "reasonable" level of price discrimination.

Although Cooley hoped popular misunderstanding of the ICA would dissipate with time, the ICC's second annual report focused on the prevalent but mistaken idea that the ICA empowered the ICC to outlaw all forms of price discrimination. Since such powers had not been conferred to the ICC, the commissioners complained: "The *great majority* of complaints . . . have . . . presented matters over which the Commission has no jurisdiction."[49] Given the complexity of the ICA, Cooley recognized that "some inconveniences must necessarily arise from putting in force a law which attempts such considerable changes," but, he hoped, such inconveniences "will be greater at first than after the working of the law has become understood and greatest while parties are hesitating to act because of doubts of construction."[50]

The ICC's commissioners were not the only ones convinced that the public was poorly informed of the railroad issue. Liberal reformers' conviction that the public did not understand railroad policy is critical to explain the institutional characteristics the ICC assumed and, more generally, why the ICC was granted discretion to determine whether price discrimination was reasonable. Despite believing that competitive pressures operated ineffectively in the American railroad industry, liberal reformers thought that popular demands for railroad regulation were irrational.[51]

A similar series of calculations informed certain Republicans' views of monetary policy. The Republicans were backed into a corner by the inflationary demands of the greenback and free silver movements, and the adoption of these demands by the Democratic Party embodied new assumptions regarding the proper scope of state authority. As Henry Adams noted, the public exhibited a "growing clamor for more government," and the state was increasingly immersed in a political culture demanding its expansion.[52] Although such support legitimized the state's actions, the bureaucratic incarnation of American government initially emerged in opposition to both the type of state and the specific policy demands that populist economic groups and public opinion endorsed.

In the Treasury Department, discretionary authority was used not to satisfy demands for inflation and free silver but to resume the gold standard, a policy that observers of all political persuasions recognized was deeply unpopular. Similarly, the ICC used its discretion over the railroad industry to exempt railroads from the prohibition on long-haul-short-haul price discrimination even though the ICC's commissioners recognized that the "most frequent" complaint submitted to the ICC involved rate discrimination.[53] If the strongest supporters of the ICA were agrarians and shippers who wanted to eliminate price discrimination, the ICC was using discretion to make exemptions they opposed.[54]

Hence, the American state's bureaucratic regulatory characteristics and the policy objectives this new form of authority was implementing were a conservative reaction to the populist demands emanating from American society. Although these demands conditioned the transformation of American state authority, they were not responsible for determining the *type* of state that emerged in the late nineteenth century. The American state was initially bureaucratized not in order to satisfy popular demands but to implement unpopular policy objectives and to insulate regulatory policy from public opinion.

Empowering the Treasury Department and the ICC with discretion to regulate economic conditions created a new type of regulatory state that had lasting implications for American politics. Subsequent reform efforts have been unable to alter the bureaucratic institutions of state authority and have instead focused on contesting its scope and its powers, indicating that the turn toward bureaucratic regulatory authority was a critical moment in American politics.

The actors responsible for creating this new regulatory institution were operating in the context of broad changes in the American economy and changes in the specific characteristics of party ideologies. These changes and the public's reactions to industrialization limited the scope of elite action and led certain conservatives to endorse bureaucratic innovations that they may have preferred never to have introduced. Despite recognizing the role of popular pressures and demands, the Republicans and liberal reformers responsible for creating this new form of bureaucratic authority were responding to political pressures, not underlying economic changes, when they empowered the Treasury Department and the ICC. Thus the creation of the American regulatory state was a response to factors associated with public opinion, but was not determined by it.

This indicates, however, that the forces responsible for creating the American regulatory state diverged from those influencing European political development. Instead of emerging from the organizational demands associated with war and war finance, the American regulatory state was created in response to pressures associated with mass democracy, changes in the issue positions espoused by the Democratic Party, and certain Republicans' efforts to minimize popular influence over politics.

The short-term nature of these pressures is perhaps most apparent in the changes that occurred within the Treasury Department. The creation of the ICC, however, was subject to slightly different concerns. While the Treasury Department was empowered to resist popular support for currency inflation, liberal reformers hoped the ICC would disseminate information and help cultivate an informed and rational public. Liberal reformers' support for independent regulatory commissions, and their views of what commissions could accomplish, were derived from their conviction that voters were endorsing irrational policy preferences that could not be implemented in a complex modern economy.

Social movements and interests that initially opposed the creation of these new institutions subsequently endorsed them, and sought to adapt them to their own purposes. This recognition should not, however, obscure recognition that the initial turn toward bureaucratic authority was a conservative response to populist demands that were emerging from American society and were increasingly adopted and espoused by the Democratic Party.

Conclusion State Autonomy in
Democratic Societies

This book has examined the creation of discretionary regulatory authority in federal bureaucracies, and has argued that this institution emerged as a consequence of the regulatory debates following the Civil War. This institutional innovation was a reaction to a cultural transformation with profound political consequences: the emergence of popular demands for regulating the economy, and the Democratic Party's abandonment of opposition to federal economic activism.

The ironies involved in these institutional and political innovations are innumerable. In bare outline, however, the first instances of what Stephen Skowronek has called "the new American state" was a reaction *against* populist agitation focused first in monetary policy and then in railroad regulation. Vestigial partisan patterns from the second party system impeded the realization that discretionary authority could be used to satisfy the very demands it had been created to oppose, and the parties fought each other to a standstill until the imaginative deadlock was broken by certain progressive Republicans in the next century, who called for populist demands to be satisfied bureaucratically—calls that would be fully adopted by the Democrats during the New Deal.[1]

Well before Theodore Roosevelt's presidency, however, a partisan transformation began when George Pendleton attempted to resuscitate his political career by endorsing currency inflation in the Ohio gubernatorial election of 1867. While he had done so simply to secure the Democratic nomination in 1868, Pendleton's demands for inflationary currency policy inadvertently began reversing the Democrats' opposition to federal regulatory activism. By conceptually linking the exercise of federal authority with the interests of the disadvantaged, Pendleton initiated "a striking departure" in American politics and in the ideology of the Democratic Party.[2] Once this idea was applied to monetary policy, similar demands spread to railroad regulation and other areas of the economy as well.[3]

It is possible that only the link between slavery and states' rights, and thus between the Democratic Party and opposition to federal power, had prevented this potential from being acted upon—as it had been acted upon, specifically in the form of currency inflation and debt relief, a hundred years before, under the Articles of Confederation. But the Democrats' dedication to states' rights and the Constitution's parchment barrier between the legislature and the executive had to be overcome before the modern American state, and our modern partisan alignment, could be actualized.

In this sense the Civil War played a crucial role, not simply in asserting the supremacy of the federal government over the states, but by removing the underlying condition, slavery, that was responsible for uniting the disparate elements of the Democratic Party against empowering federal authority. Nor was it a coincidence that inflationary monetary policy was initially associated with the Radical Republicans, the faction of the Republican Party most committed to using federal power to accomplish humanitarian objectives.

So long as this conception of national authority rested on greenback inflation, however, it had limited appeal. It was only after the conspiratorial imagery of the Crime of '73 was popularized and the Democrats endorsed free silver that the ideological reversal Pendleton initiated was popularized at the national level. Although the conspiratorial claims associated with the Crime of '73 were widely adopted, the silver issue exhibited a series of factual errors and mythic arguments that ensured those responsible for the Coinage Act of 1873 were never identified. However, the Coinage Act was not due to Eastern or European financiers, as the Populists and media claimed, but was drafted at the behest of William Ralston in a failed attempt to aid his financial empire.

As few understood Ralston's role in the Coinage Act, the inaccuracies in the subsequent newspaper coverage of the Coinage Act forced Ralston's coconspirators to either remain silent, deny anything conspiratorial had occurred, or echo fictitious claims to mask their role in the act's passage. The resulting inaccuracies ensured nineteenth-century Americans never understood the interests that influenced the Coinage Act, or the reasons why silver had been eliminated as a legal tender currency.

Ralston's legislative allies were not responsible for creating the bimetallic groups that preceded the Populists, nor were they responsible for the adoption of free silver by William Jennings Bryan and the Democratic Party. However, their role in facilitating the Coinage Act's passage created the underlying condition, silver's demonetization, that made free silver a political issue in the first place. Although it was not a particularly radical economic policy, the silver issue was critical for the ideological development of the Democratic Party. For when Bryan adopted demands for free silver in 1896, the Democratic Party affirmed a new willingness to use the powers of the federal government, and in this sense Ralston's actions, and those of his legislative allies, inadvertently influenced the ideology of the Democratic Party.

Although Bryan lost the election of 1896, his adoption of free silver, and the proactive federal regulatory action necessary for this policy, transformed the Democratic Party. After 1896 there was "a persistent drift" away from the antebellum Democrats' antistatism and a turn toward a modern liberal conception of the state's role in the economy.[4] While opposition to economic inequality was retained from the second party system, the transformation in the Democrats' ideas regarding the use of state authority to combat inequality was "quite novel."[5]

This ideological development had additional effects upon American state formation. For once the state's regulatory operations were legitimized by their claims to aid the disadvantaged, enlarging federal authority seemed like a natural corollary to protecting the public welfare.[6] Increasingly the state was viewed "as a savior," and agrarians gradually "ceased to fear it, as they had been taught by Jefferson and Jackson to do, and instead besought its aid against the railways, the banks, and the 'trusts.'"[7]

Yet while the Democrats were increasingly demanding the application of Hamiltonian means to serve Jeffersonian ends, it is notable that Bryan failed to institutionalize this conception in the form of the classic Weberian state, in which discretionary authority is vested in executive bureaucrats or independent commissions. While fully developed by the Democrats during the New Deal, this "statist" institutional form was, ironically, forged by the Republican successors to the Federalists and the Whigs.

The Democrats' ideological innovation inspired an institutional reaction from Republicans and certain liberal reformers, who were convinced that the public exhibited irrational policy demands. Just as populist demands forced John Sherman to delegate authority to the Treasury Department, liberal reformers influenced by the ideas of Charles Francis Adams Jr. helped delegate regulatory authority over the railroads to an independent commission. Although they would come to oppose bureaucracy, members of the Republican Party helped create this form of administrative authority in an attempt to blunt populist demands that were increasingly espoused by the Democratic Party.

Bureaucracy was hardly championed as a means of satisfying popular policy preferences; its appeal was derived from its capacity to insulate policy from public opinion, and in the vain hope that independent commissions could help inform voters of the complex regulatory policies that liberal reformers believed few understood. Thus the activist vision of the bureaucratic state that became central to the progressive movement, and to contemporary American politics, initially emerged from the political debates sweeping across the United States in the final decades of the nineteenth century.[8]

There is a tendency to view these institutional innovations as the inevitable, and rational, response to problems created by industrialization. According to such explanations, political institutions were created in response social needs, and if ineffective, were discarded or amended. There is a certain heuristic value to such understandings of social processes; they impose the appearance of comprehensibility on the great buzzing confusion of modern societies and reassure contemporaries that political institutions were created as a rational response to real problems.

It is not clear, however, that the social issues prompting these institutions were self-evident. Pendleton's demands for currency inflation were a simple attempt to secure the presidential nomination of 1868, and the forces that demonetized silver were never understood despite widespread media attention and popular debate. Similarly, John Reagan's railroad bill was not introduced to placate public outrage toward industrialization but was a short-term response to political forces unleashed by the collapse of the Compromise of 1877 and the unique pressures facing Thomas Scott's faltering railroad empire.

Furthermore, Pendleton, Reagan, and the various social movements and political actors who shared their policy demands initially *opposed* efforts to satisfy their policy preferences through bureaucratic institutions. Such opposition was partially due to the ambiguous position bureaucracy had within the Democratic Party's ideology and to Republican desires to use bureaucracy to oppose Democratic policies. Thus, distinctly conservative forces were responsible for an institutional innovation that was subsequently replicated in other areas of American government.

While certain aspects of these ideological and institutional transformations have been retained, there have been significant reversals and recombinations of the ideas and issue positions bundled together by party ideologies since the late nineteenth century. Although the Republican Party abandoned the Whigs' support for state-led industrialization and opposition to executive authority, the Republicans initially endorsed bureaucracy to combat the politicization of economic regulatory policy. Certain Republicans retained their support for bureaucracy through the Progressive Era, support that was jettisoned only after the New Deal.

Similarly, after abandoning their antebellum antistatism the Democrats came to demand federal regulatory activism, first in monetary policy and railroad regulation, and then in other areas of the economy as well. However, the Democrats initially preferred relying on state and federal legislatures to combat economic centralization and monopoly.[9] The Democrats' opposition to bureaucracy was only fully abandoned after the New Deal, just as the Republicans began to reject bureaucracy.

This is not to attribute our contemporary American partisan alignments to nineteenth-century political conflicts. Rather, these nineteenth-century ideological developments are important for understanding how changes in party ideologies are necessary to explain certain institutional transformations. It is difficult to explain the initial timing or bureaucratic features of the American regulatory state without recognizing how changes in the Democratic Party's ideology led certain Republicans to endorse bureaucracy to insulate regulatory decisions from public opinion. Instead of being created to aid social groups critical of markets and industrialization, the initial expansion of bureaucratic authority was intended to isolate policy decisions from public opinion and to inform voters of regulatory decisions that certain elites believed were poorly understood.

To recognize the causes of these transformations and the ways certain policies and institutions influenced various interests one must first recognize how political ideologies bundle positions together in ways that often seem illogical to contemporary observers. However, the institutional innovations created in response to these ideological shifts initiated a new developmental sequence, marking the beginning of a bureaucratic expansion that has continued into the twenty-first century. Once the state was seen to be responsible for economic growth and fairness, bureaucracy eventually became necessary to organize government to deal with America's market economy. Although certain conservatives initially endorsed bureaucracy, bureaucratic institutions were gradually enlisted to serve goals conservatives opposed.

Aside from altering the nature of American political institutions, this transformation had significant implications for democratic representation and popular understanding of politics. As the state expanded into a proliferating number of social spheres, regulating various economic activities, redistributing wealth, and producing disparate goods and services, the expanding scope of government increased the amount of information voters need to understand politics, enhancing state autonomy while simultaneously making it impossible for anyone to become politically informed.

Although these tendencies have become pronounced in contemporary America, they were hardly masked from nineteenth-century observers. In 1895, after years of discussion and publicity, one free silver partisan complained: "Not one in a thousand knew the meaning of the term 'free coinage.'"[10] Recognizing the complexity of monetary debates and issues, some nineteenth-century voters complained that even after examining all "the facts concerning coinage and monies . . . it seemed impossible to get any clear understanding of the subject."[11] Much like the transformation of American economic life, distant and anonymous actors were increasingly wielding political authority for reasons that were unknown, and perhaps largely unknowable. As government actions and offices proliferated, some complained: "There are so many different divisions and *Bureaus* . . . that it is very easy to forget which Commissioner is referred to."[12]

The state that emerged from these transformations, and the political culture surrounding it, exhibited a developmental pattern shared by all Western democratic governments. Legitimated by a political culture that assumes democracy ensures popular control of politics, and promising to secure a more just and equitable society, the American state expanded its capacities into an increasing number of social realms.

Yet instead of ensuring societal control of politics, the coexistence of an expansive state alongside an ignorant public has removed an increasing number of political decisions from popular awareness or control. Hardly a consequence of any conscious or deliberate design, state autonomy in democratic societies is an unintended consequence of voter ignorance, the vast scope of public decisions, and the resulting impossibility of anyone becoming aware of the state's actions.

Unfortunately, state autonomy is not the only consequence of voter ignorance. As public decisions have become more numerous and complex, it has also become more difficult to assess the accuracy of rival explanations of political events. Thus, in addition to making it impossible to become aware of the state's actions, voters are increasingly reliant upon political elites for explanations of public decisions. This has empowered the elites who produce and disseminate explanations for political events that voters cannot directly experience.

Of course opinion leaders, media elites, and political parties have incentives to inform voters if officials pursue unpopular or harmful policies, or popularize inaccurate explanations for political events. However, even relatively informed political elites may not understand the forces responsible for regulatory decisions when critical interests and causal relationships are complicated or masked. Furthermore, even if political elites understand the effects of regulatory policies and the actors responsible for them, these relationships may be too complicated to explain to the public. This indicates that there may be incentives for political elites to craft simple explanations that are widely adopted, despite their inaccuracies, because they confirm existing stereotypes or offer simple explanations for complex decisions.

Insofar as politics involves complicated technical questions, there may be an inverse correlation between the complexity of political explanations and their probability of adoption by the mass public. Much like Gresham's Law, accurate political ideas have a tendency to be driven from the popular mind by those that are simple, easy to communicate, and highly inaccurate.[13] Just as modern market economies produce goods designed to satisfy popular tastes, an analogous relationship exists for the crude ideas political elites disseminate for public consumption.

Thus it is hardly surprising that Western culture has produced the ostentatious frivolities of the private sphere, or that the public sphere has followed suit. People know little, and they are entertained by even less. Meanwhile, they have created in the modern state a mighty engine that caters to their petty whims as readily as does capitalism in the private sphere. The engine is, of necessity, run by thousands of officials who will forever remain nameless—as nameless as John Sherman or Henry Linderman would be to anyone who had not read these pages.

This has generated one of the simplest, and most disturbing, trends of modern political development: the rise of the regulatory state in the midst of an ignorant electorate, and the corresponding tendency for the state to free itself from popular oversight, awareness, or control. This development is the product of unintended decisions and poorly understood tendencies; no one is responsible for the public's ignorance or for the state's autonomy. Yet little can arrest this trend. The public is simply too ignorant, and the scope of government too extensive, to expect popular control or understanding of modern politics.

Unfortunately, the expansion of state power in the midst of an ignorant electorate indicates that focusing on how mass opinion fuels state autonomy is perhaps even more necessary for the study of contemporary politics than of earlier periods of American political development.[14] For if public officials enjoyed autonomy when participation was high and the state regulated few aspects of society, contemporary states may enjoy even higher levels of autonomy when voters are uninformed, participation is low, and the scope of public decisions is extensive.

Notes

INTRODUCTION

1. See, for example, Adam Przeworski and Henry Tune, *The Logic of Comparative Social Inquiry* (Malabar: Krieger, 1970), 74–75; Philip Converse, "Generalization and the Social Psychology of 'Other Worlds," 42–60, in *Metatheory in Social Science: Pluralisms and Subjectivities,* ed. Donald W. Fiske and Richard A. Shweder (Chicago: University of Chicago Press, 1986).

2. Max Weber, "Objectivity in Social Science and Social Policy," in *Methodology of the Social Sciences,* ed. Edward A. Shils and Henry L. Fluch (New York: Free Press, 1949), 78–79.

3. For a discussion of timing and sequencing see Paul Pierson, *Politics in Time: History, Institutions, and Social Analysis* (Princeton: Princeton University Press, 2004), 54–58, 74–78.

4. Developmental questions are hardly specific to the social sciences; disciplines such as astronomy and evolutionary biology exhibit similar characteristics. See R. G. Collingwood, *Essays in the Philosophy of History* (New York: McGraw Hill, 1965), 27–28.

5. Since this selection decision is conceptually unrelated to my theoretical argument, it avoids concerns regarding selection on the dependent variable.

6. Ernest Nagel, *The Structure of Science: Problems in the Logic of Scientific Explanation* (Indianapolis: Hackett, 1979), 485–487.

7. James Fearon, "Counterfactuals and Hypothesis Testing in Political Science," *World Politics* 43 (1991): 173–175.

8. Gary King, Robert O. Keohane, and Sidney Verba, *Designing Social Inquiry: Scientific Inference in Qualitative Research* (Princeton: Princeton University Press, 1994), 209.

9. James N. Druckman, Donald P. Green, James H. Kuklinski, and Arthur Lupia, "The Growth and Development of Experimental Research in Political Science," *American Political Science Review* 100 (2006): 627–635; Thad Dunning, "Improving Causal Inference: Strengths and Limitations of Natural Experiments," *Political Research Quarterly* 61 (2008): 282–293.

10. See Alexander L. George and Andrew Bennett, *Case Studies and Theory Development in the Social Sciences* (Cambridge, MA: MIT Press, 2005), chap. 10; David Collier, "Understanding Process Tracing," *PS: Political Science and Politics* 4 (2011): 824–826; Edwin Amenta, "Making the Most of a Case Study: Theories of the Welfare State and the American Experience," *International Journal of Comparative Sociology,*" 32 (1991): 172–194.

11. For "most difficult" research designs, see John Gerring, "Is There a (Viable) Crucial-Case Method?" *Comparative Political Studies* 40, no. 3: 346–347.

12. I draw upon the issues discussed in Fearon, "Counterfactuals and Hypothesis Testing," 180–181, 194–195.

CHAPTER 1. THE MODERN REGULATORY STATE

1. Max Weber, "Politics as a Vocation," in *From Max Weber: Essays in Sociology,* ed. H. H. Gerth and C. Wright Mills (New York: Oxford University Press, 1958), 77; Samuel Finer, *The History of Government from the Earliest Times* (New York: Oxford University Press, 1997), 806–854, 896–949, 963–979; Gianfranco Poggi, *The State: Its Nature, Development and Prospects* (Stanford: Stanford University Press, 1990), 40–44.

2. William Novak, "The Myth of the 'Weak' American State," *American Historical Review* 113 (2008): 752–772; Desmond King and Robert Lieberman, "American State Building: The Theoretical Challenge," 299–300, in *The Unsustainable American State,* ed. Lawrence Jacobs and Desmond King (New York: Oxford University Press, 2009).

3. Tuong Vu, "Studying the State through State Formation," *World Politics* 62 (2010): 148–175; Charles Tilly, *Coercion, Capital, and European States, AD 990–1992* (Cambridge: Blackwell, 1992); Thomas Ertman, *Birth of the Leviathan: Building States and Regimes in Medieval and Early Modern Europe* (Cambridge: Cambridge University Press, 1997); Brian Downing, *The Military Revolution and Political Change* (Princeton: Princeton University Press, 1992).

4. Joseph Strayer, *On the Medieval Origins of the Modern State* (Princeton: Princeton University Press, 1970); W. O. Henderson, *The State and the Industrial Revolution in Prussia 1740–1870* (Liverpool: Liverpool University Press, 1958); Hans Rosenberg, *Bureaucracy, Aristocracy and Autocracy: The Prussian Experience 1660–1815* (Boston: Beacon Press, 1958); John Brewer, *The Sinews of Power: War, Money, and the English State, 1688–1783* (New York: Alfred A. Knopf, 1989); Philip Gorski, *The Disciplinary Revolution, Calvinism and the Rise of the State in Early Modern Europe* (Chicago: University of Chicago Press, 2003).

5. Victoria Tin-bor Hui, *War and State Formation in Ancient China and Early Modern Europe* (New York: Cambridge University Press, 2005), chap. 2.

6. David Epstein and Sharyn O'Halloran, *Delegating Powers: A Transaction Cost Politics Approach to Policy Making under Separate Powers* (Cambridge: Cambridge University Press, 1999); John Huber and Charles Shipan, *Deliberate Discretion? The Institutional Foundations of Bureaucratic Autonomy* (Cambridge: Cambridge University Press, 2002); Mathew McCubbins, Roger Noll, and Barry Weingast, "Administrative Procedures as Instruments of Political Control," *Journal of Law, Economics, and Organization* 3: 243–277.

7. Robert Heilbroner, *Between Capitalism and Socialism: Essays in Political Economics* (New York: Vintage Books, 1970), 4; Robert Higgs, *Crisis and Leviathan: Critical Episodes in the Growth of American Government* (New York: Oxford University Press, 1987).

8. Herbert McClosky and John Zaller, *The American Ethos: Public Attitudes toward Capitalism and Democracy* (Cambridge, MA: Harvard University Press, 1984), 169, 274; Stanley Feldman and John Zaller, "The Political Culture of Ambivalence: Ideological Response to the Welfare State," *American Journal of Political Science* 36 (1992): 268–307; Philip Tetlock, "A Value Pluralism Model of Ideological Reasoning," *Journal of Personality and Social Psychology* 50 (1986): 819–827; Linda L. M. Bennett and Stephen Earl Bennett, *Living with Leviathan*, 102–103; Robert E. Lane, *Political Ideology: Why the American Common Man Believes What He Does* (New York: Free Press of Glencoe, 1962), 188.

9. Gabriel Almond, "The Return to the State," *American Political Science Review* 82 (1988): 855.

10. Richard T. Ely, *An Introduction to Political Economy* (New York: Hunt and Eaton, 1894), 85–88.

11. Claus Offe, *Modernity and the State: East, West* (Cambridge, MA: MIT Press, 1996), 89; Adam Przeworski and Michael Wallerstein, "Popular Sovereignty, State Autonomy, and Private Property," *European Journal of Sociology* XLII: 21.

12. Martin Shefter, *Political Parties and the State: The American Historical Experience* (Princeton: Princeton University Press, 1994), chap. 2.

13. Sean Wilentz, "On Class and Politics in Jacksonian America," *Reviews in American History* 10 (1982): 51; Glen Altschuler and Stuart M. Blumin, "Limits of Political Engagement in Antebellum America: A New Look at the Golden Age of Participatory Democracy," *Journal of American History* 84 (1997): 855; Michael E. McGerr, *The Decline of Popular Politics: The American North, 1865–1928* (New York: Oxford University Press, 1986); James A. Morone, *The Democratic Wish: Popular Participation and the Limits of American Government* (New Haven: Yale University Press, 1990); Joel Silbey, *The American Political Nation, 1838–1893* (Stanford: Stanford University Press, 1991).

14. Richard Bensel, The *Political Economy of American Industrialization, 1877–1900 (New York: Cambridge University Press, 2000),* xvii; William Gienapp, "'Politics Seem to Enter into Everything': Political Culture in the North, 1840–1860," in *Essays on American Antebellum Politics, 1840–1860,* ed. Stephen Maizlish and John Kushma (College Station: Texas A & M University Press, 1982), 6.

15. Elizabeth Sanders, *Roots of Reform: Farmers, Workers, and the American State, 1877–1917* (Chicago: University of Chicago Press, 1999), 1, 6; Robert Wiebe, *Self-Rule: A Cultural History of American Democracy* (Chicago: University of Chicago Press, 1995).

16. Stephen Skowronek and Karen Orren, *The Search for American Political Development* (Cambridge: Cambridge University Press, 2004), 19.

17. Daniel Carpenter, *The Forging of Bureaucratic Autonomy: Reputations, Networks, and Policy Innovation in Executive Agencies, 1862–1928* (Princeton: Princeton University Press, 2001); William Nelson, *The Roots of American Bureaucracy, 1830–1900* (Cambridge, MA: Harvard University Press, 1982).

18. Daniel Carpenter and Keith Whittington, "Executive Power in American Institutional Development," *Perspectives on Politics* (2003): 505; Carpenter, *Forging of Bureaucratic Autonomy,* 14. This claim is admittedly imprecise, as Carpenter argues that bureaucrats can alter social groups' preferences, which otherwise would not have occurred.

19. Ronald Formisano, "The 'Party Period' Revisited," *Journal of American History* 86 (1999): 94; Richard John, "Farewell to the 'Party Period': Political Economy in Nineteenth-Century America," *Journal of Policy History* 16 (2004): 118; Peter Nardulli, *Popular Efficacy in the Democratic Era: A Re-examination of Electoral Accountability in the U.S., 1828–2000* (Princeton: Princeton University Press, 2005).

20. Gordon Wood, *Radicalism of the American Revolution* (New York: Vintage Books, 1991), 87.

21. Harry Watson, *Liberty and Power: The Politics of Jacksonian America* (New York: Hill and Wang, 1990), 240; Michael Holt, *The Rise and Fall of the American Whig Party: Jacksonian Politics and the Onset of the Civil War* (New York: Oxford University Press, 2003), 66.

22. Orestes Augustus Brownson, *The Laboring Classes: An Article from the Boston Quarterly Review* (Boston: Benjamin H. Greene, 1840), 23; William Leggett, "Democratic Editorials," as quoted in *Social Theories of Jacksonian Democracy,* ed. Joseph L. Blau (New York: Liberal Arts Press, 1954), 76–77; Rush Welter, *The Mind of America, 1820–1860* (New York: Columbia University Press, 1975), 92.

23. Welter, *The Mind of America,* 94.

24. Watson, *Liberty and Power,* 239.

25. Sean Wilentz, *The Rise of American Democracy: Jefferson to Lincoln* (New York: W. W. Norton, 2005).

26. Sean Wilentz, *Chants Democratic: New York City and the Rise of the American Working Class, 1788–1850* (Oxford: Oxford University Press, 1984 [2004]), 186; Edward Pessen, *Most Uncommon Jacksonians: The Radical Leaders of the Early Labor Movement* (Albany: State University of New York Press, 1967), 176, 184.

27. Pessen, *Most Uncommon Jacksonians,* 146.

28. George Fitzhugh, *Sociology for the South: Or, The Failure of Free Society* (Ithaca: Cornell University Press, 1992).

29. Daniel Walker Howe, *The Political Culture of the American Whigs* (Chicago: University of Chicago Press, 1970), 13, 16; Holt, *The Rise and Fall of the American Whig Party,* 66–67.

30. Robert McCloskey, *American Conservatism in the Age of Enterprise, 1865–1910* (New York: Harper and Row, 1951), 23–24.

31. Walter Licht, *Industrializing America: The Nineteenth Century* (Baltimore: Johns Hopkins University Press, 1995), 88, italics added.

32. Watson, *Liberty and Power*, 239; Sidney Fine, *Laissez Faire and the General-Welfare State: A Study of Conflict in American Thought, 1865–1901* (Ann Arbor: University of Michigan Press, 1956), 12.

33. Donald Lutz, *Popular Consent and Popular Control: Whig Political Theory in the Early State Constitutions* (Baton Rouge: Louisiana State University Press, 1980), 58.

34. Larry Schweikart, *Banking in the American South from the Age of Jackson to Reconstruction* (Baton Rouge: Louisiana State University Press, 1987), 1–2; Louis Hartz, *The Liberal Tradition in America: An Interpretation of American Political Thought since the Revolution* (New York: Harcourt Brace, 1955), 215–216; Charles Beard, *Economic Origins of Jeffersonian Democracy* (New York: Macmillan, 1915), 418.

35. Daniel Walker Howe, *What Hath God Wrought: The Transformation of America, 1815–1848* (New York: Oxford University Press, 2009), 358–362; Larry Schweikart, "Jacksonian Ideology, Currency Control and Central Banking: A Reappraisal," *Historian* 51 (1988): 78–102.

36. Oscar Handlin and Mary Handlin, *Commonwealth: A Study of the Role of Government in the American Economy, Massachusetts, 1774–1861* (Cambridge, MA: Harvard University Press, 1947); Louis Hartz, *Economic Policy and Democratic Thought: Pennsylvania, 1776–1860 (Cambridge, MA: Harvard University Press, 1948);* Colleen Dunlavy, *Politics and Industrialization: Early Railroads in the United States and Prussia* (Princeton: Princeton University Press, 1994); Harry Scheiber, *Ohio Canal Era: A Case Study of Government and the Economy, 1820–1861* (Athens: Ohio University Press, 1969); William Novak, *The People's Interest: Law and Regulation in Nineteenth-Century America* (Chapel Hill: University of North Carolina Press, 1996).

37. Dunlavy, *Politics and Industrialization*, 18–19.

38. Leonard White, *The Jacksonians: A Study in Administrative History 1829–1861* (New York: Free Press, 1954), 437, 458.

39. Morton Keller, *Affairs of State: Public Life in Late Nineteenth-Century America* (Cambridge, MA: Harvard University Press, 1977), 410.

40. Samuel Hays, *The Response to Industrialism: 1885–1914* (Chicago: University of Chicago Press, 1957); Robert Wiebe, *The Search for Order, 1877–1920* (New York: Hill and Wang, 1966).

41. Thomas Cochran, "Did the Civil War Retard Industrialization?" *Mississippi Valley Historical Review* 48 (1961): 197–210.

42. Harvey Perloff, Edgar Dunn, and Eric Lampard, *Regions, Resources, and Economic Growth* (Baltimore: Johns Hopkins University Press, 1961); Albert Fishlow, *American Railroads and the Transformation of the Ante-bellum Economy* (Cambridge, MA: Harvard University Press, 1965).

43. Howard Bodenhorn, "Capital Mobility and Financial Integration in Antebellum America," *Journal of Economic History* 52 (1992): 585–610; Howard Bodenhorn, *A History of*

Banking in Antebellum America: Financial Markets and Economic Development in an Era of Nation-Building (Cambridge: Cambridge University Press, 2000); Sumner la Croix and Christopher Grandy, "Financial Integration in Antebellum America: Strengthening Boderhorn's Results," *Journal of Economic History* 53 (1993): 653–658.

44. Charles Sellers, *The Market Revolution: Jacksonian America, 1815–1846* (New York: Oxford University Press, 1994).

45. Stephen Skowronek, *Building a New American State: The Expansion of National Administrative Capacities, 1877–1920* (New York: Cambridge University Press, 1982), 253; William Novak, "A State of Legislatures," *Polity* 40 (2008): 340–347.

46. David Montgomery, *Beyond Equality: Labor and the Radical Republicans, 1862–1872* (New York: Alfred A. Knopf, 1967), 432.

47. John Ashworth, *"Agrarians" and "Aristocrats": Party Ideology in the United States, 1837–1846* (New York: Cambridge University Press, 1983); James Kloppenberg, *The Virtues of Liberalism* (New York: Oxford University Press 1998), 61; William Brock, *Parties and Political Conscience: American Dilemmas, 1840–1850* (New York: KTO Press, 1979), chap. 3; Wilentz, *The Rise of American Democracy,* 486.

48. H. Clay to G. Verplanck, Washington, DC, December 8, 1837, in *The Papers of Henry Clay,* ed. Robert Seager and Melba Porter Hay, vol. 9 (Lexington: University Press of Kentucky, 1982), 99; *The Works of Henry Clay: Comprising His Life, Correspondence and Speeches,* ed. Calvin Colton (New York: G. P. Putnam's Sons, 1904), 313.

49. Sanders, *Roots of Reform,* 6, 389, italics added.

50. Epstein and O'Halloran, *Delegating Powers*; Huber and Shipan, *Deliberate Discretion?*; McCubbins, Noll, and Weingast, "Administrative Procedures as Instruments of Political Control"; Gary Bryner, *Bureaucratic Discretion: Law and Policy in Federal Regulatory Agencies* (New York: Pergamon Press, 1987).

51. Lynton K. Caldwell, *The Administrative Theories of Hamilton and Jefferson: Their Contribution to Thought on Public Administration* (New York: Russell and Russell, 1964), 136, 133; Gordon Wood, "Knowledge, Power, and the First Congress," 52, in *Knowledge, Power, and the Congress,* ed. William Robinson and Clay Welborn (Washington, DC: Congressional Quarterly, 1992).

52. Rush Welter, *The Mind of America, 1820–1860* (New York: Columbia University Press 1975), 170; Joseph Cooper, *The Origins of the Standing Committees and the Development of the Modern House* (Huston: Rice University Press, 1970), 29; Fine, *Laissez Faire and the General-Welfare State,* 16.

53. James Q. Wilson, "The Rise of the Bureaucratic State," 33, in *Perspectives on the Administrative Process,* ed. Robert Rabin (Boston: Little, Brown, 1979).

54. See Jerry Mashaw, *Creating the Administrative Constitution: The Lost One Hundred Years of American Administrative Law* (New Haven: Yale University Press, 2012), particularly chaps. 6, 7, 9, and 11.

55. Jerry Mashaw, "Recovering American Administrative Law: Federalist Foundations, 1787–1801," *Yale Law Journal* (2006): 1256–1334; Leonard White, *The Federalists: A Study in Administrative History* (New York: Macmillan, 1959), 448–459.

56. Mark R. Wilson, *The Business of Civil War: Military Mobilization and the State, 1861–1865* (Baltimore: Johns Hopkins University Press, 2006); Steven Rockwell, *Indian Affairs and*

the Administrative State in the Nineteenth Century (New York: Cambridge University Press, 2010); Steven W. Usselman and Richard R. John, "Patent Politics: Intellectual Property, the Railroad Industry, and the Problem of Monopoly," *Journal of Policy History* 18 (2006): 96–125.

57. John G. Burke, "Bursting Boilers and the Federal Power," *Technology and Culture* 7 (1966): 1–23; Jerry Mashaw, "Administration and 'The Democracy': Administrative Law from Jackson to Lincoln," *Yale Law Journal* 17 (2008): 1628–1666.

58. Malcolm Rohrbough, *The General Land Office: The Settlement and Administration of American Public Lands, 1789–1837* (New York: Oxford University Press 1968).

59. Richard Sylla, Robert E. Wright, and David J. Cowen, "Alexander Hamilton, Central Banker: Crisis Management during the U.S. Financial Panic of 1792," *Business History Review* 83 (2009): 61–86.

60. Richard Timberlake Jr., "The Independent Treasury and Monetary Policy before the Civil War," *Southern Economic Journal* 27 (1960): 92–103.

61. Mashaw, *Creating the Administrative Constitution,* 168.

62. Mashaw, *Creating the Administrative Constitution,* 167–169.

63. Mashaw, *Creating the Administrative Constitution,* 372.

64. See Eric Lomazoff, "Turning (Into) 'The Great Regulating Wheel': The Conversion of the Bank of the United States, 1791–1811," *Studies in American Political Development* 26 (2012): 1–23.

65. See Woodbury's comments in *Reports of the Secretary of the Treasury of the United States, Annual Report on the State of the Finances, 1837* (Washington, DC: John C. Rives, 1851), 14.

66. *Reports of the Secretary of the Treasury, 1839,* 248; Timberlake, "The Independent Treasury," 95.

67. See generally Williamjames Hull Hoffer, *To Enlarge the Machinery of Government: Congressional Debates and the Growth of the American State, 1858–1891* (Baltimore: Johns Hopkins University Press, 2007).

68. Martin Sklar, *The United States as a Developing Country: Studies in U.S. History in the Progressive Era and the 1920s* (New York: Cambridge University Press, 1992), 39.

69. For the consolidation of American capitalism see Martin Sklar, *The Corporate Reconstruction of American Capitalism, 1890–1916: The Market, the Law, and Politics* (Cambridge: Cambridge University Press, 1988); Naomi Lamoreaux, *The Great Merger Movement in American Business, 1895–1904* (New York: Cambridge University Press, 1988).

70. One notable exception to this generalization would be the Populists' views of the Post Office.

CHAPTER 2. STATE AUTONOMY IN DEMOCRATIC SOCIETIES

1. Donald Wittman, *The Myth of Democratic Failure* (Chicago: University of Chicago Press, 1996); Benjamin Page and Robert Shapiro, "Effects of Public Opinion on Policy" *American Political Science Review* 77 (1983): 175–190; Benjamin Page and Robert Shapiro, *The Rational Public: Fifty Years of Trends in Americans' Policy Preferences* (Chicago: University of Chicago Press, 1992).

2. Michael Mann, "The Autonomous Power of the State: Its Origins, Mechanisms and Results," in *The State: Critical Concepts,* ed. John A. Hall (New York: Routledge, 1994), 114, 117.

3. Ilya Somin, "Voter Ignorance and the Democratic Ideal," *Critical Review* 12 (1999): 413–458; James Kuklinski and Paul Quirk, "Reconsidering the Rational Public: Cognition, Heuristics, and Mass Opinion," in *Elements of Reason: Cognition, Choice, and the Bounds of Rationality,* ed. Matthew McCubbins and Samuel Popkins (Cambridge: Cambridge University Press, 2000), 153–182.

4. Kenneth Waltz, *Theory of International Politics* (Reading: Addison-Wesley, 1979), 103.

5. Joseph Schumpeter, *Capitalism, Socialism, and Democracy* (New York: Harper and Row, 1942), 269.

6. Aspects of this definition can be found in Anthony Downs, *An Economic Theory of Democracy* (New York: Harper, 1957), 22–23; and Robert A. Dahl and Charles E. Lindblom, *Politics, Economics, and Welfare: Planning and Politico-Economic Systems Resolved into Basic Social Processes* (New York: Harper and Row, 1953), 42.

7. Religious organizations do not meet this definition of the state because their decisions can be appealed. Thus while, for example, the pope may make religiously sanctioned decisions, he lacks the ability to enforce compliance with such decisions within a defined geographic area.

8. See Theda Skocpol, "Bringing the State Back In," in Peter Evans et al., *Bringing the State Back In* (Cambridge: Cambridge University Press, 1985), 9.

9. Theda Skocpol, *States and Social Revolutions: A Comparative Analysis of France, Russia, and China* (New York: Cambridge University Press, 1979).

10. For Marxist theories of the state see Ralph Miliband, *The State in Capitalist Society* (New York: Basic Books, 1969); G. William Domhoff, *Who Rules America?* (Englewood Cliffs: Prentice-Hall, 1967); Nicos Poulantzas, "The Problem of the Capitalist State," *New Left Review* 58 (1970): 67–78; Nicos Poulantzas, *Political Power and Social Classes* (London: New Left Books, 1973); Nicos Poulantzas, *State, Power, Socialism* (London: New Left Books, 1978); David Gold, Clarence Lo, and Erik Olin Wright, "Recent Developments in Marxist Theories of the Capitalist State," *Monthly Review* 43 (1975): 29–41; Bob Jessop, *State Theory: Putting the Capitalist State in Its Place* (Cambridge: Polity, 1990); Stanley Aronowitz and Peter Bratsis, eds., *Paradigm Lost: State Theory Reconsidered* (Minneapolis: University of Minnesota Press, 2002). For a critique of Marxist state theory see Axel Van den Berg, *The Immanent Utopia: From Marxism on the State to the State of Marxism* (Princeton: Princeton University Press, 1988).

11. Angus Campbell, Philip E. Converse, Warren E. Miller, and Donald E. Stokes, *The American Voter* (Ann Arbor: University of Michigan Press, 1960), 170, 541–545; Stephen Bennett, "Trends in Americans' Political Information, 1967–1987," *American Politics Quarterly* 17 (1989): 422–435; John Ferejohn, "Information and the Electoral Process." In *Information and Democratic Processes,* ed. John Ferejohn and James Kuklinski (Urbana: University of Illinois Press, 1990), 3; Stephen Bennett, "Trends in Americans' Political Information, 1967–1987," *American Politics Quarterly* 17 (1989): 422–435; Larry Bartels, "Uninformed Votes: Information Effects in Presidential Elections," *American*

Journal of Political Science 40 (1996): 194–230; Donald Kinder, "Opinion and Action in the Realm of Politics," in *The Handbook of Social Psychology, 4th Edition,* ed. Daniel T. Gilbert, Susan T. Fiske, and Gardner Lindzey (New York: McGraw-Hill 1998), 778–867.

12. Barbara Hinckley, "The American Voter in Congressional Elections" *American Political Science Review* 74 (1980): 644; Michael Delli Carpini and Scott Keeter, *What Americans Know about Politics and Why It Matters* (New Haven: Yale University Press, 1996), 71.

13. Delli Carpini and Keeter, *What Americans Know about Politics,* 71, 75, 81.

14. Delli Carpini and Keeter, *What Americans Know about Politics,* 81.

15. Richard Bensel, "The American Ballot Box: Law, Identity, and the Polling Place in the Mid-Nineteenth Century," *Studies in American Political Development* 17 (2003): 1–27.

16. Ronald Formisano, *The Birth of Mass Political Parties in Michigan, 1827–1861* (Princeton: Princeton University Press, 1971), 12.

17. Robert Wiebe, *The Opening of American Society: From the Adoption of the Constitution to the Eve of Disunion* (New York: Vintage Books, 1985), 351.

18. Campbell et al., *The American Voter,* 544, 128.

19. See Arthur Lupia and Mathew McCubbins, *The Democratic Dilemma: Can Citizens Learn What They Need to Know?* (New York: Cambridge University Press, 1998). For studies of heuristics see Paul Sniderman, Richard A. Brody, and Philip E. Tetlock, *Reasoning and Choice: Explorations in Political Psychology* (New York: Cambridge University Press, 1991); Pamela Johnston Conover and Stanley Feldman, "Candidate Perception in an Ambiguous World: Campaigns, Cues and Inference Processes," *American Journal of Political Science* 33 (1989): 912–940; Arthur Lupia, "Shortcuts versus Encyclopedias: Information and Voting Behavior in California Insurance Reform Elections," *American Political Science Review* 88 (1994): 63–76; Robert Erikson, Michael MacKuen, and James Stimson, *The Macro Polity* (Cambridge: Cambridge University Press, 2002); Donald Kinder and D. Roderick Kiewiet, "Economic Discontent and Political Behavior: The Role of Personal Grievances and Collective Economic Judgments in Congressional Voting." *American Journal of Political Science* 23 (1979): 495–527; Morris Fiorina, *Retrospective Voting in American National Elections* (New Haven: Yale University Press, 1981); G. Bingham Powell, *Elections as Instruments of Democracy* (New Haven: Yale University Press, 2000); Samuel Popkin, *The Reasoning Voter* (Chicago: University of Chicago Press, 1991); Samuel Popkin, "Information Shortcuts and the Reasoning Voter," in *Information, Participation and Choice,* ed. Bernard Grofman (Ann Arbor: University of Michigan Press, 1993), 17–35.

20. See Paul Pierson, "The Problem of Democratic Control in an Age of Big Government," in *Politics at the Turn of the Century,* ed. Arthur M. Melzer, Jerry Weinberger, and M. Richard Zinman (Lanham: Rowman and Littlefield, 2001).

21. Warren Miller and Donald Stokes, "Constituency Influence in Congress," *American Political Science Review* 57 (1963): 55; John Kingdon, *Congressmen's Voting Decisions* (Ann Arbor: University of Michigan Press, 1989); R. Douglas Arnold, *The Logic of Congressional Action* (New Haven: Yale University Press, 1990).

22. Arnold, *The Logic of Congressional Action,* 48–51.

23. Lee Benson, *Toward the Scientific Study of History: Selected Essays* (Philadelphia: J. B. Lippincott, 1972), chap. 4.

24. See Walter Lippmann, *Public Opinion* (New York: Harcourt, Brace, 1922); John Zaller, *The Nature and Origins of Mass Opinion* (Cambridge: Cambridge University Press, 1992).

25. Mancur Olson, *The Logic of Collective Action: Public Goods and the Theory of Groups* (Cambridge, MA: Harvard University Press, 1965); George Stigler, "The Theory of Economic Regulation," *Bell Journal of Economics and Management Science* 2 (1971): 3–21; Marver Bernstein, *Regulating Business by Independent Commission* (Princeton: Princeton University Press, 1955).

26. Michael Hunt, "Ideology," *Journal of American History* 77 (1990): 108.

27. For classical treatments of ideology see Karl Marx with Friedrich Engels, *The German Ideology: Including Theses on Feuerbach and the Introduction to the Critique of Political Economy* (Amherst: Prometheus Books, 1998); Georg Lukács, *History and Class Consciousness: Studies in Marxist Dialectics* (Cambridge, MA: MIT Press, 1968); Antonio Gramsci, *Selections from the Prison Notebooks* (New York: International, 1971); Robert K. Merton, "The Sociology of Knowledge," *Isis* 27 (1937): 493–503; Karl Mannheim, *Ideology and Utopia: An Introduction to the Sociology of Knowledge* (New York: Harcourt Brace, 1985).

28. For classical elite theory see Gaetano Mosca, *The Ruling Class* (New York: McGraw-Hill, 1939); Roberto Michels, *Political Parties* (New York: Free Press, 1958); Vilfredo Pareto, *Mind and Society* (New York: Harcourt-Brace, 1935); Geraint Perry, *Political Elites* (New York: Frederick A. Praeger, 1969).

29. Philip Converse, "The Nature of Belief Systems in Mass Publics" in *Ideology and Discontent,* ed. David Apter (New York: Free Press, 1964), 206–261; Michael Freeden, *Ideologies and Political Theory: A Conceptual Approach* (Oxford: Oxford University Press, 1996), chaps. 1 and 2; Walter Carlsnaes, *The Concept of Ideology and Political Analysis: A Critical Examination of Its Usage by Marx, Lenin, and Mannheim* (Westport, CT: Greenwood Press, 1981).

30. Converse, "The Nature of Belief Systems," 211.

31. Converse, "The Nature of Belief Systems," 211.

32. Parry, *Political Elites,* 55.

33. Converse, "The Nature of Belief Systems," 211.

34. Walter Lippmann, *A Preface to Politics* (New York: Mitchell Kennerley, 1913), 215; Giovanni Sartori, "Politics, Ideology, and Belief Systems," *American Political Science Review* 63 (1969): 401.

35. Lane, *Political Ideology.*

36. Converse, "The Nature of Belief Systems," 212.

37. Converse, "The Nature of Belief Systems," 213.

38. Converse, "The Nature of Belief Systems," 213.

CHAPTER 3. CIVIL WAR FINANCE AND
THE AMERICAN STATE

1. Michael Roberts, *Essays in Swedish History* (London: Weidenfeld and Nicolson, 1967), 195–225; J. R. Hale, *War and Society in Renaissance Europe, 1450–1620* (Baltimore: Johns Hopkins University Press, 1985), chaps. 2 and 9. Critiques of Roberts's thesis focus on the timing and origins of this transition; they do not dispute that it occurred. See Geoffrey Parker, "The 'Military Revolution,' 1560–1660—A Myth?" *Journal of Modern History* 48 (1976): 195–214.

2. Richard Bensel, *Yankee Leviathan: The Origins of Central State Authority in America, 1859–1877* (New York: Cambridge University Press, 1991), 95.

3. For a review of American public finance see John Joseph Wallis, "American Government Finance in the Long Run: 1790–1990," *Journal of Economic Perspectives* 14 (2000): 61–82.

4. Richard Timberlake, *Monetary Policy in the United States: An Intellectual and Institutional History* (Chicago: University of Chicago Press, 1993), 82–83.

5. White, *Jacksonians,* 39–43, 85, 164, 170, 180.

6. Mark Wilson, *The Business of Civil War: Military Mobilization and the State, 1861–1865* (Baltimore: Johns Hopkins University Press, 2006); James McPherson, *Battle Cry of Freedom: The Civil War Era* (New York: Oxford University Press, 1988), chap. 10.

7. See the retrospective discussion by F. Conkling to E. Spaulding, October 17, 1875, New York, NY, in Elbridge Spaulding, *History of the Legal Tender Paper Money Issued during the Great Rebellion: Being a Loan without Interest and a National Currency* (Westport: Greenwood Press [1869], 1971), 84–85.

8. Robert Sharkey, *Money, Class, and Party: An Economic Study of Civil War and Reconstruction* (Baltimore: Johns Hopkins University Press, 1967), 19.

9. S. Chase to S. Hooper, May 7, 1861, quoted in Fritz Redlich, *The Molding of American Banking* (New York: Hafner, 1951), 88; David Gische, "The New York City Banks and the Development of the National Banking System, 1860–1870," *American Journal of Legal History* 23 (1979): 32.

10. *Bankers Magazine and Journal of the Money Market,* January 1860, vol. 20, p. 48; J. Cisco to J. Cooke, May 20, 1861, Cooke MSS.

11. Sven Beckert, *The Monied Metropolis: New York City and the Consolidation of the American Bourgeoisie, 1850–1896* (New York: Cambridge University Press, 2001), 92–95.

12. Beckert, *The Monied Metropolis,* 117–122. My analysis departs from Beckert's in that I believe Beckert overestimates the New York financial community's influence over the government's funding operations.

13. *Report of the Secretary of the Treasury on the State of the Finances, for the Year Ending June 30, 1861* (Washington, DC: Government Printing Office, 1861), 7–10.

14. *Report of the Secretary of the Treasury on the State of the Finances, 1861,* 18.

15. *Report of the Secretary of the Treasury on the State of the Finances, 1861,* 23.

16. *Report of the Secretary of the Treasury on the State of the Finances, 1861,* 23.

17. Bray Hammond, *Sovereignty and an Empty Purse: Banks and Politics in the Civil War* (Princeton: Princeton University Press, 1970), 18–24; Bray Hammond, *Banks and Poli-*

tics in America from the Revolution to the Civil War (Princeton: Princeton University Press, 1957), 542–553.

18. J. Cooke to H. D. Cooke, Philadelphia, PA, May 15, 1861, Cooke MSS; S. Nash to S. Chase, Gallipolis, OH, November 11, 1861, Chase MSS. For the New York Clearinghouse Association see Gary Gorton, "Clearinghouses and the Origin of Central Banking in the United States," *Journal of Economic History* 45, no. 2: 277–283; Howard Bodenhorn, *State Banking in Early America: A New Economic History* (New York: Oxford University Press, 2003), 96.

19. Hammond, *Sovereignty and an Empty Purse,* 80.

20. J. Cisco to S. Chase, December 7, 1861, New York, NY, Chase MSS.

21. S. Chase to W. Fessenden, July 15, 1861, Washington DC, RG 56, Letters Sent to Individual Senators and Representatives ("E" Series). 1834–1874. National Archives College Park, MD.

22. Timberlake, *Monetary Policy in the United States,* 29.

23. Gische, "New York City Banks," 33; Hammond, *Sovereignty and an Empty Purse,* 168.

24. Quoted in John Niven, *Salmon Chase: A Biography* (New York: Oxford University Press, 1995), 265–266.

25. *Report of the Secretary of the Treasury on the State of the Finances, 1861,* 19–20.

26. Redlich, *The Molding of American Banking,* 103.

27. J. Williams to S. Chase, December 13, 1861, New York, NY, Chase MSS.

28. R. Latham to S. Chase, December 26, 1861, New York, NY, Chase MSS, J. E. Williams to S. Chase, December 13, 1861, New York, NY, Chase MSS.

29. *The Merchants' Magazine and Commercial Review,* February 1862, p. 114.

30. Spaulding, *History of the Legal Tender,* 14; Hammond, *Sovereignty and an Empty Purse,* 161.

31. Spaulding, *History of the Legal Tender,* 17.

32. J. Gallatin to W. Fessenden, New York, NY, December 14, 1861, Fessenden MSS.

33. L. Lockwood to J. Sherman, January 13, 1862, New York, NY, Sherman MSS.

34. W. Cutter to W. Fessenden, New York, NY, July 27, 1861, Fessenden MSS; George Coe quoted in the *New York Times,* December 25, 1861.

35. *New York Herald,* December 6, 1861, *New York Tribune,* December 24, 1861; Hammond, *Sovereignty and an Empty Purse,* 162.

36. H. Vail to E. Spaulding, February 24, 1869, New York, NY, quoted in Spaulding, *History of the Legal Tender,* 57; Sharkey, *Money, Class, and Party,* 35; John Sherman, *John Sherman's Recollections of Forty Years in the House, Senate and Cabinet* (Chicago: Werner, 1896), 223.

37. J. Ganson to E. Spaulding, Buffalo, NY, quoted in Spaulding, *History of the Legal Tender,* 23.

38. M. Grinell to E. Spaulding, New York, NY, January 30, 1862, quoted in Spaulding, *History of the Legal Tender,* 23.

39. G. Opdyke to S. Chase, New York, NY, December 14, 1862, Chase MSS.

40. *Congressional Globe,* 37th Cong., 2nd Sess., February 13, 1862, p. 789; Irwin Unger, *The Greenback Era: A Social and Political History of American Finance, 1865–1879* (Princeton: Princeton University Press, 1964), 15; Spaulding, *History of the Legal Tender,* 22.

41. *Report of the Secretary of the Treasury on the State of the Finances, 1861,* 18; S. Chase to W. Fessenden, February 10, 1862; S. Chase to J. Bingham, February 6, 1862, RG 56, Letters Sent to Individual Senators and Representatives ("E" Series). 1834–1874, National Archives College Park, MD.

42. *Congressional Globe,* 37th Cong., 2nd Sess., February 13, 1862, p. 789.

43. H. Cooke to J. Cooke, February 25, 1862, Washington, DC, Cooke MSS.

44. Hammond, *Sovereignty and an Empty Purse,* 176.

45. *Congressional Globe,* 37th Cong., 2nd Sess., February 13, 1862, p. 789.

46. *Congressional Globe,* 37th Cong., 2nd Sess., January 29, 1862, p. 549.

47. *Congressional Globe,* 37th Cong., 2nd Sess., January 29, 1862, p. 549.

48. *Appendix to the Congressional Globe* 37th Cong., 2nd Sess., February 3, 1862, p. 43.

49. See Michael Kent Curtis, "Lincoln, Vallandigham, and Anti-War Speech in the Civil War," *William and Mary Bill of Rights Journal* 7 (1998): 111–114.

50. *Congressional Globe,* 37th Cong., 2nd Sess., February 13, 1862, p. 788, *Congressional Globe,* 37th Cong., 2nd Sess., February 4, 1862, p. 636.

51. *Congressional Globe,* 37th Cong., 2nd Sess., February 20, 1862, p. 900.

52. E. Case to S. Chase, December 16, 1861, Patriot, IN, Chase MSS; J. Cooke to S. Chase, Philadelphia, PA, September 7, 1861, Cooke MSS.

53. S. Pooley to S. Hooper, n.p., February 7, 1862, Hooper MSS.

54. *New York Times,* December 25, 1861.

55. A. Campbell to W. Fessenden, n.p., January 2, 1862, Fessenden MSS.

56. Allan Peskin, *Garfield* (Kent: Kent State University Press, 1978), 122.

57. Randall C. Jimerson, *The Private Civil War: Popular Thought during the Sectional Conflict* (Baton Rouge: Louisiana State University Press, 1988), 133.

58. S. Chase to W. Fessenden, February 10, 1862, RG 56. Letters Sent to Individual Senators and Representatives ("E" Series). 1834–1874, National Archives College Park, MD; S. Chase to J. Cisco, Washington, DC, December 10, 1862, in *The Salmon P. Chase Papers,* ed. John Niven, James P. McClure, Leigh Johnsen, William M. Ferraro, and Steve Leikin (Kent: Kent University Press, 1993).

59. S. Chase to W. Fessenden, February 10, 1862, RG 56. Letters Sent to Individual Senators and Representatives ("E" Series). 1834–1874, National Archives College Park, MD.

60. David Moss and Sarah Brennan, "Managing Money Risk in Antebellum New York: From Chartered Banking to Free Banking and Beyond," *Studies in American Political Development* 15 (2001): 138–162.

61. Phillip Paludan, *A People's Contest: The Union and the Civil War 1861–1865* (New York: Harper and Row, 1988), 123–124.

62. Theodore Burton, *John Sherman* (Boston: Houghton and Mifflin, 1908), 135.

63. S. Chase to H. Greeley, Washington DC, January 28, 1863, in *Salmon Chase Papers;* Sharkey, *Money, Class, and Party,* 26.

64. S. Chase to S. D. Gloodgood, Washington DC, December 11, 1862, in *Salmon Chase Papers;* Hammond, *Sovereignty and an Empty Purse,* 285; S. Chase to T. Lathrop, Washington DC, January 2, 1869, in *Salmon Chase Papers.*

65. *The Merchants' Magazine and Commercial Review,* January 1863, p. 65.

66. *New York Times,* January 10, 1863; Paludan, *A People's Contest,* 124.

67. Hammond, *Sovereignty and an Empty Purse,* 285.

68. Hammond, *Sovereignty and an Empty Purse,* 148.

69. *New York Times,* February 15, 1863.

70. J. Williams to H. Greeley, n.p., January 5, 1864, Sherman MSS.

71. J. Williams to J. Sherman, Strawberry Hill, NY, January 17, 1864, Sherman MSS.

72. G. Opdyke to S. Chase, New York, NY, December 14, 1862, Chase MSS.

73. Gary Gorton and Donald Mullineaux, "The Joint Production of Confidence: Endogenous Regulation and Nineteenth-Century Commercial-Bank Clearinghouses," *Journal of Money Credit and Banking* 19 (1987): 460; Redlich, *The Molding of American Banking.*

74. *Congressional Globe,* 37th Cong., 3rd Sess., January 13, 1863, p. 296; E. N. Sill, President of the Summit County Savings Bank, to J. Sherman, Cuyahoga Falls, OH, January 28, 1863, Sherman MSS; M [?] to J. Cooke, January 29, 1863, Cooke MSS; J. Andrews to S. Chase, February 5, 1863, Chase MSS; W. Mellen to S. Chase, Cincinnati, OH, December 25, 1862, Chase MSS; Ellis P. Oberholtzer, *Jay Cooke: Financier of the Civil War, Volume 1* (New York: Sentry Press, 1907), 338.

75. H. Curtis to J. Sherman, Mount Vernon, OH, March 2, 1863, Sherman MSS.

76. Sharkey, *Money, Class, and Party,* 249.

77. J. Gaidiuer, President of the Cleveland and Toledo Railroad, to J. Sherman, Newark, OH, January 21, 1863. Sherman MSS.

78. As quoted in *The Merchants' Magazine and Commercial Review,* October 1863.

79. J. Henderson to A. Lincoln, New York, NY, June 29, 1864, Lincoln Papers.

80. James Gallatin, *The National Debt, Taxation, Currency, and Banking System of the United States: With Some Remarks on the Report of the Secretary of the Treasury* (New York: Hosford and Ketcham Stationers and Printers, 1864), 7.

81. D. Wilder to W. Fessenden, Boston, MA, January 6, 1862, Fessenden MSS.

82. James G. Blaine, *Twenty Years of Congress: From Lincoln to Garfield: With a Review of the Events Which Led to the Revolution of 1860* (Norwich: Henry Bill, 1886), 407.

83. *Congressional Globe,* 37th Cong., 3rd Sess., January 13, 1863, p. 296.

84. Hammond, *Sovereignty and an Empty Purse,* 316; *New York Times,* January 20, 1863.

85. S. Chase to W. Fessenden, Washington, DC, April 11, 1864, Lincoln Papers.

86. H. Cooke to J. Cooke, Washington, DC, December 16, 1862, Cooke MSS.

87. S. Chase to H. Greeley, January 28, 1863, in *Salmon Chase Papers.*

88. Hammond, *Sovereignty and an Empty Purse,* 290.

89. Oberholtzer, *Jay Cooke,* vol. 1, 332; H. Cooke to J. Cooke, Washington, DC, February 11, 1863, Cooke MSS.

90. S. Chase to T. Lathrop, Washington, DC, January 2, 1869, in *Salmon Chase Papers;* H. Cooke to J. Cooke, Washington, DC, February 5, 1863, Cooke MSS.

91. *Congressional Globe,* 37th Cong., 3rd Sess., February 10, 1863, p. 840; Chase quoted in Andrew McFarland Davis, *The Origin of the National Banking System* (New York: Arno Press, [1910], 1980), 77.

92. *Merchants' Magazine and Commercial Review,* January 1863, p. 29; *Congressional Globe,* 37th Cong., 3rd Sess., February 10, 1863, p. 840.

93. H. Cooke to J. Cooke, Washington, DC, February 11, 1863, Cooke MSS.

94. R. Larkin to J. Cooke, Columbus, OH, December 9, 1862, Cooke MSS.

95. R. Clarkson to J. Cooke, Dayton, OH, December 11, 1862, Cooke MSS.

96. E. Case to S. Chase, Patriot, IN, December 16, 1861, Chase MSS.

97. R. Clarkson to J. Cooke, Dayton, OH, December 11, 1862, Cooke MSS.

98. E. Case to S. Chase, Patriot, IN, December 16, 1861, Chase MSS.

99. Davis, *Origin of the National Banking System,* 87.

100. Susan E. Van de Vort Emery, *Seven Financial Conspiracies Which Have Enslaved the American People* (Lansing: Robert Smith, State Printers and Binders, 1894), 25–32.

101. John James and David Weiman, "The National Banking Acts and the Transformation of New York City Banking during the Civil War Era," *Journal of Economic History* 71 (2011): 341–344.

102. W. Mellen to S. Chase, Cincinnati, OH, December 25, 1862, Chase MSS. Chase was exposed to the malleability of public opinion in the 1850s. One of Chase's associates noted: "You say well, we want a *public Opinion* which political men may thence shape into form. But we want one thing more a man who can wisely & bravely embody what public Opinion there is already. Such a man is one of the Forces that *made* public Opinion; for while the *thinker* can only *persuade* and convince men, one by one, and act on thoughtful men, the magistrate, in a high place, affects men by his Position by the authority thereof, and moves such as do not think much." T. Parker to S. Chase, Boston, MA, March 29, 1858, Chase MSS.

103. J. Cooke to J. Sherman, Philadelphia, PA, February 13, 1863, Sherman MSS.

104. J. Andrews to J. Sherman, Columbus, OH, February 23, 1863, Sherman MSS.

105. Sharkey, *Money, Class, and Party,* 226; *Congressional Globe,* 37th Cong., 2nd Sess., February 20, 1862, p. 900.

106. *Congressional Globe,* 37th Cong., 3rd Sess., February 12, 1863, pp. 897, 1148.

107. H. Cooke to J. Cooke, Washington, DC, February 12, 1863, Cooke MSS.

108. H. Cooke to J. Cooke, Washington, DC, February 12, 1863, Cooke MSS.

109. H. Cooke to J. Cooke, Washington, DC, February 12, 1863, Cooke MSS.

110. H. Cooke to J. Sherman, Washington, DC, July 9, 1863, Sherman MSS. Others attributed the measure to Chase. See J. Williams to H. Greeley, n.p., January 5, 1864, Sherman MSS.

111. H. McCulloch to M. Kitchum, Washington, DC, May 11, 1863, McCulloch MSS; Sharkey, *Money, Class, and Party,* 226.

112. E. Spaulding to H. McCulloch, Buffalo, NY, December 4, 1866, as quoted in Spaulding, *History of the Legal Tender,* Appendix, 18.

113. H. Cooke to J. Cooke, Washington, DC, February 5, 1863, H. Cooke to J. Cooke, February 11, 1863, Cooke MSS.

114. *Merchants' Magazine and Commercial Review,* January 1863, pp. 65–66.

115. Hoffer, *To Enlarge the Machinery of Government,* chap. 2.

116. Leonard D. White, *The Republican Era: 1869–1901: A Study in Administrative History* (New York: Free Press, 1958), 232.

117. Fred Shannon, *The Farmer's Last Frontier: Agriculture, 1860–1897* (New York: Farrar and Rinehart, 1945), 270–271; Charles H. Greathouse, *Historical Sketch of the U.S. Depart-*

ment of Agriculture: Its Objects and Present Organization (Washington, DC: Government Printing Office, 1907).

CHAPTER 4. GEORGE PENDLETON AND MASS OPINION

1. Hugh McCulloch, *Men and Measures of Half a Century* (New York: Charles Scribner's Sons, 1900), 249–251.
2. *Report of the Secretary of the Treasury,* 1865, 4.
3. *Report of the Secretary of the Treasury,* 1865, 4.
4. H. McCulloch to C. Sumner, n.p., August 15, 1865, McCulloch MSS.
5. *Report of the Secretary of the Treasury,* 1865, 14.
6. *Report of the Secretary of the Treasury,* 1865, 14.
7. *Report of the Secretary of the Treasury,* 1865, 14.
8. *Commercial and Financial Chronicle,* December 23, 1865.
9. D. Ross, President of the Tenth National Bank, to H. McCulloch, New York, NY, March 15, 1865, McCulloch MSS.
10. Ellis Paxson Oberholtzer, *Jay Cooke: Financier of the Civil War, Volume 2* (Philadelphia: George W. Jacobs, 1907), 37–38.
11. J. Cooke to H. Cooke, Philadelphia, PA, September 20, 1867, Cooke MSS.
12. J. Cooke to H. Cooke, Philadelphia, PA, September 19, 1867, Cooke MSS.
13. A. Moss to J. Sherman, Sandusky, OH, January 28, 1867, Sherman MSS.
14. A. Moss to J. Sherman, Sandusky, OH, January 28, 1867, Sherman MSS.
15. L. Lockwood to J. Sherman, New York, NY, October 23, 1867, Sherman MSS.
16. J. Cooke to J. Sherman, Philadelphia, PA, April 20, 1866; J. G [?] of the Cincinnati Chamber of Commerce, to J. Sherman, March 29, 1866, Sherman MSS.
17. E. Spaulding to H. Hulburd, Comptroller of the Currency, Washington, DC, quoted in Spaulding, *History of the Legal Tender,* Appendix, 14.
18. E. Spaulding to H. Hulburd, Comptroller of the Currency, Washington, DC, quoted in Spaulding, *History of the Legal Tender,* Appendix, 14.
19. E. Atkins to H. McCulloch, Boston, MA, August 7, 1867, McCulloch MSS.
20. *Congressional Globe,* 39th Cong., 1st Sess., April 9, 1866, p. 1845.
21. McCulloch, *Men and Measures,* 211.
22. *Congressional Globe,* 39th Cong., 1st Sess., April 9, 1866, p. 1845.
23. *Congressional Globe,* 39th Cong., 1st Sess., April 9, 1866, p. 1846.
24. *Congressional Globe,* 39th Cong., 1st Sess., April 9, 1866, p. 1846.
25. *Congressional Globe,* 39th Cong., 1st Sess., April 9, 1866, p. 1846.
26. *Congressional Globe,* 39th Cong., 1st Sess., April 9, 1866, p. 1846.
27. *Congressional Globe,* 39th Cong., 1st Sess., April 9, 1866, p. 1846.
28. *Congressional Globe,* 39th Cong., 1st Sess., April 9, 1866, p. 1846, italics added.
29. *Nation,* June 13, 1867.
30. *Commercial and Financial Chronicle,* May 26, 1866; *Nation,* June 13, 1867.
31. F. A. Conkling to E. Spaulding, New York, NY, October 17, 1875, as quoted in Spaulding, *History of the Legal Tender,* 85–86.

32. Mashaw, *Creating the Administrative Constitution,* 5.

33. Montgomery, *Beyond Equality,* 65; Sharkey, *Money, Class, and Party,* 74, 78.

34. *Annual Report of the Secretary of the Treasury,* 1866, 8.

35. *Annual Report of the Secretary of the Treasury,* 1866, 17.

36. J. Haddock to B. Butler, Philadelphia PA, September 16, 1867, Butler MSS.

37. Michael Les Benedict, *A Compromise of Principle: Congressional Republicans and Reconstruction, 1863–1869* (New York: W. W. Norton, 1974), 270, 272; H. D. Cooke to J. Cooke, Washington, DC, October 2, 1867, Cooke MSS.

38. J. Sherman to H. Greeley, Washington, DC, February 5, 1865, Greeley MSS.

39. *Nation,* June 27, 1867.

40. *Nation,* June 27, 1867.

41. Sharkey, *Money, Class, and Party,* 83–87.

42. Richard Timberlake Jr., "Ideological Factors in Specie Resumption and Treasury Policy," *Journal of Economic History* 24 (1964): 31–32.

43. H. McCulloch to Boston Merchants, May 11, 1867, McCulloch MSS.

44. Max Shipley, "The Background and Legal Aspects of the Pendleton Plan," *Mississippi Valley Historical Review* 24 (1937): 329; Frank Klement, *The Limits of Dissent: Clement L. Vallandigham and the Civil War* (Lexington: University Press of Kentucky, 1970), 304.

45. Robert A. McGuire, "Economic Causes of Late-Nineteenth Century Agrarian Unrest: New Evidence," *Journal of Economic History* 41 (1981): 840.

46. See Isaac Newton to O. Kelley, Washington, DC, January 1, 1866, Box 7, National Grange of the Patrons of Husbandry Records, 1842–1994.

47. See John Gjerde, *Minds of the West: Ethnocultural Evolution in the Rural Middle West, 1830–1917* (Chapel Hill: University of North Carolina Press, 1997), 293, 310–312.

48. O. Kelley to W. Saunders, "Outline of the Order," n.p., August 5, 1867, Box 2, National Grange of the Patrons of Husbandry Records, 1842–1994.

49. O. Kelley to W. Saunders, "Outline of the Order," n.p., August 5, 1867, Box 2, National Grange of the Patrons of Husbandry Records, 1842–1994.

50. O. Kelley to W. Saunders, "Outline of the Order," n.p., August 5, 1867, Box 2, National Grange of the Patrons of Husbandry Records, 1842–1994.

51. Kellogg made inconsistent statements regarding which branch of government should issue currency. Compare Edward Kellogg, *Remarks upon Usury and Its Effects: A National Bank A Remedy; In a Letter &c.* (New York: Whitehook, 1841), 61, 62, with *Labor and Other Capital: The Rights of Each Secured and the Wrongs of Both Eradicated* (New York: Published by the Author, 1849), 262.

52. Kellogg, *Labor and Other Capital,* 251–252; Jonathan Grossman, *William Sylvis, Pioneer of American Labor: A Study of the Labor Movement during the Era of the Civil War* (New York: Columbia University Press, 1954).

53. Chester McArthur Destler, *American Radicalism, 1865–1901: Essays and Documents* (New London: Connecticut College, 1946), 173–174; Sharkey, *Money, Class, and Party,* 98.

54. For Pendleton see Thomas Mach, *"Gentleman George" Hunt Pendleton: Party Politics and Ideological Identity in Nineteenth-Century America* (Kent: Kent State University Press, 2007).

55. Klement, *Limits of Dissent,* 40.

56. Thomas Mach, "George Hunt Pendleton, the Ohio Idea and Political Continuity in Reconstruction America," *Ohio History* 108 (1999): 128. Republican inflationists also believed that voters had to be led to adopt inflationary monetary views. See O. White to B. Butler, New York, NY, November 18, 1867, A. Spies to B. Butler, October 4, 1867, New York, NY, Butler MSS.

57. *Congressional Record*, 37th Cong., 2nd Sess., January 29, 1862, pp. 549–551; Unger, *Greenback Era*, 80.

58. Jennifer L. Weber, *Copperheads: The Rise and Fall of Lincoln's Opponents in the North* (New York: Oxford University Press, 2006), 95–97.

59. R. Clarkson to J. Cooke, Dayton, Ohio, December 11, 1862, Cooke MSS.

60. Sharkey, *Money, Class, and Party,* 282; *Cincinnati Enquirer,* May 27, 1867.

61. Speech of Hon. George Pendleton Delivered at Lima, Allen County, Ohio, Thursday, August 15, 1867.

62. Klement, *Limits of Dissent,* 305; A. Denny to B. Wade, Eaton, OH, July 1867, Wade MSS; J. C. Devin to J. Sherman, September 30, 1867, Sherman MSS.

63. C. Aylsworth to E. Washburne, Fulton, IL, November 12, 1867, J. Cochrane to E. Washburn, New York, NY, November 4, 1867, Washburne MSS; *Elyria Democrat,* February 13, 1867.

64. James Vallandigham, *A Life of Clement Vallandigham* (Baltimore: Turnbull Brothers, 1872), 412.

65. Unger, *Greenback Era,* 98.

66. Sharkey, *Money, Class, and Party,* 82; Sherman, *Recollections,* 324; Destler, *American Radicalism,* 36.

67. M. Sutliff to B. Butler, Warren, OH, October 8, 1867, Butler MSS; E. Ward to B. Wade, Detroit, MI, October 13, 1867, Wade MSS; W. Wilkeson to J. Sherman, December 21, 1867, Buffalo, NY, J. Belden to J. Sherman, New Orleans, LA, December 22, 1867, Sherman MSS.

68. J. Sherman to W. T. Sherman, Mansfield, OH, August 9, 1867, *The Sherman Letters: Correspondence between General and Senator Sherman from 1837 to 1891,* ed. Rachel Sherman Thorndike (New York: Charles Scribner's Sons, 1894); T. Ewing to "Father" Ewing, OH [?], September 4, 1867, Ewing Family Papers.

69. W. Carroll to A. Johnson, Montreal, September 16, 1867, *The Papers of Andrew Johnson,* ed. LeRoy P. Graf and Ralph W. Haskins (Knoxville: University of Tennessee Press, 1970).

70. W. Carroll to A. Johnson, Montreal, September 16, 1867, *Papers of Andrew Johnson;* J. C. Devin to J. Sherman, September 30, 1867, Sherman MSS.

71. *Ohio Democrat,* August 30, 1867.

72. *Ohio Democrat,* April 24, 1868.

73. *Ohio Democrat,* May 15, 1868.

74. *Ohio Democrat,* April 24, 1868.

75. *Defiance Democrat,* February 2, 1867.

76. Sharkey, *Money, Class, and Party,* 86, italics added.

77. J. Cooke to H. D. Cooke, Philadelphia, PA, September 20, 1867, Cooke MSS.

78. J. Williams to H. Greeley, [New York, NY?] January 5, 1864, Sherman MSS.

79. Hammond, *Banks and Politics,* 731.

80. Hammond, *Banks and Politics,* 731.

81. James and Weiman, "The National Banking Acts and the Transformation of New York City Banking during the Civil War Era," 342–343; J. Henderson to A. Lincoln, New York, NY, June 29, 1864, Lincoln Papers.

82. Sharkey, *Money, Class, and Party,* 82.

83. Sharkey, *Money, Class, and Party,* 82.

84. McCulloch, *Men and Measures,* 211–212.

85. McCulloch, *Men and Measures,* 211–212.

86. *Appendix to the Congressional Globe,* 37th Cong., 2nd Sess., February 3, 1862, 44.

87. *Appendix to the Congressional Globe,* 37th Cong., 2nd Sess., February 3, 1862, 44.

88. *Tioga County Agitator,* October 14, 1868.

89. S. Chase to H. Greeley, Washington, DC, November 29, 1867, Greeley MSS.

90. J. Calkins to J. Sherman, Cincinnati, OH, February 2, 1867, Sherman MSS.

91. J. Medill to E. Washburne, Chicago, IL, May 1, 1868, Washburne MSS.

92. J. Cooke to B. Butler, November 5, 1867, Philadelphia, PA, Butler MSS.

93. J. Doyle to M. Marble, San Francisco, CA, December 26, 1867, Marble MSS.

94. P. Cooper to J. Sherman, New York, NY, April 13, 1868, Sherman MSS.

95. J. Shelton to E. Washburne, February 6, 1868, Buffalo, NY, Washburne MSS.

96. E. Ward to B. Wade, Detroit, MI, October 13, 1867, Wade MSS; M. Pomeroy to M. Marble, La Cross, WIS, January 3, 1868, Marble MSS; A. Denny to J. Sherman, October 14, 1867, Sherman MSS.

97. A. Grover to B. Butler, Leavenworth KS, October 20, 1867, Butler MSS; A. Denny to J. Sherman, October 14, 1867, Sherman MSS.

98. R. A. Harrisson to T. Ewing, London, OH, September 9, 1867, Ewing Family Papers.

99. Eric Foner, *Reconstruction: America's Unfinished Revolution* (New York: Harper and Row, 1988), 267; Daniel Corwin to J. Sherman, n.p., October 23, 1863, Sherman MSS.

100. D. Taylor to J. Sherman, Washington, DC, September 6, 1867, Sherman MSS; C. Davenport to J. Sherman, October 15, 1867, Sherman MSS.

101. A. Denny to B. Wade, Eaton, OH, July 1867, Wade MSS.

102. A. Tyrrell to E. Washburne, Sterling, IL, January 27, 1868, Washburne MSS.

103. *Commercial and Financial Chronicle,* September 16, 1876.

104. P. Freeman to B. Butler, New York, NY, October 12, 1867, Butler MSS.

105. P. Freeman to B. Butler, New York, NY, October 12, 1867, Butler MSS.

106. S. Colfax to J. Sherman, October 12 1867, Sherman MSS.

107. S. Colfax to J. Sherman, Washington, DC, December 28, 1867, Sherman MSS.

108. Sherman, *Recollections,* I, 433.

109. J. Medill to J. Sherman, Chicago, IL, March 9, 1868, Sherman MSS.

110. S. Colfax to J. Sherman, Washington, DC, December 26, 1867, Sherman MSS; C. Davenport to J. Sherman, Barnesville, OH, December 27, 1867, Sherman MSS.

111. Welles Diary, October 9, 1867, *Diary of Gideon Welles, Secretary of the Navy under Lincoln and Johnson, Volume* III, January 1, 1867–June 6, 1869 (Boston: Houghton Mifflin, 1911), 232.

112. *Merchants' Magazine and Commercial Review,* November 1867, p. 378.

113. B. Close to E. Washburne, Fulton, IL, October 1, 1868, M. Brown to E. Washburne, St. Louis, MO, December 9, 1867, Washburne MSS.

114. A. Denny to J. Sherman, Eaton, OH, October 14, 1867, Sherman MSS.

115. F. Lieber to U. Grant, New York City, NY, October 19, 1867, Grant MSS; H. Raymond to U. Grant, New York City, NY, October 13, 1867, Grant MSS.

116. A. Campbell to T. Stevens, La Salle, IL, November 15, 1867, Stevens MSS.

117. G. Pendleton to M. Marble, November 13, 1867, Cincinnati, OH, Marble MSS.

118. R. Hart to D. Wells, Rochester, NY, November 4, 1867, Wells MSS; [?] Finch to B. Butler, Milwaukee WIS, October 23, 1867, Butler MSS; T. Ewing to T. Ewing Jr., Lancaster, OH, June 14, 1868, Ewing Family Papers; G. Pendleton to H. Greeley, November 13, 1867, Cincinnati, OH, Greeley MSS.

119. Allan G. Bogue, *The Earnest Men: Republicans of the Civil War Senate* (Ithaca: Cornell University Press, 1981), 25.

120. Douglass Irwin, "Antebellum Tariff Policies: Regional Coalitions and Shifting Economic Interests," *Journal of Law and Economics* 51 (2008): 715–742.

CHAPTER 5. THE ELECTION OF 1868

1. Martin Mantell, *Johnson, Grant, and the Politics of Reconstruction* (New York: Columbia University Press, 1973), 64.

2. Eric Foner, *Free Soil, Free Labor, Free Men: The Ideology of the Republican Party before the Civil War* (New York: Oxford University Press, 1970); William E. Gienapp, *The Origins of the Republican Party, 1852–1856* (New York: Oxford University Press, 1987), 353–373; Michael Holt, *The Political Crisis of the 1850s* (New York: W. W. Norton, 1978), chaps. 6 and 7.

3. Holt, *The Political Crisis,* 180–181.

4. Gienapp, *The Origins of the Republican Party,* 358, 365–367.

5. Foner, *Free Soil, Free Labor, Free Men;* Holt, *The Political Crisis,* 152.

6. Gienapp, *The Origins of the Republican Party,* 364–365.

7. Gienapp, *The Origins of the Republican Party,* 360.

8. Amy Bridges, *A City in the Republic: Antebellum New York and the Origins of Machine Politics* (Ithaca: Cornell University Press, 1984), 141. The state of New York had voted Republican in the presidential elections of 1860 and 1856. However, the city of New York, which had emerged as a leading center of American finance, was far less supportive.

9. Welles Diary, October 9, 1867, *Diary of Gideon Welles,* III, 232; *Merchants' Magazine and Commercial Review,* November 1867, p. 378.

10. B. Close to E. Washburne, Fulton, IL, October 1, 1868, Washburne MSS.

11. "Bass" to E. Washburne, Chicago, IL, December 3, 1867, Washburne MSS; M. Sutliff to B. Butler, Warren, OH, October 8, 1867, Butler MSS.

12. A. Grover to B. Butler, Leavenworth, KS, October 20, 1867, Butler MSS.

13. M. B. Brown to E. Washburne, St. Louis, MO, December 9, 1867, Washburne MSS.

14. S. Colfax to J. Sherman, Washington, DC, December 26, 1867, C. Davenport to J. Sherman, Barnesville, OH, December 27, 1867, Sherman MSS.

15. P. Yates to B. Butler, Milwaukee, WI, October 22, 1867, Butler MSS.

16. Brooks D. Simpson, *Let Us Have Peace: Ulysses S. Grant and the Politics of War and Reconstruction, 1861–1868* (Chapel Hill: University of North Carolina Press, 1991), 207.

17. M. Brown to E. Washburne, St. Louis, MO, December 9, 1867, Washburne MSS.

18. U. Grant to W. Sherman, n.p., June 21, 1868, Blaine Papers.

19. U. Grant to W. Sherman, n.p., June 21, 1868, Blaine Papers.

20. Foner, *Reconstruction*, 339; Montgomery, *Beyond Equality*, 350.

21. *Ohio Democrat,* January 17, 1868; *Fort Wayne Daily Gazette,* January 10, 1868.

22. Wilentz, *Chants Democratic,* 240; Sellers, *Market Revolution,* 164.

23. James Roger Sharp, *The Jacksonians versus the Banks: Politics in the States after the Panic of 1837* (New York: Columbia University Press, 1970), 182, 184–185, italics added.

24. Pendleton as quoted in the *St. Joseph Herald,* January 18, 1868; Robert Remini, *The Life of Andrew Jackson* (New York: Harper and Row, 2001), 234–235; Arthur M. Schlesinger Jr., *The Age of Jackson* (Boston: Little, Brown, 1945), chap. 10; Charles Sellers, *The Market Revolution: Jacksonian America, 1815–1846* (New York: Oxford University Press, 1991).

25. Charles Hubert Coleman, *The Election of 1868: The Democratic Effort to Regain Control* (New York: Octagon Books, 1971), 31; J. Morrow to M. van Buren, Elliot Hills, MD, August 9, 1837, van Buren MSS.

26. Speech of Hon. H. P. Baldwin, At the Dedication of Republican Wigwam at Detroit, August 13, 1868, quoted in the *Hillsdale Standard,* August 25, 1868.

27. J. Medill to E. Washburne, Niagara Falls, NY, July 10, 1868, Washburne MSS.

28. J. Cochrane to E. Washburne, New York, NY, February 16, 1868, Washburne MSS.

29. E. Cowles to J. Sherman, Cleveland, OH, February 20, 1868, Sherman MSS.

30. A. A. Low, *The Finances of the United States: An Address Delivered by A. A. Low, Esq., At the Centennial Celebration of the Chamber of Commerce of the State of New York, At Irving Hall, New York, April 6, 1868* (New York: John W. Amerman, 1868), 7.

31. J. Wilson to E. Washburne, Davenport, IL, October 12, 1867, Washburne MSS.

32. M. B. Brown to E. Washburne, St. Louis, MO, December 9, 1867, Washburne MSS; E. Cowles to J. Sherman, Cleveland, OH, February 20, 1868, Sherman MSS.

33. E. Warner to E. Washburne, Marrison, IL, November 12, 1867, Washburne MSS.

34. G. Grow to E. Washburne, New York, October 13, 1867, A. Powell to E. Washburne, Brooklyn, NY, January 24, 1868; E. Hathaway to E. Washburne, Damascus, IL, March 17, 1868, Washburne MSS.

35. Garfield to Hinsdale, Washington, DC, February 2, 1868, Garfield-Hinsdale Letters; William McFeely, *Grant: A Biography* (New York: W. W. Norton, 1978).

36. C. Aylsworth to E. Washburne, Fulton, IL, November 12, 1867, Washburne MSS.

37. A. Tyrrell to E. Washburne, Sterling, IL, January 27, 1868, Washburne MSS.

38. J. Cooke to J. Sherman, Philadelphia, PA, March, 1868, Sherman MSS; M. Ward to E. Washburne, Fenton NJ, December 17, 1867, Washburne MSS.

39. J. Medill to J. Sherman, Chicago, IL, June 25, 1868, Sherman MSS.

40. E. Cowles to J. Sherman, Cleveland, OH, February 20, 1868, Sherman MSS.

41. *The American Annual Cyclopedia and Register of Important Events of the Year 1868* (New York: D. Appleton, 1869), 351.

42. Foner, *Free Soil, Free Labor, Free Men,* 19; Holt, *The Rise and Fall of the American Whig Party,* 66–67. In 1875 one voter identifying himself as "an old Henry Clay Whig," who had converted into "a *Rabid* Republican," proclaimed: "I am in favor of the U.S. treasury legal tender notes, believing in a paper currency." See E. R. Clarke to B. Bristow, Michigan, November 10, 1875, Bristow MSS.

43. P. Yates to B. Butler, Milwaukee, WI, October 23, 1867, Butler MSS.

44. Montgomery, *Beyond Equality,* 340–341.

45. George Pendleton quoted in the *Cincinnati Daily Enquirer,* October 17, 1867.

46. Roman Zorn, "The Working Men's Parties of 1828–1831," *Arkansas Academy of Science* 4 (1951): 173–182.

47. C. Carroll to E. Washburne, West Newton, MA, March 16, 1868, Washburne MSS; S. Arnold to J. Sherman, Mount Pleasant, DE, November 3, 1873, Sherman MSS.

48. Montgomery, *Beyond Equality,* 355.

49. *Coshocton Democrat,* October 20, 1868; Unger, *Greenback Era,* 123.

50. J. Medill to E. Washburne, Niagara Falls, NY, July 10, 1868, Washburne MSS.

51. J. Adams to H. Seymour, n.p., March 19, 1868, Fairchild MSS.

52. J. D. van Buren to H. Seymour, New York, NY, May 20, 1868; H. Seymour to G. Miller, n.p., February 28, 1876, Fairchild MSS.

53. Coleman, *Election of 1868,* 291; S. Tilden to [?], New York, NY, February 28, 1868, Tilden MSS.

54. S. Tilden to [?], New York, NY, February 28, 1868, Tilden MSS.

55. *New York Times,* July 3, 1868.

56. *New York Times,* July 4, 1868.

57. *New York Times,* July 3, 1868.

58. Coleman, *Election of 1868,* 39.

59. J. Medill to E. Washburne, Niagara Falls, NY, July 10, 1868, Washburne MSS.

60. McFeely, *Grant,* 279.

61. *Fort Wayne Daily Gazette,* July 6, 1868.

62. *Fort Wayne Daily Gazette,* July 6, 1868.

63. *Fort Wayne Daily Gazette,* February 11, 1868.

64. Coleman, *Election of 1868,* 310.

65. W. Pierce to E. Washburne, Indianapolis, IN, October 24, 1868, Washburne MSS.

66. Quoted in A. Nettleton to J. Cooke, Chicago, IL, September 4, 1869, Cooke MSS.

67. H. Lamb to D. Wells, Jamestown, November 11, 1868, Wells MSS.

68. W. Cade to D. Wells, Charleston, SC, January 9, 1869, Wells MSS.

69. J. Sherman to W. T. Sherman, St. Louis, MO, December 20, 1868, *Sherman Letters;* J. Sherman to J. W. Ellis, Washington DC, June 10, 1877, Sherman MSS.

70. J. Tallant to D. Wells, Burlington, IA, January 11, 1869, J. Garfield to D. Wells, Hiram, OH, November 24, 1868, Wells MSS.

71. N. M. B. to D. Wells, n.p., December 26, 1869, Wells MSS.

72. W. Cade to D. Wells, Charleston, SC, January 9, 1869, Wells MSS.

73. Sharkey, *Money, Class, and Party,* 132; A. Walker to E. Spaulding, North Brookfield, September 1, 1869, as quoted in Spaulding, *History of the Legal Tender,* 73.

74. H. McCulloch to E. Spaulding, October 23, 1869, Prince George's Co., MD, as quoted in Spaulding, *History of the Legal Tender,* 49.

75. Sharkey, *Money, Class, and Party,* 122–123.

76. Sharkey, *Money, Class, and Party,* 124.

77. J. Sherman to W. T. Sherman, St. Louis, MO, December 20, 1868, *Sherman Letters.*

78. S. Tilden to D. Wells, New York, NY, February 2, 1870, Wells MSS.

79. *Congressional Globe,* 40th Cong., 3rd Sess., January 27, 1869, p. 626.

80. *Congressional Globe,* 40th Cong., 3rd Sess., January 27, 1869, p. 632.

81. *Congressional Globe,* 40th Cong., 3rd Sess., January 27, 1869, p. 632.

82. *Congressional Globe,* 40th Cong., 3rd Sess., January 27, 1869, p. 632.

83. James Oakes, *Freedom National: The Destruction of Slavery in the United States, 1861–1865* (New York: W. W. Norton, 2012), chap. 1. For a discussion of how conflicts over slavery influenced issues such as taxation see Robin Einhorn, "Slavery and the Politics of Taxation in the Early United States," *Studies in American Political Development* 14 (2000): 156–183.

CHAPTER 6. THE CRIME OF 1873

1. "Demonetization" is the term describing eliminating the silver dollar's legal tender properties, preventing silver dollars from being exchanged for a dollar of gold at the Treasury or sub-Treasuries.

2. Jeffrey Ostler, "The Rhetoric of Conspiracy and the Formation of Kansas Populism," *Agricultural History* 69 (1995): 1–27; Emery, *Seven Financial Conspiracies Which Have Enslaved the American People,* 51–59.

3. See Richard Bensel, *Passion and Preferences: William Jennings Bryan and the 1896 Democratic National Convention* (Cambridge: Cambridge University Press, 2008), chap. 7.

4. For the Populists see Charles Postel, *The Populist Vision* (New York: Oxford University Press, 2007); Michael Kazin, *The Populist Persuasion: An American History* (New York: Basic Books, 1995); Lawrence Goodwyn, *Democratic Promise: The Populist Moment in America* (New York: Oxford University Press, 1976); Bruce Palmer, *"Man over Money": The Southern Critique of American Capitalism* (Chapel Hill: University of North Carolina Press, 1980); Peter Argersinger, *The Limits of Agrarian Radicalism: Western Populism and American Politics* (Lawrence: University Press of Kansas, 1995); Steven Hahn, *The Roots of Southern Populism: Yeoman Farmers and the Transformation of the Georgia Up-country, 1850–1890* (Oxford: Oxford University Press, 1983); James E. Wright, *The Politics of Populism: Dissent in Colorado* (New Haven: Yale University Press, 1974); Robert Larson, *Populism in the Mountain West* (Albuquerque: University of New Mexico Press, 1986); John Hicks, *The Populist Revolt: A History of the Farmers' Alliance and the People's Party* (Minneapolis: University of Minnesota Press, 1931).

5. William Jennings Bryan, *The First Battle: A Story of the Campaign of 1896* (Chicago: W. B. Conkey, 1896), 154–155.

6. Bryan, *The First Battle,* 153–154.

7. Bryan, *The First Battle*, 71.

8. Unger, *Greenback Era*, 331; Milton Friedman and Anna Schwartz, *A Monetary History of the United States* (Princeton: Princeton University Press, 1963); Milton Friedman, "The Crime of 1873," *Journal of Political Economy* 98 (1990): 1159–1194; Lawrence Laughlin, *The History of Bimetallism in the United States* (New York: Greenwood Press, 1968). See generally Angela Redish, *Bimetallism: An Economic and Historical Analysis* (New York: Cambridge University Press, 2000), chap. 7.

9. Richard Hofstadter, *The Paranoid Style in American Politics and Other Essays* (New York: Alfred A. Knopf, 1965), 3–40.

10. Allen Weinstein, *Prelude to Populism: Origins of the Silver Issue, 1867–1878* (New Haven: Yale University Press, 1970), 14; Paul O'Leary, "The Scene of the Crime of 1873 Revisited: A Note," *Journal of Political Economy* 68 (1960): 1159–1194; Allen Weinstein, "Was There a 'Crime of 1873'? The Case of the Demonetized Dollar," *Journal of American History* 54 (1967): 307–326; Walter Nugent, *Money and American Society 1865–1880* (New York: Free Press, 1968).

11. Walter Nugent, *The Money Question during Reconstruction* (New York: W. W. Norton, 1967), 146.

12. Unger, *Greenback Era*, 331; Hofstadter, *Paranoid Style*, 255.

13. Peter Viereck, "The Revolt against the Elite," 94, in *The New American Right*, ed. Daniel Bell (New York: Criterion Books, 1955); Mark Fenster, *Conspiracy Theories: Secrecy and Power in American Culture* (Minneapolis: University of Minnesota Press, 2001).

14. Weinstein, "Was There a 'Crime of 1873'?" 325.

15. Laughlin, *The History of Bimetallism*, 76–85.

16. For biographical information on Linderman see Allen Johnson and Dumas Malone, eds., *Dictionary of American Biography*, 22 vols. (New York: Charles Scribner's Sons, 1932), 273; *Pennsylvania Magazine of History and Biography*, vol. 51, no. 1 (1927).

17. *Annual Report of the Director of the Mint*, 1867, 326 in the Report of the Secretary of the Treasury on the State of the Finances for the Year 1867 (Washington, DC: Government Printing Office, 1868).

18. S. Ruggles to J. Sherman, Paris, France, May 17, 1867, Ruggles MSS.

19. *Congressional Globe*, 40th Cong., 3rd Sess., January 27, 1869, p. 627.

20. For Ralston see David Lavender, *Nothing Seemed Impossible: William C. Ralston and Early San Francisco* (Palo Alto: American West, 1975); George D. Lyman, *Ralston's Ring: California Plunders the Comstock Lode* (New York: Charles Scribner's Sons, 1937); Cecil Tilton, *William Chapman Ralston: Courageous Builder* (Boston: Christopher, 1935).

21. Neill C. Wilson, *400 California Street: The Story of The Bank of California, National Association and Its First 100 Years in the Financial Development of the Pacific Coast* (San Francisco: Hooper Printing and Lithograph, 1964), 27.

22. Lyman, *Ralston's Ring*, 86.

23. Lyman, *Ralston's Ring*, 57–58, 125.

24. H. Linderman to W. Ralston, Washington, DC, May 19, 1872, Ralston MSS.

25. Giulio Gallarotti, "The Scramble for Gold: Monetary Regime Transformation in the 1870s," in *Monetary Regimes in Transition*, ed. Michael Bordo and Forrest Capie (Cambridge: Cambridge University Press, 1993), 15–67; John Kemp and Ted Wilson, "Mon-

etary Regime Transformation: The Scramble to Gold in the Late Nineteenth Century," *Review of Political Economy* 11 (1999): 125–149.

26. See Steven Reti, *Silver and Gold: The Political Economy of International Monetary Conferences, 1867–1892* (New York: Praeger, 1998). Economists disagree over the bimetallism's effects. Compare Friedman, "The Crime of 1873" and "Bimetallism Revisited," with Gallarotti, "The Scramble for Gold," 63.

27. F. Barsalou, "The Concentration of Banking Power in Nevada: An Historical Analysis," *Business History Review* 29 (1955): 352.

28. Lavender, *Nothing Seemed Impossible,* 321.

29. Lavender, *Nothing Seemed Impossible,* 332.

30. Weinstein, *Prelude to Populism,* 16–17.

31. Lavender, *Nothing Seemed Impossible,* 280–281.

32. J. Knox to W. Ralston, Washington, DC, November 16, 1869, Ralston MSS.

33. G. Boutwell to H. Linderman, Washington, DC, October 27, 1869, RG 104, NA.

34. G. Boutwell to H. Linderman, Washington, DC, October 27, 1869, RG 104, NA.

35. Russell R. Elliott, *Servant of Power: A Political Biography of Senator William M. Stewart* (Reno: University of Nevada Press, 1983), 119.

36. G. Boutwell to H. Linderman, Washington, DC, May 4, 1869, G. Boutwell to H. Linderman, June 9, 1869, G. Boutwell to H. Linderman, June 23, 1869, G. Boutwell to H. Linderman, July 23, 1869, Records of the Office of the Secretary of the Treasury, Letters Sent, 1836–1878, Record Group 104, National Archives College Park, MD. National Archives sources are subsequently identified by their record group (RG) number.

37. Lavender, *Nothing Seemed Impossible,* 331.

38. Lavender, *Nothing Seemed Impossible,* 326.

39. H. Linderman, as quoted in J. Knox to G. Boutwell, April 25, 1870, Washington, DC, Records of the Office of the Secretary of the Treasury, Letters Sent, 1836–1878, RG 104, NA.

40. Linderman quoted in J. Knox, Deputy Comptroller of the Currency to G. Boutwell, Secretary of the Treasury, April 25, 1870, Washington, DC, RG 104, NA.

41. Knox sought the advice of Robert Patterson, Franklin Peale, and J. Ross Snowden of Philadelphia, L. A. Garnett and John Hewston Jr. of San Francisco, and E. B. Elliott of the Treasury Department. See J. Knox, Deputy Comptroller of the Currency to G. Boutwell, Secretary of the Treasury, April 25, 1870, Washington, DC, RG 104, NA.

42. J. Knox to G. Boutwell, April 25, 1870, Washington, DC, RG 104, NA.

43. J. Knox to G. Boutwell, April 25, 1870, Washington, DC, RG 104, NA.

44. Porter Garnett, "The History of the Trade Dollar," *American Economic Review* 7 (1917): 91–97.

45. J. Knox to G. Boutwell, April 25, 1870, Washington, DC, RG 104.

46. "Guyescutes" to W. Ralston, Washington, DC, January 14, 1870, Ralston MSS. Linderman often wrote using the pseudonyms "Guyescutes" and "Old Man" when discussing sensitive issues with Ralston. These pseudonyms appear on letterhead from the Director of the Philadelphia Mint, and are written in Linderman's handwriting. The meaning of "Guyescutes" is unknown.

47. "Guyescutes" to W. Ralston, Washington, DC, January 14, 1870, Ralston MSS.

48. Wells Drury, *An Editor on the Comstock Lode* (Reno: University of Nevada Press, [1936,] 1984), 22. For Stewart see Elliott, *Servant of Power*; Ruth Hermann, *Gold and Silver Colossus: William Morris Stewart and His Southern Bride* (Sparks: Dave's, 1975); Dennis Drabelle, *Mile-High Fever: Silver Mines, Boom Towns, and High Living on the Comstock Lode* (New York: St. Martin's Press, 2009).

49. Lavender, *Nothing Seemed Impossible*, 324.

50. Hermann, *Gold and Silver Colossus*, 200.

51. W. Stewart to A. Bull and W. Ralston, April 30, 1867, Washington, DC, Ralston MSS.

52. W. Stewart and E. Casserly to W. Ralston, April 22, 1869, n.p., Ralston MSS.

53. W. Stewart to W. Ralston, February 10, 1870, Washington, DC, Ralston MSS.

54. R. Stevens to W. Ralston, December 11, 1870, Washington, DC, Ralston MSS.

55. W. Stewart to W. Ralston, February 10, 1870, Washington, DC, Ralston MSS.

56. F. Smith to W. Ralston, June 2, 1870, Washington, DC, Ralston MSS.

57. *Congressional Globe,* 41st Cong., 2nd Sess., April 28, 1870, p. 3051.

58. R. Stevens to W. Ralston, December 11, 1870, Washington, DC, Ralston MSS.

59. *Congressional Globe,* 41st Cong., 3rd Sess., January 9, p. 368.

60. *Congressional Globe,* 41st Cong., 3rd Sess., January 9, p. 368.

61. *Congressional Globe,* 41st Cong., 3rd Sess., January 9, p. 369.

62. *Congressional Globe,* 41st Cong., 3rd Sess., January 9, p. 369.

63. *Congressional Globe,* 41st Cong., 3rd Sess., January 9, p. 369.

64. *Congressional Globe,* 41st Cong., 3rd Sess., January 9, p. 369.

65. *Congressional Globe,* 41st Cong., 3rd Sess., January 9, p. 369.

66. *Congressional Globe,* 41st Cong., 3rd Sess., January 9, p. 370.

67. *Congressional Globe,* 41st Cong., 3rd Sess., January 9, p. 370.

68. *Congressional Globe,* 41st Cong., 3rd Sess., January 9, pp. 376–377.

69. *Congressional Globe,* 41st Cong., 3rd Sess., January 9, p. 370.

70. *Congressional Globe,* 41st Cong., 3rd Sess., January 9, p. 376.

71. *Congressional Globe,* 41st Cong., 3rd Sess., January 9, p. 376.

72. W. Huntington to W. Ralston, January 11, 1871, n.p., Ralston MSS.

73. H. Linderman to W. Ralston, Washington, DC, February 3, 1871, Ralston MSS.

74. H. Linderman to W. Ralston, Washington, DC, March 26, 1871, Ralston MSS.

75. H. Linderman to W. Ralston, Washington, DC, February 3, 1871, Ralston MSS.

76. H. Linderman to W. Ralston, Washington, DC, March 26, 1871, Ralston MSS.

77. H. Linderman to W. Ralston, n.p., March 9, 1873, Ralston MSS.

78. H. Linderman to W. Ralston, Washington, DC, February 3, 1871, Ralston MSS.

79. H. Linderman to W. Ralston, Washington, DC, March 26, 1871, Ralston MSS.

80. H. Linderman to W. Ralston, Washington, DC, March 26, 1871, Ralston MSS.

81. E. Casserly to W. Ralston, Washington, DC, December 23, 1872, Ralston MSS; W. Huntington to W. Ralston, January 25, 1871, Washington, DC, Ralston MSS.

82. G. Williams to W. Ralston, January 11, 1871, Washington, DC, Ralston MSS.

83. H. Linderman to W. Ralston, Washington, DC, March 26, 1871, Ralston MSS.

84. H. Linderman to W. Ralston, Washington, DC, March 26, 1871, Ralston MSS.

85. H. Linderman to W. Ralston, Washington, DC, March 26, 1871, Ralston MSS.

86. Grant Smith, *The History of the Comstock Lode, 1850–1920* (Reno: Nevada State Bureau of Mines, 1943), 186; Friedman, "The Crime of 1873," 1165.

87. H. Linderman to W. Ralston, Washington, DC, March 26, 1871, Ralston MSS.

88. Weinstein, "Was There a 'Crime of 1873'?" 325; Lavender, *Nothing Seemed Impossible,* 333.

89. Lavender, *Nothing Seemed Impossible,* 333; W. Ralston to H. Linderman, April 5, 1871, San Francisco, CA, Ralston MSS.

90. W. Ralston to H. Linderman, April 5, 1871, San Francisco, CA, Ralston MSS.

91. Ralston's check is an example of data that unambiguously falsifies claims that bribery was not associated with the Coinage Act. For "smoking gun" tests in process tracing see Collier, "Understanding Process Tracing," 827.

92. H. Linderman to W. Ralston, Washington, DC, March 26, 1871, Ralston MSS.

93. Nugent, *Money Question,* 146.

94. Weinstein, "Was There a 'Crime of 1873?'" 324.

95. H. Linderman to W. Ralston, Washington, DC, March 26, 1871, Ralston MSS.

96. J. Henston Jr. to W. Ralston, June 25, 1868, Washington, DC, Ralston MSS.

97. *Congressional Globe,* 42nd Cong., 2nd Sess., January 10, 1872, p. 338.

98. *Congressional Globe,* 42nd Cong., 2nd Sess., January 9, 1872, p. 322–323.

99. *Congressional Globe,* 42nd Cong., 2nd Sess., January 9, 1872, p. 322.

100. Weinstein, "Was There a 'Crime of 1873'?" 319.

101. H. Linderman to W. Ralston, Washington, DC, May 19, 1872, Ralston MSS.

102. W. Ralston to G. Williams, June 7, 1872, San Francisco, CA, Ralston MSS.

103. W. Ralston to G. Williams, June 7, 1872, San Francisco, CA, Ralston MSS.

104. J. Pollock to G. Boutwell, Philadelphia PA, December 6th, 1872, RG 104, NA.

105. Quoted in the *Bankers Magazine,* March 1873, 710.

106. *Bankers Magazine,* March 1873, 710.

107. Henry R. Linderman, *Money and Legal Tender in the United States* (New York: G. P. Putnam's Sons, 1878), 45.

108. Weinstein, *Prelude to Populism,* 20.

109. Nugent, *Money Question,* 158.

110. Weinstein, *Prelude to Populism,* 21.

111. Weinstein, "Was There a 'Crime of 1873'?" 311–312; Weinstein, *Prelude to Populism,* 14.

112. *Annual Report of the Secretary of the Treasury,* 1872.

113. *Annual Report of the Secretary of the Treasury,* 1872.

114. Weinstein, "Was There a 'Crime of 1873'?" 317.

115. Weinstein, *Prelude to Populism,* 25.

116. The draft of the bill is contained in John J. Knox to John Sherman, December 14, 1872, RG 104, NA; see also Weinstein, *Prelude to Populism,* 24–25; Nugent, *Money Question,* 157.

117. H. Linderman to W. Richardson, Lake Ward, NY, August 29, 1873, General Records of the Department of the Treasury, Correspondence of the Office of the Secretary of the Treasury, Letters Received from the Director of the Bureau of the Mint, 1873–1910. Box No. 1, National Archives College Park, MD.

118. Linderman quoted in the *Bankers Magazine,* VII, March 1873, 711.

119. H. Linderman to W. Richardson, Philadelphia PA, August 18, 1873, Correspondence of the Office of the Secretary of the Treasury, Letters Received from the Director of the Bureau of the Mint, 1873–1910. Entry 168, Box No. 1. National Archives College Park, MD.

120. H. Linderman to W. Ralston, n.p., March 9, 1873, Ralston MSS.

121. Paul O'Leary, "The Scene of the Crime of 1873 Revisited: A Note," *Journal of Political Economy* 68 (1960): 392.

122. *Congressional Globe,* 42nd Cong., 3rd Sess., January 17, 1873, p. 672.

123. *Congressional Globe,* 42nd Cong., 3rd Sess., January 17, 1873, p. 668.

124. Weinstein, *Prelude to Populism,* 14.

125. Weinstein, "Was There a 'Crime of 1873'?" 323.

126. *Congressional Globe,* 42 Cong., 3rd Sess., January 17, 1873, pp. 668–672.

127. *Congressional Globe,* 42 Cong., 3rd Sess., January 17, 1873, p. 672. At its annual meeting, the Chamber noted "the usefulness in commerce of the new silver 'trade' dollar, introduced into the Coinage Act on the recommendation contained in the valuable report to the Secretary of the Treasury in November last, by Dr. Linderman, now Director of the Mint." As quoted in "Report of the Committee on Coinage, Samuel B. Ruggles, Chairman, New York, April 30, 1873," in proceedings of the *Annual Report of the Corporation of the Corporation of the Chamber of Commerce, of the State of New-York, for the Year 1873–'74.*

128. *Congressional Globe,* 42nd Cong., 3rd Sess., January 17, 1873, p. 672.

129. *Congressional Globe,* 42nd Cong., 3rd Sess., January 17, 1873, p. 672.

130. Porter Garnett, "The History of the Trade Dollar," *American Economic Review* 7 (1917): 96; Weinstein, *Prelude to Populism,* 25.

131. Edward McPherson, *A Hand-Book of Politics for 1874* (Washington City: Philp and Solomons, 1874), 134–135.

132. Garfield Diary, May 27, 1872, Garfield MSS.

133. E. Casserly to W. Ralston, January 23, 1873, Washington, DC, Ralston MSS.

134. H. Linderman to W. Ralston, n.p., March 9, 1873, Ralston MSS.

135. W. Ralston to B. Bristow, April 13, 1875, San Francisco, CA, Bristow MSS.

136. Lavender, *Nothing Seemed Impossible,* 336.

137. H. Linderman to W. Ralston, n.p., March 9, 1873, Ralston MSS.

138. H. Linderman to W. Ralston, March 9, 1873, Ralston MSS, italics added.

139. Nugent, *Money Question,* 144; George M. Weston, *The Silver Question* (New York: I. S. Homans, 1878), 54.

140. *Daily Nevada State Journal,* April 26, 1876.

141. Weston, *The Silver Question,* 61.

142. *Annual Report of the Director of the Mint,* 1873, 477; H. R. Linderman to J. B. Floyd, August 7, 1873, Records of the Bureau of the Mint, Correspondence, Letters Sent, 1873–1917, RG 104, NA.

143. Nugent, *Money Question,* 140; Weston, *The Silver Question,* 54.

144. *Annual Report of the Director of the Mint,* 1873, 477.

145. *Annual Report of the Director of the Mint,* 1874, 198–199.

146. H. Linderman to S. Ruggles, Philadelphia, PA, January 22, 1873, Ruggles MSS.

147. H. Linderman to W. Ralston, n.p., March 9, 1873, Ralston MSS.

148. Lavender, *Nothing Seemed Impossible,* 334.

149. Nugent, *Money Question,* 312.

150. Weston, *The Silver Question,* 558–559.

151. Kingdon, *Congressmen's Voting Decisions;* Arnold, *The Logic of Congressional Action.*

152. Both Hofstadter and Weinstein recognized the problems complexity posed for their interpretations, and for the understanding of this period of American history. See R. Hofstadter to A. Weinstein, January 23, 1968, New York, NY, Box 9, Hofstadter MSS.

CHAPTER 7. DISCRETION AND THE
TREASURY DEPARTMENT

1. Elmus Wicker, *Banking Panics of the Gilded Age* (Cambridge: Cambridge University Press, 2000), chap. 2.

2. T. Brady to D. Pratt, October 15, 1874, n.p., Julian MSS; J. Amos to W. Allen, August 12, 1873, Springfield, OH, Allen MSS.

3. H. Sanford to S. Fish, December 18, 1874, Jacksonville, FL, Hamilton Fish MSS.

4. W. Kuhns to J. Logan, March 27, 1874, Chicago, IL, Logan Family MSS.

5. S. Bayless to D. Pratt, October 20, 1874, Pratt MSS.

6. Sherman, Recollections, 434; James G. Blaine, *Twenty Years of Congress: From Lincoln to Garfield: With a Review of the Events Which Led to the Political Revolution of 1860* (Norwich: Henry Bill, 1886), 563, 565; J. Jones to Benjamin Bristow, San Francisco, CA, Bristow MSS.

7. Sherman, *Recollections,* 426; J. Garfield, April 10, 1874, November 9, 1875, Garfield Diary, Garfield MSS.

8. M. Marble to [?], August [?], 1875, Marble MSS.

9. J. Buchanan to T. Ewing, Indianapolis, IN, June 29, 1875, Ewing Family Papers.

10. Report of the Special Committee, New York Chamber of Commerce, A. A. Low Chairman, November 28, 1873, in *Annual Report of the Corporation of the Corporation of the Chamber of Commerce, of the State of New-York, for the Year 1873–'74,* 87–88.

11. B. Bristow to J. Sherman, Washington, DC, August 27, 1875, B. Bristow to H. Maynard, Washington, DC, September 25, 1875, Bristow MSS.

12. J. Partnoy to H. Fish, December 24, 1874, Rio de Janeiro, Fish MSS.

13. *Annual Report of the Secretary of the Treasury,* 1874, 11.

14. *Annual Report of the Secretary of the Treasury,* 1874, 12.

15. *Annual Report of the Secretary of the Treasury,* 1874, 14–16, 22.

16. Garfield Diary, December 8, 1874, Garfield MSS; Unger, *Greenback Era,* 252.

17. Garfield Diary, December 8, 1874, Garfield MSS; Sherman, *Recollections,* 509.

18. *Commercial and Financial Chronicle,* November 7, 1874.

19. Unger, *Greenback Era,* 250; Irwin Unger, "The Business Community and the Origins of the 1875 Resumption Act," *Business History Review* 35 (1961): 252; Clifford H. Moore,

"Ohio in National Politics, 1865–1986," *Ohio Archaeological and Historical Publications* 37 (1928): 294.

20. As early as December 12, Garfield reported having a "long interview with Secretary Bristow in reference to a bill for specie payments." Garfield Diary, December 12, 1874, Garfield MSS.

21. Weinstein, *Prelude to Populism*, 41–48; Unger, *Greenback Era*, 249–260. Fractional greenbacks were small-denomination greenbacks. Although the Resumption Act included a free-banking clause at the insistence of John Logan of Illinois, presumably to placate his inflationary constituents, those close to the proceedings dismissed the relevance of the clause, noting that "the amendment in the Sixth Section, making free banking after 6 mos. from the passage of the act is in deference to a supposed popular wish, harmless, and . . . is expedient." B. Nourse to B. Bristow, Washington, DC, December 15, 1874, Bristow MSS.

22. B. Nourse to B. Bristow, Boston, MA, April 3, 1876, Bristow MSS.

23. *Commercial and Financial Chronicle,* January 16, 1875.

24. *Commercial and Financial Chronicle,* January 16, 1875.

25. Unger, "Business Community," 247–262.

26. *Commercial and Financial Chronicle,* June 20, 1874.

27. *Congressional Record,* 43rd Cong., 2nd Sess., December 22, 1874, 188.

28. *Commercial and Financial Chronicle,* February 20, 1875.

29. *Congressional Record,* 43rd Cong., 2nd Sess., December 22, 1874, 187.

30. *Congressional Record,* 43rd Cong., 2nd Sess., December 22, 1874, 187.

31. *Congressional Record,* 43rd Cong., 2nd Sess., December 22, 1874, 187.

32. *Congressional Record,* 43rd Cong., 2nd Sess., December 22, 1874, 204.

33. Sherman, *Recollections,* 433.

34. Unger, "Business Community," 248; *Commercial and Financial Chronicle,* January 2, 1875.

35. *Commercial and Financial Chronicle,* December 26, 1874.

36. Clipping in George McCartee to B. Bristow, December 9, 1874, Bristow MSS.

37. *Commercial and Financial Chronicle,* January 16, 1875.

38. *Commercial and Financial Chronicle,* January 8, 1875.

39. Quoted in Burton, *John Sherman,* 184.

40. *Congressional Globe,* 39th Cong., 1st Sess., April 9, 1866, p. 1846.

41. Sherman criticized Grant in his *Recollections,* claiming that Grant did not understand the "essential requisite of a republican government," because he "regarded these heads of departments, *invested by law with specific and independent duties,* as mere subordinates, whose functions he might assume. This is not the true theory of our government. The President is intrusted by the constitution and laws with important powers, and so by law are the heads of departments. The President has no more right to control or exercise the powers conferred by law upon them than they have to control him in the discharge of his duties. It is especially the custom of Congress to intrust to the Secretary of the Treasury specific powers over the currency, the public debt and the collection of the revenue . . . but the President cannot exercise or control *the discretion reposed by law in the Secretary of the Treasury,* or in any head or subordinate of any department of the

government" (Sherman, *Recollections,* 377, italics added). This indicates that by the time he wrote his *Recollections* Sherman had come to believe that discretionary executive (but not presidential) authority was an integral part of American republicanism. In 1866 he had denied this, explicitly arguing that by granting the treasury secretary the "power to reduce the currency," Congress was granting "a power that has not heretofore been granted to any Secretary of the Treasury." See *Congressional Globe,* 39th Cong., 1st Sess., April 9, 1866, p. 1846.

42. W. Chilton to B. Bristow, January [28?], Louisville, KY, Bristow MSS.

43. W. Chilton to B. Bristow, January [28?], Louisville, KY, Bristow MSS.

44. W. Grosvenor to B. Bristow, November 29, 1875, New York, NY, Bristow MSS.

45. *Financier,* November 27, 1875.

46. Unger, "Business Community," 248.

47. Unger, *Greenback Era,* 255.

CHAPTER 8. THE OHIO GUBERNATORIAL ELECTION OF 1875

1. B. Bristow to Judge D. M. Wooldridge, Washington, DC, October 11, 1875, Bristow MSS.

2. Unger, *Greenback Era,* 275; J. Smith to J. Sherman, Ashland, OH, August 6, 1875, Sherman MSS; W. Sweet to R. Hayes, Washington, DC, June 25, 1875, Hayes MSS.

3. Hayes Diary, April 18, 1875, in *Diary and Letters of Rutherford Birchard Hayes, Nineteenth President of the United States,* ed. Charles Williams, *Volume III, 1865–1881* (Columbus: Ohio State Archaeological and Historical Society, 1924).

4. Ward McAfee, *Religion, Race, and Reconstruction: The Public School in the Politics of the 1870's* (Albany: State University of New York Press, 1998), 178; Hayes Diary, May 31, 1875, in *Hayes Diary and Letters.*

5. G. E. Howe to R. Hayes, Lancaster, OH, May 13, W. Knapp to R. Hayes, Massillon, OH, May 25, 1875, Isaac Newton to R. Hayes, Renton, OH, May 27, 1875, Hayes MSS.

6. R. Hayes to J. Garfield, Fremont Ohio, June 28, 1875, in *Hayes Diary and Letters.* Democrats echoed this conclusion noting that "a portion of the Germans and a few others, complain of the financial plank in the platform, but with the masses it has positive strength" G. W. Morgan to W. Allen, July 4, 1875, Cleveland, OH, Allen MSS.

7. R. Hayes to J. Sherman, Fremont Ohio, June 29, 1875, July 5, 1875, in *Hayes Diary and Letters.* Hayes noted in his diary that "Winthrop says something like this: Each one of us is engaged in the formation of public opinion. Each of us is in some degree responsible for its course and character. 'Opportunity, powers, and employment of them.'" Hayes Diary, April 21, 1878, in *Hayes Diary and Letters.*

8. W. Knapp to R. Hayes, Massillon, OH, May 25, 1875, Hayes MSS.

9. Foner, *Reconstruction,* 557; Unger, *Greenback Era,* 275; William A. Clonts, "The Political Campaign of 1875 in Ohio," *Ohio Archeological and Historical Society Publications* 31 (1922): 38–97; C. E. Henry to J. A. Garfield, December 21, 1874, Pond, OH, in *Politics and Patronage in the Gilded Age: The Correspondence of James A. Garfield and Charles E.*

Henry, ed. James D. Norris and Arthur H. Shaffer (Madison: State Historical Society of Wisconsin, 1970).

10. Ross Web, *Benjamin Helm Bristow: Border State Politician* (Lexington: University Press of Kentucky, 1969), 186; B. Bristow to Senator J. P. Jones, Washington DC, August 6, 1875, Bristow MSS.

11. J. Blaine to A. Wikoff, October 28, 1875, Blaine Papers.

12. B. Bristow to Senator J. P. Jones, Washington, DC, August 6, 1875, Bristow MSS.

13. Clonts, "The Political Campaign of 1875," 41–46; Reginald McGrane, "Ohio and the Greenback Movement," *Mississippi Valley Historical Review* 11 (1925): 532.

14. P. Luther to J. Stoll, November 10, 1875, Stoll MSS; A. Warner to T. Ewing, Marietta, OH, August 22, 1875, Ewing Family Papers.

15. *Ohio Democrat,* August 19, 1875.

16. Sherman, *Recollections,* 435.

17. A. Gilstrap to C. Schurz, Macon, MO, 1874, Schurz MSS.

18. A. Campbell to T. Ewing, La Salle, June 14, 1875, Ewing Family Papers.

19. A. Campbell to T. Ewing, La Salle, June 14, 1875, Ewing Family Papers.

20. J. Smith to J. Sherman, Ashland, OH, August 6, 1875, Sherman MSS.

21. J. Smith to J. Sherman, Ashland, OH, August 6, 1875, Sherman MSS.

22. G. Morgan to W. Allen, Cleveland, OH, July 4, 1875, Allen MSS.

23. C. Woolley to M. Marble, Kelly's Island, OH, September 1, 1875, Marble MSS.

24. Hayes to Wikoff, Youngstown, OH, September 20, 1875, in *Hayes Diary and Letters.*

25. H. Rawson to R. B. Hayes, Heartland Ohio, September 5, 1875, Hayes MSS.

26. H. Bundy to R. Hayes, Wellston, OH, June 2, 1875, Hayes MSS.

27. See T. Ewing to Hon. Senator Reese, Lancaster, OH, March 22, 1875, T. Ewing to Gen. Charles [?], Lancaster, OH, March 21, 1875, Ewing Family Papers.

28. R. Stimson to R. Hayes, Marietta, OH, June 14, 1875, Hayes MSS. The *Steubenville Daily Herald and News* noted: "There has been less fault found with the famous Geghan bill itself . . . than the means which were used to secure its enactment into a law." Letters were printed demonstrating that Catholics were demanding the Democrats pass the bill. See *Steubenville Daily Herald and News,* June 14, 1875.

29. Daniel Porter, "Governor Rutherford B. Hayes," *Ohio History* 77 (1968): 71.

30. Hayes Diary, June 4, in *Hayes Diary and Letters.*

31. Ward M. McAfee, *Religion, Race, and Reconstruction: The Public School in the Politics of the 1870s* (Albany: State University of New York Press, 1998), 178.

32. Gienapp, *The Origins of the Republican Party,* 60–63.

33. *Appletons' Annual Cyclopaedia and Register of Important Events of the Year 1875,* 606.

34. *Appletons' Annual Cyclopaedia and Register of Important Events of the Year 1875,* 606.

35. R. Stimson to R. Hayes, Marietta, OH, June 14, 1875, Hayes MSS.

36. J. Blaine to A. Wikoff, Augusta, ME, October 2, 1875, Blaine MSS.

37. *The Athens Messenger,* September 30, 1875.

38. J. Bickerstaff to R. Hayes, Cincinnati, OH, June 6, 1875, Hayes MSS.

39. R. Hayes to J. Garfield, Fremont, OH, June 28, 1875, *Hayes Diary and Letters.*

40. J. Dalzell to R. Hayes, Caldwell, OH, August 5, 1875, Hayes MSS.

41. For the actual bill see *Appletons' Annual Cyclopaedia and Register of Important Events of the Year 1875* (New York: D. Appleton and Company, 1875), 605.

42. *The Ohio Democrat,* February 10, 1876, *The Portsmouth Times,* August 21, 1875.

43. *Appletons' Annual Cyclopaedia and Register of Important Events of the Year 1875,* 607; *The Cambridge Jeffersonian,* September 9, 1875.

44. As quoted in the *Ohio Democrat,* September 9, 1875.

45. George Pendleton quoted in the *Ohio Democrat,* September 9, 1875.

46. *Ohio Democrat,* September 16, 1875, February 10, 1876.

47. *Steubenville Daily Herald,* September 4, 1875.

48. Geghan reportedly granted the interview only "after forcibly ejecting a tablespoonful of amber colored saliva," after which "he remarked: 'Well, my old boy, my little bill raised hell in the State, didn't it?'" *Athens Messenger,* September 2, 1875.

49. *Coshocton Age,* May 28, 1875; *Elyria Republican,* September 25, 1875.

50. Unlike the "American Lutheran" movement, which drew its theological positions from Lutheran pietists such as Franke Spener, the Ohio Lutheran Synod was led by conservative theologians, like Matthias Loy, who rejected the pietists' evangelism. Many Ohio Lutherans supported slavery and expressed hostility to the Republican Party, precluding Lutherans in Ohio from homogeneously supporting the Republican Party as they did in areas where the pietistic Lutherans dominated. See Charles William Heathcote, *The Lutheran Church and the Civil War* (New York: Fleming H. Revell, 1919), 82; C. George Fry, "Matthias Loy, Leader of Ohio's Lutherans," *Ohio History* 76 (1967): 198–199; Paul Kuenning, *The Rise and Fall of American Lutheran Pietism* (Macon: Mercer University Press, 1988); 58, 134; Paul Kleppner, *The Cross of Culture: A Social Analysis of Midwestern Politics 1850–1900* (New York: Free Press), 43–51.

51. As quoted in Frederic Bancroft and William Dunning, eds., *The Reminiscences of Carl Schurz, III Volumes* (New York: McClure Company, 1908), 363.

52. See John Gerring, "Culture versus Economics: An American Dilemma," *Social Science History* 23 (1999): 129–173.

53. C. E. Henry to J. A. Garfield, Pond, OH, April 17, 1875, *Garfield-Henry Correspondence.* Despite such uncertainty, Henry noted: "The republicans are pretty sure of the German vote in '76 as matters stand now." C. E. Henry to J. A. Garfield, Pond, OH, April 17, 1875, *Garfield-Henry Correspondence.*

54. T. Hubbard to R. Hayes, New Vienna, OH, June 12, 1875, Hayes MSS.

55. W. McKinley to R. Hayes, Canton, OH, June 8, 1875, Hayes MSS.

56. W. McFarland to R. Hayes, Cleveland, OH, June 25, 1875, Hayes MSS.

57. R. Hayes to A. Wikoff, Fremont, OH, July 8, 1875, in *Hayes Diary and Letters.*

58. C. E. Henry to J. A. Garfield, Pond, OH, July 25, 1875, *Garfield-Henry Correspondence;* G. B. Smith to R. B. Hayes, Elkader Iowa, August 12, 1875, Hayes MSS.

59. E. Noyes to B. Bristow, Cincinnati, OH, September 5, 1875, Bristow MSS.

60. H. Sheldon to R. Hayes, Oberlin, OH, July 5, 1875, Hayes MSS; A. Wikoff to R. Hayes, Columbus, OH, August 6, 1875, T. Wildes to R. Hayes, Akron, OH, June 8, 1875, Hayes MSS; C. H [?] to R. Hayes, Pomeroy, OH, June 8, 1875, Hayes MSS; J. Smith to J. Sherman, Oakland, OH, October 18, 1875, Sherman MSS.

61. R. Hayes to W. Bickham, Fremont, OH, July 10, 1875, in *Hayes Diary and Letters,* E. E. Henry to R. B. Hayes, Geanga Lake, OH, September, 1875, Hayes MSS.

62. J. Barns [?] to W. Allen, May 18, 1875, Allen MSS.

63. R. Hayes to W. Bickham, Fremont, OH, July 10, 1875, in *Hayes Diary and Letters.*

64. Unger, *Greenback Era,* 286.

65. J. Smith to J. Sherman, Oakland, OH, October 18, 1875, Sherman MSS; J. Allison to B. Bristow, Oil City, PA, October 20, 1875, Bristow MSS.

66. M. Halstead to M. Marble, October 12, 1875, Marble MSS.

67. G. Morgan to W. Allen, October 16, 1875, Allen MSS.

68. Ralph Morrow, *Northern Methodism and Reconstruction* (East Lansing: Michigan State University Press, 1956), 217–218.

69. Morrow, *Northern Methodism,* 218; F. Fonton [?] to M. Marble, New York, NY, December 8, 1875, Marble MSS.

70. R. Hayes to J. Sherman, Fremont, OH, August 7, 1876, Sherman MSS.

71. [?] to U. Grant, Philadelphia, PA, December 9, 1875, I. Gore to U. Grant, Erie, PA [?], December 10, 1875, Grant MSS.

72. J. Buchanan Henry to S. Tilden, New York, NY, November 23[?], 1875, Tilden Papers.

73. J. Garfield, November 3, 1875, *Garfield Diary.*

74. B. Bristow to Judge D. M. Wooldridge, Washington, DC, October 11, 1875, Bristow MSS; A. Walker to M. Marble, North Brookfield, [NY,] September 18, 1875, Marble MSS.

75. Keith Polakoff, *The Politics of Inertia: The Election of 1876 and the End of Reconstruction* (Baton Rouge: Louisiana State University Press, 1973), 90.

76. Roy Morris, *Fraud of the Century: Rutherford B. Hayes, Samuel Tilden, and the Stolen Election of 1876* (New York: Simon and Schuster, 2003), 113–114.

77. M. Marble to [?], August 1875, Marble MSS.

78. B. Frech to S. Tilden, Whitley, VA, November 21, 1875, Tilden Papers.

79. B. Frech to S. Tilden, Whitley, VA, November 21, 1875, Tilden Papers; *New York Times,* June 3, 1876.

80. D. Wells to S. Tilden, n.p., November 9, 1875, B. Frech to S. Tilden, Whitley, VA, November 21, 1875, S. Tilden to A. Hewitt, Albany, NY, July 15, 1876, Tilden Papers.

81. Unger, *Greenback Era,* 308–310; William Wallace to S. Tilden, Washington, DC, July 7, 1876; A. Hewitt to S. Tilden, Washington, DC, July 6, 1876; L. De La Court to S. Tilden, Hamilton, OH, July 6, 1876; T. A. Hendricks to S. Tilden, Indianapolis, IN, July 6, 1874, Tilden Papers.

82. *Annual Cyclopedia for 1876,* 785; Unger, *Greenback Era,* 309.

83. Weinstein, *Prelude to Populism,* 177.

84. G. Curtis to S. Tilden, New York, NY, July 10, 1876, Tilden Papers.

85. D. Wells to S. Tilden, November 9, 1875, Tilden Papers.

86. J. Madigan to C. Kimball, Houlton, ME, November 11, 1875, J. M. to "dear Son," Bedford, November 21, 1875, Tilden Papers.

87. Polakoff, *Politics of Inertia,* 44–52; E. H. Henry to J. A. Garfield, Geauga Lake, OH, January 22, 1876, *Garfield-Henry Correspondence.*

88. William Rehnquist, *Centennial Crisis: The Disputed Election of 1876* (New York: Alfred Knopf, 2004), 47.

89. For a general treatment of political manipulation see William Riker, *The Art of Political Manipulation* (New Haven: Yale University Press, 1986).

90. Moore, "Ohio in National Politics," 294; Sherman, *Recollections,* 453–455.

91. [?] to O. Morton, n.p. 1875, Oliver Morton Papers.

92. I. Sherman to D. Wells, Saratoga Springs, July 16, 1876, Wells MSS.

93. Unger, *Greenback Era,* 286.

CHAPTER 9. THE COMPROMISE OF 1877
AND RAILROAD REGULATION

1. For the election of 1876 see C. Vann Woodward, *Reunion and Reaction: The Compromise of 1877 and the End of Reconstruction* (Boston: Little, Brown, 1951); Polakoff, *Politics of Inertia;* Michael Holt, *By One Vote: The Disputed Presidential Election of 1876* (Lawrence: University Press of Kansas, 2007).

2. Michael Les Benedict, *Preserving the Constitution: Essays on Politics and the Constitution in the Reconstruction Era* (New York: Fordham University Press, 2006), 200–201; Allan Peskin, "Was There a Compromise of 1877?" *Journal of American History* 60(1): 63–75; C. Vann Woodward, "Yes, There Was a Compromise of 1877," *Journal of American History* 60(1): 215–223.

3. David Mayhew, *Electoral Realignments: A Critique of an American Genre* (New Haven: Yale University Press, 2004).

4. R. Hayes to G. Bryan, Fremont, OH, July 27, 1875, Folder 7, Box 2N246, Guy Bryan Papers.

5. Woodward, *Reunion and Reaction;* Holt, *By One Vote.*

6. Gerald Nash, "Selections from the Reagan Papers: The Butler-Reagan Ticket of 1884," *The Journal of Southern History,* 21(3): 379; Woodward, *Reunion and Reaction,* 86.

7. Scott James, *Presidents, Parties, and the State: A Party System Perspective on Democratic Regulatory Choice, 1884–1936* (New York: Cambridge University Press, 2000), 39.

8. James, *Presidents, Parties, and the State,* 42; Morris Fiorina, "Legislator Uncertainty, Legislative Control, and the Delegation of Legislative Power," *Journal of Law, Economics, and Organization* 2 (1986): 36; Marver H. Bernstein, *Regulating Business by Independent Commission* (Princeton: Princeton University Press, 1955); Ari Hoogenboom and Olive Hoogenboom, *A History of the ICC: From Panacea to Palliative* (New York: W. W. Norton, 1976).

9. Solon Justus Buck, *The Granger Movement* (Cambridge: Cambridge University Press, 1913); Wiebe, *The Search for Order;* Sanders, *Roots of Reform;* Bensel, *Political Economy;* Thomas Gilligan, William Marshall, and Barry Weingast, "Regulation and the Theory of Legislative Choice: The Interstate Commerce Act of 1887," *Journal of Law and Economics* 32, no. 1: 36; Samuel Huntington, "The Marasmus of the ICC: The Commission, the Railroads, and the Public Interest," *Yale Law Journal* 61 (1952): 467–509; Anne Mayhew, "A Reappraisal of the Causes of Farm Protest in the United States, 1870–1900,"

Journal of Economic History 32 (1974): 464–475; Postel, *Populist Vision*, 146–148; Matthew Hild, *Greenbackers, Knights of Labor, and Populists: Farmer-Laborer Insurgency in the Late-Nineteenth-Century South* (Athens: University of Georgia Press, 2007); D. Sven Nordin, *Rich Harvest: A History of the Grange 1867–1900* (Jackson: University Press of Mississippi, 1974); Thomas Woods, *Knights of the Plow: Oliver H. Kelley and the Origins of the Grange in Republican Ideology* (Ames: Iowa State University Press, 1991).

10. Gabriel Kolko, *Railroads and Regulation 1877–1916* (Princeton: Princeton University Press, 1961); *The Triumph of Conservatism* (New York: Free Press, 1963); Robert Wiebe, *Businessmen and Reform (Cambridge, MA: Harvard University Press, 1962);* Lee Benson, *Merchants, Farmers, and Railroads: Railroad Regulation and New York Politics, 1850–1887* (Cambridge, MA: Harvard University Press, 1955); George Miller, *Railroads and the Granger Laws* (Madison: University of Wisconsin Press, 1971); Gerald Nash, "Origins of the Interstate Commerce Act of 1887," *Pennsylvania Magazine of History* 24 (1957): 182.

11. Skowronek, *Building a New American State;* James, *Presidents, Parties, and the State.*

12. James, *Presidents, Parties, and the State,* 40.

13. Benson, *Merchants, Farmers, and Railroads,* 212.

14. Kolko, *Railroads and Regulation,* 20.

15. Benson, *Merchants, Farmers, and Railroads,* 214.

16. Ben Proctor, *Not without Honor: The Life of John H. Reagan* (Austin: University of Texas Press, 1962), 218–219. For Reagan's view of states' rights see John Reagan, *Memoirs: With Special Reference to Secession and Civil War,* ed. Walter McCaleb (New York: Neale, 1906), 247–248; J. Reagan to T. McRea, Washington, DC, May 25, 1890, Folder 8, Box 2K330, Reagan Papers.

17. Reagan, *Memoirs,* 244, 246, 248.

18. David W. Blight, *Race and Reunion: The Civil War in American Memory* (Cambridge, MA: Harvard University Press, 2001), 136; F. Ruffin to J. Stevenson, Richmond, VA, December 13, 1876, Volume 33, Stevenson Family Papers.

19. Woodward, *Reunion and Reaction,* 28.

20. Wallace D. Farnham, "Grenville Dodge and the Union Pacific Railroad: A Study of Historical Legends," *Journal of American History* 51 (1965): 632–650.

21. See Robert Fogel, *The Union Pacific Railroad: A Study in Premature Enterprise* (Baltimore: Johns Hopkins University Press, 1960); Wallace Farnham, "'The Weakened Spring of Government': A Study in Nineteenth-Century American History," *American Historical Review* 68 (1963): 662–680.

22. T. Scott to C. Huntington, Philadelphia, PA, January 6, 1877, Huntington MSS; H. Boynton to B. Bristow, Washington DC, January 5, 1877, Bristow MSS.

23. A. Towne to C. Huntington, San Francisco, CA, March 22, 1877, Huntington MSS.

24. A. Towne to C. Huntington, n.p., December 19, 1876, Huntington MSS.

25. For Standard Oil see Ida Tarbell, *The History of the Standard Oil Company* (New York: Cosimo, [1904,] 2009); Allan Nevins, *Study in Power: John D. Rockefeller, Industrialist and Philanthropist* (New York: Charles Scribner's Sons, 1953); Ron Chernow, *Titan: The Life of John D. Rockefeller, Sr.* (New York: Vintage Books, 1998); Daniel Yergin, *The Prize: The Epic Quest for Oil, Money, and Power* (New York: Free Press, 1991).

26. The most comprehensive analysis of the railroads and the oil region remains Ronald Harper Maybee, *Railroad Competition and the Oil Trade, 1855–1873* (Philadelphia: Porcupine Press, 1974).

27. Maybee, *Railroad Competition,* 62–74.

28. Elizabeth Granitz and Benjamin Klein, "Monopolization by 'Raising Rivals' Costs': The Standard Oil Case," *Journal of Law and Economics* 39 (1996): 18–19.

29. Chernow, *Titan,* 167, 169–170.

30. *National Republican,* January 2, 1877.

31. *Congressional Record,* 44th Cong., 2nd Sess., January 17, 1877, p. 702.

32. *National Republican,* February 18, 1877.

33. Proctor, *Not without Honor,* 207, 196–197.

34. William Childs, *The Texas Railroad Commission: Understanding Regulation in America to the Mid-Twentieth Century* (College Station: TAMU Press, 2005), 18.

35. F. Bond to W. Rosecrans, Philadelphia, PA, September 18, 1876, Box 31A, Folder 29, Rosecrans MSS.

36. See John Brown's comments in *To the People of the South: A Letter from Jno. C. Brown, Vice-President of the Texas and Pacific Railway Co.* (Pulaski, TN: The Company, 1878), 10.

37. For Reagan's actions to aid Galveston see J. Reagan to G. Bryan, Washington, DC, March 10, 1876, Folder 6, Box 2K330, A. Smith to J. Reagan, Evergreen, TX, March 20, 1876, Folder 6, Box 2K330, Reagan Papers.

38. G. Bryan to J. Reagan, Galveston, TX, January 29, 1877, Folder 6, Box 2K330, Reagan Papers.

39. G. Bryan to J. Reagan, Galveston, TX, January 29, 1877, Folder 6, Box 2K330, Reagan Papers.

40. G. Bryan to J. Reagan, Galveston, TX, January 29, 1877, Folder 6, Box 2K330, Reagan Papers.

41. B. Holladay to C. Huntington, Washington DC, May 2, 1877, H. D. Morey to C. P. Huntington, May 5, 1877, MS, Huntington MSS.

42. C. Crocker to C. Huntington, San Francisco, CA, May 9, 1877, Huntington MSS. For similar comments made prior to the Compromise of 1877 see L. Stanford to C. Huntington, San Francisco, CA, May 1, 1875, Hopkins MSS.

43. *Galveston Daily News,* May 18, 1878.

44. C. Schurz to R. Hayes, St. Louis, MO, February 2, 1877, Schurz MSS.

45. R. Hayes to C. Schurz, Columbus, OH, February 4, 1877, Schurz MSS.

46. R. Hayes to C. Schurz, Columbus, OH, January 4, 1877, Schurz MSS.

47. R. Hayes to C. Schurz, Columbus, OH, January 29, 1877, Schurz MSS.

48. *Galveston Daily News,* March 15, 1877.

49. R. Conkling to E. Pierrepont, Utica, NY, March 27, 1877, RG 400, Box 1, Folder 20, Pierrepont MSS; A. Sheridan to J. Sherman, Philadelphia, PA, May 24, 1878, Sherman MSS.

50. Henry Watterson quoted in Woodward, *Reunion and Reaction,* 6; A. Hewitt to E. M. Shepard, New York [?], NY, March 5, 1889, Hewitt MSS.

51. H. Boynton to W. Smith, Washington, DC, January 5, 1877, Bristow MSS.

52. C. Nordhoff to S. Bowles, Washington, DC, February 21, 1877, Bowles MSS.

53. J. Lee to J. Black, Upper Marlboro, MD, July 28, 1877, Black MSS.

54. Frank Vazzano, "The Louisiana Question Resurrected: The Potter Commission and the Election of 1876," *Louisiana History: The Journal of the Louisiana Historical Association* 16(1975): 53–55.

55. Cincinnati *Daily Gazette,* December 22, 1877; Woodward, *Reunion and Reaction,* 234.

56. M. Spaulding to C. Huntington, Chicago, IL, April 30, 1878, Huntington MSS. For the Central Pacific Railroad and the American railroad industry more generally, see Richard White's *Railroaded: The Transcontinentals and the Making of Modern America* (New York: W. W. Norton, 2011).

57. Walter Borneman, *Rival Rails: The Race to Build America's Greatest Transcontinental Railroad* (New York: Random House, 2010), 123.

58. Borneman, *Rival Rails,* 123.

59. Polakoff, *Politics of Inertia,* 318.

60. H. Boynton to B. Bristow, Washington, DC, January 8, 1878, Bristow MSS.

61. *Commercial and Financial Chronicle,* September 1, 1877; F. Bond to W. Rosecrans, Marshall, TX, March 20, 1878, Box 33, Folder 94, Rosecrans Papers.

62. *Congressional Record,* 45th Cong., 2nd Sess., June 5, 1878, pp. 4124–4130. Although the profitability of the Texas and Pacific's line to California was questionable, the threat of forfeiture of their charter was probably responsible for Scott's efforts to extend his line West.

63. *Railroad Gazette,* February 1, 1878.

64. Harry Barnard, *Rutherford B. Hayes and His America* (New York: Bobbs-Merrill, 1954), 438.

65. H. Boynton to B. Bristow, n.p., December 18, 1877, Bristow MSS.

66. B. Bristow to H. Boynton, n.p., December 18, 1877, Bristow MSS.

67. Nevins, *Study in Power,* 106.

68. Granitz and Klein, "Monopolization," 18–19.

69. Granitz and Klein, "Monopolization," 18.

70. Granitz and Klein, "Monopolization," 28.

71. S. Randall to J. Black, August 14, 1877, Philadelphia, PA, Black MSS.

72. Chester Arthur Destler, *Roger Sherman and the Independent Oil Men* (Ithaca: Cornell University Press, 1967).

73. Chernow, *Titan,* 171.

74. Granitz and Klein, "Monopolization," 28.

75. Granitz and Klein, "Monopolization," 29.

76. Granitz and Klein, "Monopolization," 18–19.

77. Granitz and Klein, "Monopolization," 31.

78. M. Spaulding to C. Huntington, Chicago, IL, April 30, 1878, Huntington MSS.

79. J. Boyd to C. Huntington, Washington, DC, May 6, 1878, Huntington MSS.

80. C. Huntington to J. Garfield, New York, NY, April 12, 1878, Garfield MSS; J. Gould to C. Schurz, New York, NY, October 9, 1878, Schurz MSS.

81. Lucas Smith Diary, Dallas, TX, March 2, 3, 1877, Smith MSS.

82. Proctor, *Not without Honor,* 216; *New York Times,* April 2, 1877.

83. *Congressional Record,* 45th Cong., 2nd Sess., May 2, 1878, p. 3097.

84. *Congressional Record,* 45th Cong., 2nd Sess., May 8, 1878, p. 3279.

85. *Congressional Record,* 45th Cong., 2nd Sess., May 8, 1878, pp. 3275–3280.

86. William Z. Ripley, *Railroads, Rates and Regulations* (Washington, DC: Beard Books, [1919,] 1999), 442.

87. C. Sherrill to C. Huntington, Washington, DC, January 19, 1879, Huntington MSS. Sherrill was a paid employee of the Central Pacific Railroad. By all accounts he was a faithful agent for Huntington's interests and did not misrepresent or exaggerate his influence over legislation.

88. G. Bardwell to C. Huntington, Washington, DC, May 14, 1878, Huntington MSS.

89. O. Payne to J. D. Rockefeller, Cleveland, OH, March 1, 1879, JDR Papers, RG1, Box 63, Folder 464, Rockefeller MSS.

90. George Blanchard, *Argument before the Committee on Commerce of the Senate of the United States, Tuesday, February 11, 1879* (New York: Martin B. Brown, Printer and Stationer, 1879), 13.

91. Blanchard, *Argument before the Committee on Commerce,* 54.

92. For William Vanderbilt's opposition to the Reagan bill see the *Railroad Gazette,* June 28, 1878.

93. Roger Sherman to [?], n.p., May 7, 1879, Box 34, Folder 255, Roger Sherman MSS.

94. Roger Sherman to [?], n.p., May 7, 1879, Box 34, Folder 255, Roger Sherman MSS, italics added.

95. See Scott's comments in the *New York Times,* February 14, 1879, *New York Times,* July 3, 1878; [J]? Phillip to J. Garfield, n.p., May 13, 1878, Garfield MSS.

96. Hoogenboom and Hoogenboom, *A History of the ICC,* 10.

97. Maybee, *Railroad Competition,* 89–90, 92.

98. Frank S. Bond, Vice President, Texas and Pacific Railway Co., to J. R. West, Chairman U.S. Senate Committee on Railroads, Philadelphia, PA, March 10, 1876, RG 46, NA, Box 115, Folder SEN 45A-E21.

99. *Argument of John C. Brown, Vice President Texas and Pacific Railway Company, before House Committee on Pacific Railroads, January 25, 1878, in Behalf of the Texas and Pacific Railway Company* (Washington, DC: Thomas McGill, 1878), 26.

100. Brown, *To the People of the South,* 22.

101. *Argument of John C. Brown,* 31.

102. *Congressional Record,* 45th Cong., 3rd Sess., December 3, 1878, p. 14.

103. *Congressional Record,* 45th Cong., 3rd Sess., December 3, 1878, p. 17.

104. C. Huntington to J. West, Chairman U.S. Senate Committee on Railroads, New York, NY, February 15, 1876, RG 46, Box 99, Folder SEN 44A-E18.

105. See the comments on commissions in John Brown, *Railway Legislation. Address of John C. Brown before the House and Senate Committees of the Texas Legislature, on Bills Affecting Railway Legislation. Delivered April 7, 1882* (Austin: E. W. Swindells Printer, 1882), 22.

106. Ernest William, *Platforms of Political Parties in Texas* (Austin: University of Texas Press, 1916), 180.

107. Reagan was a member of the Texas Grange. See Proctor, *Not without Honor.*

108. David Cloud, *Monopolies and the People* (Davenport: Day, Egbert, and Fidlar, 1873), 90.

109. *Congressional Record*, 45th Cong., 2nd Sess., May 11, 1878, pp. 3394–3395.

110. Benson, *Merchants, Farmers, and Railroads*, 215; Miller, *Railroads and the Granger Laws*, 196.

111. *Congressional Record*, 45th Cong., 2nd Sess., May 11, 1878, p. 3393. For Scott's influence over Pennsylvania legislators see Ted Nance, *Gangs of America: The Rise of Corporate Power and the Disabling of Democracy* (San Francisco: Berrett-Koehler, 2005), 61–64.

112. *Congressional Record*, 45th Cong., 2nd Sess., May 11, 1878, p. 3393.

113. *Congressional Record*, 45th Cong., 2nd Sess., May 11, 1878, p. 3394.

114. *Congressional Record*, 45th Cong., 2nd Sess., May 11, 1878, p. 3394.

115. *Congressional Record*, 45th Cong., 2nd Sess., May 11, 1878, p. 3394.

116. *Congressional Record*, 45th Cong., 2nd Sess., May 8, 1878, p. 3276; *Railroad Gazette*, March 8, 1878.

117. *Railroad Gazette*, May 24, 1878. In 1877 the New York Grange endorsed legislation to prevent price discrimination. See *Proceedings of the Fourth Annual Session of The New York State Grange of the Patrons of Husbandry. Held at Rochester, January 23d, 24th, and 25th, 1877* (Elmira, NY: Husbandman Press, Farmers' Club-Hall, 1877), 23, 60.

118. *Congressional Record*, 45th Cong., 2nd Sess., May 11, 1878, p. 3396.

119. *Galveston Daily News*, July 7, 1878.

120. *New York Times*, April 18, 1878.

121. *Congressional Record*, 46th Cong., 2nd Sess., June 1, 1880, p. 4022; Benson, *Merchants, Farmers, and Railroads*, 217.

122. Kolko, *Railroads and Regulation*, 3.

123. *Congressional Record*, 45th Cong., 3rd Sess., December 3, 1878, p. 17.

124. C. P. Huntington to J. R. West, Chairman U.S. Senate Committee on Railroads, New York, NY, February 15, 1876, RG 46, Records of Committees Relating to Commerce, 1816–1988, National Archives, Washington, DC, Box 99, Folder SEN 44A-E18.

125. J. Gould to C. Huntington, New York, NY, January 29, 1880, Huntington MSS.

126. C. Sherrill to C. Huntington, Washington, DC, December 16, 1879, N. Towne to C. Huntington, San Francisco, CA, December 24, 1879, Huntington MSS.

127. Roger M. Olien and Diana Davids Olien, "Oil Men Conspiring and Cats Making Love: The Manipulation of Anti-Monopoly Discourse for Competitive Advantage in the Domestic Petroleum Industry, 1870–1911," *Business and Economic History* 24 (1995): 135–146.

128. *Galveston Daily News*, December 12, 1878.

129. *Galveston Daily News*, December 15, 1878.

130. *Congressional Record*, 42nd Cong. 2nd Sess., January 21, 1885, p. 884; J. Kernns to C. Huntington, Washington, DC, February 14, 1880, Huntington MSS.

131. *Congressional Record*, 45th Cong., 3rd Sess., December 11, 1878, p. 99.

132. *Congressional Record*, 45th Cong., 3rd Sess., December 11, 1878, p. 99.

133. *Congressional Record*, 45th Cong., 3rd Sess., December 11, 1878, p. 98.

134. *Congressional Record*, 45th Cong., 2nd Sess., May 11, 1878, p. 3406.

135. *Congressional Record*, 45th Cong., 2nd Sess., May 11, 1878, p. 3393.

136. *Congressional Record,* 45th Cong., 2nd Sess., May 11, 1878, p. 3396.

137. *Congressional Record,* 45th Cong., 2nd Sess., May 11, 1878, p. 3394.

138. *Cincinnati Commercial,* May 12, 1878.

139. Proctor, *Not without Honor,* 218–219. For Reagan's view of states rights see John Reagan, *Memoirs,* 247–248.

140. C. Adams Jr. to C. Schurz, Boston, MA, March 23, 1878, Schurz MSS.

141. G. Vilas to A. Townsend, Cleveland, OH, February 28, 1880, Box 70, Folder 522, RG 1; G. Vilas to J. Rockefeller, Cleveland, OH, February 28, 1880, Box 70, Folder 522, RG 1, Rockefeller MSS.

142. Scott may have bribed Reagan, as this was standard practice for the railroads. However, there is no evidence that Scott was bribing Reagan, and since Scott did not retain his correspondence, and resisted committing many critical agreements to paper, it is unlikely that any evidence of bribery will ever be found.

143. *Railroad Gazette,* August 9, 1878.

144. C. Schurz to C. F. Adams Jr., Washington DC, January 8, 1879, Schurz MSS.

145. J. Rollins to C. Schurz, Columbia, MO, July 29, 1879, Schurz MSS.

146. Thomas Gilligan, William J. Marshall, and Barry R. Weingast, "Legislative Choice: The Interstate Commerce Act of 1887," *Journal of Law and Economics* 32 (1989): 48.

147. *Report of the Select Committee on Transportation-Routes to the Seaboard: With Appendix and Evidence* (Washington, DC: Government Printing Office, 1874), 242.

148. *Report of the Select Committee on Transportation-Routes to the Seaboard,* 242–243. For the decline of railroad rates relative to the general price level see Robert Higgs, "Railroad Rates and the Populist Uprising," *Agricultural History* 44 (1970): 291–297.

149. See Handlin and Handlin, *Commonwealth,* pp. 240–241, for a discussion of the Massachusetts General Court's involvement in rate regulation.

150. Reagan to the *Galveston News,* March 4, 1884, Folder 7, Box 2K330, Reagan Papers.

151. Gerald W. McFarland, *Mugwumps, Morals and Politics, 1884–1920* (Amherst: University of Massachusetts Press, 1975), chap. 3.

152. Liberal reformers' ideas, and attitudes toward bureaucracy, seem paradoxical only when examined from our contemporary ideological perspectives, which are themselves subject to the same quasi-logic that configured Gilded Age American political ideologies. See generally Converse, "The Nature of Belief Systems."

CHAPTER 10. CHARLES FRANCIS ADAMS JR. AND BUREAUCRACY

1. Skowronek, *Building a New American State,* 148; David Welborn, *Governance of Federal Regulatory Agencies* (Knoxville: University of Tennessee Press, 1977).

2. William E. Nelson, *The Roots of American Bureaucracy, 1830–1900* (Cambridge, MA: Harvard University Press, 1982).

3. Reagan was familiar with commissions, as Richard Coke, Texas governor and Reagan's ally, had endorsed a state commission modeled after the Massachusetts Railroad Commission. See Charles Shirley Potts, "Railroad Transportation in Texas," *Bulletin of the University of Texas* (Austin: University of Texas, 1909), 116.

4. *Congressional Record,* 46th Cong., 2nd Sess., June 1, 1880, p. 4021; Gerald Nash, "The Reformer Reformed: John H. Reagan and Railroad Regulation," *Business History Review* 20 (1955): 192.

5. *Report of the Special Committee on Railroad Transportation of the Chamber of Commerce of the State of New York on the Subject of the Regulation of Commerce by Railroads and the Reagan and Henderson Bills, Now Pending in Congress* (New York: Press of the Chamber of Commerce, 1881), 7–8; *Congressional Record,* 46th Cong., 2nd Sess., June 1, 1880, p. 4022.

6. *Congressional Record,* 46th Cong., 2nd Sess., June 1, 1880, p. 4023–4024.

7. *Congressional Record,* 46th Cong., 2nd Sess., June 1, 1880, p. 4025.

8. *Congressional Record,* 46th Cong., 2nd Sess., June 1, 1880, p. 4026.

9. *Congressional Record,* 46th Cong., 2nd Sess., June 1, 1880, p. 4026.

10. *Congressional Record,* 46th Cong., 2nd Sess., June 1, 1880, p. 4027; Hoogenboom and Hoogenboom, *A History of the ICC,* 17.

11. H. Yerington to R. Colcord, n.p., November 2, 1882, Letterpress Books, Volume 24, pp. 67–68, Yerington Papers.

12. Gerald Berk, *Alternative Tracks: The Constitution of American Industrial Order, 1865–1917* (Baltimore: Johns Hopkins University Press, 1997), 83–85.

13. See John Sproat, *The Best Men: Liberal Reformers in the Gilded Age* (New York: Oxford University Press); Nancy Cohen, *The Reconstruction of American Liberalism, 1865–1914* (Charlotte: University of North Carolina Press, 2001); Leslie Butler, *Critical Americans: Victorian Intellectuals and Transatlantic Liberal Reform* (Chapel Hill: University of North Carolina Press, 2007); Andrew Slap, *The Doom of Reconstruction: The Liberal Republicans in the Civil War Era* (New York: Fordham University Press, 2010).

14. C. Adams Jr. to E. Godkin, Boston, MA, February 23, 1887, Godkin MSS.

15. Thomas McCraw, *Prophets of Regulation: Charles Francis Adams, Louis D. Brandeis, James M. Landis, Alfred E. Kahn* (Cambridge, MA: Belknap Press of Harvard University Press, 1986), 20–22.

16. C. Adams Jr. to H. Adams, Boston, MA, February 14, 1859, Adams MSS.

17. Charles Francis Adams Jr., *Charles Francis Adams, 1835–1915: An Autobiography* (Boston: Houghton Mifflin Company, 1916), 179. See John Stuart Mill, *Auguste Comte and Positivism* (Ann Arbor: University of Michigan Press, 1961).

18. Adams, *Autobiography,* 179.

19. Adams, *Autobiography,* 179. Adams does not appear to have understood that Mill was *critical* of Comte's writings.

20. Charles Francis Adams Jr., *Railroads: Their Origin and Problems* (New York: G. P. Putnam's Sons, 1878), 140, 80.

21. Adams in the *Railroad Gazette,* March 1, 1878.

22. Adams in the *Railroad Gazette,* March 1, 1878.

23. Adams, *Autobiography,* 175.

24. Adams, Charles Francis Adams Jr., "Boston," *North American Review* 106 (1868): 15; Cohen, *Reconstruction,* 130.

25. Adams, *Autobiography,* 175–176.

26. Adams, "Boston," 15; C. F. Adams Jr. to H. Adams, Boston, MA, June 4, 1880, Adams Family Papers.

27. C. F. Adams to H. C. Adams, Boston, MA, December 15, 1877, Henry Carter Adams Papers.

28. Charles Francis Adams Jr., *The Regulation of All Railroads Through the State-Ownership of One: Speech of Charles Francis Adams Jr. on Behalf of the Board of Railroad- Commissioners, Made before the Joint Standing Legislative Committee on Railways, February 14, 1873* (Boston: James R. Osgood, 1872), 16.

29. C. F. Adams Jr. to W. Sumner, Quincy, MA, July 1, 1877, Sumner MSS.

30. Adams, *Railroads*, 88; Adams, *The Regulation of All Railroads*, 18.

31. Adams, *The Regulation of All Railroads*, 15.

32. Adams, *Ninth Annual Report of the Board of Railroad Commissioners* (Boston: Rand, Abery, Printers to the Commonwealth, 1878), 88.

33. Charles Francis Adams Jr., *The Federation of the Railroad System: Argument of Charles Francis Adams Jr., February 27, 1880, before the Committee of Commerce of the United States House of Representatives on the Bills to Regulate Interstate Railroad Traffic* (Boston: Estes and Lauriat, 1880), 10; Adams, *Ninth Annual Report*, 90.

34. Adams, *Federation of the Railroad System*, 22.

35. Adams, *Railroads*, 187–189.

36. Adams, *Ninth Annual Report*, 92.

37. James, *Presidents, Parties, and the State*, 77–80.

38. C. Adams Jr. to S. Bowles, Boston, MA, January 23 1877, Bowles MSS.

39. C. Adams Jr. to S. Bowles, Boston, MA, January 23 1877, Bowles MSS.

40. Charles Francis Adams Jr., "Railway Commissions," *Journal of Social Science* 2 (1870): 235.

41. C. Adams Jr. to C. Schurz, Boston, MA, October 31, 1878, Schurz MSS.

42. Charles Francis Adams Jr. quoted in the *New York Times*, April 11, 1878.

43. C. Adams Jr. to C. Schurz, Boston, MA, October 31, 1878, Schurz MSS.

44. Adams, *Railroads*, 93.

45. Adams, *Railroads*, 120.

46. Daniel T. Rodgers, *Atlantic Crossings: Social Politics in a Progressive Age* (Cambridge, MA: Harvard University Press, 2000); Adams, *Federation of the Railroad System*, 20.

47. Adams, *Federation of the Railroad System*, 20.

48. C. Adams Jr. to C. Nordhoff, Boston, MA, April 21, 1879, Adams Family Papers.

49. Adams quoted in William Crafts, *State Railroad Commissions: Ten Years' Working of the Massachusetts Railroad Commission* (New York: Railroad Gazette, 1883), 11.

50. Lippmann, *Public Opinion*, 31; W. Lippmann to Dr. Albert C. Dieffenbach, n.p., July 12, 1920, Series I, Reel 6, Walter Lippmann Papers. For Lippmann's criticism of expertise see W. Lippmann to Editor, *Democratic Chronicle*, Rochester, NY, April 26, 1919, Series I, Reel 7, Walter Lippmann Papers.

51. Herbert Croly, *The Promise of American Life* (New York: Capricorn Books, 1964), 360–366.

52. Croly, *The Promise of American Life*, 362.

53. Herbert Croly, *Progressive Democracy* (New York: Macmillan, 1914), chap. 17.

54. Croly, *Progressive Democracy,* 353–354.

55. For American progressives and the state see Marc Stears, *Progressives, Pluralists, and the Problems of the State: Ideologies of Reform in the United States and Britain, 1909–1926* (New York: Oxford University Press, 2002).

56. C. Adams Jr. to C. Nordhoff, Boston, MA, April 21, 1879, Adams Family Papers.

57. Charles Francis Adams Jr., "Railroad Inflation," *North American Review* 108 (1869): 163–164; Charles Francis Adams Jr. and Henry Adams, *Chapters of Erie, and Other Essays* (Boston, J. R. Osgood, 1871), 426.

58. Adams in the *Railroad Gazette,* March 1, 1878.

59. Adams, "Railroad Inflation," 133.

60. Adams, "Railroad Inflation," 133.

61. Adams, *Autobiography,* 175; C. Adams Jr. to S. Bowles, Boston, MA, January 19, 1877, Bowles MSS.

62. Frank Dobbin, *Forging Industrial Policy: The United States, Britain, and France in the Railway Age* (New York: Cambridge University Press, 1997), 78, 87.

63. Adams, *Railroads,* 81.

64. *Congressional Record,* 45th Cong., 3rd Sess., December 11, 1878, p. 95.

65. *Congressional Record,* 45th Cong., 3rd Sess., December 11, 1878, p. 95; *Railroad Gazette,* December 20, 1878; Adams, *Railroads,* 81, 186.

66. *Congressional Record,* 45th Cong., 3rd Sess., December 11, 1878, p. 95.

67. *Congressional Record,* 46th Cong., 2nd Sess., June 1, 1880, p. 4031.

68. Shelby Cullom, *Fifty Years of Public Service: Personal Recollections of Shelby M. Cullom* (Chicago: A. C. McClurg, 1911), 308.

69. [J.] Green, Vice President Pennsylvania Railroad, to J. Sherman, Philadelphia, PA, December 23, 1886, Sherman MSS.

70. *Congressional Record,* 49th Cong., 2nd Sess., January 11, 1887, p. 526.

71. *Congressional Record,* 49th Cong., 2nd Sess., January 10, 1887, p. 475.

72. *Congressional Record,* 49th Cong., 2nd Sess., January 10, 1887, p. 475.

73. *Congressional Record,* 49th Cong., 2nd Sess., January 11, 1887, pg. 526.

74. *Congressional Record,* 49th Cong., 2nd Sess., January 10, 1887, pg. 484.

75. Cullom, *Fifty Years of Public Service,* 306.

76. *Congressional Record,* 49th Cong., 2nd Sess., January 11, 1887, p. 525.

77. *Congressional Record,* 49th Cong., 2nd Sess., January 11, 1887, p. 576.

78. Miller, *Railroads and the Granger Laws,* 92–93.

79. Richard John, *Spreading the News: The American Postal System from Franklin to Morse* (Cambridge, MA: Harvard University Press, 1998), 81, 95–100; William Nelson, *The Roots of American Bureaucracy, 1830–1900* (Cambridge, MA: Harvard University Press, 1982), 122–123.

80. *Congressional Record,* 49th Cong., 2nd Sess., January 6, 1887, p. 400.

81. J. Reagan to Hon. W. Morrison, Palestine, TX, May 10, 1887, Folder 8, Box 2K330, Reagan Papers.

82. Cohen, *Reconstruction,* 113.

83. E. Atkinson to C. Schurz, Boston, MA, December 15, 1879, Schurz MSS.

84. E. Atkinson to C. Schurz, Boston, MA, December 15, 1879, Schurz MSS.
85. *Cincinnati Commercial,* March 4, 1878.
86. Charles Francis Adams Jr., "The Granger Movement," *North American Review* (1875): 399–400.
87. Adams, "Boston," 16–18; Charles Francis Adams Jr., "The Government and the Railroad Corporations," 421, in Adams and Adams, *Chapters of Erie.*
88. C. Adams Jr. to S. Bowles, Boston, MA, January 19, 1877, Bowles MSS.
89. F. Wayland to W. Sumner, New Haven, CT, November 5, 1893, Sumner MSS.
90. C. Adams Jr. to H. Adams, Boston, MA, June 4, 1880, Adams Family Papers.
91. Cohen, *Reconstruction,* 129.
92. J. Bryce to E. L. Godkin, n.p., February 6, 1886, Godkin MSS.

CHAPTER 11. FREE SILVER AND THE DEMOCRATIC PARTY

1. For the election of 1896 see Stanley L. Jones, *The Presidential Election of 1896* (Madison: University of Wisconsin Press, 1964).
2. Michael Kazin, *A Godly Hero: The Life of William Jennings Bryan* (New York: Anchor Books, 2007), 55–56.
3. For the development of bimetallic organizations in the 1880s and 1890s see Jones, *The Presidential Election of 1896,* chap. 2.
4. Weston in the *Chicago Tribune,* September 9, 1876. All citations to Weston are taken from newspapers reproduced in Weston, *The Silver Question.*
5. Weston in the *Chicago Tribune,* September 9, 1876.
6. Weston in the *Boston Globe,* March 2, 1876.
7. Weston in the *Chicago Tribune,* September 9, 1876.
8. Weston in the *Chicago Tribune,* September 9, 1876.
9. Weston in the *Chicago Tribune,* September 9, 1876.
10. Weston in the Washington *National Republican,* January 22, 1878.
11. A. Campbell to T. Ewing, January 30, 1878, La Salle [OH?], Ewing Family Papers.
12. Unger, *Greenback Era,* 336.
13. John P. Jones, *Resumption and the Double Standard: Or, The Impossibility of Resuming Specie Payments in the United States without Restoring the Double Standard of Gold and Silver. A Speech Delivered in the Senate of the United States, April 24, 1876* (Washington, DC, 1876), 63.
14. Jones, *Resumption and the Double Standard,* 64.
15. Jones, *Resumption and the Double Standard,* 3.
16. Weinstein, *Prelude to Populism,* 53, 78.
17. Weinstein, *Prelude to Populism,* 247, J. Jones to G. Jones, September 24, 1877, Jones Family Papers.
18. Weinstein, *Prelude to Populism,* 78.
19. *Trenton Times,* May 13, 1890.
20. *Daily Nevada State Journal,* April 26, 1876.
21. John P. Jones quoted in *Daily Nevada State Journal,* April 26, 1876.

22. Speech of John P. Jones in the *Virginia Chronicle,* September 6, 1894, clipping in the Jones Family Papers, *Trenton Times,* May 13, 1890.

23. Weinstein, *Prelude to Populism,* 80.

24. Thomas Ewing quoted in the *Ohio Democrat,* September 6, 1877.

25. *Defiance Democrat,* September 6, 1877.

26. Weston in the *Boston Herald,* March 19, 1876, italics added.

27. Baron Edmond de Rothschild to B. Bristow, Paris, March 6, 1876, Bristow MSS.

28. Ernst Seyd, *Bullion and Foreign Exchanges Theoretically and Practically Considered; Followed by a Defense of the Double Valuation, With Special Reference to the Proposed System of Universal Coinage* (London: E. Wilson, 1868).

29. *Burlington Hawkeye,* July 27, 1878.

30. *Burlington Hawkeye,* July 27, 1878.

31. Testimony of H. R. Linderman to the Monetary Commission of 1876, quoted in *Documents Accompanying the Report of the United States Monetary Commission* (Washington, DC, 1876).

32. *Ohio Democrat,* September 6, 1877.

33. *Standard,* April 2, 1892.

34. *Standard,* April 2, 1892.

35. Sherman, *Recollections,* 469.

36. Sherman, *Recollections,* 468.

37. H. Linderman to J. Sherman, Washington, DC, June 3, 1875, Sherman MSS.

38. E. Thornton to J. Sherman, Washington, DC, September 13, 1876, Sherman MSS.

39. George Boutwell, *Reminiscences of Sixty Years in Public Affairs* (New York: Greenwood Press, 1902), 150.

40. Linderman, *Money and Legal Tender,* 44.

41. H. Linderman to J. B. Floyd, August 7, 1873, RG 104, NA.

42. H. Linderman to B. Bristow, June 3, 1875, Washington, DC, Bristow MSS.

43. As printed in the *Bankers Magazine,* March 1873, p. 710.

44. George G. Evans, *Illustrated History of the United States Mint: With a Complete Description of American Coinage, From the Earliest Period to the Present Time* (Philadelphia: George G. Evans, 1889), 105.

45. *Proceedings of the First National Silver Convention* (St. Louis: Buxton and Skinner Stationary, 1889), 111.

46. As quoted in Hermann, *Gold and Silver Colossus,* 267.

47. Hofstadter, *The Age of Reform,* 89; Friedman, "The Crime of 1873," 1159.

48. Elliot, *Servant of Power,* 92.

49. William M. Stewart, *Reminiscences of Senator William M. Stewart of Nevada* (New York: George Rothwell Brown, 1908), 277.

50. Robert Larson, *Populism in the Mountain West* (Albuquerque: University of New Mexico Press, 1986), 141.

51. Drury, *An Editor on the Comstock Lode,* 22–23.

52. Elliot, *Servant of Power,* 92.

53. Stewart, *Reminiscences,* 317.

54. Hermann, *Gold and Silver Colossus,* 265.

55. W. Stewart to W. Ralston, February 10, 1870, Washington, DC, Ralston MSS.

56. Elliot, *Servant of Power,* 121.

57. William Stewart, *The Silver Question* (San Francisco: Geo. Spaulding, 1885), 17.

58. Stewart, *The Silver Question,* 18.

59. Elliot, *Servant of Power,* 120.

60. Paul W. Glad, *McKinley, Bryan and the People* (New York: J. P. Lippincott), 115–116.

61. Elliot, *Servant of Power,* 101.

62. Stewart, *The Silver Question,* 25.

63. Robert Van Ryzin, *Crime of 1873: The Comstock Connection* (Iola, WI: Karuse Publications, 2001), 122.

64. Stewart, *Reminiscences,* 288–289.

65. Stewart, *Reminiscences,* 288.

66. Stewart, *The Silver Question,* 25.

67. Stewart, *The Silver Question,* 25.

68. Stewart, *Reminiscences,* 317.

69. Elliott, *Servant of Power,* 165.

70. E. Casserly to W. Ralston, January 23, 1873, Washington, DC, Ralston MSS.

71. "Guyescutes" to W. Ralston, January 14, 1870, Washington, DC, Ralston MSS.

72. A. Sargent to W. Ralston, January 31, 1871, Washington, DC, Ralston MSS.

73. *Congressional Record,* 45th Cong., 2nd Sess., February 15, 1878, p. 1079.

74. J. Jones to B. Bristow, August 14, 1875, San Francisco, CA, Bristow MSS.

75. H. Linderman to B. Bristow, July 25, 1875, San Francisco, CA, Bristow MSS.

76. J. Jones to B. Bristow, July 24, 1875, San Francisco, CA, Bristow MSS.

77. Kleppner, *Cross of Culture,* 302.

78. *New York Daily Tribune,* May 1, 1893.

79. *Silver Knight-Watchman,* January 6, 1898.

80. *Evening Gazette,* July 17, 1877.

81. *Silver Knight-Watchman,* January 20, 1898.

82. Jones, *The Presidential Election of 1896,* 20–21.

83. Jones, *The Presidential Election of 1896,* 48–49, 60.

84. Norman Pollack, *The Just Polity: Populism, Law, and Human Welfare* (Urbana: University of Illinois Press, 1987), 306, 298.

85. G. Johnson to I. Donnelly, St. Paul, MN, June 19, 1896; H. Taubeck to I. Donnelly, St. Louis, MO, June 29, 1896, Donnelly MSS.

86. Francis Butler Simkins, *Pitchfork Ben Tillman, South Carolinian* (Baton Rouge: Louisiana State University Press, 1967), 311.

87. William Jennings Bryan, *The First Battle: A Story of the Campaign of 1896 Together with a Collection of His Speeches and a Biographical Sketch by His Wife* (Chicago: W. B. Conkey, 1896), 71.

88. Bryan, *The First Battle,* 155.

89. Bryan, *The First Battle,* 155.

90. Pollack, *The Just Polity,* 324.

91. The only exceptions being David Lavender's biography of Ralston and the coinage expert Robert Van Ryzin's *Crime of 1873.*

92. J. Tait to W. J. Bryan, October 25, 1896, Santa Cruz, CA, William Jennings Bryan Papers.

93. Sanders, *Roots of Reform,* 109.

94. Hofstadter, *Age of Reform,* 71.

95. Peter Novick, *That Noble Dream: The 'Objectivity Question' and the American Historical Profession* (Cambridge: Cambridge University Press, 1988), 337.

CHAPTER 12. THE CONSERVATIVE ORIGINS OF
THE AMERICAN REGULATORY STATE

1. Daniel Rogers, *Atlantic Crossings: Social Politics in a Progressive Age* (Cambridge, MA: Harvard University Press, 1998).

2. Rogers, *Atlantic Crossings,* 90–93, 97–101.

3. Dorothy Ross, *The Origins of American Social Science* (New York: Cambridge University Press, 1991), chap. 3.

4. Ross recognizes this tendency existed among certain "gentry" economists and thinkers such as John W. Burgess, who were influenced by German historicism but wrote before the Progressive Era. See Ross, *The Origins,* 62, 68, 74–75.

5. Weston in the *New York Bankers Magazine,* November 1877.

6. Weston in the *New York Bankers Magazine,* November 1877.

7. W. Stewart to C. Power, June 24, 1895, Book 7, Box 11, pp. 26–27; W. Stewart to H. Ashby, July 15, 1895, Book 7, Box 11, pp. 63–66, Stewart MSS.

8. Nash, *Railroads and the Granger Laws,* 92–96. At their 1878 convention, the Grange members endorsed creating a department of agriculture. However, Grangers did not want the department to function as a regulatory agency but instead sought distributive benefits such as seed distribution. See *Journal of Proceedings of the Twelfth Session of the National Grange of the Patrons of Husbandry* (Philadelphia: J. A. Wagenseller, 1878), 15–18.

9. See Eugene B. Patton, "Secretary Shaw and Precedents as to Treasury Control over the Money Market," *Journal of Political Economy* 15 (1907): 65–87.

10. J. Sherman to F. Bowen, August 4, 1877, Sherman MSS.

11. J. Sherman to A. Belmont, June 1877, quoted in Burton, *John Sherman,* 260.

12. Burton, *John Sherman,* 272.

13. Sherman, *Recollections,* 557.

14. Sherman, *Recollections,* 377.

15. Michael J. Gerhardt, "Constitutional Construction and Departmentalism: A Case Study of the Demise of the Whig Presidency," *Journal of Constitutional Law* 12 (2010): 11.

16. White, *The Federalists,* 94.

17. *Annual Report of the Secretary of the Treasury,* 1880, xiv.

18. Clipping of the *Galveston News,* November 29, 1886, Folder 9, Box 2K331, Reagan MSS. Reagan was also reported to have offered more supportive comments. See clipping of the *Galveston News,* December 8, 1886, Folder 9, Box 2K331, Reagan MSS.

19. J. Brown to D. Pratt, n.p., October 14, 1874, Pratt MSS. For the argument that monetary policy and railroad regulation were conceptually linked by anticommercial ideol-

ogy see Keith Poole and Howard Rosenthal, "Railroad Regulation and Congress," in *The Regulated Economy: A Historical Approach to Political Economy,* ed. Claudia Goldin and Gary Libecap (Chicago: University of Chicago Press, 1994), 94–95.

20. In this sense my argument departs from Kolko's *Triumph of Conservatism.*
21. Richard H. K. Vietor, "Businessmen and the Political Economy: The Railroad Rate Controversy of 1905," *Journal of American History* 64, no. 1: 50–53.
22. Fine, *Laissez Faire and the General-Welfare State,* 232.
23. Croly, *The Promise of American Life,* 361–364. For Croly's defense of bureaucracy see *Progressive Democracy,* chap. 17.
24. C. F. Adams Jr. quoted in the *New York Times,* December 16, 1888.
25. See T. Cooley to J. Hanley, Washington, DC, May 18, 1887, pp. 30–46, RG 134, Records of the Interstate Commerce Commission, General Letters 1887–1942, Vol. 1 of 523, pp. 30–46.
26. White, *Railroaded,* 159.
27. W. Morrison to the Secretary of the Treasury, Washington, DC, December 11, 1895, RG 134, Records of the Interstate Commerce Commission, General Letters 1887–1942, Vol. 19 of 523, pp. 190–193.
28. See Albro Martin, *Enterprise Denied: Origins of the Decline of American Railroads, 1897–1917* (New York: Columbia University Press, 1971), 128–139 and chap. 5.
29. Edward Chase Kirkland, *Charles Francis Adams Jr. 1835–1915: The Patrician at Bay* (Cambridge, MA: Harvard University Press, 1965), 55–56.
30. Henry Carter Adams, *Relation of the State to Industrial Action* (Baltimore: Guggenheimer, Weil, 1887), 29.
31. Adams, *Relation of the State to Industrial Action,* 50.
32. Albert Fink, *Argument before the Committee of Commerce of the House of Representatives of the United States, on the Reagan Bill, for the Regulation of Interstate Commerce by Albert Fink, Washington, January 14, 15, 16, 1880* (New York: Russell Brothers, 1880), 4.
33. White, *Railroaded,* 161.
34. Thomas Cooley, "State Regulation of Corporate Profits," *North American Review* 137 (1883): 217.
35. Cooley, "State Regulation of Corporate Profits," 217.
36. Skowronek, *Building a New American State,* 269.
37. Skowronek, *Building a New American State,* 149.
38. *First Annual Report of the Interstate Commerce Commission* (Washington, DC: Government Printing Office, 1887), 16.
39. *First Annual Report of the Interstate Commerce Commission,* 67.
40. W. Veazey, Commissioner, to T. Moore, Washington, DC, January 19, 1891, RG 134, Records of the Interstate Commerce Commission, General Letters 1887–1942, Vol. 7 of 523, pp. 167.
41. A. Schoonmaker to Hon. Charles S. Baker, House of Representatives, Washington, DC, March 14, 1890, RG 134, Records of the Interstate Commerce Commission, General Letters 1887–1942, Vol. 5 of 523, pp. 24–25.
42. Mashaw, *Creating the Administrative Constitution,* 194–195.

43. H. Johnson, General Counsel of the East Tennessee, Virginia & Georgia Railway Co., to T. Cooley, New York, NY, April 9, 1887, RG 134, Files of the Operating Division, 1887–1906, Box 1, Folder 150–199.

44. Miller, *The Railroads and the Granger Laws,* 19; W. Morrison, A. Schoonmaker, W. Bragg, W. Veazey, to Attorney General, RG 134, Records of the Interstate Commerce Commission, General Letters 1887–1942, Vol. 6 of 523, pp. 410–418; G. Davis to T. Cooley, Farmville, VA, April 4, 1887, RG 134, Files of the Operating Division, 1887–1906, Box 1, Folder 150–199; *First Annual Report of the Interstate Commerce Commission,* 8.

45. S. Elkins to N. Aldrich, n.p., October 11, 1905, Nelson Aldrich Papers.

46. T. Cooley to B. Ines, Washington, DC [?], April 14, 1887, RG 134, Files of the Operating Division, 1887–1906, Box 1, Folder 1–149; T. Cooley to A. Raymond and C. Bowen, Washington DC, June 17, 1887, RG 134, Records of the Interstate Commerce Commission, General Letters 1887–1942, Vol. 1 of 523, p. 462.

47. T. Cooley to J. Hanley, Washington DC, May 18, 1887, RG 134, Records of the Interstate Commerce Commission, General Letters 1887–1942, Vol. 1 of 523, pp. 30–46.

48. T. Cooley to J. Hanley, Washington DC, May 18, 1887, RG 134, Records of the Interstate Commerce Commission, General Letters 1887–1942, Vol. 1 of 523, pp. 30–46.

49. *Second Annual Report of the Interstate Commerce Commission,* 9, italics added.

50. T. Cooley quoted in an unknown newspaper clipping, Ann Arbor, MI, May 9, 1887, RG 134, Records of the Interstate Commerce Commission, General Letters 1887–1942, Vol. 1 of 523, p. 6.

51. Charles Francis Adams Jr., "A Decade of Federal Railway Regulation," *Atlantic Monthly* 81 (April): 433.

52. Adams, *Relation of the State to Industrial Action,* 12.

53. *Second Annual Report of the Interstate Commerce Commission,* 9.

54. Gilligan, Marshall, and Weingast, "Regulation and the Theory of Legislative Choice," 57–58.

CONCLUSION

1. Alan Brinkley, "The New Deal and the Idea of the State," in *The Rise and Fall of the New Deal Order, 1930–1980,* ed. Steven Fraser and Gary Gerstle (Princeton: Princeton University Press, 1989), 93.

2. Foner, *Reconstruction,* 237, 231.

3. Norman Pollack, *The Populist Response to Industrial America* (New York: W. W. Norton, 1962), 136; Sanders, *Roots of Reform,* 108; Destler, *American Radicalism,* 31.

4. Vernon Louis Parrington, *The Beginnings of Critical Realism in America: 1860–1920* (New York: Harcourt, Brace, 1930), 283, 286.

5. John Gerring, *Party Ideologies in America, 1828–1996* (New York: Cambridge University Press, 2001), 222.

6. Pollack, *The Just Polity,* 324, 328.

7. Hammond, *Sovereignty and an Empty Purse,* 360.

8. Gerring, *Party Ideologies in America,* 188–189.

9. James, *Presidents, Parties, and the State,* 119, 158–161.

10. J. Ewing to W. Bryan, Mechanicsburg, OH, November 8, 1896, Bryan MSS.
11. A. Tressel to W. Bryan, Allegheny, PA, November 9, 1896, Bryan MSS.
12. M. Owen to M. Waite, n.p., March 17, 1887, Box 26, Folder 8, Waite Papers.
13. See Richard Hofstadter, "*Coin's Financial School* and the Mind of 'Coin' Harvey," 34, in William Harvey, *Coin's Financial School* (Cambridge, MA: Belknap Press of Harvard University Press, 1963).
14. See Jeffrey Friedman, "Public Ignorance and Democratic Theory," *Critical Review* 12 (1998): 397–411; Ilya Somin, "Voter Ignorance and the Democratic Ideal," *Critical Review* 12 (1998): 413–458; Larry Bartels, *Unequal Democracy: The Political Economy of the New Gilded Age* (Princeton: Princeton University Press, 2008); Martin Gilens, "Inequality and Democratic Responsiveness," *Public Opinion Quarterly* 69 (2005): 778–896.

Primary Sources

COLLECTIONS OF PAPERS

Adams Family Papers. Massachusetts Historical Society, Boston MA.

Charles Francis Adams Jr. Papers. Massachusetts Historical Society, Boston, MA.

Henry Carter Adams Papers. Massachusetts Historical Society, Boston, MA.

Nelson W. Aldrich Papers. Library of Congress, Washington, DC.

William Allen Papers. Library of Congress, Washington, DC.

Edward Atkinson Papers. New York Public Library, New York, NY.

James Bigelow Papers. Library of Congress, Washington, DC.

Jeremiah Black Papers. Library of Congress, Washington, DC.

James G. Blaine Papers. Library of Congress, Washington, DC.

Samuel Bowles Papers. Yale University, New Haven, CT.

Benjamin Bristow Papers. Library of Congress, Washington, DC.

Guy Morrison Bryan Papers, 1795–1901. Dolph Briscoe Center for American History, University of Texas at Austin.

William Jennings Bryan Papers. Library of Congress, Washington, DC.

Martin van Buren Papers. Library of Congress, Washington, DC.

Benjamin Butler Papers. Library of Congress, Washington, DC.

Salmon Chase Papers. Library of Congress, Washington, DC.

Cole Family Papers. Charles E. Young Research Library, University of California, Los Angeles.

Jay Cooke Papers. Pennsylvania Historical Society, Philadelphia, PA.

Thomas M. Cooley Papers. Bentley Historical Library, University of Michigan, Ann Arbor, MI.

Peter Cooper Manuscripts. Cooper Union Library, New York, NY.

Grenville Dodge Papers. Iowa Department of History and Archives, Des Moines, IA.

Ignatius Donnelly Papers. Minnesota Historical Society, St. Paul, MN.

Ewing Family Papers. Library of Congress, Washington, DC.

The Fairchild Collection. New York Historical Society, New York, NY.

William Fessenden Papers. Library of Congress, Washington, DC.

Hamilton Fish Papers. Library of Congress, Washington, DC.

James Garfield Papers. Library of Congress, Washington, DC.

E. L. Godkin Papers. Harvard University, Cambridge, MA.

Ulysses Grant Papers. Library of Congress, Washington, DC.

Horace Greeley Papers. Library of Congress, Washington, DC.

Rutherford Hayes Papers. Library of Congress, Washington, DC.

Abraham Hewitt Papers. Cooper Union Library, New York, NY.

Richard Hofstadter Papers, 1944–1970. Rare Book and Manuscript Library, Columbia University, New York, NY.

Samuel Hooper Papers. Library of Congress, Washington, DC.

Mark Hopkins Papers. Bancroft Library, University of California, Berkeley.

Collis P. Huntington Papers. Iowa Department of History and Archives, Des Moines, IA.

Jones Family Papers. Charles E. Young Research Library, University of California, Los Angeles.

George Julian Papers. Indiana Historical Society, Indianapolis, IN.

Kernan Family Papers. Division of Rare and Manuscript Collections, Cornell University Library, Ithaca, NY.

Abraham Lincoln Papers. Library of Congress, Washington, DC.

Walter Lippmann Papers. Yale University Library, New Haven, CT.

Logan Family Papers. Library of Congress, Washington, DC.

Manton Marble Papers. Library of Congress, Washington, DC.

Hugh McCulloch Papers. Library of Congress, Washington, DC.

Oliver Morton Papers. Indiana Historical Society, Indianapolis, IN.

National Grange of the Patrons of Husbandry Records, 1842–1994. Division of Rare and Manuscript Collections, Cornell University Library, Ithaca, NY.

Edward Pierrepont Papers. Yale University, New Haven, CT.

Daniel Pratt Papers. Indiana Historical Society, Indianapolis, IN.

William Ralston Papers. Bancroft Library, University of California, Berkeley.

John Henninger Reagan Papers, 1847–1949. The Center for American History, University of Texas at Austin.

Record Group 46, Records of Committees Relating to Commerce, 1816–1988, National Archives, Washington, DC.

Record Group 56, Letters Sent to Individual Senators and Representatives ("E" Series), 1834–1874, National Archives College Park, MD.

Record Group 104, Records of the Office of the Secretary of the Treasury, Letters Sent, 1836–1878, National Archives College Park, MD.

Record Group 134, Records of the Interstate Commerce Commission, General Letters, 1887–1942, National Archives College Park, MD.

Record Group 134, Records of the Interstate Commerce Commission, Files of the Operating Division, 1887–1906, National Archives College Park, MD.

Rockefeller Foundation Archives. Tarrytown, NY.

William Rosecrans Papers. Charles E. Young Memorial Library, University of California, Los Angeles.

Samuel Ruggles Papers. New York Public Library, New York, NY.

Carl Schurz Papers. Library of Congress, Washington, DC.

John Sherman Papers. Library of Congress, Washington, DC.

Roger Sherman Papers. Yale University Library, New Haven, CT.

Sherman Family Papers. Library of Congress, Washington, DC.

Lucas F. Smith Diaries and Notebooks. Beinecke Library, Yale University, New Haven, CT.

Thaddeus Stevens Papers. Library of Congress, Washington, DC.

John B. Stoll Papers. Indiana Historical Society, Indianapolis, IN.

William Henry Smith Papers. Ohio Historical Society, Columbus, OH.

Andrew and John Stevenson Family Papers. Library of Congress, Washington, DC.

William Graham Sumner Papers. Yale University Library, New Haven, CT.

William Stewart Manuscripts. Nevada Historical Society, Reno, NV.

Samuel Tilden Papers. New York Public Library, New York, NY.

Morrison Waite Papers, Library of Congress, Washington, DC.

Elihu Washburne Papers. Library of Congress, Washington, DC.

Benjamin Wade Papers. Library of Congress, Washington, DC.

Alexander S. Webb Papers. Yale University Library, New Haven, CT.

David Wells Papers. Library of Congress, Washington, DC.

C. Vann Woodward Papers. Yale University Library, New Haven, CT.

Henry M. Yerington Papers, 1864–1950. Bancroft Library, University of California, Berkeley.

PRINTED COMPILATIONS OF PAPERS

Hinsdale, Mary L., ed. *Garfield-Hinsdale Letters: Correspondence between James Abram Garfield and Burke Aaron Hinsdale* (Ann Arbor: University of Michigan Press, 1943).

Graf, LeRoy P., and Ralph W. Haskins, eds. *The Papers of Andrew Johnson* (Knoxville: University of Tennessee Press, 1970).

Niven, John, James P. McClure, Leigh Johnsen, William M. Ferraro, and Steve Leikin, eds. *The Salmon P. Chase Papers* (Kent: Kent State University Press, 1993).

Norris, James D., and Arthur H. Shaffer, eds. *Politics and Patronage in the Gilded Age: The Correspondence of James A. Garfield and Charles E. Henry* (Madison: State Historical Society of Wisconsin, 1970).

Thorndike, Rachel S. *The Sherman Letters: Correspondence between General and Senator Sherman from 1837 to 1891* (New York: Scribner's Sons, 1894).

Williams, Charles, ed. *Diary and Letters of Rutherford Birchard Hayes, Nineteenth President of the United States* (Columbus: Ohio State Archaeological and Historical Society, 1924).

NEWSPAPERS

The Athens Messenger
Bankers Magazine and Journal of the Money Market
Bankers Magazine
Boston Globe
Burlington Hawkeye
Boston Commercial Bulletin
The Cambridge Jeffersonian
The Chicago Tribune
Commercial and Financial Chronicle
Cincinnati Daily Enquirer
The Commercial and Financial Chronicle
The Coshocton Age
Daily Nevada State Journal
The Daily Independent
Defiance Democrat
The Elyria Democrat
The Elyria Independent Democrat
The Elyria Republican
The Evening Gazette
The Financier
Fort Wayne Daily Gazette
Galveston Daily News
Hillsdale Standard
Idaho Statesman
Journal of Commerce
McKean County Miner
Merchants' Magazine and Commercial Review
The Portsmouth Times
The Nation
New York Bankers Magazine
New York Evening Sun
New York Herald
The New York Times
New York Tribune
New York Daily Tribune
North American Review
The Ohio Democrat
The Public

The Railroad Gazette
The San Francisco Daily Alta
The Silver Knight-Watchman
The Standard
St. Joseph Herald
The Steubenville Daily Herald and News
The Tioga County Agitator
Trenton Times
Virginia Chronicle
Virginia City Territorial Enterprise
The Waterloo Daily Reporter

Index